Bristol Studies in Law and Social Justice

Series Editors: **Alan Bogg**, University of Bristol, UK and **Virginia Mantouvalou**, University College London, UK

This series explores the role of law in securing social justice in society and the economy. The focus is on 'social justice' as a normative ideal, and the law as a critical tool in influencing (for good or for ill) the social structures that shape people's lives.

Forthcoming

Low Paid EU Migrant Workers
The House, The Street, The Town
By **Catherine Barnard**, **Fiona Costello** and **Sarah Fraser Butlin**

Labour Law and Social Justice
The Promise of Relational Autonomy
By **Lisa Rodgers**

Discrimination, Equality and Health Care Rationing
By **Rachel Horton**

Find out more at
bristoluniversitypress.co.uk/
bristol-studies-in-law-and-social-justice

International advisory board

Find out more at

bristoluniversitypress.co.uk/
bristol-studies-in-law-and-social-justice

CLIMATE LITIGATION AND JUSTICE IN AFRICA

Edited by
Kim Bouwer, Uzuazo Etemire, Tracy-Lynn Field
and Ademola Oluborode Jegede

BRISTOL
UNIVERSITY
PRESS

First published in Great Britain in 2024 by

Bristol University Press
University of Bristol
1–9 Old Park Hill
Bristol
BS2 8BB
UK
t: +44 (0)117 374 6645
e: bup-info@bristol.ac.uk

Details of international sales and distribution partners are available at bristoluniversitypress.co.uk

British Library Cataloguing in Publication Data
A catalogue record for this book is available from the British Library

ISBN 978-1-5292-2895-3 hardcover
ISBN 978-1-5292-2896-0 ePub
ISBN 978-1-5292-2897-7 ePdf

Cover design: Blu inc
Front cover image: Alamy/Jack Maguire
Bristol University Press uses environmentally responsible print partners.
Printed and bound in Great Britain by CPI Group (UK) Ltd, Croydon, CR0 4YY

FSC www.fsc.org MIX Paper | Supporting responsible forestry FSC® C013604

Contents

Series Editors' Preface

Alan Bogg and Virginia Mantouvalou

Bristol Studies in Law and Social Justice explores the role of law in securing social justice in society and the economy. The focus is on 'social justice' as a normative ideal, and the law as a critical tool in influencing (for good or for ill) the social structures that shape people's lives. This international series is designed to be inclusive of a wide range of methodologies and disciplinary approaches. Contributions examine these issues from multiple legal perspectives, including constitutional law, discrimination law, human rights, contract law, criminal law, migration law, labour law, social welfare law, property law, international and supranational law. The Series has broad jurisdictional coverage, including single-country, comparative, international and regional legal orders, and encourages a critical and interdisciplinary approach to legal analysis.

List of Tables

Notes on Contributors

Fiona Batt is an independent researcher and consultant, based mainly in Tanzania and Kenya.

Elsabé Boshoff is a PhD candidate at the Norwegian Centre for Human Rights.

Kim Bouwer is Assistant Professor in Law at Durham Law School.

Eghosa O Ekhator is Senior Lecturer in Law at the University of Derby.

Uzuazo Etemire is Associate Professor of Law at the University of Port Harcourt.

Riyad Fakhri is Director of the Business Law Research Laboratory at the Hassan University of Settat.

Tracy-Lynn Field is Professor of Law and Claude Leon Chair in Earth Justice and Stewardship at the University of the Witwatersrand.

Ademola Oluborode Jegede is Professor of Law and Director at Ismail Mahomed Centre for Human and Peoples' Rights, School of Law at the University of Venda, Thohoyandou.

Youness Lazrak Hassouni is Professor of Law at Hassan University of Settat.

Nicole Loser is an attorney and activist, and is Consultant to the Just Transition Energy Africa Initiative, Natural Justice, Cape Town.

Judge John Mativo is a Judge of the Kenya Court of Appeal.

Bright Nkrumah is Assistant Professor at Florida Gulf Coast University.

Pedi Obani is Associate Professor of Law at the University of Bradford.

Edward O Okumagba is Lecturer in Law at Delta State University.

Daniel Armel Owona Mbarga is a PhD candidate at the Catholic University of Central Africa and an advisor at Field Legality Advisory Group in Cameroon.

Pia Rebelo is Lecturer in Law at City, University of London.

Xavier Rebelo is a PhD candidate at the University of Cape Town.

Sanita van Wyk is Lecturer in Law at Tilburg Law School and the University of Stellenbosch, and Attorney of the High Court of South Africa.

Acknowledgements

The editors thank our authors and everyone who has collaborated with us on, or supported, this project. We also appreciate the support from our many friends and colleagues.

We are very grateful to Bristol University Press for their support during the development and publication process.

Mostly, we thank our families, including our ancestors and future generations. This book is dedicated to them.

1

Africa, Climate Justice and the Role of the Courts

Kim Bouwer, Uzuazo Etemire, Tracy-Lynn Field and Ademola Oluborode Jegede

This volume is a collection of scholarly reflections on the theme of climate litigation in Africa. The book spans a range of approaches and jurisdictions and aims to be a relevant yet lasting volume of reflective contributions both in relation to transnational, regional and local climate litigation scholarship, but also to our understanding of the plural nature of climate justice and climate governance in Africa.

In developing this project we have delved into, and supported, the creation of a body of rich, complex and interesting work.[1] The range of insights, perspectives and analyses has much to offer on its own terms. The richness of this scholarship emerges to some extent from its truly global nature; as our authors work within the diversity of a global field, as well as learning from and citing the works of other African scholars. But why does pursuing

---

[1] This includes the contributions in this volume, the special issue edited by two of us, see from K Bouwer and T-L Field, 'Editorial: The Emergence of Climate Litigation in Africa' (2021) 15 *Carbon & Climate Law Review* 123; J Lin and DA Kysar (eds), *Climate Change Litigation in the Asia Pacific* (Cambridge University Press 2020). Also see J Peel and J Lin, 'Transnational Climate Litigation: The Contribution of the Global South' (2019) 113 *American Journal of International Law* 679; J Setzer and L Benjamin, 'Climate Litigation in the Global South: Constraints and Innovations' (2020) 9 *Transnational Environmental Law* 77; PK Oniemola, 'A Proposal for Transnational Litigation against Climate Change Violations in Africa' (2020) 38 *Wisconsin International Law Journal* 301; M Murcott and E Webster, 'Litigation and Regulatory Governance in the Age of the Anthropocene: The Case of Fracking in the Karoo' (2020) 11 *Transnational Legal Theory* 144; LJ Kotzé and A du Plessis, 'Putting Africa on the Stand: A Bird's Eye View of Climate Change Litigation on the Continent' (2020) 50 *Environmental Law* 615.

and asserting an African identity of climate litigation matter? The answer to this question lies in an understanding of what it means to pursue a 'global' endeavour, but also in an understanding of the dignity of African scholars, practitioners and activists in the face of the climate crisis.

As the study of climate change litigation continues to emerge as a scholarly field, the conversation about the characteristics of litigation in Global South countries is still nascent. The meaning and identity of climate litigation, and the scholarly response to it, are mostly shaped around the priorities and pressures of Global North countries. This is understandable, to some extent. Much (but by no means all) of the activity in the courts in the Global North was and is brought in response to a deficit in mitigation ambition of historically high-emitting states, and the contribution of corporations registered in those states.[2] We are of course not suggesting that mitigating climate change is something that Global South countries should not care about; African countries share the goals and objectives of Paris Agreement with other nation states. However, the mitigation obligations they bear do not carry the same urgency or moral weight. Core to this is the question of what constitutes a 'fair share' to the global goals of climate action, and the question of whether most African countries may already be doing enough in terms of climate change mitigation. In some instances – such as disputes arising in connection with new coal extraction or production, which have additional implications for local pollution – climate action can seem at face value to be targeted at mitigation ambition even though the legal bases for such actions, and the complexities underlying them, are distinct. Simultaneously, many African states carry the burden of adapting to climate change and seeking a just transition to a low carbon economy, with limited resources and other pressures. Therefore, the issues in Global South, and certainly most African countries, are not the same as in historically high-emitting states in the Global North. The meaning of climate justice, and what might be done to pursue it in this context, is distinct.

For this and other reasons, as activity in the courts increases globally, African climate jurisprudence has been slow to emerge. This however does not mean that African countries are 'lagging behind' the rest of the world when it comes to climate action,[3] but rather that African climate

[2] Global adaptation cases are still significantly underrepresented, see J Setzer and C Higham, 'Global Trends in Climate Change Litigation: 2021 Snapshot', Grantham Research Institute on Climate Change and the Environment and Centre for Climate Change Economics and Policy, London School of Economics and Political Science, 2021, https://www.lse.ac.uk/granthaminstitute/wp-content/uploads/2021/07/Global-trends-in-climate-change-litigation_2021-snapshot.pdf, accessed 10 July 2021, 17.

[3] As suggested in the otherwise very helpful Kotzé and du Plessis (n 1).

action – including litigation – has been slow to be recognized,[4] and is not well understood. Our research, and the research of the contributors to this book, shows a complex and diverse range of mobilization strategies, employed in diverse contexts and for different purposes. In some respects, the strategies used by litigators do – at face value – fit easily with the global model of climate litigation. But this does not entail an adoption of strategies that have succeeded elsewhere. Rather, the model of successful litigation in the African context demonstrates a willingness of climate activists and litigators to make use of their own plural legal opportunities, and to craft campaigns that work given the demands posed by climate change in the African context.

In addition, the slightly distorted nature of the 'global' field means that in many respects some African climate jurisprudence has not been framed or recognized as such. In this connection, the editors reject the notion that Africa is in any way behind, and take the view that the status of climate litigation will reflect what is needed and relevant, but that this requires analysis. Some of the chapters in this volume highlight disputes or engagements where climate change issues are implicit or peripheral, but have not been mapped or framed as climate cases. To some extent, this matters less to the litigants if they have achieved their desired outcome; it does, however, matter to us as scholars if we wish properly to understand the field. It also matters when it comes to the development of strategy for future and ongoing actions, as we discuss further below.

The writing and analysis in this book will support an understanding of the plural but also distinctive nature of a 'climate case' – and how and why the pursuit of justice may not culminate in a climate case – in the African context.[5] This is not a story of a few cases mimicking other strategies that have worked elsewhere. It is a story of – to some extent – constrained legal opportunities being put to work where they are most effective, by those with the expertise to know how.

Structure of book and contributions

The book is in three parts. The first part includes the introductory chapters, which outline how climate litigation in Africa is distinct. This includes several chapters that explore African climate litigation from various

4 See the chapters by T-L Field and DA Owona Mbarga in this volume, as well as HI Majamba, 'Emerging Trends in Addressing Climate Change through Litigation in Tanzania' (2023) 18 *Utafiti* 1.

5 This builds on and is complemented by the work done by ourselves and others previously – see n 1.

perspectives and based on different definitions, including doctrinal analyses of common and civil law countries, and an overview of existing litigation and activism strategies.

After this introductory chapter, Tracy-Lynn Field engages with the methodological and conceptual approaches that could be used to identify climate change cases decided in African courts, positing an approach based on climate risk with reference to the findings of climate science on the key climate risks in Africa. The value of a climate risk approach is demonstrated through a discussion of three 'drought litigation' cases from South Africa. In chapter 3, Ademola Jegede explores the tension between doctrinal potential and practical realities. He argues that due regard by a state to its obligation to protect human rights may help address procedural hurdles and thereby advance climate litigation for success in African countries. He highlights the need for reform that addresses legal obstacles to climate litigation. Chapter 4, by Nicole Loser, offers a series of case studies of climate litigation in South Africa, highlighting the importance of fundamental rights protection, and tensions between climate commitments and government energy policy. She outlines the strategies that have been used to target projects that would undermine South Africa's climate commitments. Owona Mbarga Daniel Armel's chapter examines the need and possibilities for climate litigation in Cameroon, a (mostly) civil law country. He demonstrates diverse and experienced civil society engagement with climate change issues in Cameroon, which, he argues, is more effective for preservation of resources needed for climate action – specifically forests – showing ways to achieve climate justice that are not limited to litigation.

Part 2 focuses entirely on human rights approaches. This is of particular relevance given the significance of human rights in shaping African legal systems. The chapters map across a range of jurisdictions and levels of law. The first three chapters in this part focus on African regional law. Elsabé Boshoff, in chapter 6, draws on African human rights norms, and substantive rights protection by regional human rights instruments, as well as the procedural considerations of climate litigation before human rights bodies. She provides a comprehensive overview of the opportunities and challenges of litigating climate change in the African human rights system. In chapter 7, Judge John Mativo highlights the growing implications of the climate crisis for displacement, illustrating that while not unique to African countries, the capacity of many states to adapt intensifies this risk. This means that the extent of displacement in African countries is particularly high. Simultaneously, the African regional system is alone in providing express legal recognition (potentially) to climate displaced persons, through the Kampala Convention, and extensive protection based on this. Judge Mativo highlights how a human rights-based approach to refugee protection could ensure better protection for climate refugees on the continent. In chapter 8, Fiona Batt highlights the value and vulnerability of the Meteorological Traditional Knowledge (MTK) of indigenous peoples; the value includes the capacity and willingness of indigenous peoples to interpret and respond to changing weather patterns. However, using MTK could make it vulnerable to appropriation and misuse. Batt demonstrates how MTK could be protected, both through international instruments, but also how human rights-based climate litigation through the African regional system have created powerful precedents that protect the cultural rights of indigenous peoples.[6]

Chapter 9, by Pia Rebelo and Xavier Rebelo, explores the role of human rights in climate litigation both globally and in other African countries, before analysing how the expansive horizontal interpretation of human rights in the South African Constitution creates unique potential for climate change litigation against private actors. They argue that the substantive protections afforded by the protection of the right to environment have not as yet been fully utilized, and demonstrate how effective this could be in holding private actors to account for climate harms. In chapter 10, Sanita van Wyk explores the influence of human rights protections and international law obligations on climate change, in the jurisprudence of the Dutch and South African courts. Using a comparative methodology, she highlights the difference in strategies and priorities in the two jurisdictions that, on opposite sides of the globe, share legal roots (South African law being derived, to some extent, from Roman Dutch law). She argues that, despite their different strategies, a study of the cases reveals 'two roads to the same destination', namely the mitigation of climate change.

The third part of the book considers various approaches related to justice, equity and activism. In chapter 11, Eghosa Ekhator and Edward Okumagba illustrate the synergies between environmental justice and climate justice in relation to litigation against fossil fuel companies in Nigeria. They provide an incisive contextual analysis of climate justice in this context, and – mapping across the dimensions of climate justice – demonstrate how litigation against multinationals in the Nigerian courts might yet tend towards climate justice. Riyadh Fakhri and Youness Lazrak Hassouni, in contrast, demonstrate that in Morocco the legislative and institutional framework for the governance of climate change – including the integration of climate change adaptation – is well-developed across a number of sectors, including energy, air pollution and the protection of water resources. However, the formal ambition is not matched by measures taken for implementation, and the judiciary – despite

6 Although not explored at length in the book, Batt also works within the ambit of what has been identified as a 'new knowledge frontier', the rise in the study of litigation seeking to ensure a just transition – see Savaresi *et al*, 'Just Transition Litigation: A New Knowledge Frontier.' Working paper available at https://papers.ssrn.com/sol3/papers.cfm?abstract_id=4561679.

being proactive in relation to discrete environmental and climate change disputes – have not exercised their power to accelerate implementation. In chapter 13, Pedi Obani examines the contingent and gendered nature of legal opportunities in climate litigation in South Africa and Nigeria, asking serious critical questions of how inclusive the litigation in the most-represented states in this context, truly are. Finally, Bright Nkrumah, in chapter 14, looks to the future by examining the principle of intergenerational equity. Mapping across African and international case law, he examines the extent to which this principle is embedded in constitutional protections, and has already featured directly and indirectly in the decisions of African courts.

Themes and reflections

This volume has two overarching themes. The first theme is that the African climate litigation must be informed by African priorities and values, and serve the purposes and needs of African peoples. From this perspective, what a climate case looks like will to some extent be informed by what necessary or desirable climate action looks like in the African context. As we highlight above, while many priorities are shared between all nations, the relative importance or urgency of them may not be the same in different context. But this does raise questions as to the relevance of 'global' strategies and what is needed locally to address the impacts of a changing climate.

The second theme relates to the tensions between global and local strategies, as well as those between barriers and opportunities both in doctrine and in practice. Most of the chapters in this book lie within this matrix of tension. The opportunities created by pluralist legal systems – particularly with entrenched human rights protection – runs parallel with constraints on standing, rules about costs or other disincentives. Also, as Obani argues in her chapter, there is some contingency in these legal opportunities, including patterns of exclusion that result in some marginalized groups being under-represented. These pressures are amplified by the global or transnational nature of the problem, which frequently means that the defendant is abroad, and out of reach due to legal or practical constraints.[7] This is associated, to some extent, with the question of why some more obvious mitigation ambition cases might not be brought.[8]

None of our contributions seek to map the field or really speak expressly to questions about how many climate cases there are in any particular

[7] Bouwer and Field (n 1), 125.

[8] Kotzé and du Plessis (n 1); S Adelman, 'Climate Change Litigation in the African System' in I Alogna, C Bakker and J-P Gauci (eds), *Climate Change Litigation: Global Perspective* (Brill 2021).

African country or the continent at large. In general, the project of mapping and tracking climate cases is useful and necessary,[9] but this is difficult to do comprehensively without an understanding of what African climate jurisprudence is. This is a task that will need to be undertaken by African scholars and activists as the field develops. It might be more interesting at this stage to ask what climate cases look like in different contexts and, more importantly, what they might hope to achieve in their own context. In this vein, Field argues that the key criteria underlying the selection of climate change cases in conventional climate litigation scholarship – climate visibility and centrality – underlie the claim that most climate cases are mitigation-related. She argues for developing a parallel archive of cases and associated scholarship that places climate risk at the centre, although what counts as climate risk will vary, spatially and temporally – even across the African continent.

This returns us again and again to definitional questions. The book does not set a definition of climate litigation, and some of our authors have either defined or clearly conceptualized climate litigation in this context in the more conventional frame, which makes sense in many ways. But as one of us has argued elsewhere:

> Climate litigation [in this context] can be understood as adjudicative activity that raises legal questions relating to climate change mitigation or adaptation or engages with some aspect of climate law or policy, whether or not these aspects are central to – or even peripheral to – the litigation. Adopting this broader understanding creates the space to read litigation in which climate issues are not front and centre or the main priority, as nonetheless worth studying. This broader approach is necessary for a proper understanding of climate litigation in ... Africa. But in addition to understanding the breadth of the field, the reasons why this broader analysis is necessary requires contextual reflection, including how legal rules fit with climate with climate change and how this 'threat multiplier' is reconciled with other challenges.[10]

Ekhator and Okumagba employ this broader definition or methodology in their work to explore how broadly defined climate litigation that targets environmental pollution can tend towards climate justice. Field's

[9] In general, climate litigation databases seek to 'catch' cases brought strategically that directly seek to improve climate action through some means, see Setzer and Higham (n 2), 13–14. This in itself is a task involving increasing challenges.

[10] K Bouwer, 'The Influence of Human Rights on Climate Litigation in Africa' (2022) 13 *Journal of Human Rights and Environment* 157, 158–9.

contribution examines these definition issues as tied to litigation priorities, raising the question of what should be the focal point for climate action on adaptation, and which methodological and conceptual approaches will assist in identifying African case law in this regard.

As highlighted above, the question is also what, in the African context, we might want climate litigation to achieve, which depends on broader questions about responsibility, relative contribution and what sustainable development looks like in the context of climate change on the African continent. African states have, with a few exceptions, made a negligible contribution to climate change. As Boshoff explains in her chapter, this could be one reason why fewer cases are brought at the regional level, and – as is a general theme in the book – why what can be called 'systemic'[11] mitigation cases have not made much of an appearance. In her chapter, Van Wyk also emphasizes the mitigation obligations that African states have adopted at the international level, how these differ to European countries, emphasizing that the pressure to mitigate is not as intense. While neither of these statements are particularly contentious in themselves, questions about responsibility, contribution and sustainable development would determine what was an appropriate or relevant target for litigation. For instance, as is clear from Nicole Loser's chapter, the case for discontinuing the use of coal in South Africa is pretty incontrovertible – but the case for discontinuing the use of fossil fuels in all states and (as Loser herself acknowledges) without viable alternatives is less clearcut.

Loser's chapter also makes very clear that the case against coal in the South African context is, but is not only, about the need to reduce greenhouse gas emissions. South Africa's reliance on coal has also caused localized air pollution, and stands to exacerbate existing vulnerabilities in the water-scarce country. The theme of vulnerabilities and the need for adaptation where possible runs through several of the chapters. Authors focus on the potential or greater scope for litigation arising in the context of climate vulnerabilities, including forests (Owona Mbarga) and water (Fakhri and Lazrak Hassouni). They also highlight how the complexities in the field and the limited scope of what could be achieved with litigation relative to its costs perhaps explain why there is a sense that there is less to do in this context. Applying a risk-based approach to the definition of climate litigation, Field's chapter incorporates a unique discussion of 'drought litigation' cases in South Africa. Boshoff's chapter also reminds us of the possibilities for systemic adaptation litigation, including before monitoring bodies of the regional system.

[11] See O Kelleher, 'A Critical Appraisal of Friends of the Irish Environment v Government of Ireland' (2021) 30 *Review of European, Comparative & International Environmental Law* 138.

What does emerge clearly from a number of the chapters, however, is an imaginative range of potential strategies that are being or could be deployed against corporate actors for their role in – and potentially against states for their complicity in – causing or contributing to the impacts of climate change on the continent. Again, Boshoff explains how the framing of rights protections at the regional level creates avenues both for state liability for complicity, as well as direct human rights responsibilities of corporations. Rebelo and Rebelo explore how the unique and radical interpretation of the horizontal application of human rights in South Africa could open up avenues towards litigation against the directors of high-emitting corporate bodies for their role in climate change. Ekhator and Okumagba demonstrate how the sustained legal response to multinational energy companies in Nigeria could advance climate justice. It should not be forgotten that, in many of the disputes where the defendants are government ministers or state parties, frequently the substance and outcome of the litigation does affect powerful – frequently transnational – corporate interests.[12]

A question that we discussed a great deal between ourselves as editors was the role and relevance of global strategies on climate litigation to the development of strategy in African countries. As we highlight above, climate litigation certainly is a global movement, but one in which the needs, priorities and context of many Global South countries are still in danger of being marginalized. This connects, to some extent, with the definitional issues we point to above and, similarly, how each author took a slightly different perspective to the role and relevance of the climate litigation movement as a whole. In general, we would suggest that global strategies are interesting and will remain influential, particularly as the climate litigation movement continues to be global and also as African scholars remain curious about the legal systems beyond their borders. For instance, in their chapters, Rebelo and Rebelo, and Van Wyk, explore how human rights have been used in climate cases in European countries. Their respective analyses inform but also illustrate the unique potential of the South African Constitution, and how judges use this in an ongoing project of legal transformation. Owona Mbarga looks to climate jurisprudence from Europe and other African countries, contrasting this both with legal constraints and contextual differences in Cameroon. Nkrumah and Judge Mativo both illustrate how international human rights protections can shape African climate change jurisprudence, but also how local or regional jurisprudence have developed their own norms based on African values. Also, each chapter demonstrates a strong

12 See Murcott and Webster (n 1). Also see S Bogojević and M Zou, 'Making Infrastructure "Visible" in Environmental Law: The Belt and Road Initiative and Climate Change Friction' (2021) 10 *Transnational Environmental Law* 35.

home-grown element, with scholars arguing that existing jurisprudence may be useful in crafting remedies – or understanding the implications of existing litigation as suggested in several chapters – that are context-specific. It goes without saying that existing knowledge and expertise on the ground has contributed to the success of many of the extant cases and, as Loser suggests, could also lend norms and strategies to other countries both in Africa and globally. Many of our chapters also discuss the strong cultures of legal activism that have developed in response to social and environmental issues more generally.

This is linked to another theme that emerges in many chapters, which is the connection between legal actions and activism, whether by pressure groups or formalized civil society organizations or non-governmental organizations (NGOs). Activists on the ground understand the potential and limits of the tools available to them, and we acknowledge that they would know best when other forms of advocacy or participation would better serve their purposes. In general, we find that many of our authors demonstrate a more sophisticated understanding of the interwoven nature of activism with the legal process than appears in much of the global legal scholarship on climate litigation. In other contexts, participation through NGOs or civil society organizations can strengthen the legitimacy of legal claims brought in response to community concerns.[13] Batt's highly original chapter illustrates how forms of adjudication in climate disputes (broadly defined) can also feature as sites of protection of indigenous peoples' Traditional Knowledge. In Loser's chapter, she explains that individual climate cases in the South African context frequently form part of ongoing campaigns targeted at defendant groups, and that this ongoing activism can reinforce and support the outcomes of individual cases.

In Owona Mbarga's work, he illustrates how evolved and experienced civil society practice to some extent replaces the need for litigation, in a context where access to courts is constrained but other forms of legal and political engagement are well-developed. There is also a strong understanding of how climate litigation as part of climate governance forms part of an overall legal framework[14] – as demonstrated by Fakhri and Lazrak Hassouni. They discuss how the effectiveness of climate legislation and the institutions created through it can provide effective and comprehensive governance solutions, to some extent supplanting the need for direct action through the courts.

[13] This is also illustrated with the 'litigation plus' approach discussed by EMA Okoth and MO Odaga, 'Leveraging Existing Approaches and Tools to Secure Climate Justice in Africa' (2021) 15 *Carbon & Climate Law Review* 129.

[14] E Fisher, 'Climate Change Litigation, Obsession and Expertise: Reflecting on the Scholarly Response to Massachusetts v. EPA' (2013) 35 *Law & Policy* 236, 242.

The question of when and how access to courts might arise is complex and varied. In some instances, either procedural rules or other considerations, including the risks of unfavourable costs orders, do represent practical barriers, as explored by Jegede.[15] However, the story emerging from the book is that there is significant untapped potential in terms of the use of the substantive law in strategic litigation. As Boshoff argues, the

> regional norms in general open pathways to, rather than hinder, climate litigation in the region, through providing for justiciable socio-economic rights and collective rights, strong obligations on duty bearers to respect, protect, promote and fulfil rights, strong norms for the protection of child rights and the possibility of individual (corporate) duties.

She, as well as Judge Mativo, highlight the under-utilized provisions that protect persons against climate-induced displacement in the African context, including through the Kampala Convention.[16] Similarly, the analysis by Rebelo and Rebelo reveals the unique potential for innovative litigation targeting corporate actors using human rights. But as much as developments in the substantive law create opportunities for litigation, some of our authors also acknowledge that they preclude the need for litigation. For instance, Fakhri and Lazrak Hassouni explain that, in Morocco, the legislature has moved forward in the legalization of climate change responses, much faster than the judiciary. This argument resonates with Jegede's position that states' duty to 'protect' rights entails the formulation of appropriate legislation that can remove barriers and aid the accountability of all actors involved in climate change and climate response measures.

Finally, the role and purpose of the science on climate change is a fundamental part of any study about climate change and the courts. In many cases, scientific proof connecting human activity to climate change or determining contribution share is fundamental for the success of climate cases. Many of our chapters demonstrate how scientific evidence has been or could be used to establish the necessary elements of an action. For instance, Van Wyk demonstrates how courts do or could use scientific evidence

---

15 Also explored in SAK Mwesigwa and PD Mutesasira, 'Climate Litigation as a Tool for Enforcing Rights of Nature and Environmental Rights by NGOs: Security for Costs and Costs Limitations in Uganda' (2021) 2 *Carbon & Climate Law Review* 139.

16 As one of us has argued elsewhere, the Kampala Convention may apply territorially and extraterritorially to protect human rights in the context of climate induced displacement: see AO Jegede, 'Rights Away From Home: Climate-Induced Displacement of Indigenous Peoples and the Extraterritorial Application of the Kampala Convention' (2016) 16 *African Human Rights Law Journal* 58–82.

to determine how much mitigation action is necessary for a state (in her chapter, the Netherlands or South Africa) to meet its emissions reductions obligations. But in this volume, the role and relevance of scientific evidence in climate change extends beyond its use as evidence in proceedings. Batt's chapter extols the value of 'other' forms of knowledge, but explains how Meteorological Traditional Knowledge of indigenous peoples should be protected if it is to be used in devising solutions to climate change. Field argues that climate science is foundational (but not exhaustive) for determining climate risk on the continent and in particular regions. As explained above, if the definitional boundaries around climate litigation are more porous in this plural space, using scientific evidence about the effects of climate change to determine sites of African climate cases presents another basis on which to use science to help us understand how the courts are responding to climate change.

In conclusion, we return to the observations we made at the beginning of the chapter. In this volume we see a picture of carefully targeted public interest litigation, embedded in grassroots campaigns that clearly make the connections between climate and environmental justice. We see a story of untapped potential arising from legal systems which are both highly plural and have a mandate to transform the law, to target corporation that drain Africa's resources, while moving the wealth this generates offshore. We also see, in some contexts, a picture of careful and responsible climate action and activism, that supplants the need to appeal to the courts. Yet we also note, as identified by several of our authors, that there is more contentious activity in Africa than has been recognized, and that this highlights the need for closer attention to how the local (and regional) courts are engaging with climate change issues, whether explicit or implicit. How can we understand the picture of climate litigation in the African context? To some extent, this work has just begun.

PART I

Legal Tools, Opportunities and Barriers

2

Towards a Risk-Thematic Approach for African Climate Litigation

Tracy-Lynn Field

Introduction

This chapter asserts a risk-thematic approach for African climate litigation. It engages with the methodological and conceptual approaches that could be used to identify climate change cases decided in African courts, and to develop a reflexive and critical scholarship on climate litigation for the African context.

There have been many attempts to define climate litigation and delineate litigation typologies.[1] However, from an African perspective, these attempts suffer from two glaring deficiencies. Firstly, they consistently position Africa on the margin of climate change litigation action, reflecting and reconstituting the continent's peripheral framing. Secondly, the climate visibility approach[2] used in mainstream 'global' climate litigation scholarship results in a case archive with a mitigation and Global North bias. This is not necessarily a bad thing for African climate litigation scholarship, as important mitigation litigation from the continent's courts has already been identified

1 D Markell and JB Ruhl, 'An Empirical Assessment of Climate Change in the Courts: A New Jurisprudence or Business as Usual?' (2012) 64 *Florida Law Review* 15; F Sindico and MM Mbengue (eds), *Comparative Climate Change Litigation: Beyond the Usual Suspects* (Palgrave 2021); NS Ghaleigh, '"Six Honest Serving Men" – Climate Change Litigation as Legal Mobilization and the Utility of Typologies' (2010) 1 *Climate Law* 31; J Lin, 'Climate Change and the Courts' (2012) 32 *Legal Studies* 35; J Peel and HM Osofsky 'Climate Change Litigation' (2020) 16 *Annual Review of Social Sciences* 21.

2 For an explanation of the 'climate visibility approach', see the discussion below.

and discussed in the mainstream literature.[3] The climate visibility approach also enables climate litigation scholars to support a transnational climate justice movement; that is, to spur ambition on greenhouse gas abatement and to position courts and citizens as strategic actors in a polycentric system of transnational climate governance.

But the climate visibility approach does not serve a more important agenda for climate law scholars from or interested in Africa, which is to study and advocate for transformation of the power relations, institutions and processes most critical to responding to the urgent and severe risks and vulnerabilities arising from already-observed and projected climate change. This is more than a call to focus on adaptation litigation, but rather an invitation to refocus the lens on the tools states and private actors have at hand to address climate change, to understand how these tools are already being used and contested, and to contribute to their evolution. A focus on the specificities of climate-related risks brings these tools into clearer view than a focus on 'climate change' *per se*.

This chapter responds to the gap in the literature on an alternative approach to developing the archive of climate cases, in two ways. Firstly, it attempts to discern the key criterion for identifying climate change cases in mainstream climate litigation scholarship, and argues that this criterion is climate visibility. Climate visibility is the Rosetta Stone of climate litigation knowledge, because it drives the selection of cases on which all the scholarship is based. The chapter reflects on the rationale underlying climate visibility, as well as its utility and limitations in an African context. Secondly, the chapter carves out space for an alternative approach to case selection, termed a risk-thematic approach. To this end, it references recent Intergovernmental Panel on Climate Change (IPCC) reports to identify the key climate risks governments and people in Africa are contending with. It then takes a methodological turn, exploring keywords associated with such risks and the case 'hits' each keyword delivers when used to search the Southern African Freedom of Legal Information Institute, an important open-access southern African legal database.[4] Finally, it analyses a sub-set of such cases – 'drought litigation' cases from South Africa – to illustrate the value of a risk-thematic approach. A discussion of these cases reveals how the South African courts are dealing with conflicts arising from drought relief and the imposition of water restrictions to deal with drought conditions, respectively. Using a risk-thematic approach, these cases constitute 'climate litigation' as

3 See, for example, K Bouwer and T-L Field, 'Editorial: The Emergence of Climate Litigation in Africa' 15 *Carbon & Climate Law Review* 123 and sources cited therein.

4 See http://www.saflii.org/.

they show how South African institutions are responding to drought as a key climate risk.

The use and limitations of a climate visibility approach to scoping climate litigation

The marginality of Global South cases in climate litigation and scholarship (and why they are still important)

Since the mid-2000s, climate litigation has emerged as a 'global phenomenon' with the potential to affect the outcome and ambition of climate governance.[5] Disillusioned with the pace and reach of domestic and international regulatory efforts stemming from international climate negotiations, actors outside of national government started turning to the courts as a way to advance (or delay) effective climate action.[6] As of May 2022, 2,002 'climate change litigation' cases had been filed before national, regional or international courts with the vast majority (71 per cent or 1,426 cases) filed before courts in the United States.[7] According to the climate change litigation database maintained by the Sabin Center for Climate Change Law and Policy, 88 climate change cases have been filed in Global South jurisdictions, of which only 13 (or 0.7 per cent) emanate from the African continent.[8]

A body of climate litigation literature has burgeoned alongside the growing archive of climate case law. From 2000 to 2019, 187 academic articles on climate change litigation were published in English law and social science journals.[9] Analyses of climate litigation in the Global North dominate this literature,[10] and the overwhelming focus is on mitigation-related litigation.[11] There are far fewer studies on adaptation litigation, or cases seeking remedies for climate-related loss and damage.[12] In their 2019 review of climate

---

[5] J Setzer and C Higham, *Global Trends in Climate Litigation: 2022 Snapshot* (Grantham Research Institute on Climate Change and the Environment and Centre for Climate Change Economics and Policy, London School of Economics and Political Science 2022), 1, 9.

[6] Peel and Osofsky (n 1), 21, 22.

[7] Setzer and Higham (n 5), 9.

[8] Setzer and Higham (n 5), 10. Cases filed in Kenya, Nigeria, South Africa, Uganda and the East Africa Court of Justice have been included in the database of Global Climate Change Litigation. Nine of the cases, however, emanate from South Africa.

[9] Peel and Osofsky (n 1), 24–5; J Setzer and LC Vanhala, 'Climate Change Litigation: A Review of Research on Courts and Litigants in Climate Governance' (2019) 10(3) *Wiley Interdisciplinary Review of Climate Change* 580.

[10] Peel and Osofsky (n 1), 28.

[11] Peel and Osofsky (n 1), 27. Mitigation-related cases include those challenging emissions reductions measures or policies, or challenges to coal-fired power stations.

[12] Peel and Osofsky (n 1).

litigation literature, Peel and Osofsky note the Global North bias of the literature, but observe a small shift in attention to climate litigation efforts in the Global South.[13]

Setzer and Benjamin concede that climate litigation in the Global South has to date received 'scant attention',[14] but note that the limited body of Global South climate cases advances the climate litigation agenda in at least two respects: The use of climate change framing to overcome, or to use, procedural requirements for access to environmental justice;[15] and the innovative ways in which climate change has been linked to human rights.[16] Here, they rely on the path-breaking work of Peel and Lin, who analysed 34 cases from 12 developing country jurisdictions to determine the Global South's contribution to 'transnational' climate litigation.[17]

Despite the low number of cases, Peel and Lin advance three reasons for paying attention to climate lawsuits in the Global South. The first is that Global South countries are the most vulnerable to climate change impacts, and many millions of people face the prospect of 'very real and tangible' climate change impacts on their homes, families, communities and livelihoods.[18] The second is that courts in the Global North and the Global South are *both* contributing to the project of global climate governance through transnational climate jurisprudence, which is a project that positions the courts (and the social actors petitioning the courts) as key actors in ensuring 'just outcomes for the most climate vulnerable'.[19] And the third is that paying attention to Global South cases adjusts the lens through which climate litigation is viewed, allowing for further growth of

13 Peel and Osofsky (n 1), 28. The authors make specific mention of litigation developments in China.

14 J Setzer and L Benjamin, 'Climate litigation in the Global South: Constraints and Innovations' (2020) 9(1) *Transnational Environmental Law* 77.

15 See further Bouwer and Field (n 3); SAK Mwesigwa and PD Mutesasira, 'Climate Litigation as a Tool for Enforcing Rights of Nature and Environmental Rights by NGOs: Security for Costs and Costs Limitations in Uganda' (2021) 15(2) *Carbon & Climate Law Review* 139; LA Omuko-Jung, 'The Evolving Locus Standi and Causation Requirements in Kenya: A Precautionary Turn for Climate Change Litigation?' (2021) 15(2) *Carbon & Climate Law Review* 171.

16 Setzer and Benjamin (n 14). The chapters on a human rights approach to climate litigation in Africa in this volume support this claim.

17 J Peel and J Lin, 'Transnational Climate Litigation: The Contribution of the Global South' (2019) 113(4) *American Journal of International Law* 679. The analysed cases are set out in supplementary material to the article. Since their article was published, the number of Global South cases (understood as cases decided in jurisdiction from state parties who were not listed in annex I to the United Nations Framework Convention on Climate Change), has increased to 136 cases from 22 jurisdictions.

18 Peel and Lin (n 17), 681–2.

19 Peel and Lin (n 17), 682.

the climate justice movement and better understanding the barriers to that movement's growth. This, in turn, highlights pragmatic considerations for strategic litigation (informing advocacy, stimulating partnership initiatives and capacity-building efforts, and so on).[20]

Curiously, Peel and Lin found that notwithstanding the great potential for adaptation-related climate litigation in the Global South, and even with employing an expanded 'lens' to net climate change cases (more on this in the section below), most Global South lawsuits focus on mitigation issues.[21] This is curious. Is it that cases arising from the 'very real and tangible impacts' of climate change on homes, families, and so on are simply not finding their way to courts in the Global South? Or is there is a deeper conceptual or methodological issue at play that is rendering these cases invisible and, with that, the knowledge claims that can be made about climate litigation? Answering these questions requires taking a step back to examine the conceptual and methodological choices underlying mainstream knowledge production on climate litigation.

The main criteria underlying the mainstream climate litigation archive: visibility and centrality

In 2019, Setzer and Vanhala observed that there are 'as many understandings of what counts as "climate change litigation" as there are authors writing on the phenomenon'.[22] Scholars have differed on the substantive criteria that distinguish a climate change case, the inclusion of quasi-judicial decision-making processes, and whether to include cases challenging climate regulatory measures in addition to those having a pro-regulatory focus.[23] Nevertheless, as the climate litigation field has evolved, two approaches to identifying the cases that fuel climate change scholarship have become dominant. The criteria that constitute these approaches are embedded in the task of defining climate litigation.

The first has been described as the narrow approach,[24] and stems from the path-finding work of Markell and Ruhl, who defined climate change litigation in 2010 in the context of the United States as 'any piece of federal, state, tribal, or local administrative or judicial litigation in which the party filings or tribunal decisions directly and expressly raise an issue of fact or law regarding the substance or policy of climate change causes and

[20] Peel and Lin (n 17), 683.

[21] Peel and Lin (n 17), 685.

[22] Setzer and Vanhala (n 9), 4.

[23] Peel and Osofsky (n 1), 23.

[24] Setzer and Higham (n 5), 6. In their latest update on global climate litigation, Setzer and Higham state that they adopt a 'narrow' approach to defining climate litigation.

impacts'.[25] According to the authors, this definition excludes cases motivated by concerns over climate change, and also cases where the consequence is aligned with climate regulatory objectives, but achieved through argument on other grounds (for example, halting the construction of a coal-fired power plant on the basis of failure to consider mercury deposition).[26] It nets cases where argument about 'fact or law' relating to 'climate change causes and impacts' (whether as substance or policy) is direct and express; that is, central and visible.

Building on scholarship advocating for a broader definition,[27] the second approach is described in Peel and Osofsky's 2020 review of climate litigation, which broadens the framing to cases where climate change features more peripherally.[28] With (1) climate change still at the core, their conception of climate litigation moves outward in a series of concentric circles to include cases where (2) climate change features as a peripheral issue, (3) litigation is motivated by climate change but is not raised as an issue, and (4) litigation has no express climate change framing but has implications for mitigation or adaptation.[29]

An expressly visible 'climate change' or 'climate policy' issue defines the first two categories, and one would be able to identify these cases by searching for the term 'climate change' in the judgment or papers. The third category is more tricky, and would require research on, for instance, media statements or the reports issued by litigating parties to determine whether climate change concerns feature as a motivation. The last category is the most nebulous of all, marking the point at which climate litigation starts fading into the more generic categories of litigation about environmental or natural resource management, raising the spectre that 'if everything is climate litigation, then nothing is'.[30] This blending should be avoided to guard the 'autonomy' of climate litigation, Kotze and Du Plessis argue 'to continue riding the wave of interest, positive sentiments, and enthusiasm surrounding it'.[31]

---

25 D Markell and JB Ruhl, 'An Empirical Survey of Climate Change Litigation in the United States' (2010) 40 *Environmental Law Reporter* 10644.

26 Markell and Ruhl (n 25), 10647.

27 See, for example, C Hilson, *Climate Change Litigation: A Social Movement Perspective* (2010), at 2, https://papers.ssrn.com/sol3/papers.cfm?abstract_id=1680362.

28 Peel and Osofsky (n 1), 24.

29 For the application of this typology in a South African context, see T-L Field, 'Climate Change Litigation in South Africa: Firmly Out of the Starting Blocks' in I Alogna *et al* (eds), *Climate Change Litigation: Global Perspectives* (Brill 2021).

30 LJ Kotze and A du Plessis, 'Putting Africa on the Stand' (2020) 50(3) *Environmental Law* 615, 622.

31 Kotze and du Plessis (n 30).

In their review of the Global South's contribution to transnational climate litigation, Peel and Lin apply their broader approach to a Global South context. They acknowledge that the visibility of climate change as the criterion to select cases has biased the scholarship toward high-profile mitigation cases,[32] and agree with Bouwer that this results in 'smaller scale' and 'lower profile' cases that nevertheless offer other valuable points of focus[33] being overlooked. They highlight the prevalence of cases where climate change is more peripheral to the arguments in non-US climate jurisprudence[34] and offer three possible reasons for the greater preponderance of peripheral climate framings in Global South jurisdictions, namely that: climate law frameworks and associated avenues to justice are absent, less well-developed or not implemented in the Global South;[35] climate change policy issues take a backseat to more pressing policy issues around economic development, poverty alleviation and public health;[36] and in many Global South countries, climate change adds a layer of complexity to, or exacerbates, existing environmental challenges such as air pollution, biodiversity loss or deforestation.[37]

To increase the number of Global South cases under analysis, Peel and Lin accordingly broaden the definition of climate litigation beyond the first category (narrow) approach, to include the second and third categories, where climate change features on the periphery of, or as a motivation for, arguments. The authors elucidate the methodological choice underlying their creation of the 'Global South docket', as the selection of cases that directly mention climate change in the pleadings, judgment, campaign materials or surrounding media.[38] They opine that with no visible climate change reference it would be difficult to distinguish a case as climate relevant. As mentioned above, with the help of this broader lens, the authors filed 34 cases in the Global South docket.

The visibility of references to 'climate' or to 'climate change' nevertheless remains paramount, and cases with climate change at the centre continue to define the 'conventional'[39] understanding of climate litigation.

Reviews of climate litigation scholarship reinforce visibility as the key definitional criteria. In their update to Setzer and Vanhala's review of climate

---

32 Peel and Lin (n 17), 689–90.

33 K Bouwer, 'The Unsexy Future of Climate Change Litigation' (2018) 30 *Journal of Environmental Law* 483.

34 Peel and Lin (n 17), 691.

35 Peel and Lin (n 17), 692.

36 Peel and Lin (n 17), 694.

37 Peel and Lin (n 17).

38 Peel and Lin (n 17), 695.

39 Peel and Lin (n 17), 690.

litigation scholarship, for example, Peel and Osofsky observe that the earlier review largely sidestepped the definitional difficulty of delimiting climate litigation.[40] But for purposes of consistency they limited their own update of the literature review to titles or abstracts in the major databases of English law and social studies containing the search terms 'climate' and 'litigation'.[41] They concede that this epistemological move limits the discussion to relevant literature self-identifying as being about climate litigation published in outlets dominated by English Global North scholars, and that this may exclude journal articles discussing cases with strong implications for mitigation or adaptation that do not expressly mention climate change.[42]

The value and limitations of the visibility approach criteria for scoping climate litigation

Narrowing the criteria for scoping climate change cases to visibility and centrality serves two very important functions. Firstly, the criterion disciplines judges and scholars to focus on the rather novel, recent idea that *the climate* can and should be governed, that is, that powers, duties and liabilities can be allocated to and vested in a wide range of actors for substances they release into (or taking into account developments in carbon capture and storage, remove from) the atmosphere. Such atmospheric governance has its roots in national and international efforts to address air pollution and control ozone-depleting substances, but has expanded massively in scope as a result of climate change science, and the understanding of how concentrations of heat-trapping gases in the atmosphere are affecting climate across the globe, over the short, medium and long term. Thus, the focus on 'mitigation-litigation', which essentially hones in on responsibilities attached to greenhouse gas abatement[43] is necessary and important to understand the continuing evolution of atmospheric governance.

Secondly, identifying climate change cases on the basis of climate visibility tends to flush out lawsuits that align with a longer tradition of strategic public interest litigation. Proponents of a transnational climate justice movement are now harnessing the resources and modalities of strategic public interest litigation to alleviate the frustration that other institutions (the negotiating parties to the United Nations Framework Convention on Climate Change, legislatures and executives, corporations) are not doing enough to stem the

40 Peel and Osofsky (n 1), 24.

41 Peel and Osofsky (n 1).

42 Peel and Osofsky (n 1).

43 J Peel and J Lin, 'Climate Change Adaptation Litigation: A View from Southeast Asia' in J Lin and D Kysar (eds), *Climate Change Litigation in the Asia Pacific* (Cambridge University Press 2019), 296–7; Bouwer (n 33), 484.

release of greenhouse gases (GHGs) into the atmosphere and deal with the already-evident impacts of climate change.[44] These are cases that, as Bouwer has astutely observed, are the 'holy grail' that:

> [T]end to be born from specific theoretical manifestos which seek to pursue climate litigation for a specific instrumental purpose: to force national governments to take more stringent action towards the reduction of their greenhouse gas emissions, and/or to force payments for climate change loss and damage based on historical responsibility.[45]

These cases cast judges, courts and litigious citizens of all stripes as the heroes, drawing attention to climate change issues and forcing greater ambition on the part of (villainous and laggardly) government regulators, administrators and corporations, sweeping change in one sexy, heroic litigious act.[46] They constitute, as Gloppen and St Claire have quipped, 'climate lawfare', a strategy climate change activists have adopted to use rights and legal institutions to deliver or at least catalyse social transformation and human development.[47] They are thus the cases that most overtly advance the cause of a transnational climate justice movement and the comforting idea that everyone can be an important player in multi-level climate governance.[48] By studying and writing about these cases, climate litigation scholars help inform advocacy, partnering initiatives and capacity building[49] and distill the 'recipes for success' that have been most effective.[50] This rights-based, public interest litigation is nevertheless seen as a vital strategy to secure just outcomes for the most climate-vulnerable.[51]

But the narrow criteria of climate visibility and centrality also has limitations and costs.[52] Leading the call to focus on smaller-scale, lower-profile and

---

44 This 'frustration' motivation encompasses Ghaleigh's typology of climate litigation (boundary-testing, defensive, promotive and perfecting cases claims), which supposedly encompass the 'entirety of climate change case law'. See Ghaleigh (n 1), 32.

45 Bouwer (n 33), 489–90, and n 4, where the 'holy grail' framing is attributed to Richard Lord QC.

46 Peel and Osofsky (n 1), 28; Kotze and Du Plessis (n 30), 622; Bouwer (n 33), 489.

47 S Gloppen and AL St Claire, 'Climate Change Lawfare' (2012) 79 *Social Research* 89, quoted in Kotze and Du Plessis (n 30), 623.

48 Peel and Lin (n 17), 681.

49 Peel and Lin (n 17), 683.

50 J Peel and R Markey-Towler, 'Recipes for Success? Lessons for Strategic Climate Litigation from the *Sharma*, *Neubauer* and *Shell* Cases' (2021) 22 *German Law Journal* 1484.

51 Peel and Lin (n 17), 682.

52 These limitations and costs have been acknowledged by authors using the conventional definition. See, for example, Peel and Lin (n 17), 690; J Setzer and L Benjamin, 'Climate Change Litigation in the Global South: Filling in Gaps' (2020) 114 *AJIL Unbound* 56, 60.

private cases,[53] as well as cases that address all elements of climate action,[54] Bouwer warns that a preoccupation with holy grail cases 'achieves little in terms of policy improvement, and distracts attention and resources from other policy areas, where litigation could have a more significant effect in terms of improving the climate change response'.[55]

One of the costs is the relative neglect of adaptation cases, which go 'unnoticed'. Ohdedar supports broadening the scope of climate litigation 'by incorporating smaller, more discrete cases that have not been argued on expressly climate grounds'[56] to start understanding the multiple ways in which climate change adaptation may be present but invisible.[57]

Put another way, the case selection criteria underlying conventional climate litigation keeps out of focus the tools that global North and South governments have at their disposal to address climate risks, and how the courts are already shaping a risk response. Scholars are thus missing out on opportunities to study and describe the evolution of these tools and advocate for their development and transformation.

But what can fill the gap of climate visibility as a case selection criterion? What happens when one moves litigation about environmental or natural resource management or, even broader, litigation happening 'in the context of climate change' to the very centre? Do we risk diluting climate litigation to the point where it means nothing, as Kotze and Du Plessis caution? Does a shift away from a visibility approach mean putting climate 'adaptation' at the core and, if so, how would one recognize cases about climate adaptation? Peel and Lin maintain that climate adaptation cases are typically managed through planning and environmental law frameworks,[58] but do we risk creating a new realm of invisibility when outside of these regulatory frames are excluded? Are planning and EIA (environmental impact assessment) legal

---

53 Bouwer (n 33), 483.

54 Bouwer (n 33), 496–9. The elements of climate action other than mitigation are finance, technology transfer, capacity building, transparency and loss and damage.

55 Bouwer (n 33), 493.

56 B Ohdedar, 'Climate Adaptation, Vulnerability and Rights-Based Litigation: Broadening the Scope of Climate Litigation Using Political Ecology' (2022) *Journal of Human Rights and the Environment* 137, 138.

57 Bouwer (n 33), 502–4.

58 Bouwer (n 33), 294. Admittedly, in their recent review, Peel and Osofsky identify a third category, namely cases seeking remedies for loss and damage (see Peel and Osofsky (n 1) 27). This category of cases may rise in prominence in climate litigation scholarship following the 'breakthrough' agreement on a new 'Loss and Damage Fund' for vulnerable countries taken at COP 27 (see UN Climate Press Release "COP27 reaches breakthrough agreement on new 'Loss and Damage' fund for vulnerable countries" (20 November 2022), available at https://unfccc.int/news/cop27-reaches-breakthrough-agreement-on-new-loss-and-damage-fund-for-vulnerable-countries.

instruments exhaustive of the tools climate-impacted governments have to address the myriad of climate risks already manifesting?

Climate risk as the basis for case selection

The remainder of this chapter is devoted to the idea that climate risk should be at the center of case selection. By foregrounding climate risk, a second overarching category of climate litigation and derivative scholarship will emerge, to complement conventional climate litigation and scholarship on mitigation (or what may be called 'atmospheric governance' litigation).

A risk-based framing has already come to the fore in recent scholarship. In their comparative review of three African cases, for example, Kotze and Du Plessis define climate litigation as 'all litigious means offered by judicial and quasi-judicial fora to adjudicate juridical conflicts emanating directly from the risks and impacts of climate change'.[59] They further highlight climate-change related risks in recent IPCC reports on Africa, which include (among others) compounded stress on water resources, extreme weather events, reduced crop productivity and increased food insecurity.[60] Yet, they do not go on to examine how a risk-thematic focus should inform criteria for case selection, and the cases they select for a comparative analysis already fall within the Global South docket.

Ohdedar posits a novel analytical approach for adaptation litigation that also incorporates risk. Drawing on political ecology, he proposes a vulnerability framing that distinguishes between the biophysical risk of climate change (a hazards framing), and a social vulnerability framing that incorporates human security and relational approaches.[61] Therefore, he opens up space to situate biophysical risk and, within that context, vulnerable groupings at the core of a climate litigation typology.

The remainder of this chapter aims to develop these nascent risk-based approaches into a more full-fledged risk-thematic approach to climate litigation in Africa.

Towards a risk-thematic approach

Putting climate risk at the centre of case selection requires taking into account the spatial and even temporal specificity of impacts. Climate change is being experienced differently in different parts of the world. Although droughts,

---

59 Kotze and Du Plessis (n 30), 622.

60 Kotze and Du Plessis (n 30), 628.

61 Ohdedar (n 56), 145. Ohdedar's approach suggests numerous other avenues of investigation which, for reasons of space, are not further explored in this chapter.

extreme weather events and wildfires are not discriminating, the IPCC has identified regional biophysical trends.[62] Risks are also temporally-specific, with many regions of the world experiencing cycles of droughts, flooding or cyclones. Risk intersects differentially with vulnerability which, once again, is comprehensively reflected in the IPCC Working Group II's regional assessments of risks and vulnerability.[63] Apart from the IPCC's assessments, National Adaptation Plans (NAPs) and, more recently, updated Nationally Determined Contributions (NDCs) to the Paris Agreement offer more granular assessments of risk and vulnerability in particular jurisdictions. The upshot of these observations is that climate risk is not going to be the same everywhere, and neither will the criteria that capture it. The IPCC's scientific reports as well as NAPs and NDCs should be the starting point to determine the criteria for case selection for a scholarship that examines more specific and granular climate risk in particular regions and countries.

With a view to contextualizing a discussion on the possible keywords that could be used to identify climate risk relevant cases for Africa, this section relies on the IPCC reports to outline the key risks the continent faces. This section also outlines some of the limitations of relying only on these reports and scientific studies of probabilistic event attribution (PEA).

The state of climate change science in Africa

The first observation one should make about climate change science and Africa is that the continent is under-represented in the datasets and models that drive climate change observations, attributions and projections. In terms of trends in annual precipitation, for example, there is not enough observational data for most regions in Africa over the last century to draw definitive conclusions, and many regions have discrepancies between different observed precipitation datasets.[64] The knowledge base is even more patchy for biophysical drivers and huge gaps remain.[65] Africa is also under-represented

62 See, for instance, JM Gutiérrez *et al*, 'Atlas' in V Masson-Delmonte *et al* (eds), *Climate Change 2021: The Physical Science Basis. Contribution to Working Group I to the Sixth Assessment Report of the Intergovernmental Panel on Climate Change* (Cambridge University Press 2021) 1927, 1968.

63 IPCC Sixth Assessment Report, 'Climate Change 2022: Impacts, adaptation and vulnerability', https://www.ipcc.ch/report/ar6/wg2/.

64 Gutiérrez (n 62), 1968.

65 See, for example, the coverage of studies on the impact of climate change on streamflow, where there is almost no coverage for much of Africa (MA Caretta and A Mukherji (eds), 'Water' in H Pörtner *et al*, *Climate Change 2022: Impacts, Adaptation and Vulnerability. Working Group II Contribution to the Sixth Assessment Report of the Intergovernmental Panel on Climate Change* (IPCC 2022), 4–26).

in the emerging field of PEA, as very few of the studies in a journal such as the American Meteorological Society's 'Explaining extreme events' focus on Africa, despite it being clear that climate change is already driving extreme weather events on the continent.[66] Any attempt to link the core of climate change litigation to 'climate change science' narrowly considered as actually completed studies cited in court filings or judgments will therefore radically restrict what counts as risk-thematic climate litigation. This does not mean that the physical and biophysical phenomenon that climate change scientists around the world are studying are not also unfolding on the continent.

Despite these limitations, the IPCC has reported that in terms of observed impacts there is a high level of confidence that mean annual surface temperature is rising rapidly over the whole continent. Significant increases of 0.1°C and 0.2°C per decade have been observed in all regions, with higher increases over the eastern and south-western regions of Sub-Saharan Africa.[67] These temperature increases can be attributed 'to strong evidence of a continent-wide anthropogenic signal'.[68] Statistically significant decreases in the amount of rainfall and the number of rainy days have been observed in the eastern, central and north-eastern parts of South Africa during spring and summer (1960–2010),[69] as well as Central Africa and the Horn of Africa. Conversely, over mountainous regions such as the southern Drakensberg in South Africa, southern West Africa, and the Sahel increased or more intense rainfall has been observed.[70]

Looking forward, the World Climate Research Programme's Coupled Model Inter-comparison Project Phases 5 and 6 (CMIP5 and CMIP6) projects continued warming across the continent.[71] Under a business-as-usual emissions scenario,[72] median projected regional warming for 2080–2100 compared to 1995–2014 will be in the order of 4°C and in some regions 5°C.[73] The south-western region of the continent (covering

[66] See American Meteorological Society, 'Explaining extreme events from a climate perspective', https://www.ametsoc.org/ams/index.cfm/publications/bulletin-of-the-american-meteorological-society-bams/explaining-extreme-events-from-a-climate-perspective/.

[67] Gutiérrez (n 62), 1968.

[68] Gutiérrez (n 62), 1969.

[69] Gutiérrez (n 62), 1968.

[70] Gutiérrez (n 62).

[71] Gutiérrez (n 62), 1971.

[72] Referenced in the climate change literature as RCP8.5. For a critique of RCP8.5 as a modelling scenario see Carbon Brief 'Explainer: The high-emissions "RCP8.5" global warming scenario', 2019, https://www.carbonbrief.org/explainer-the-high-emissions-rcp8-5-global-warming-scenario/, accessed 16 July 2022.

[73] Gutiérrez (n 62), 1969. Under the Shared Socio-Economic Pathways (SSP) scenario 1–2.6 these median projected temperature increases are 1°C and 2°C respectively.

parts of Namibia, Botswana and South Africa) is expected to experience the largest increase in temperature, greater than global mean warming, as the interior of southern Africa will warm faster than equatorial and tropical regions.[74] The enhanced warming over southern Africa is projected to result in a reduction in mean rainfall as well as an increase in rainfall intensity. In other parts of Sub-Saharan Africa, however, large uncertainties remain.[75] These projections point to an intensified and disrupted hydrological cycle.[76]

Notwithstanding the patchy science on the impacts of climate change on biophysical drivers, observed changes in soil moisture between 1978 and 2018 show a 10–20 per cent reduction in soil moisture over much of southern Africa, increases of up to 10 per cent over eastern Africa, and more of a drying than a wetting trend across central and west Africa.[77] Much of Sub-Saharan Africa is already subject to moderate to high drought risk,[78] and the likelihood of agricultural drought (driven by soil moisture) increases by 100–250 per cent under a 4°C global warming in south-west Africa.[79]

Turning to completed PEA studies, Kam *et al* estimated that the 2015–2019 drought in South Africa's Western Cape, for example, was at least double as likely as a result of anthropogenic greenhouse forcing.[80] The same is true of the drought in Tanzania, Ethiopia and Somalia that occurred over more or less the same time period, which contributed to extreme food insecurity.[81] Table 2.1 cites attribution studies pertinent to disruption of the hydrological cycle in Africa.

These studies may not be raised in any particular litigation proceeding as a basis to pin liability on a greenhouse gas emitter, but they are important for grounding an understanding of the biophysical stressors African people are facing as a result of anthropogenic climate change.

---

[74] Gutiérrez (n 62), 1971.

[75] Gutiérrez (n 62), 1971.

[76] Caretta and Mukherji (n 65), 4–41.

[77] Caretta and Mukherji (n 65),4–21–22. Changes to the balance of precipitation and evapotranspiration drive changes in soil moisture.

[78] Caretta and Mukherji (n 65), 4–33.

[79] Caretta and Mukherji (n 65), 4–72.

[80] J Kam *et al*, 'CMIP6 Model-Based Assessment of Anthropogenic Influence on the Long-Sustained Western Cape Drought over 2015–2019' *Explaining Extremes of 2019 from a Climate Perspective* (2021) 102(1)*Bulletin of the American Meteorological Society* S45–S50. The vast majority of studies in this series, however, are concentrated on developing world regions and/or Asia.

[81] IPCC Sixth Assessment Report (n 63), 4–35.

Table 2.1: PEA studies on the disruption of the water cycle in Africa

Sector	African attribution studies
Agricultural production	South Southern Africa: anthropogenic emissions increased the chances of October to December droughts over south southern Africa by 1.4–4.3 times[a]
Hydropower	Ghana: between 1970 and 1990 rainfall variability accounted for 21% of inter-annual variations in hydropower generation[b]
Outbreaks of water-related and neglected tropical disease	• Senegal: rainy season associated with 84% increase in relative risk of childhood diarrhea[c] • Mozambique: additional wet day per week associated with 2% increase in diarrheal disease[d]
Cities	South Africa: likelihood of prolonged rainfall deficit in Cape Town during 2015–2017 made more likely by factor of 3.3 (1.4–6.4)[e]

[a] Nangombe *et al* (n 106).

[b] SA Boadi and K Owusu, 'Impact of Climate Change and Variability on Hydropower in Ghana' (2019) 38(1) *African Geographical Review* 19.

[c] S Thiam *et al*, 'Association between Childhood Diarrhoeal Incidence and Climatic Factors in Urban and Rural 41 Settings in the Health District of Mbour, Senegal' (2017) 14(9) *International Journal of Environmental Research and Public Health* 42.

[d] LM Horn *et al*, 'Association between Precipitation and Diarrheal Disease in Mozambique' (2018) 15(4) *International Journal of Environmental Research and Public Health* 22.

[e] FEL Otto *et al*, 'Anthropogenic Influence on the Drivers of the Western Cape Drought 2015–2017' (2018) 13(12) *Environmental Research Letters* 124010.

Climate science's consensus on Africa's key risks

Working Group II's key risks[82] for particular regions crystallize the impact of climate-related physical and biophysical drivers on social, cultural, economic and political pathways (impacts the Working Group has characterized as 'multifaceted and severe').[83] The key risks build on detailed sectoral studies that link physical and biophysical drivers and vulnerabilities. Table 2.2 below sets out the relationship among impacts, drivers and vulnerabilities for the sectors used in Working Group II's most recent assessment of water insecurity.

In Africa, water and energy insecurity arising from hydropower shortages[84] is a stand-alone risk, but precipitation changes feature in all other key risks, which are: loss of food production; reduced economic output and

[82] Defined as 'potentially severe' risk. See CH Trisos, IO Adelekan and E Totin, 'Chapter 9' in IPCC Sixth Assessment Report Pörtner (n 63), 9–18.

[83] IPCC Sixth Assessment Report (n 63), 4–41.

[84] Which would in turn also impact irrigation as an adaptive response to drought.

Table 2.2: Sectoral impacts of an intensified hydrological cycle and associated vulnerabilities[a]

Sector	Observed impact	Driver	Vulnerability	Confidence
Agricultural production	Negative	Drought[b]	Food insecurity	High
Hydropower	Negative	Rainfall variability	Shortage of hydropower generation	Medium
Thermal power production	Negative	Drought, increased ambient water temperatures	Loss of coal-fired capacity	High
Mining, metal, agro-processing sectors	Risk	Lack of water availability	Operational impacts	Low
Outbreaks of water-related and neglected tropical disease (WaSH)	Negative	Increase in temperature, precipitation and extreme weather events	Increase in diarrheal disease, mortality and morbidity from infectious diseases	High
Disruption of water supply	Negative	Extreme weather events[c]	Morbidity, morality and mental health	Very high
Some cities	Negative	Exacerbation of existing flood and drought hazard	Management and supply of water to cities, economic loss	High
Freshwater ecosystems	Negative	Increasing temperatures, declining rainfall	Limited food supply for freshwater species, physiological stress and death, migration	High
Water-related conflict	Increase (exacerbation not causal)	Reduction of water availability exacerbates tensions (especially in groups dependent on agriculture)	Conflict, conflict-ridden societies unable to manage climate-related stressors	High
Bilateral migration	Increase	Slow- or rapid-onset climate-related events	Temporary or permanent migration	Medium
Cultural uses of water	Negative	Inundation, relocation, scarcity of water	Non-economic loss of culture and traditions,[d] mental health impacts	Medium

[a] Based on information presented in Pörtner (n 66), 4–41–4–54.

[b] According to research conducted by Vogel *et al*, mean climate and climate extremes are responsible for 20–49 per cent yield anomalies variance. Between 18 per cent and 49 per cent of this variance is attributable to droughts and heatwaves. See E Vogel *et al*, 'The Effects of Climate Extreme on Global Agricultural Yields' 14(5) *Environmental Research Letters*, https://iopscience.iop.org/article/10.1088/1748-9326/ab154b/meta. Yield delinks of major crops such as maize, soy beans and rice are more marked in semi-arid regions, which include sub-Saharan Africa (see IPCC Sixth Assessment Report (n 63), 4–42).

[c] Extreme weather events can exacerbate existing WaSH vulnerabilities, cause WaSH infrastructure failure or be associated with inadequate WaSH facilities in emergency treatment centres. The loss of electricity during extreme weather events may also detrimentally impact WaSH coverage.

[d] Exacerbated by ongoing processes of colonialism and capitalism.

growth; mortality and morbidity from infectious disease; the cascading and compounding risks of loss of life, livelihoods and infrastructure in human settlements; and reduction in or irreversible loss of ecosystem function and species extinction.[85]

Crop and livestock production is affected by the overlapping and synergistic impacts of drought, heatwaves and diseases and pests. Impacts on agriculture and associated loss of food production from crops, livestock and fisheries looms large because 55–62 per cent of the Sub-Saharan Africa workforce is employed in agriculture, and 95 per cent of cropland is rainfed.[86] There is high confidence that since 1961 climate change has already reduced total agricultural productivity growth by 34 per cent, which is more than any other region.[87] Lost food production will make even more Africans food insecure, but subsistence farmers, the rural poor and pastoralists will feel the impact of variable precipitation and drought most keenly.[88]

Aggregate macroeconomic impacts of climate change in Africa have largely manifested through losses in agriculture.[89] According to Diffenbaugh and Burke's analysis, for example, GDP per capita would on average be 13.6 per cent higher for African countries in the absence of global warming since 1991.[90] Warming in poorer, drier African countries has thus increased global inequality relative to the temperate Northern hemisphere.[91]

Precipitation changes (both increases and decreases) drive mortality and morbidity arising from infectious disease, a situation compounded by the existing inadequacy of water and sanitation infrastructure, and burgeoning population growth and urbanization. Increased malaria incidents and outbreaks have already been observed as a result of shifting rainfall patterns and extreme flooding.[92] In drought conditions, species of virus-transmitting mosquitos thrive in open water storage facilities near human settlements, while flooding enables mosquitos to proliferate and spread diseases such as dengue, Zika and Rift Valley fever even further. Kraemer *et al* suggest that

85 Trisos, Adelekan, Totin (n 82), 9–22.

86 L Abrams *et al* (2018), *Unlocking the Potential of Enhanced Rainfed Agriculture*, Report No. 39, SIWI, Stockholm, https://siwi.org/wp-content/uploads/2018/12/Unlocking-the-potential-of-rainfed-agriculture-2018-FINAL.pdf.

87 A Ortiz-Bobea *et al*, 'Anthropogenic Climate Change Has Slowed Global Agricultural Productivity Growth' (2021) 11(4) *Nature Climate Change* 306.

88 Trisos, Adelekan, Totin (n 82), 9–21.

89 S Barrios, L Bertinelli and E Strobl, 'Trends in Rainfall and Economic Growth in Africa: A Neglected Cause of the African Growth Tragedy' (2010) 92(2) *The Review of Economics and Statistics* 350.

90 NS Diffenbaugh and M Burke, 'Global Warming Has Increased Global Economic Inequality' (2019) 116(20) *Proceedings of the National Academy of Sciences* 9808–13.

91 Diffenbaugh and Burke (n 90), 9808.

92 AM Adeola *et al*, 'Predicting Malaria Cases Using Remotely Sensed Environmental Variables in Nkomazi, South Africa' (2019) 14(1) *Geospatial Health*.

by 2050 the African population exposed to mosquito-borne viruses may double, and by 2080 nearly triple at >2°C warming.[93] Africa already has the highest death rates from diarrheal disease in the world and even if children don't die, repeated episodes of diarrhea cause stunting, impaired growth and reduced cognitive performance. Water supply disruptions, whether during droughts or flooding, will further jeopardize access to safe water and sanitation, with a projected 20,000 to 30,000 additional child deaths by 2050 under a 1.5° to 2°C scenario. West Africa will be most affected, followed by East, Central and southern Africa.[94]

Floods and coinciding drought and heat will have cascading and compounding effects on life, livelihoods and infrastructure in African human settlements. Africa is the most rapidly urbanizing region in the world and almost 60 per cent of the population of Sub-Saharan Africa lives in informal settlements.[95] Decreased rainfall in rural areas drives increased migration to informal settlements, and such informal settlements heighten exposure to climate hazards such as floods and landslides.[96] Flooding, however, is a more significant threat, as floods accounted for 80 per cent of the 337 million African people displaced by climate hazards from 2000 to 2019. Africa is the only region in the world where flood mortality has increased since the 1990s, and exposure to flood shocks has been associated with extreme poverty and up to 35 per cent reduction in consumption.[97] Floods have also had a devastating impact on Sub-Saharan Africa's already-fragile road transport, energy, and water and sanitation infrastructure, and yet it is not clear how major planned infrastructure investments such as the African Union's Programme for Infrastructure Development or China's Belt and Road Initiative will integrate planning for future climate change risks.[98]

Last, but by no means least, precipitation changes will contribute to reduction in or irreversible loss of ecosystem function and species extinction. Changes in African terrestrial and freshwater ecosystems has already been observed (for example, the overall continental trend is woody plant expansion into savannas and grasslands, with knock-on effects for the bird, reptile and mammal species dependent on those habitats as well as cattle production and

---

[93] MUG Kraemer *et al*, 'Past and Future Spread of the Arbovirus Vectors Aedes Aegypti and Aedes Albopictus' (2019) 4(5) *Nature Microbiology* 854.

[94] SM Moore *et al*, 'El Nino and the Shifting Geography of Cholera in Africa' (2017) 114(17) *Proceedings of the National Academy of Sciences* 4436–41.

[95] UN-Habitat, *World Cities Report 2016. Urbanization and Development: Emerging Futures* (UN-Habitat 2016).

[96] D Satterthwaite *et al*, 'Building Resilience to Climate Change in Informal Settlements' (2020) 2(2) *One Earth* 143.

[97] C Azzarri and S Signorelli, 'Climate and Poverty in Africa South of the Sahara' (2020) 125 *World Development* 104691.

[98] Trisos, Adelekan and Totin (n 82), 9–98.

water supply).[99] At 2°C global warming, 11.6 per cent of African species are at risk of global extinction, increasing to 20 per cent for certain species at >2°C.[100] These species losses and extinctions will also have deleterious effects on African nature-based tourism. Heat and drought has already had an effect on ecosystem services in Africa by reducing crop and livelihood activity, fish stocks and water provisioning. But were global warming to exceed 3°C, 1.2 billion Africans are projected to be negatively affected by polluted drinking water and reduced ecosystem water regulation.[101]

These key risks should be defining which cases are climate relevant for an African context: not climate change policies or laws as such, or cases launched against GHG regulators or emitters, but rather the ways in which particular risk themes arise in cases. These themes include, but are not confined to: agriculture (particularly as affected by drought), flood damage, the spread of waterborne diseases, hydropower shortages or disruptions, and the loss of savannas and grasslands. Instead of (or as well as) using 'climate' as a search term, for example, African scholars should be searching for cases with terms such as 'drought', 'floods', 'agricultural relief', or possibly 'hydropower' in the pleadings or judgment as a first-level screening tool. The facts of the case will then indicate the extent to which climate change impacts featured in the case.[102]

The following section presents the results of various climate risk keyword searches of an open-access legal database containing judgments from southern Africa.

Applying a risk-thematic approach to African case law

Identifying climate change cases based on the thematic messiness of key risks is more complicated than a clean-cut search for cases that mention 'climate change' or 'greenhouse gas emissions'. To test the utility of a risk-thematic approach, a variety of keywords were tested to find case law, literature and (to a lesser extent) legislation in the Southern African Freedom of Legal Information Institute (SAFLII) database of legal materials, which contains legal materials from across southern Africa.[103]

99 CR Axelsson and NP Hanan, 'Rates of Woody Encroachment in African Savannas Reflect Water Constraints and Fire Disturbance' (2018) 45(6) *Journal of Biogeography* 1209–18.

100 Trisos, Adelekan and Totin (n 82), 9–65.

101 R Chaplin-Kramer *et al*, 'Global Modeling of Nature's Contributions to People' (2019) 366 *Science* 255.

102 Attribution studies may assist in this analysis but should not be regarded as essential.

103 SAFLII purports to incorporate case law from the national courts of Botswana, Lesotho, Malawi, Mozambique, Namibia, the Seychelles, South Africa, Tanzania, Uganda, Zimbabwe and Zambia as well as the East Africa Courts of Justice and Appeal. However, the content is heavily biased in favour of South Africa.

Table 2.3: Number of hits on the SAFLII database using varying keywords for identifying climate change cases and literature

Keyword	No. of hits
Climate change	87
Greenhouse gas	26
Greenhouse gas AND oil OR gas OR coal	18
Water security	25
Drought	217
Agriculture AND climate change	42
Agriculture AND heat stress	2
Agricultural relief	0
Agricultural loss	2
Veldfire	25
Flooding	150
Sanitation AND floods or droughts	78
Ecosystem services	22
Ecosystem loss	0

Table 2.3 records the number of hits using various combinations of climate risk keywords.

The keyword of 'climate change', which aligns with the visibility criterion for identifying climate relevant cases, yielded 87 hits on this database, but of those only 21 were distinct judgments, all from South Africa. The remaining hits are literature hits, with a number of double entries. Five of those literature hits deal with water security.[104] The narrower search terms of 'greenhouse gas' or 'greenhouse gas AND oil OR gas OR coal' yield 26 and 18 hits respectively (of which six and four hits are actual cases).

Using the alternative key word of 'water security' results in nine case hits, of which six do not overlap with so-called climate change cases.

[104] T Honkonen, 'Water Security and Climate Change: The Need for Adaptive Governance' (2017) 20 *Potchefstroom Electronic Law Journal* 52; B Qumbu, 'The Role of the Courts in Advancing Water Security in South Africa' 24 (2021) *Potchefstroom Electronic Law Journal* 18; C Soyapi and T Honkonen, 'Special Edition: Water Security' (2017) 20 *Potchefstroom Electronic Law Journal* 6; T Kuokkanen, 'Water Security and International Law' (2017) 20 *Potchefstroom Electronic Law Journal* 57; CB Soyapi, 'Water Security and the Right to Water in Southern Africa: An Overview' (2017) 20 *Potchefstroom Electronic Law Journal* 72; A Rieu-Clarke and C Spray, 'Ecosystem Services and International Water Law: Towards a More Effective Determination and Implementation of Equity' (2013) 16 *Potchefstroom Electronic Law Journal* 19.

But the keywords of 'drought' or 'flooding'[105] nets a much broader set of cases, including cases from Zimbabwe and Botswana. Although there is literature mentioning 'drought', there was no single literature contribution discussing the adequacy of drought governance mechanisms in the face of the climate crisis. That 120 of the drought hits are from 2014 and later is suggestive that the cases were responding to the drought conditions in Sub-Saharan Africa during the second decade of the twentieth century, for which there are already some PEA studies.[106] Three of these cases are described below.

The keywords of 'agriculture' and 'climate change' show less promise as screening criteria, as the cases they net overlap to a large extent with cases identified using the keyword of 'climate change' and most of the hits refer to non-climate relevant literature. An interesting couple of cases, however, examine the relationship between animal welfare and heat stress.[107] The keyword of 'agricultural relief' had no hits, and 'agricultural loss' yielded only two hits. However, 25 hits related to 'veldfire' and most are case law. The relationship between drought conditions, heat and fire is well-established and these cases may therefore also be valuable for discerning how law is being used deal with the impacts of veldfire, and how affected parties are adapting to the impacts of climate change.

Similarly to 'drought' the keyword of 'flooding' brought a larger number of cases to the fore – 150 in total – of which 124 (82 per cent) are cases. These cases would need to be examined to determine whether the factual matrix can be linked to an extreme flooding event that could be attributed to climate change. Like the 'drought' dataset, the flooding cases include cases from Botswana.

The keywords of 'sanitation' AND 'drought OR floods' responds to the intersectional risks of extreme weather events and the lack of water, sanitation and hygiene (WaSH) facilities in southern Africa. These keywords generated 78 hits of which 47 (60 per cent) are cases, with the overwhelming majority decided after 2015. This could be an indication of attempts to use the law

[105] The keyword 'flooding' was preferred to 'flood' or 'floods' given courts' penchant for referring to themselves being flooded by case law.

[106] S Nangombe, T Zhou, L Zhang and W Zhang, 'Attribution of the 2018 October–December Drought Over South Southern Africa (2020) 101(1) *Bulletin of the American Meteorological Society* S135–S140.

[107] *National Council for the Prevention of Cruelty to Animals v Al Mawashi (Pty) Ltd* [2020] ZAECGHC 118 (15 October 2020), *Al Mawashi (Pty) Ltd v National Council of Societies for the Prevention of Cruelty to Animals* [2020] ZAECGHG 74 (30 June 2020). In these cases the National Council sought an interdict from the court banning the practice of transporting sheep from anywhere in South Africa to anywhere north of the Equator by anyone on any vessel during any time of the year. In their argument, the National Council placed great reliance on the heat stress which sheep purportedly suffer during these journeys, which they maintain causes extreme cruelty to the sheep.

to address the intersectional vulnerability arising lack of WaSH access and extreme weather events, but an analysis of this set of cases would need to be conducted to make any definitive claim.

Finally, the keywords of 'ecosystem services' and 'ecosystem loss' were less generative, yielding only 22 and zero hits respectively. Of the ecosystem services hits, 12 include the keyword of 'climate change', but only five of these hits were case law.

To illustrate the value of a risk-thematic approach to climate case selection, the following section considers three 'drought litigation' cases from South Africa.

Drought litigation in South Africa

Contextualizing drought in South Africa

South Africa is naturally drought-prone and extreme droughts are often triggered by the El-Nino Southern Oscillation (ENSO).[108] Between 2015 and 2017 South Africa experienced the combined effects of a severe drought and an ENSO event that affected the whole country, but was particularly severe in the south-western parts of the country, which scientists estimated to be a 1-in-100, to 1-in-300 year event.[109] As noted in the discussion of Africa's key climate risks above, the south-western region of the continent is projected to experience the largest increases in temperature, which will result in a reduction in mean rainfall.

South Africa's first NDC (updated in 2021)[110] states that since 1990 the national average temperature has increased at more than twice the rate of global temperature increases. This has already resulted in more frequent droughts and extreme weather events.[111] Since 1980, the country has recorded 86 weather-related disasters, which affected more than 22 million South Africans and cost the economy in excess of R133 billion (US$ 6.81 billion).[112] It also projects that droughts over the central interior of the country will become more frequent and severe.[113] In South Africa, therefore, drought is a clear and present climate risk.

---

[108] M-A Baudoin *et al*, 'Living With Drought in South Africa: Lessons Learnt from the Recent El Nino Drought Period' (2017) 23 *International Journal of Disaster Risk Reduction* 128.

[109] P Wolski *et al*, 'Spatio-Temporal Patterns of Rainfall Trends and the 2015–2017 Drought over the Winter Rainfall Region of South Africa' (2020) *International Journal of Climatology* E1303.

[110] Republic of South Africa, *South Africa – First Nationally Determined Contribution under the Paris Agreement*, 2021, https://unfccc.int/sites/default/files/NDC/2022-06/South%20Africa%20updated%20first%20NDC%20September%202021.pdf.

[111] Republic of South Africa (n 110), 3.

[112] Republic of South Africa (n 110), 6–7.

[113] Republic of South Africa (n 110), 6.

The country's National Climate Change Adaptation Strategy (NCCAS), adopted in 2020, incorporates a drought risk mapping of settlements most at risk,[114] notes the impact of droughts on the availability of water resources,[115] and highlights existing 'products and services' in South Africa to deal with the vagaries of extreme events such as droughts. These include drought early warning systems, the drought monitoring desk, and the Severe Weather Warning Systems (SAWS).[116] It links early warning systems to the capacity to impose early water restrictions,[117] and recognizes that some companies are already developing drought-resistant seeds, supporting adaptation.[118] The NCCAS is otherwise silent on the social relief measures that may support vulnerable groups during times of drought, affirming Ohdedar and others' observations that adaptation policies have tended to be narrow, apolitical and technocratic.[119] The cases discussed as part of drought litigation, a sub-set of broader climate risk cases in South Africa, nevertheless bring a variety of other governance tools to light and shows their impact on vulnerable groupings.

Ohdedar discusses drought and vulnerability in the courts in an Indian context, highlighting the governance tools of drought declaration (a highly-politicized tool)[120] and state support for agricultural debt,[121] in his analysis. The discussion of South African drought litigation in the following section adds knowledge about the range of governance tools available to address drought conditions, highlights the kinds of conflicts that have emerged in the state's use of such tools and describes how the courts have responded to drought-related social vulnerability.

Drought litigation in South Africa: three illustrative cases

As noted above, searching the SAFLII database using the keyword 'drought' netted 156 case hits from courts in South Africa. In the majority of these cases, 'drought' is a passing reference (at times also misspelled as 'draught'), but in a number of cases drought plays a central role as the driver of public or private action. From the sub-set of drought cases, three cases were selected to illustrate two governance tools, how the state used them, and the courts response.

---

[114] Republic of South Africa, *National Climate Change Adaptation Strategy* (2020), 18 (*NCCAS*).

[115] *NCCAS* (n 114), 20.

[116] *NCCAS* (n 114), 33.

[117] *NCCAS* (n 114), 38.

[118] *NCCAS* (n 114), 53.

[119] Ohdedar (n 56), 137.

[120] Ohdedar (n 56), 11.

[121] Ohdedar (n 56), 19.

In *Astral Operations Ltd v Ekurhuleni Metropolitan Municipality*[122] a private company contested the state's lack of consultation in imposing so-called 'water-shedding' during the severe 2015–2017 drought. And in two cases decided in the Northern Cape division of the High Court – *Mweza v MEC for Social Services and Population Development (Northern Cape)*[123] and *Windvöel v MEC for Social Development (Northern Cape)*[124] – the courts reviewed the state's handling of requests for drought relief on the part of the rural poor in the context of the 2002–2004 drought that affected northern South Africa. None of the cases referenced climate change, meaning that they would not have been flagged as climate relevant using the climate visibility criterion of mainstream climate litigation scholarship. The cases are presented as illustrative of climate risk cases and the discussion below is not intended to be exhaustive of drought litigation in South Africa. Given space constraints and the focus of this chapter (methodological and conceptual), the case discussions are also not intended to be exhaustive.[125]

Contesting water shedding in Ekurhuleni Metropolitan Municipality

In *Astral Operations*, a company active in the broiler industry (growing and slaughtering broiler chickens for human consumption), approached the Johannesburg High Court for an interdict preventing the Ekurhuleni Metropolitan Municipality (EMM) from implementing its water-shedding programme in relation to Astral, pending a consultative process with the company or, in the alternative, granting the company 12 weeks' grace to implement a contingency plan to deal with water cuts (no water) lasting from 21:00 in the evening to 5:00 the following morning on Tuesdays, Thursdays and Saturdays. EMM's hand in imposing these restrictions had been forced by the bulk water supplier, Rand Water, after earlier attempts to reduce water consumption in the municipality in response to the severe drought had not met the anticipated targets. Astral maintained that the cuts caused it substantial financial loss, as it interrupted water supply to its abattoir and processing facility.

[122] Case No. 39702/2016 [2016] ZAGPJHC 380, 18 November 2016, http://www.saflii.org/cgi-bin/disp.pl?file=za/cases/ZAGPJHC/2016/380.html&query=astral%20 Operations.

[123] Case No. 376/06 [2008] ZANCHC 74, 12 December 2008, http://www.saflii.org/cgi-bin/disp.pl?file=za/cases/ZANCHC/2008/74.html&query=mweza.

[124] Case No. 1014/09 [2011] ZANCHC 31, 21 October 2011, http://www.saflii.org/cgi-bin/disp.pl?file=za/cases/ZANCHC/2011/31.html&query=mweza.

[125] There is clearly scope for considerable work to be done in the analysis of this body of case law and it is hoped that this will spark broader study in this area. By drawing attention to these kinds of cases, it is anticipated that they will begin to be decided in a manner that is not climate blind (Bouwer (n 33), 504). The author will be continuing this work over the coming years under the auspices of the Claude Leon Chair.

As referenced in South Africa's NCCAS, the capacity to impose water restrictions in response to drought early warnings is an important adaptation response, and herein lies its climate relevance. In South Africa, the National Water Act 38 of 1998 allows the Minister of Water and Sanitation to limit or prohibit the use of water, and failure to comply with any direction in this regard is an offence. In August 2016, the acting Minister of Water and Sanitation issued a ministerial notice limiting the taking of water from the Integrated Vaal System (which also fed the EMM), in an effort to conserve water in the drought conditions. Various provisions of the Water Services Act 108 of 1997 allowed for a water services provider such as the EMM to in turn impose water restrictions on its customers. These powers were elaborated in the EMM's water supply by-laws, which included a provision stating:

> If the Council considers it necessary as a matter of urgency to prevent any wastage of water, unauthorised use of water, damage to property, danger to life or pollution of water, and national disaster or if sufficient water is not available for any other reason the Council may, without prior notice and without prejudice to the Council's power under section 9(2)(*b*) . . . suspend the supply of water to any premises.[126]

The court dismissed Astral's application and confirmed EMM's imposition of the water-shedding programme, notwithstanding the lack of prior consultation. Finding that the law imposed no obligation on the municipality to consult before imposing such water restrictions, the court pointed out that other consumers would be prejudiced if Astral were to be exempted from the water-shedding programme. Specifically, the court noted that 'the consequences of providing uninterrupted water to Astral will be borne by the occupants of Ekurhuleni who, in the light of the drought being experienced in South Africa, face the risk of severe water shortages or more stringent restrictions'.[127] The court found that Astral had not established a clear right in this instance – the first requirement for the granting of an interdict – as it has not made averments relating to 'a right to a continued uninterrupted supply of water' in its pleadings.[128]

The *Astral* case thus stands as an important decision affirming a municipality's power to restrict water under drought conditions, in a manner that upheld the concerns of other water consumers and prevented a special exemption for a single corporate actor. It showed the court's awareness of the need to look beyond the parties appearing before it, and the importance of fairness in the

[126] Section 11(2)(a) Water Supply By-Law, Ekurhuleni Metropolitan Municipality. Section 12 of the by-law further provided for Special Water Restrictions.

[127] *Astral Operations* (n 122), para. 16.

[128] *Astral Operations* (n 122), para. 17.

distribution of a diminishing public good. It will thus serve as an important precedent in further cases where water restrictions are imposed as a result of drought risk.

Reviewing the state's handing of drought relief measures in the Northern Cape

In *Mweza* and *Windvöel* the applicants sought a review of state action under the Promotion of Administrative Justice Act 3 of 2000. In *Mweza* the applicants asked the court to direct the state respondents to decide on their applications for drought relief and the validity of so-called 'settlements agreements' (signed while the litigation was ongoing, purportedly in full and final settlement of the applicants' claims); and in *Windvöel* the court was asked to direct the state respondents to decide drought relief grants, in circumstances where officials denied that a community meeting relating to the relief had even taken place. In both cases the applicants belonged to a group that might be termed the 'rural poor': Functionally illiterate persons dependent on social grants engaged in modest or subsistence vegetable and maize farming businesses. In both cases, the value of the drought relief grant was a paltry R900. This relatively tiny amount, however, would have made the difference between crisis and survival for the applicants.

In 2004, the President of South African had proclaimed the Northern Cape as a disaster area in accordance with, curiously, section 26 of the Fund-Raising Act 107 of 1978. Section 16 of this Act also established the Disaster Relief Fund Board, cited as a respondent in both cases. The applicants sought assistance, however, in terms of section 5(2) of the Social Assistance Act 59 of 1992, which vested a discretion in the Director-General 'make a financial award to a person if he or she is satisfied that such person is in need of social relief of distress'.

The climate relevance of disaster relief is obvious. If climate change is exacerbating drought conditions, vulnerable groups need access to various forms of social assistance. This brings the doctrinal and statutory bases for granting such relief squarely into focus. Intriguingly, drought relief is not addressed in the country's NCCAS or, if it is, the idea is hidden beneath technical jargon such as the delivery of 'targeted climate change vulnerability reduction programmes'.[129]

The court granted the relief sought by the applicants in both cases, directing the Member of the Executive Council (MEC) responsible for social development in the Northern Cape, the Disaster Relief Fund Board, and the Minister of Social Development to consider and decide the applicants'

[129] *NCCAS* (n 114), 27.

applications for disaster relief under the Social Assistance Act within a set time period, and to provide written reasons in the event that the applicants were found to not be entitled to such. In *Mweza*, the court in fact found that the applicants were entitled to drought relief under the Social Assistance Act and lambasted officials for treating the applicants 'in the most unsympathetic manner imaginable'.[130] The court also pointed out the relevance of the rights to social assistance and to dignity (enshrined in sections 27(1)(c) and 10 of the South African Constitution) to the facts at hand. In *Windvöel*, the court described the state's conduct toward the destitute, poverty-restricted applicants as shameful, and affirmed their eligibility to apply for relief funding under the Social Assistance and Fund-Raising Act.[131]

In *Mweza* and *Windvöel*, one can see, therefore, how the courts came to the relief of the rural poor in a situation where state officials were unwilling, recalcitrant or incapable of coming to their aid with drought relief. The cases also potentially highlight a key policy gap in South Africa's adaptation response, namely the expeditious administration of drought relief, to address the human welfare of a vulnerable group. The need to fill this gap will become only more pressing as drought risk as a result of anthropogenic climate change.

Conclusion

This chapter has a conceptual and methodological orientation and engages with the question of the criteria that should be used to identify a case as climate litigation, or as climate relevant. It assumes that Africans need a climate litigation definition that will not only transcend the continent's marginal framing, but also will enable African actors to cognize, target and transform the governance institutions most critical to responding to the multi-faceted and severe social, cultural, economic and political vulnerabilities arising from already-observed and projected climate change on the continent.

The chapter engages with recent climate scholarship to argue that the keystone criterion for identifying a climate change case is climate visibility. While this criterion is important and valuable for identifying cases that show the evolution of the atmospheric governance strand of climate litigation, it obscures cases that exhibit the tools governments are already using (or not using) to alleviate the impacts of climate change. The chapter accordingly proposes an alternative approach where climate risk features as the central criterion for developing a parallel body of case law centered on adaptation (but not restricted to a state's official adaptation response).

---

130 *Mweza* (n 123), para. 13.

131 *Windvöel* (n 124), para. 20.

In developing a risk-thematic approach to identifying climate relevant case law, the chapter turns to climate science with a view to identifying key risks that have already been identified for the African continent. The chapter argues that the thematic content of these risks – agriculture, hydropower, WaSH, extreme events such as droughts and floods, and ecosystem loss – should ground the methodological strategy to identify cases dealing with climate change in Africa. The chapter presents the results of using different keywords to find climate relevant cases in the SAFLII database and finds that in addition to 'climate change' or 'greenhouse gas emissions', 'droughts', 'flooding and 'sanitation' should be used to identify the true archive of African climate jurisprudence and commentary. Finally, the chapter illustrates the value of a risk-thematic approach to identifying climate-relevant cases by describing three drought litigation cases in South Africa, which bring to the fore the importance of governance tools relating to water restrictions and drought relief.

By using a risk-thematic approach to identifying climate case, scholars in and interested in Africa will be in a better position to frame, categorize, analyse and compare. This work will enable diverse African climate change actors to discern patterns, predict future trends, and orientate their own actions within a broader stream of multi-level, multi-jurisdictional, poly-vocal and intersecting climate action.

3

State Duty to 'Protect' Rights and Legal Obstacles to Climate Litigation

Ademola Oluborode Jegede

Introduction

Climate change has disproportionate adverse consequences on populations, including those within Africa.[1] Nigeria, for instance, faces extreme climate change events,[2] with significant adverse consequences on agriculture and food security,[3] health,[4] and energy,[5] among others. These have implications for the realization of rights,[6] and may trigger future rise in rights-based climate litigation on behalf of the public in Nigeria.[7] Under international

---

1 CH Trisos *et al*, 'Africa' in H-O Pörtner and others (eds), *Climate Change 2022: Impacts, Adaptation and Vulnerability. Contribution of Working Group II to the Sixth Assessment Report of the Intergovernmental Panel on Climate Change* (Cambridge University Press 2022) 1285–455.

2 Such as increased flooding, drought, rise in sea level, and so on. H Haider, *Climate Change in Nigeria: Impacts and Responses* (Institute of Development Studies 2019) 2.

3 ME Ikehi *et al*, 'Assessing Climate Change Mitigation and Adaptation Strategies and Agricultural Innovation Systems in the Niger Delta' (2022) *Geojournal* 1–16.

4 S-UO Akanbi *et al*, 'Vulnerability of Rice Farmers to Climate Change in Kwara State, Nigeria' (2022) 10(2) *Turkish Journal of Agriculture – Food Science and Technology* 374–80.

5 OO Ajayi, G Mokryani and BM Edu, 'Sustainable Energy for National Climate Change, Food Security and Employment Opportunities: Implications for Nigeria' (2022) 10 *Fuel Communications* 1–6.

6 AO Jegede, 'Climate Change and Socio-Economic Rights Duties in Nigeria' (2017) 73/74 *Dignitas – The Slovene Journal of Human Rights* 14–43.

7 On the fragility of human rights approach to climate litigation in Nigeria, see M Adigun and AO Jegede, 'A Human Rights Approach to Climate litigation in Nigeria: Potentialities and Agamben's State of Exception Theory' 16(3) *Carbon & Climate Law Review* 179–91.

human rights law, states have the duty to 'respect', 'protect' and 'fulfil' human rights,[8] The duty to 'protect' rights, which is the context of this paper, demands that measures – mainly legislative – be established by states to ensure that individual and groups are protected from human rights abuses, non-state actors are regulated, and effective remedies are provided.[9] Therefore, this chapter asks the question of whether groups or individuals could seek relief from the courts – relying on human rights law – if those legislative commitments are either inadequate or not met.

Nigeria's new 2021 Climate Change Act[10] provides for an ambitious framework for mainstreaming climate actions in line with national development priorities, and sets a net-zero target for 2050–2070.[11] This legislation appears promising as it offers some basis to challenge climate actions or inactions on the part of the government. In fact, recent writings indicate challenges as well as possibilities within emerging law and case law to enhance climate litigation,[12] and boost a rights-based approach.[13] The Climate Change Act is a potential game-changer as it creates duties that can serve as a benchmark to evaluate both ambition and compliance.

In writings commenting on Global North climate litigation, procedural hurdles still loom large.[14] These include: founding causal links between a country's greenhouse gas (GHG) emissions, or proving exactly how let-downs in adaptation and mitigation policies result in human rights violations.[15] These procedural hurdles may also feature in the African

---

[8] H Shue, *Basic Rights: Subsistence, Affluence, and US Foreign Policy* (Princeton University Press 1980) 2nd ed 52; A Eide, 'Realisation of Social and Economic Rights and the Minimum Threshold Approach' (1989)10 *Human Rights Law Journal* 35–51.

[9] IE Koch, 'Dichotomies, Trichotomies or Waves of Duties?'(2005) 5 *Human Rights Law Review* 81–103.

[10] Climate Change Act 2021, https://faolex.fao.org/docs/pdf/NIG208055.pdf.

[11] Section 1, Climate Change Act 2021 (n 10).

[12] U Etemire, 'The Future of Climate Change Litigation in Nigeria: COPW v NNPC in the Spotlight' (2021) 15(2) *Carbon & Climate Law Review* 158–70. Also see the chapter by Eghosa Ekhator and Edward Okumagba in this volume.

[13] MT Ladan, 'A Review of Nigeria's 2021: Climate Change Act: Potential for Increased Climate Litigation' (2022) *Climate Law Blog*, https://blogs.law.columbia.edu/climatechange/2022/03/16/guest-blog-a-review-of-nigerias-2021-climate-change-act-potential-for-increased-climate-litigation/, accessed 15 January 2023.

[14] V Adelmant, P Alston and M Blainey, 'Human Rights and Climate Change Litigation: One Step Forward, Two Steps Backwards in the Irish Supreme Court' (2021) 13(1) *Journal of Human Rights Practice* 1–23; K Bouwer, 'Lessons from a Distorted Metaphor: The Holy Grail of Climate Litigation'(2020) 9(2) *Transnational Environmental Law* 347–378.

[15] J Peel and HM Osofsky, 'A Rights Turn in Climate Change Litigation?' (2018) 7(1) *Transnational Environmental Law* 37–67; S McInerney-Lankford, 'Climate Change and Human Rights: An Introduction to Legal Issues' (2009) 33(2) *Harvard Environmental Law Review* 431–7.

context when states are challenged for their compliance – or otherwise – with domestic climate policy and law put in place to help achieve their international commitments to address climate change. While there is a 'good feeling' about developments in the legal environment relating to climate change, it is not well understood how principles relating to costs, disclosure, standing, delay and burden of proof may still be problematic in climate litigation.[16] It is even more less well-understood what the state duty to 'protect' human rights means for climate litigation and whether it can overcome the procedural hurdles. Hence, using Nigeria as a case study, this chapter argues that due regard by the state to its duty to 'protect' human rights may help address procedural hurdles and thereby advance the success of potential climate litigation in African countries. In making this argument, the chapter engages with the following questions: What does a state duty to 'protect' rights means for climate litigation? What are the difficult hurdles to climate litigation in the African context? How have existing frameworks addressed the hurdles? And how can the state duty to protect rights advance climate litigation?

State duty to 'protect' rights and climate litigation

The duty to comply with globally acknowledged human rights requires three levels of duty from states: the duty to 'respect', 'protect' and 'fulfil' human rights.[17] The conceptualization of these duties owes its introduction and current influence on international human rights law to the pioneering work of Shue and Eide. The typology of duties, argues Shue, is tripartite (1) duties to avoid the deprivation of the right concerned, (2) duties to 'protect' rights holders from deprivation, and (3) duties to aid rights holders who have been deprived.[18]

The duty to 'protect' rights is of significance to climate litigation in that it requires the state to adopt legislation, to provide effective remedies to protect right holders, and to regulate non-state actors to ensure that their

[16] See K Bouwer and T-L Field, 'Editorial: The Emergence of Climate Litigation in Africa' (2021) 15(2) *Carbon & Climate Law Review* 123–8; International Bar Association, 'Model Statute for Proceedings Challenging Government Failure to Act on Climate Change' An International Bar Association Climate Change Justice and Human Rights Task Force Report February 2020.

[17] Shue (n 8); Koch (n 9).

[18] Shue (n 8), 52; also see Eide (n 8), 37; General Comment No. 12: The right to adequate food, UN ESCOR, Comm. on Econ., Soc. & Cult. Rts., 20th Sess., 14–20, UN Doc. E/C.12/1999/5 (1999) (United Nations General Comment No. 12); General Comment No. 13: The right to education, UN ESCOR, Comm. on Econ., Soc. & Cult. Rts., 21st Sess., 46–8 (1999) (United Nations General Comment No. 13).

actions do not hinder the realization of rights.[19] Ideally, the enactment and enforcement of legislation would signify that enough is done to protect rights without resorting to courts. Where such effort proves inadequate, however, it questions states' duty to 'protect' rights. The adoption of legislation is central to effective remedies which include the regulation of state actors and implies a legally supportive environment for climate change litigation. It is also difficult to effectively regulate non-state actors where legislation is weak or patchy. Seen in this context, the state duty to 'protect' rights, arguably, has three foundations for climate litigation to thrive: (1) climate legislation; (2) effective remedies for climate wrongs; and (3) accountability of non-state actors for climate actions or inactions, considering that failure to regulate corporations is a failure of state's duty to 'protect'. The linking of these three elements to climate litigation merits a deeper reflection as it is rarely clarified.

The necessity of climate legislation

The provisions of climate instruments, namely, the United Nations Framework Convention on Climate Change (UNFCCC),[20] and the Paris Agreement,[21] are clear on the global goals on mitigation and adaptation, which require the response of law at different levels. While reflecting the global aim on mitigation, article 2 of the Paris Agreement calls on states to limit the global temperature increase to 1.5°C above pre-industrial levels and make nationally determined contributions in pursuit of mitigation measures.[22] Building on article 4 of the UNFCCC, article 7 of the Paris Agreement formulates the global goal on adaptation as entailing the improvement of adaptive capacity, the bolstering of resilience and reducing vulnerability to climate change. Hence, there is need for legislation in some form at the domestic level to actualize states' commitments made at international negotiations on climate change. The availability of such legislation will also allow for legal assessment of the extent to which a state is responsive to global climate change normative and institutional standards on climate change adaptation and mitigation.

For instance, legislation that purports to address adaptation offers potentials for litigation where it does not adequately improve adaptive capacity, bolster resilience and reduce vulnerability to climate change. Regarding mitigation, questions can be raised about the adequacy or otherwise of legal frameworks

---

19 Shue (n 8); also see Eide (n 8).

20 United Nations Framework Convention on Climate Change (UNFCCC) (1992) *ILM* 851.

21 Paris Agreement under the UNFCCC adopted 30 November–11 December 2015 at the 21st Sess., Conference of the Parties, FCCC/CP/2015/L.9/Rev.1 (Paris Agreement 2015).

22 Paris Agreement 2015 (n 21), art. 4(2).

for the reduction of emissions of GHG. It may raise a concern if the spectrum of mitigation legislation does not touch or impact established sectors that are known to influence CO_2 emissions.[23] An adequate legislative coverage of the above provides a sound basis for litigation, as litigants can test the compliance of government with the existing law and test the adequacy of law against the constitutional or legal duties of the state in bill of rights or international human rights instruments,[24] or against the aspirations of Paris Agreement, which urges states to respect, promote and consider their respective duties in climate interventions.[25]

The state duty to 'protect' demands the establishment of adequate climate legislation since climate litigation often challenges laws and policies and resultant actions or inactions. The nature of this kind of challenge is revealed by Ruhl and Salzman who argue that it generally focuses on the adequacy or otherwise of law and policies about climate change.[26] However, it is not always well-defined what climate legislation or policy means. Scholars have questioned the viability of framing sets of rules and principles on climate change arguing that it is problematic to have standalone legislation, for instance, to govern every aspect of climate adaptation.[27] The logic behind such a viewpoint is that it can only be effectively addressed through a variety of law and policies,[28] or across various existing legal fields.[29] The imprecision of the phenomenon and the fuzziness of its scope and boundaries, argue Dupuis and Biesbroek, makes legislation less useful.[30] In Mayer's view, the need to adapt existing legal frameworks to climate change is more urgent than the call to create new ones.[31] At any rate, where the legislative framework relating to climate change is inadequate or gives rise to threats to human

23 G Van Calster *et al* (eds), *Research Handbook on Climate Change Mitigation Law* (Edward Elgar 2016).

24 On the link of rights to climate change, see recent Resolution by the Human Rights Council on human rights and climate change (*Resolution 4/24*), adopted 26 July 2021 at the 47th Session of the Human Rights Council, A/HRC/RES/47/24.

25 Paris Agreement (n 21), preamble.

26 JB Ruhl and J Salzman, 'Climate Change Meets the Law of the Horse' (2013) 62 *Duke Law Journal* 975–1020; for different typologies of litigation, see K Bouwer, 'The Unsexy Future of Climate Change Litigation' (2018) 30(3) *Journal of Environmental Law* 483–506.

27 D van Niekerk, 'Climate Change Adaptation and Disaster Law' in J Verschuuren (ed), *Research Handbook on Climate Change Adaptation Law* (Edward Elgar 2013) 142–70, 146.

28 Verschuuren (n 27), 3.

29 Ruhl and Salzman (n 26), 975, 993.

30 J Dupuis and R Biesbroek, 'Comparing Apples and Oranges: The Dependent Variable Problem in Comparing and Evaluating Climate Change Adaptation Policies' (2013) 23(6) *Global Environmental Change* 1476–87.

31 B Mayer, 'Reflection 1: Climate Change Adaptation Law: Is There Such a Thing?' in B Mayer and A Zahar, *Debating Climate Law* (Cambridge University Press 2021) 310–28.

rights, litigants can raise arguments on the effectiveness of the state duty to 'protect' rights.

Effective remedies for climate wrongs

Irrespective of the substantive right, the duty to 'protect' can only be realized where complainants have meaningful access to justice and can pursue remedies without impediment. Litigants might substantively be able to show that their rights are not adequately protected by bad climate legislation, but without proper access to justice these rights mean little.

Access to remedies is a crucial component of the state duty to 'protect' rights; hence, an effective remedy is difficult to achieve unless states take their duties to protect rights seriously. A state duty to 'protect' requires accessibility to appropriate remedies for violation of rights. The duty to provide an effective remedy, according to Human Rights Committee General Comment 31, demands that appropriate judicial and administrative mechanisms and compensations should be established for addressing claims of rights violation.[32] It is trite in international human rights law that a remedy is only available where there are no impediments on its accessibility. In *Jawara v The Gambia*, the African Commission on Human and Peoples' Rights remarks that a remedy is available if the petitioner can pursue it without impediment; it is effective if it offers a prospect of success; and it is sufficient if it is capable of redressing the complaint.[33] As the removal of impediments is key to access remedy, the ensuing section examines what the state duty to 'protect' means to legal principles on costs, disclosure, standing, and burden of proof in the climate litigation context. The state duty to 'protect' must not only address substantive issues (such as mitigation reduction targets, for example) but must consciously create the 'field' for climate litigation by addressing well-known procedural hurdles.

Cost

Litigation on climate change, similar to any other type of litigation, involves costs depending on the cause of action, complexity and duration of the suit.[34] In some jurisdictions, a litigant may be asked to provide security for

---

32 UN Human Rights Committee (HRC), *General Comment No. 31 [80], The Nature of the General Legal Obligation Imposed on States Parties to the Covenant*, 26 May 2004, CCPR/C/21/Rev.1/Add.13 paras 14–16.

33 *Jawara v The Gambia* Comm. 147/95–149/96.

34 SAK Mwesigwa and PD Mutesasira, 'Climate Litigation as a Tool for Enforcing Rights of Nature and Environmental Rights by NGOs: Security for Costs and Costs Limitations in Uganda' (2021) 15(2) *Carbon & Climate Law Review* 139–49, 144.

the costs of the defendants, a development that may discourage the pursuit of public interest litigation.[35] Often, litigants in public interest litigation are non-governmental organizations (NGOs) that generally have few or no assets to provide for such security.[36] In pursuing litigation, litigants may also incur considerable costs, which may be a disincentive in suing government and private companies for harm to the environment and for human rights violations.[37] Such costs, include filing fees, payments to expert witnesses, travel expenses, legal practitioners' fees and miscellaneous other fees.[38] Even where complainants are publicly funded or lawyers are acting pro bono, the expenses payable on litigation may be a deterrent to litigation.

The meaningfulness of a state's duty to 'protect' in the context of climate litigation can be measured by the applicable approach to costs in environmental proceedings. The award of costs in litigation is one of the procedural aspects of various legal systems.[39] Though a court hearing a matter has a wide discretion when it comes to awarding costs,[40] the traditional approach in various legal systems is that costs follow the outcome.[41] This implies that a party losing a case is usually required to pay the costs of the successful party. Costs may be a very sizeable figure if litigation has gone through different courts until being finalized, especially since the losing party will be required to pay the costs of the winning party and his or her own costs.[42]

Costs matter to the state duty to 'protect' rights in the climate change litigation context, because the prospects of an adverse cost order can be a real deterrent to public interest litigation. Climate change is a phenomenon of public significance, as it affects all. Applicants who may ordinarily litigate a climate change matter on behalf of the public may refrain from doing so due to the fear of being slammed by cost awards should their matter be adjudged unsuccessful. Consequently, for individuals or NGOs with an

---

35 'Taking Action to Protect the Environment', https://queenslandlawhandbook.org.au/the-queensland-law-handbook/living-and-working-in-society/laws-affecting-the-environment/taking-action-to-protect-the-environment/, accessed 14 January 2023.

36 'Taking Action to Protect the Environment' (n 35).

37 G Mayeda, 'Access to Justice: The Impact of Injunctions, Contempt of Court Proceedings, and Costs Awards on Environmental Protestors and First Nations' (2010) 6(2) *McGill International Law Journal of Sustainable Development Law & Policy* 143–76, 166.

38 Mayeda (n 37), 147.

39 S Budlender, G Marcus and N Ferreira, *Public Interest Litigation and Social Change in South Africa: Strategies, Tactics and Lessons* (The Atlantic Philanthropies 2014) 136.

40 *Naylor v Jansen* 2007 (1) SA 16 (SCA).

41 C Theophilopoulos *et al*, *Fundamental Principles of Civil Procedure* (LexisNexis 2020) 4th ed 499.

42 Theophilopoulos (n 41).

interest in such matters, the willingness to litigate despite risks of punitive costs may be undermined by the risk of high costs.

For the Global South, it has been noted that what might be framed or analysed as climate challenges will take the form of environmental harm or pollution control, or authorization relating to natural resources or infrastructure projects.[43] With limited costs protection and high competition for representation, litigants are unlikely to take steps that protect the climate for its own sake. For instance, in South Africa most litigations focus on challenges linked to mining and coal-based energy production and the adverse consequences of retaining the status quo are a commonality running through the cases.[44]

Disclosure

The principle of disclosure is linked with the right to access to information, which is an important tool for success in public interest climate litigation. Access to information is a recognized procedural environmental right.[45] Access to information empowers citizens and NGOs in examining compliance with legal requirements to protect the environment, and address climate change.[46] Without access to the necessary information, the knowledge of populations will be restricted and advocacy for change will be difficult. Hence, access to information on climate change is crucial to climate activism and litigation. It is also important for climate education in Africa. The protection against the adverse consequences of climate change, and proving the cause of its impacts, demand proper information. Therefore, it is incompatible with the idea of state responsibility to protect to maintain a regime of evidential law that inhibits disclosure and encourages parties or stakeholders in climate litigation to play a 'hide and seek' game with information on climate-related matters.

---

[43] J Peel and J Lin, 'Transnational Climate Litigation: The Contribution of the Global South' (2019) 113 *American Journal of International Law* 679–726; J Setzer and L Benjamin, 'Climate Litigation in the Global South: Constraints and Innovations' (2020) 9(1) *Transnational Environmental Law* 77–101.

[44] Bouwer and Field (n 16), 4. Also see the chapter by Nicole Loser in this volume.

[45] See, for instance, the African Convention on the Conservation of Nature and Natural Resources (Revised version 2003) (Conservation Convention), art. 16(1)(a)(b) enjoins states to adopt legislative and regulatory measures necessary to ensure timely and appropriate dissemination and access of the public to environmental information.

[46] AO Salau, 'Right of Access to Information and its Limitation by National Security in Nigeria: Mutually Inclusive or Exclusive?' Thesis Presented for the Degree of Doctor of Philosophy in the Department of Public Law, Faculty of Law University of Cape Town (2017) 143.

Globally, the tensions around access to information are already presenting in climate activism and litigation. For instance, companies may elect not to disclose to their investors the risks that their activities pose to the climate system. In October 2018, a complaint was lodged against Exxon Mobil for misleading investors about the risks that climate change regulations posed to its business.[47] Corporations may fail to reveal measures that they have taken to achieve climate change intervention objectives.[48] Even where there is disclosure, such information may be misleading in relation to a corporation's knowledge of the risks of fossil fuels or investment assets.[49] They may elect to ignore or misrepresent the adverse consequences of climate change on their operations and finances.[50]

The concept of disclosure concerns the provision of documents and all evidence in any form that relates to the matter at hand.[51] However, requests may not succeed where evidence is regarded as privileged or confidential. Such information may include communications regarding legal advice and any confidential document or communication made for the sole or dominant purpose of pending or existing litigation between a company and its representatives.[52] A possible implication of this exemption is that, without an adequate legislative safeguard, corporations and state institutions may, under the cover of protecting confidential information, exclude communications of relevance to the determination of the causes and consequences of climate change.

Standing

Remedies can only be assured where states ensure that applicants can access courts. Standing relates to whether an applicant is entitled to seek redress from the courts about an issue.[53] Standing is an essential requirement for accessing

---

47 Clifford Chance, 'Climate Change Litigation Tackling Climate Change Through the Courts', October 2019, https://www.cliffordchance.com/content/dam/cliffordchance/briefings/2019/10/growing-the-green-economy-climate-change-litigation.pdf, accessed 13 January 2023.

48 United Nations Environment Programme, *Global Climate Litigation Report: 2020* Status Review 2.

49 *Global Climate Litigation Report* (n 48).

50 R Wasim, 'Corporate (Non)Disclosure of Climate Change Information' (2019) 119(5) *Columbia Law Review* 1311–54.

51 DK Brown, 'Evidence Disclosure and Discovery in Common Law Jurisdictions' in DK Brown and others (eds), *The Oxford Handbook of Criminal Process* (Oxford University Press 2019) 543–61.

52 HL Ho, 'Legal Advice Privilege and the Corporate Client' (2006) *Singapore Journal of Legal Studies* 231–63.

53 C Loots, 'Locus Standi to Claim Relief in the Public Interest in Matters Involving the Enforcement of Legislation' (1989) *South African Law Journal* 131–48; AK Abebe, 'Towards

justice and the realization of human rights.[54] While in some African states, anyone can file an action to redress human rights violations whether the person has an interest or not,[55] in other states the requirement is different. Only the persons whose fundamental human rights are in issue are allowed to litigate. In Lesotho, for instance, section 22(1) of the Constitution allows litigation in relation to human rights only where a

> person alleges that any of the provisions of sections 4 to 21 (inclusive) of this Constitution has been, is being or is likely to be contravened in relation to him (or, in the case of a person who is detained, if any other person alleges such a contravention in relation to the detained person).[56]

Courts have often invoked section 22(1) to exclude litigants who are not 'directly and substantially' affected by the case being brought before the court.[57]

Exclusion from litigating on the ground of lack of or insufficient interest anywhere in Africa is problematic in climate litigation where a person may wish to litigate in the interest of the public, and not based on a real or potential violation of his or her own rights. For a similar reason, courts may also not want to hear actions brought by a person challenging legislation that does not sufficiently protect his rights in the climate change context.

The need for a state to create an enabling legal environment that liberalizes standing is needed for effective access to justice and the most fundamental requirement of a legal system that claims to guarantee legal rights.[58] A narrow interpretation of the rules of standing may undermine needed actions on climate change. It may frustrate activists and organizations that wish to litigate not owing to personal harm suffered but purely in the interests of protecting the climate. Hence, a state duty to 'protect' rights is not fully

---

More Liberal Standing Rules to Enforce Constitutional Rights in Ethiopia' (2010) *African Human Rights Law Journal* 407–31.

54 L Chiduza and PN Makiwane, 'Strengthening Locus Standi in Human Rights Litigation in Zimbabwe: An Analysis of the Provisions in the New Zimbabwean Constitution [2016] *Potchefstroom Electronic Law Journal* 11.

55 See for instance, s. 38 of the Republic of South Africa Constitution 1996.

56 Lesotho's Constitution of 1993 with Amendments through 2018.

57 *Mosito v Letsika* (C OF A (CIV) 9/2018) [2018] LSCA 1 (26 October 2018). See also *Justice Maseshophe Hlajoane v Letsika* (C OF A (CIV) 66/2018) [2019] LSCA 27 (1 February 2019); for a reflection on this narrow approach, see H Nyane and T Maqakachane, 'Standing to Litigate in the Public Interest in Lesotho: The Case for a Liberal Approach' (2020) 20(2) *African Human Rights Law Journal* 799–824.

58 M Cappelletti, *The Judicial Process in Comparative Perspective* (Oxford University Press 1989) 36.

achieved where the standing rules in environmental – and hence climate – litigation are not fully liberalized.

Burden of proof

The litigant who makes an allegation – whether the plaintiff or the defendant – is required to prove it. The principle is an established legal principle, and is relevant in climate litigation in particular, as frequently so much that the plaintiff needs to prove is in the control or knowledge of the defendant. For instance, plaintiffs in climate change litigation face the challenge of demonstrating the cause and nature of the harm of climate change when seeking redress or asking for improved climate action. This problem applies across the variety of climate change litigation, whether based in private, public law or international causes of action; the plaintiff will often need to prove that carbon emissions by a particular activity or company or entity will, or have a tendency to, give rise to specific impacts on a local area or population.[59] The need for such proof may also form part of a court's analysis of standing questions or go to the merits of a claim that GHG emissions from a certain corporation may have a significant impact on the environment.[60] The onus of proving the causation and consequences suffered from climate change is a difficult one for plaintiffs, and may require innovative legal rules, or a relaxation of the burden of proof, if the plaintiff is to satisfy this requirement.

Regulation of non-state actors for climate-related activities

Operations by non-state actors often create a need for interventions in environmental and climate law.[61] Non-state actors are not only involved in the combustion of fossil fuel;[62] along with international organizations they are also involved in climate change mitigation measures.[63] The application of human rights to non-state actors, in particular, before regional and international human rights bodies is problematic as they are non-parties

[59] *Massachusetts v EPA* 549 US 497 (2007).

[60] *Massachusetts v EPA* (n 59).

[61] RM Bratspies, 'The Intersection of International Human Rights and Domestic Environmental Regulation' (2010) 38 *Georgia Journal of International & Comparative Law* 649–71.

[62] Bratspies (n 61), 652.

[63] JF Green, 'Delegation and Accountability in the Clean Development Mechanism: The New Authority of Non-State Actors' (2008) 4 *Journal of International Law & International Relations* 21–53. Also see the discussion by Eghosa Ekhator and Edward Okumagba in this volume.

to the regional instruments.[64] It is also difficult at the domestic level since international organizations generally enjoy effective immunity,[65] with the de facto authorization of states.[66]

Yet, as a critical component of a state duty to 'protect', states in Africa must ensure that appropriate regulation is established to guide or coordinate the actions of non-state actors. This is no less required in the context of climate change as the activities of non-state actors are linked to climate change and may result in litigation.

The 2019 Report of the United Nations Special Rapporteur on the issue of human rights duties relating to the enjoyment of a safe, clean, healthy and sustainable environment affirms that fossil fuels combustion produces 70 per cent of GHG emissions and biomass for electricity and heat.[67] This development is supported in another report showing that the world's total energy supply through fossil fuels corporations has remained unchanged at 81 per cent.[68] This confirms the energy supply sector remains the largest contributor to global GHG emissions.[69] These emissions are either generated through extractive activities or sources over which a company enjoys state-given control. Yet, a study concluded that 82 per cent of known coal reserves, 49 per cent of gas reserves, and 33 per cent of oil reserves should remain in the ground if the world is to avoid dangerous climate change of more than 2°C.[70]

The Intergovernmental Panel on Climate Change (IPCC) Sixth Assessment Report (AR6) estimates that in 2018 Africa contributed only 3 per cent to global fossil fuel industry CO_2 emissions (on a consumption-based

64 However, see the discussion about potential liability of non-state actors in the chapter in this volume by Elsabé Boshoff.

65 For instance, international organizations generally enjoy immunity in their operations, see K Tesfagabir, 'The State of Functional Immunity of International Organisations and their Officials and Why It Should Be Streamlined' (2011) 10 *Chinese Journal of International Law* 97–128, 99.

66 GC Jimenez and E Pulos, *Good Corpn, Bad Corpn: Corporate Social Responsibility in the Global Economy* (Open Suny 2016).

67 United Nations General Assembly, 'Report of the Special Rapporteur on the issue of human rights obligations relating to the enjoyment of a safe, clean, healthy and sustainable environment' Seventy-fourth session A/74/161, 15 July 2019, para. 12.

68 UNEP, *Global Environment Outlook 6: Healthy Planet, Healthy People* (UNEP 2019).

69 T Bruckner *et al*, 'Energy Systems' in Ottmar Georg Edenhofer *et al* (eds), *Climate Change 2014: Mitigation of Climate Change. Contribution of Working Group III to the Fifth Assessment Report of the Intergovernmental Panel on Climate Change* (Cambridge University Press 2014) 511–97.

70 C McGlade and P Ekins, 'The Geographical Distribution of Fossil Fuels Unused When Limiting Global Warming to 2°C' (2015) 517 *Nature* 187–90.

calculation).[71] However, this percentage is expected to increase as African economies grow.[72] The real winner, of course, is large corporates that cause localized environmental harm, form a significant proportion of Africa's contribution to climate change and take substantial amounts of their revenue offshore.

While MNCs commit to climate action by signing the Paris Pledge for Action,[73] these are aspirational, and non-binding commitments, which themselves constitute a challenge to enforcement. Without an appropriate legal framework specifying duties for private actors, states cannot make these commitments count at the domestic level, nor can courts maximize their importance in climate-related matters. Therefore, emissions regulations that require corporate entities to take proactive measures on carbon emission reduction are an imperative.[74] Better legislation is required at the domestic level to regulate such activities in a manner that is compatible with the global objective to address climate change.

The following section analyses the legal framework in Nigeria as an example of the extent to which the approach of a state to the duty to 'protect' can aid climate litigation in Africa.

Legal frameworks in Nigeria: a hurdle or catalyst to climate litigation

This section argues that while there are developments in the legal framework in Nigeria that may be relied upon in proceedings against the state or non-state actors, many of the factors identified in the previous sections are still lacking. This could mean any proceedings that could be classified as 'climate litigation' may still face challenges in Nigeria.

Inadequacy of existing climate legislation

Nigeria has signed and ratified international climate instruments, namely the UNFCCC and the Paris Agreement.[75] Along similar lines, while the

---

71 V Masson-Delmotte *et al* (eds), 'Summary for Policymakers' in *Climate Change 2021: The Physical Science Basis. Contribution of Working Group I to the Sixth Assessment Report of the Intergovernmental Panel on Climate Change* (2021) (IPCC Summary for Policymakers) 1–32.

72 OE Olubusoye and D Musa, 'Carbon Emissions and Economic Growth in Africa: Are They Related?' (2020) 8(1) *Cogent Economics & Finance* 1–21.

73 University of Cambridge Institute for Sustainability Leadership (CISL), 'Paris Pledge for Action' (2015) http://www.parispledgeforaction.org/, accessed 13 January 2023.

74 EM Reid and MW Toffel, 'Responding to Public and Private Politics: Corporate Disclosure of Climate Change Strategies' (2009) 30(11) *Strategic Management Journal* 1157–78.

75 'Nigeria', https://unfccc.int/node/61130, accessed 13 January 2023.

ICCPR and the ICESCR are not yet domesticated in Nigeria, the country has acceded to and ratified the instruments relating to human rights.[76] Under the terms of the Vienna Convention,[77] Nigeria cannot use its national law as an excuse for not complying with the provisions of international climate change instruments that it ratifies and signs.[78] Nigeria also has a bill of rights section in its national constitution.[79]

However, the commitment at the international level has not translated to wholesale implementation at the domestic level in Nigeria. Existing instruments in Nigeria that conform to or aim at advancing the goals in key climate instruments are both soft and hard in nature.

The soft instruments in the form of policy documents are the National Adaptation Strategy and the Plan of Action on Climate Change,[80] and the National Policy on Climate Change for Nigeria.[81] Arguably, these are documents of intent that do not contain legally enforceable commitments; hence, they may have limited significance in litigation on the extent of compliance or non-compliance with international standards.

There are instruments that fall into the hard law category in the sense that they contain legally enforceable commitments on climate change. For instance, the recent Climate Change Act has unique provisions that have been lauded in emerging scholarship as creating potential pathways to holding the state accountable in climate litigation, if needed.[82] The Act imposes duties on ministries, departments, and agencies to establish desk officers for ensuring compliance with the National Climate Change Action Plan.[83] The National Council on Climate Change established by section 3 of the Climate Change Act can further impose duties relating to climate action on public and private entities. The Act empowers a federal or state High Court, before which a suit regarding climate change or environmental matters is instituted, to make an order to: (1) prevent, stop or discontinue the performance of any act that is harmful to the environment; (2) compel any public official to act to prevent or stop the performance of any act that

[76] Ratification Status for CCPR – International Covenant on Civil and Political Rights, https://tbinternet.ohchr.org/_layouts/15/TreatyBodyExternal/Treaty.aspx, accessed 13 January 2023; Ratification Status for CESCR – International Covenant on Economic, Social and Cultural Rights, https://tbinternet.ohchr.org/_layouts/15/TreatyBodyExternal/Treaty.aspx, accessed 13 January 2023.

[77] Vienna Convention on the Law of Treatises United Nations, Treaty Series, vol. 1155, p. 331, art. 27.

[78] 'Nigeria', https://unfccc.int/node/61130, accessed 13 January 2023.

[79] 1999 Constitution of Nigeria, chapter IV.

[80] Nigeria National Adaptation Strategy and Plan of Action on Climate Change 2011.

[81] National Policy on Climate Change for Nigeria, 2015.

[82] Etemire (n 12); Ladan (n 13).

[83] Nigeria Climate Change Act (n 10), ss 22–26.

is harmful to the environment; (3) compensate victims directly affected by the acts that are harmful to the environment.[84]

The Act obligates any private entity with employees numbering 50 and above to put in place measures to achieve the annual carbon emission reduction targets in line with the National Climate Change Action Plan; and designate a climate change officer responsible for submitting annual reports to the National Climate Change Secretariats regarding meeting its carbon emission reduction targets and climate adaptation plan. The National Council on Climate Change,[85] is chaired by the President of Nigeria, with members from both the public and private sectors, including members of the civil society, women, youth, and persons with disabilities. It empowers the Council with significant powers to coordinate national climate actions, administer the newly established Climate Change Fund,[86] mobilize resources to support climate actions, and collaborate with the Nigerian Sovereign Green Bond in meeting Nigeria's NDC. The Climate Change Fund is envisioned as a financing mechanism for prioritized climate actions and intervention.

However, even at its infancy, the Act is not without a number of institutional and potential enforcement shortcomings. It is doubtful that some of the entities created and entrusted with responsibilities under the Act will be useful in addressing climate change. For instance, the National Council on Climate Change is largely composed of political office holders and rarely includes specialist members of academia or civil society, who may contribute to the realization of the objectives of global climate instruments. While the Act provides for the role of the courts in climate litigation, it is silent on the issue of enforcement of decisions; this has been a major problem even where litigation has been successful against corporations for harmful environmental practices in Nigeria.[87]

In terms of the enforcement component of the Act, while it is promising that the courts can make an order to prevent harmful activities, in only targeting environmental harmful activities, the human dimension of the impact of climate change has been overlooked. Climate change does not only impact the physical environment; an inadequate application of adaptation and mitigation measures may have adverse consequences on vulnerable populations, a development that may impact on the enjoyment of their rights.

Another weakness in climate legislation is both the lack of supportive constitutional provisions and the lack of reference made in the Act to

84 Nigeria Climate Change Act (n 10), s. 34.
85 Nigeria Climate Change Act (n 10), Part II, ss 3–5.
86 Nigeria Climate Change Act (n 10), s. 15.
87 Adigun and Jegede (n 7).

other environmental laws. There is no constitutional backing as the right to environment is not guaranteed by the Constitution.[88] The protection of the environment is only found in the fundamental directive principles of state policy (FDPSP) part of the Nigeria Constitution. While these provisions may be deployed indirectly to protect the climate system, they fall short of the commanding presence that the protection of the environment – and by extension the climate – has in other constitutions.[89] Other notable legislation prior to the Climate Change Act include the National Environmental Standards and Regulations Enforcement Agency Act (NESREA),[90] supplemented by the Environmental Impact Assessment Act.[91] The environmental agency established under the terms of part 1 of the NESREA was given the power to enforce compliance with environmental regulations and standards. This legislation have not been able to ensure accountability or prevent the wanton destruction of the environment in the oil-producing region of Nigeria.

Also, if the meaning of the phrase 'private entities' includes corporations, then the imposition of a duty to cut emissions on organizations with more than 50 employees is awkwardly placed. Climate change does not result from how large a number of employees a corporation has, but by the intensity of its carbon-emitting activities. This arises from the nature of the corporation, their technologies and activities, not by their staff volume. It is problematic also in the sense that a corporation may limit its employee to below 50, while still having very high emissions, to escape the duty imposed on private entities.

In all, while it is encouraging that Nigeria has enacted climate change legislation, the adequacy of both the normative and institutional standards to effectively address climate change is doubtful. There is lack of clarity on the specific measures to be taken to improve adaptive capacity and reduce vulnerability to climate change. Much also remains vague regarding the accountability of corporations and public entities for climate actions or inactions that are in breach of rights. The existing legislative framework in Nigeria remains rather too fragile to achieve global climate change objectives. This makes the potential need for recourse to the courts to seek human rights protection – through climate litigation – more pronounced. But also, a lack of clear standards and duties may make it more challenging. The procedural context in which it takes place adds further challenges, as discussed below.

88 1999 Constitution of the Federal Republic of Nigeria.

89 See the Constitution of Tunisia 2014, art. 45.

90 National Environmental Standards and Regulations Enforcement Agency Act 25 of 2007.

91 Environmental Impact Assessment Act 2004, Cap E12 LFN.

Fluctuating hurdles of access to remedies

An analysis of the approach in Nigeria to established hurdles to climate litigation – namely to costs, disclosure, standing and burden of proof – reveals that there is a lot of room for improvement.

In Nigeria, there are no provisions in existing legislation or rules that an unsuccessful litigation of environmental matters should be exempted from an award of cost. No such position is accommodated in section 1(c) of NESREA, which allows the Agency to sue or be sued in its corporate name,[92] or the Fundamental Rights (Enforcement Procedure) Rules.[93] The latter allows the court to exercise its discretion in awarding costs or to act otherwise in matters relating to the variation or discharge of ex parte orders.[94] The rules of courts of some states are not as ambivalent, as they provide that a successful party is generally entitled to be indemnified for the expenses used in enforcing his/her civil rights.[95] Where a litigant unsuccessfully litigates against the state or other entity on climate change issues, in terms of the provisions of rules and legislation, there is no guarantee that such litigant can be exempted from costs. Such costs may include not only the expenses of witnesses and scientific experts, but also the costs of legal representation.

Generally, courts have a discretion to exercise in the matter of costs, including the making of an order that parties should bear their individual cost. For instance, some courts in the past have stated that it is against public policy to saddle an unsuccessful litigant with the solicitors' fees of the successful litigant.[96] More recently, however, the approach is changing, as evident in *Ajibola v Anisere* where the Court of Appeal ruled that a claim for solicitor's fees for the prosecution of a matter may succeed if specifically and properly pleaded.[97] In the context of climate litigation, based on the case law, a possibility still exists that an unsuccessful litigant, for instance against an MNC, may be saddled with the burden of paying the litigation cost of the other party.[98]

---

92 National Environmental Standards and Regulations Enforcement Agency (Establishment) Act 2007.

93 Fundamental Rights (Enforcement Procedure) Rules 2009.

94 Fundamental Rights (Enforcement Procedure) Rules 2009, r. 6.

95 Order 49 of the High Court of Ogun State (Civil Procedure Rules) 2014; Ord. 53 of the High Court of Lagos State (Civil Procedure Rules) 2019; and Ord. 25 of the Federal High Court (Civil Procedure) Rules 2019.

96 *Guinness v Nwoke* [2005] 15 NWLR (Pt 689) 135.

97 *Ajibola v Anisere* (2019) LPELR-48204(CA); also *see Naude v Simon* (2013) LPELR – 20491 (CA).

98 *Ajibola v Anisere* (2019) LPELR-48204(CA); also *see Naude v Simon* (2013) LPELR – 20491 (CA).

There is the risk that a potential climate change litigant may face a challenge in accessing information in the possession of the respondent. Section 39 of the Constitution provides that 'everyone is entitled to freedom of expression, including freedom to hold opinions and receive and impart information'. Section 39(3), however, permits statutory limitations on access to information on grounds including national security. The exception on national security grounds is strengthened by other legislation such as the Criminal Code Act[99] and the Official Secrets Act,[100] which impose restrictions on the disclosure of official information by public officials in the interest of defence and public safety, among others. The Freedom of Information Act was passed to prevent information concealment by administrative bodies; it does this by guaranteeing access to official information and records.[101] It does not affect existing legislation that allows vague national security exemptions to the access to official information.[102] Hence, as 'national security' has no precise meaning in Nigerian law, it may constitute a hurdle to receiving necessary information on the activities of the state and its organs in collaboration with corporate actors.

Also, in matters relating to court evidence, the disclosure of information may be subject to many reservations in climate litigation. For instance, solicitor–client privilege is codified and found in sections 192–195 of the Evidence Act.[103] Under the terms of section 192(1), a legal practitioner cannot, without the consent of his client, disclose any communication made to him during and for the purpose of his employment, or reveal the contents or condition of any document he possesses for the purpose of his professional employment, or disclose any advice given by him to his client during and for the purpose of such employment. The exceptions to this rule are the communication of documents concealed for any illegal purpose, crime or fraud. Section 195 protects everyone from being compelled to disclose to the court any confidential communication between him and a legal practitioner, unless he offers himself as a witness to explain his evidence.

These rules can make plaintiffs' access to information very complicated. Crucial information may be exchanged between a corporation (the client) and legal practitioner in relation to their knowledge of climate risks, earnings from carbon-emitting activities and the involvement of the state. Under sections 192(1) and 195, such communications and documents may be privileged and deemed confidential, in that they are not necessarily

99 Criminal Code Act, Cap. 38 LFN 2004.
100 Official Secrets Act Cap O3 LFN 2004.
101 Freedom of Information Act 2011.
102 Salau (n 46), 115.
103 Nigerian Evidence Act Cap. E14 LFN 2011.

being concealed for illegal purpose, or a crime or fraud. They are not so because there is no law criminalizing activities underlying climate change or rendering such activities illegal in Nigeria. Rather, activities underlying climate change result from projects that are legal and permissible. Generally, it may be possible to compel the disclosure of such communications and documents under section 3 of the Evidence Act, which provides that 'nothing in this Act, shall prejudice the admissibility of any evidence that is made admissible by any other legislation validly in force in Nigeria'. However, in this context, section 3 appears inapplicable as there is no legislation that authorizes the disclosure of such climate-related communications or documents. These wide-ranging factors, again, mean that plaintiffs wishing to bring climate cases will have real difficulties obtaining disclosure from the defendants.

Concerning standing to sue, accountability for environmental issues formerly rested largely in tort law, where the proof of specific harm is crucial to admissibility.[104] Under the Fundamental Human Right Rules, the court encourages public interest litigations in the human rights field, urging that no human rights case may be dismissed or struck out for want of locus standi.[105] This provision has been applauded for increasing the access to justice for all classes of litigants, especially the poor, the illiterate, the uninformed, the vulnerable, the incarcerated and the unrepresented.[106] The application of the provision to NGOs to litigate in the interest of the environment was considered and upheld by the Supreme Court in the case of *Centre for Oil Pollution Watch v Nigerian National Petroleum Corn*,[107] and was subsequently followed in *Olumide Babalola v Attorney General of The Federation*.[108] It has been argued that the foregoing approach of the courts is positive for climate litigation in Nigeria.[109] This is more so as the Climate Change Act encourages that actions can be brought against the state and other entities for the failure to implement, or the inadequate implementation of, the Act.[110]

---

104 A Babalola, 'The Right to a Clean Environment in Nigeria: A Fundamental Right?' (2020) 25(1) *Hastings Environmental Law Journal* 3–14.

105 Fundamental Right (Enforcement Procedure) Rules, preamble 3(e).

106 JN Mbadugha, 'Environmental Public Interest Litigation in Nigeria: A case comment on Centre for Oil Pollution Watch v Nigerian National Petroleum Corporation' (2021) 11 *UNIZIK Journal of Public and Private Law* 53–65.

107 *Centre for Oil Pollution Watch (COPW) v Nigerian National Petroleum Corpn (NNPC)* (2019) 15 NWLR 1666.

108 *Olumide Babalola v Attorney General of The Federation* [2019] 5 NWLR 518.

109 Etemire (n 12); Ladan (n 13). Also see Eghosa Ekhator and Edward Okumagba in this volume.

110 Ladan (n 13).

However, it is too early to tell whether there is going to be significant and effective climate litigation in Nigeria. The Fundamental Rights (Enforcement Procedure) Rules remain a set of subsidiary procedural rules that do not carry influence at a par with a principal legislation. The Climate Change Act, as explained above, does not create a strong basis for public interest-based environmental litigation, as its sections 33 and 34 are silent about who can sue. Further, section 33 of the Climate Change Act allows a very short limitation period only. It refers to a provision in the Public Officers Protection Act, which specifies proceedings must be brought within three months of an allegation, or within six months in the case of continuing damage or injury.[111] Also, it is uncertain how litigation under the Climate Change Act will compete with other legislation, which confers on the Attorney General (AG) of the Federation the powers to institute legal action for the purpose of asserting a public right or the enforcement of the performance of a public duty by public office holders in Nigeria.[112] The possibility of deferring to the AG in the matter of instituting a climate action in the interest of the public against the state is not remote as climate change is a phenomenon of public significance that may be argued to fall with the AG's remit. As the office of the AG is political in nature,[113] climate change litigation in the interest of the public could be worse off where the AG is considered the more appropriate office to litigate such matter. Or, more probably, the AG office may simply have no interest in litigating climate change issues against the state, even if the measures taken are plainly inadequate.

The burden of proof and the onus in terms of section 131 of the Evidence Act places the duty to prove on the person asserting.[114] However, considering the uniqueness of environmental litigation, it can turn into an almost impossible task for an applicant to discharge.[115] There are numerous strong cases of environmental breaches that highlight that burden of proof will be challenging for litigants in climate litigation. In *Chinda v Shell BP Petroleum Co. Nigeria Ltd,* the plaintiff filed a lawsuit against the defendant on the grounds of thermal vibration and noise pollution, for neglecting to handle the defendant's gas flare work that damaged the plaintiff's property.

111 Public Officers Protection Act 2004, s. 2.

112 Supreme Court Act 2004, s. 20; Nigeria Constitution 1999 (as amended), ss 150(1–2), 174(a)–(c), 195(1)–(2) and 211(a)–(c).

113 OI Usang, 'Public Interest Litigation: A Veritable Avenue for the Fight Against Corruption in Nigeria' (2021) 8(1) *Nnamdi Azikwe University. Journal of Commercial and Property Law* 26–38, 35.

114 Nigerian Evidence Act (n 105), s. 131.

115 N-A Odong, 'Burden of Proof: Real Burden in Environmental Litigation for the Niger-Delta of Nigeria' (2020) 35 *Journal for Environmental Law and Litigation* 193–226.

The court of first instance dismissed the plaintiff's proceedings based on the absence of objective evidence that the defendant failed to oversee exploration activities.[116] This evidence, of course, would be under the control of the defendant.

It is unlikely that the burden of proof in alleged environmental breaches will be positively impacted by the decision of the Supreme Court in the *Centre for Oil Pollution Watch (COPW)* case, which liberalizes the notion of standing. In that case the Supreme Court only set out criteria that an applicant will have standing where the action was: for the public interest; for the maintenance of the environment; to vindicate the rule of law; and that the appellant has shown that public nuisance endangers life.[117] While the case is helpful to climate litigation in the sense that it does not require a proof of special harm as a ground for standing, the decision does not negate the need to prove specific harm for the award of specific damages. Consequently, where an applicant seeks damages from the state for climate-related wrongs committed against his or her human rights, there is still the need to prove specific damages based on the principle of he who asserts must prove. In the circumstance, it seems the long-established authorities on specific damage will apply. In *KE Nwanewu Onyiorah v Benedict C Onyiorah*,[118] the Supreme Court followed its trite position that special damages must be specially pleaded and strictly proved by giving necessary particulars and adducing credible evidence in support. No court is allowed to make its own assessment or speculate on special damages without supporting credible evidence.[119] Challenges arising in relation to costs, access to information and evidentiary proof will therefore still present real hurdles for the person bringing the case.

The constitutional provisions of Nigeria do not impose human rights duties directly on companies, which makes their accountability for wrong linked to human rights unjusticiable. There is other legislation that regulates the activities of multinational corporations, such as the Petroleum Act, which provides that oil companies' operations have to conform in a manner that is in accordance with good oil field practices.[120] Also, the Environmental Impact Assessment Act requires an environmental impact assessment (EIA) to be carried out where the scope, nature or location of a proposed project or activity are likely to affect the environment significantly.[121] The utility of these provisions to aid the accountability of non-state actors is disputed. For instance, there was a successful litigation against the respondent in *Gbemre*

[116] *Chinda v Shell Bp Petroleum Co.* (1974) 2 RSLR 1.

[117] COPW (n 107), 590–1, 597–8.

[118] In *KE Nwanewu Onyiorah v Benedict C Onyiorah* NOR LER [2019] SC254/2008.

[119] *SPDC Nig Ltd v Terbo* (1996) 4 NWLR (Pt 445) 657.

[120] Petroleum Act P10 LFN 2004.

[121] Environmental Impact Assessment Act 2004, Cap. E12 LFN.

v Shell Petroleum Development Co Nigeria Lt.[122] However, due to a lack of political will on the part of the state, the judgment in *Gbemre* has not been effectively enforced, and gas flaring continues largely unabated in the Niger Delta area.[123] The power of multinational corporations and the lack of the political will of the state to implement courts' decisions often render remedies hollow. The unlikelihood of successful litigation and the implementation of court decisions against multinational corporations in Nigeria has given rise to a spate of transnational litigation in different parts in Europe.[124] Without effective guidelines on enforceability and implementation measures against multinational corporations in Nigeria, the eventual remedies if awarded or made in climate litigation stand little chance of being implemented or enforced.

Enhancing the state's duty to 'protect' – the way forward

Experience from Nigeria shows that while there are positive developments on certain aspects of climate change law, reforms are necessary to establish a legislative environment that can ensure that meaningful action is taken on climate change both by state and non-state actors. There also needs to be reform that is supportive of effective remedies against and the accountability of non-state actors for activities that cause, and the impacts of, climate change. Therefore, there is the need for reform that addresses the legal obstacles to climate litigation.

For adequate accountability mechanisms – both in relation to climate change and other issues – a number of things are needed. The review of government initiatives or involvement in activities that trigger climate change should be legally possible. These may include a specific reference to state disinvestment in coals or other fossil-based energy resources and time-bound afforestation and reforestation measures. Similarly, the inactions of government, especially the failure to comply with its climate commitments under its policies or official papers and regional and international instruments to which it is a state party, should fall within the coverage of comprehensive and adequate climate legislation. Functional legislation should make enforceable action points set out for reducing climate change in the NDC. For instance, Nigeria NDC commits to reduction from business as usual

[122] *Gbemre v Shell Petroleum Development Co. Nigeria Ltd* (2005) AHRLR 151 (Federal High Court, Nigeria).

[123] World Data Atlas. 2021. Nigeria-CO_2 emissions, https://knoema.com/atlas/Nigeria/CO2-emissions.

[124] See, for instance, *Okpabi v Royal Dutch Shell* [2021] UKSC 3.

(BAU) and 20 per cent unconditional mitigation objectives. It specifies key strategies to be implemented across high emission sectors such as agriculture (crops and livestock, forests, energy, transportation and communications, vulnerable groups, industry and commerce).[125] While it is important that the state get these right, in the interest of addressing climate change, an applicant should also be able to hold the government accountable for is failure to fulfil these commitments. It is not currently certain that they can. As they stand presently, these are statements of intention that are merely aspirational and not binding. They are merely reflective of the commitments under the Paris Agreement, which itself is not an instrument of binding obligations.[126] However, their inclusion in legislation may mean they can be introduced in any future proceedings, if litigants want to hold the government to what they have previously promised to do.

The reform of procedural law relating to access to remedies is equally important in the context of climate change litigation. The impediments, as have been demonstrated, relating to costs, disclosure, standing and burden of proof need to be ameliorated, both in climate and other public interest cases. The state needs a reflection and reformation of its framework relating to costs in climate litigation. Such reforms should exempt persons or groups litigating in the interest of climate protection from costs, including the expenses of legal representation, witnesses, the value of wasted time, or at least introduce a costs cap for environmental cases. The rationale for such exemption is based on the reality that climate change is a global concern and, as watchmen of the global climate, it is in the interest of all to encourage a positive step such as litigation aimed at ensuring a safe climate. The risk of a costs order should not be allowed to deter climate activists or NGOs from taking action on behalf of everyone.

Access to information relating to climate change should be exempted from the application of statutory limitations on access to information. The application of the disclosure principle should exclude communications – and especially scientific evidence – relating to causation and the effects of climate change from privileged or confidential status. This may help in addressing the frustration that litigants often face in climate change and environmental proceedings. Such reforms should make disclosable reports, memoranda or other internal defence documents made by the defendant, or the defendant's attorneys or agents, or of assertions made by the defendant, or by government or any of its agents, defence witnesses, to the defendant,

[125] Nationally Determined Contribution (NDC) to the Paris Agreement: Nigeria 15 February 2022.

[126] P Sands, 'Climate Change and the Rule of Law: Adjudicating the Future in International Law' (2016) 28(1) *Journal Environmental Law* 19–35, 22.

the defendant's agents or attorneys in connection with climate change cases. Such an approach would ease the struggle often faced by applicants, in particular where they are in need of information at the custody of the respondents to prove elements of their case.

This is connected to questions about the burden of proof, which becomes a very high hurdle where the applicant cannot access vital information. The general rule of he who asserts must prove is not helpful in litigation involving the actions or inactions of the state – including climate litigation – where, for instance, a litigant may struggle to generate and produce evidence necessary to establish crucial facts. Approaches such as employing a reverse burden of proof, or allowing the plaintiff to rely on publicly available scientific evidence as evidence in the case, could help in such cases.

Finally, when it comes to questions about the contribution to the problem of climate change, a court could order that any attempt to rely on arguments that climate change is caused by others (as a way for the defendant to reduce his own responsibility), could be regarded as a special defence that the defendant should prove. It is arguable in any event that this is required in the context of human rights where, as a matter of principle in the realization of rights, a state cannot refuse to discharge its obligations by resorting to the actions or inactions of other states.[127] Hence, in relation to addressing the cause and impact of climate change, the omission or inaction of one party should not be an excuse for other parties not to act.[128]

The accountability of non-state actors for climate change needs to be made possible through appropriate law and regulations. Appropriate domestic guidelines need to be formulated to bring domestic law and procedure in line with the emerging international law position on accountability in the context of business and human rights. The Ruggie guiding principles that apply to businesses call for the respect for human rights by avoiding the infringement of rights and addressing the adverse human rights impacts with which they are involved.[129] Also these guidelines specify that businesses should seek to prevent or mitigate adverse human rights impacts that are directly linked to their operations, even if they have not contributed to those impacts.[130] To

[127] O De Schutter *et al*, 'Commentary to the Maastricht Principles on Extraterritorial Obligations of States in the Area of Economic Social and Cultural Rights' (2012) 34 *Human Rights Quarterly* 1084, 1096.

[128] AO Jegede, *The Climate Change Regulatory Framework and Indigenous Peoples' Lands in Africa: Human Rights Implications* (Pretoria University Law Press 2016).

[129] UN Human Rights Council, *Protect, Respect and Remedy: a Framework for Business and Human Rights: Report of the Special Representative of the Secretary-General on the Issue of Human Rights and Transnational Corpns and Other Business Enterprises, John Ruggie*, 7 April 2008, A/HRC/8/5, (Ruggie Principles) principle 13.

[130] *Protect, Respect and Remedy* (n 129).

perform this role, they are required to put in place appropriate policies and processes.[131] A similar approach could be followed in Nigeria in relation to climate litigation; the interpretation of the content of the new Climate Change Act could benefit greatly from the principles. The basis for such application is found in one of the primary objectives of the Act, which is to set emission targets to achieve zero emissions in line with the international obligations of Nigeria.[132]

Finally, while legal developments in Nigeria in relation to standing are promising, the textual basis for it remains fragile. It is a necessity to constitutionalize the standing rule in Nigeria. A similar provision as exists in the South African provision would leave nobody in any doubt as to legal status of standing to sue in Nigeria.[133] This would assist in removing any doubt that may arise from uncertainties that, as earlier shown, are likely to emerge from the implementation of the new Climate Change Act, which is silent on who can sue.

Conclusion

In the main, this chapter interrogates what the state duty to 'protect' human rights signifies for the difficult hurdles in climate litigation. As shown in the chapter, the state duty to 'protect' human rights in the context of climate change may be achieved by a number of things, namely: effective climate legislation; effective remedies for climate wrongs; and the accountability of non-state actors for climate actions or inactions. Using the realities in Nigeria as an example, the chapter has demonstrated that while there are positive developments, much uncertainty remains around the viability of the application of the three pillars. Consequently, reforms are necessary in a range of areas. As has been discussed, there is the general urgency to formulate an adequate legislative environment that supports a variety of cause of actions on climate change against the state. There is a need for changes in procedural law to improve access to remedies. The effective implementation of the duty to 'protect' human rights may help improve Nigerian action on climate change but, if needed, may also reduce the fragility of success in climate litigation in Africa.

[131] *Protect, Respect and Remedy* (n 129), principle 9.

[132] Climate Change Act (n 10), s.1(f).

[133] Republic of South Africa Constitution 1996, s. 38.

4

Litigation Against Coal-Fired Power in South Africa: Lessons from and for Global Climate Litigation to Reduce Greenhouse Gas Emissions

Nicole Loser

Introduction

South Africa is both villain and victim in the climate crisis. South Africa is a major contributor to the impacts of climate change, as the fourteenth largest emitter of greenhouse gases (GHGs) globally[1] and the highest emitter in Africa. The exploitation of, and further reliance on, fossil fuels is still very much on South Africa's agenda and entrenched in national policy.[2] At the same time, South Africa and its neighbouring countries are identified by the United Nation's Intergovernmental Panel on Climate Change (IPCC) as a climate change 'hotspot' – a location where climate change impacts are abnormally high in a global context.[3] South Africa is already a water-stressed

---

1 Global Carbon Project's Carbon Atlas 2020, www.globalcarbonatlas.org, accessed 22 October 2022.

2 Policies that support the proliferation of fossil fuels in South Africa include the 'Integrated Resource Plan for Electricity 2019' and the 'National Development Plan 2030 Our Future-make it work'.

3 This finding stems from the region's subtropical climate, already warm and dry, which under climate change is projected to become drastically warmer and likely also drier. Hoegh-Guldberg, Jacob, Taylor *et al*, 'Impacts of 1.5°C Global Warming on Natural and Human Systems' in *Global Warming of 1.5°C. An IPCC Special Report on the impacts of global warming of 1.5°C above pre-industrial levels and related global greenhouse gas emission pathways, in the context of strengthening the global response to the threat of climate change, sustainable development, and efforts to eradicate poverty* (IPCC 2018) 3.5.4.7. FA Engelbrecht *et al*,

country and we face future drying trends and weather variability with cycles of droughts and sudden excessive rains.

South Africa's own Climate Change Response Policy 2011 recognizes that South Africa is extremely vulnerable and exposed to the impacts of climate change due to our socio-economic and environmental context. It also recognizes that climate variability, including the increased frequency and intensity of extreme weather events, will disproportionately affect the poor[4] – an important example being the floods in South Africa's KwaZulu-Natal province in April 2022, which resulted in at least 435 deaths, with 54 people declared missing. At least 13,500 houses were damaged or destroyed. More than 600 schools were affected.[5] A World Weather Attribution report concludes that the probability of an event such as the rainfall that resulted in the April 2022 KwaZulu-Natal floods has approximately doubled due to human-induced climate change, and the intensity of the event has increased by 4–8 per cent.[6]

South Africa (and the southern African region) has increased plans for fossil fuel exploitation as well as greater exposure to climate harms. Therefore, litigation and other legal strategies will become increasingly relevant in seeking to prevent these harms.

Lawyers, activists and academics are implementing creative legal and non-legal strategies[7] to tackle GHG emissions from fossil fuels in the face of the climate crisis. Litigation, which will be the focus of this chapter, is increasingly relied on as a last resort to achieve GHG emission reductions in South Africa and globally. In some instances, the strategy has been to litigate on government plans and inaction. In others, the focus has been on using the law and litigation to stop fossil fuel projects. All of these strategies come with their own challenges and opportunities, in which external contexts and available legal mechanisms play a major role.

While there are a number of groundbreaking legal and litigation strategies underway in southern Africa, and Africa more broadly, to address climate change, this chapter focuses on South Africa. It delves into the practical learnings and experiences of some of the litigation strategies that have been, and are being, deployed in South Africa to challenge coal-fired power – as

---

'Projections of Rapidly Rising Surface Temperatures Over Africa Under Low Mitigation' (2015) *IOP Science* 10(8).

4 National Climate Change Response White Paper, South Africa (2011), 8.

5 Pinto, Wolski, Zachariah, Wolski *et al*, 'Climate Change Exacerbated Rainfall Causing Devastating Flooding in Eastern South Africa' (2022) *World Weather Attribution*, 2.

6 Pinto *et al* (n 5).

7 Other non-legal strategies focusing on financing, research, media, education and other forms of community mobilization, for example, are and have been crucial in the fight to stop the climate crisis.

an important avenue to achieve climate change mitigation. The author bases these insights on her own experience as a legal practitioner, having acted as attorney in a number of the cases mentioned herein.[8]

The chapter is structured as follows: first, it looks into South Africa's political and socio-economic context as relevant to understanding the litigation strategies being discussed. Second, a brief overview of South Africa's legal mechanisms is provided – this is also relevant to, and a key component of, the litigation strategies discussed. Next, the chapter speaks to some of the litigation strategies used in South Africa to challenge and address the harms of coal-fired power. It discusses the different types of cases – litigation to stop coal projects; legal challenges to broader government decisions that call for new coal power; and challenges to government's failure to address the harmful impacts of coal power – providing case study examples (we refer to this body of cases as 'South Africa's coal litigation'). Finally, the chapter draws on learnings from South Africa's coal litigation, and the effectiveness of these cases as a means to mitigate GHG emissions and the effects of climate change.

South African context

South Africa is a country of extreme poverty and inequality. It is one of the most unequal countries in the world,[9] with a staggering unemployment rate.[10] As a result, economic development and jobs are prioritized in all decision making.[11]

South Africa is historically dependent on coal, as the initial backbone of the country's economy and electricity sector. Roughly 80 per cent of South Africa's GHG emissions come from the energy sector,[12] with

8 Many of the claims I make about these strategies are based on my own knowledge and experience.

9 Statistics South Africa, Department of Statistics South Africa, *Inequality Trends in South Africa: A Multidimensional Diagnostic of Inequality* (2019) 2.

10 The unemployment rate in the second quarter of 2022 (April–June 2022) was 33.9 per cent (Quarterly Labour Force Survey Quarter 2 2022).

11 Examples of this position can be found in: South Africa's National Development Plan 2030 (p. 27), where raising employment through faster economic growth is flagged as a priority, 7; and South Africa's Nationally Determined Contribution update of 2021, which states that a well-resourced just transition strategy will be needed to shift to low-carbon technologies, to maximize benefits and minimize adverse impacts on communities, workers and the economy, 4.

12 Department of Environmental Affairs' 7th National Greenhouse Gas Inventory for South Africa 2000–2017, 24 August 2021, 6. The Draft 8th GHG Inventory for South Africa: 2000–2020 estimates that total emissions from the Energy sector for 2020 were 380 033 Gg CO2e (Table ES 3) which is 79.4 per cent of the total emissions (excl. FOLU) for South Africa (Figure ES 2), p. xii.

87 per cent of those emissions coming from public sector electricity (coal-fired power emissions) produced by South Africa's state-owned electricity utility, Eskom.[13]

Eskom is in a state of financial crisis and its coal-fired power stations are in poor condition, exacerbating their devastating pollution, with little consequence in the way of enforcement action, and regular nationwide blackouts.[14] Eskom's compliance with environmental laws is not prioritized, nor is its expenditure on needed retrofits to comply with the law and reduce polluting emissions from its coal-fired power stations.[15]

In many ways, South Africa's government is sending out mixed signals. While it is saying the right things on climate change mitigation and response,[16] it is also implementing contradictory steps and policy decisions. Examples of these mixed messages include plans to develop new coal and gas power capacity, which are not aligned with government's own acknowledged need for a climate change response and a just transition away from coal and fossil fuels more generally.

South Africa's 2021 revised First Nationally Determined Contribution under the Paris Agreement (2021 NDC) confirms that South Africa is already experiencing significant impacts of climate change, particularly as a result of increased temperatures and rainfall variability, and is warming at more than twice the global rate of temperature increase.[17] It also notes that South Africa's economy and energy system is one of the most coal-dependent in the world, featuring a large stock of high-carbon infrastructure, particularly in the energy sector. The 2021 NDC records that South Africa is also fortunately blessed with abundant renewable energy resources, and that developments

---

13 Department of Environmental Affairs (n 12), 147, and Draft GHG Inventory for South Africa: 2000–2020, 80.

14 See, for instance, C Ramaphosa, 'While We All Desperately Want to, We Cannot End load Shedding Overnight' *Daily Maverick*, 23 January 2023, https://www.dailymaverick.co.za/article/2023-01-23-its-easy-to-blame-eskom-for-load-shedding-but-reality-is-different/; DR Walwyn, 'Explosive Revelations About South Africa's Power Utility: Why New Electricity Minister Should Heed the Words of Former Eskom CEO', *The Conversation*, 14 March 2023, https://theconversation.com/explosive-revelations-about-south-africas-power-utility-why-new-electricity-minister-should-heed-the-words-of-former-eskom-ceo-201508.

15 Eskom Powerpoint Presentation, 'The MES and Eskom's 2035 JET strategy', presented by André de Ruyter, Group Chief Executive (July 2022).

16 At the Virtual Leaders' Summit on Climate Change, April 2021, President Cyril Ramaphosa, in his speech, referred to climate change as the most pressing issue of our time. President Cyril Ramaphosa: Virtual Leaders' Summit on Climate Change, https://www.gov.za/speeches/president-cyril-ramaphosa-virtual-leaders-summit-climate-22-apr-2021-0000, accessed 22 October 2022.

17 South Africa First Nationally Determined Contribution under the Paris Agreement Updated September 2021, 6.

in the economics of renewable energy technologies over the last decade are very favourable to low-carbon development in the country.[18]

New fossil fuel projects are being proposed, in line with government's stated position that coal is necessary for 'baseload' electricity security;[19] and, according to the country's Integrated Resource Plan for Electricity 2019 (IRP 2019),[20] which reflects a decision that government should not 'sterilize' South Africa's coal resources.[21] South Africa's government takes the position that 'cleaner coal' is the lifeline that will enable continued reliance on coal into the future,[22] while also arguing that gas is the bridge that will enable and complement increased uptake of renewables and maintain security of supply.[23]

Communities within the areas where coal plants and mines are proposed are often divided in terms of the support for big fossil fuel projects, where there are prospects (or at least promises) of employment and access to services.[24] Understandably, people want to be presented with opportunities and – if not new coal plants or mines – then alternatives to those projects.

Global coal use in electricity generation needs to be reduced by 80 per cent below 2010 levels by 2030[25] to avoid temperature increases exceeding 1.5°C – the limit recognized by the IPCC as the safe limit for our climate.[26] Achieving this substantial cut in coal use requires ambitious action to stop not only new coal plants, but to achieve the speedy retirement (or at least substantially reduced capacity) of existing coal plants as well.

18 South Africa First Nationally Determined Contribution under the Paris Agreement Updated September 2021, 3–4.

19 Consultation Paper: Concurrence with the Ministerial Determination on the Procurement of New Generation Capacity from renewables (wind and PV), storage, gas and coal technologies, 18 March 2020, 15 and Independent Power Producer webpage for the 'Coal Baseload IPP Procurement Programme', https://www.ipp-coal.co.za, accessed on 22 October 2022.

20 GN1360, Gazette number 42784, of 18 October 2019.

21 IRP 2019, 46.

22 IRP 2019.

23 Department of Mineral Resources and Energy's South African Gas Master Plan: Basecase Report, version 01 for stakeholder consultation (September 2021) 1, 45; and IRP 2019, 13.

24 The South African Human Rights Commission, National Hearing on the Underlying Socio-Economic Challenges of Mining-Affected Communities in South Africa, 13–14 September, 26 and 28 September and 3 November 2016.

25 R Brecha *et al,* 'Global and Regional Coal Phase Out Requirements of the Paris Agreement: Insights from the IPCC Special Report on 1.5°C' (2019) *Climate Analytics*, 1.

26 IPCC, 2018: Global Warming of 1.5°C. An IPCC Special Report on the impacts of global warming of 1.5°C above pre-industrial levels and related global greenhouse gas emission pathways, in the context of strengthening the global response to the threat of climate change, sustainable development, and efforts to eradicate poverty (V Masson-Delmotte *et al* (eds)).

While the government acknowledges the need for a just transition away from coal, in line with global trends and the commitment to decarbonize the economy to address climate concerns,[27] a number of contradictory decisions mentioned above, that would see new fossil fuel capacity being developed, suggest otherwise. South Africa's government adopts the narrative that, if it is to be just and sustainable, the transition needs to be carried out in a phased and gradual manner.[28] Available evidence shows that a low carbon development path for the country is also in the country's best interests from an economic perspective.[29] South Africa faces transition risk of more than USD120 billion in present value terms (R2 trillion) if it fails to take timeous steps to move away from coal and avoid locking into new coal power and coal infrastructure.[30] Yet, the government has shown no signs of any intention to abandon new coal-fired power.

Legal mechanisms in South Africa have the potential to address some of these challenges and underpin several climate litigation strategies. These are addressed in the next section.

South Africa's legal mechanisms

South Africa has a strong legal framework supporting potential options for climate litigation.

As a signatory and ratifying party to the Paris Agreement,[31] the South African government has undertaken international commitments to address climate change. The Constitution states the following in relation to international commitments: 'when interpreting the Bill of Rights, a court, tribunal or forum must consider international law'[32] and 'an international agreement binds the Republic only after it has been approved by resolution in both the National Assembly and the National Council of Provinces'.[33]

27 South Africa First Nationally Determined Contribution under the Paris Agreement Updated September 2021, 4.

28 Government of South Africa, 'Accelerating Coal Transition Investment Plan for South Africa', 23 September 2022; J Burton, T Caetano, B McCall 'Coal transitions in South Africa Understanding the implications of a 2°C-compatible coal phase-out plan for South Africa' (2018) The Institute for Sustainable Development and International Relations (IDDRI) and the Energy Research Centre University of Cape Town.

29 J Burton *et al* in collaboration with the CSIR Energy Centre, 'A Vital Ambition: Determining the Cost of Additional CO_2 Emission Mitigation in the South African Electricity System' (2020) *Meridian Economics* 60–1.

30 M Anwar *et al* 'Understanding the Impact of a Low Carbon Transition on South Africa' (2019) *Climate Policy Initiative* 11, 13, 31.

31 United Nations Framework Convention on Climate Change (2015) Adoption of the Paris Agreement, 21st Conference of the Parties, Paris: United Nations.

32 Section 39(1)(b), Constitution of RSA 1996.

33 Section 231(2), Constitution of RSA 1996.

The parties (including South Africa) to the Paris Agreement commit to 'ambitious efforts'[34] and successive NDCs must represent a progression beyond the party's then current nationally determined contribution and reflect its highest possible ambition.[35] The Paris Agreement will – by its own provisions – be implemented to reflect the principle of common but differentiated responsibilities and respective capabilities, in the light of different national circumstances.

In September 2021, South Africa adopted the update to its First Nationally Determined Contribution – the 2021 NDC. The 2021 NDC is more ambitious than the 2015 NDC.[36] Still, the 2021 NDC emissions target range[37] for 2030 is criticized as being 'insufficient'[38] and is inconsistent with keeping temperatures below the needed 1.5°C, in order to avoid the worst impacts of the climate crisis. It is therefore not yet Paris Agreement compatible.[39]

The Constitution of the Republic of South Africa 1996[40] (the Constitution) is the supreme law of the country.

South Africa recognizes an unqualified right to an environment not harmful to health or wellbeing in its Constitution. Section 24 reads:

> Everyone has the right—
> (a) to an environment that is not harmful to their health or wellbeing; and
> (b) to have the environment protected, for the benefit of present and future generations, through reasonable legislative and other measures that—
> (i) prevent pollution and ecological degradation;
> (ii) promote conservation; and
> (iii) secure ecologically sustainable development and use of natural resources while promoting justifiable economic and social development.

34 Article 3.

35 Article 4(3).

36 The lower end of the new target range for 2030 (350 MtCO2e) is aligned with the upper end of the range for a 1.5°C fair share emission target for South Africa, namely 274–350 MtCO2e). Climate Equity Reference Project, 'Comparison of South Africa's draft updated mitigation NDC to its mitigation fair share' (2021).

37 350–420 MtCO2e for 2030.

38 'Climate Action Tracker, South Africa Country Summary, 21 September 2022 Update', available at https://climateactiontracker.org/countries/south-africa/, accessed on 8 August 2023.

39 'Climate Action Tracker, ibid.

40 Act 108 of 1996.

The judgment in the case of *Trustees for the time being of Groundwork Trust v Minister of Environmental Affairs,*[41] which is addressed as a case study in this chapter, distinguishes section 24(a) from section 24(b) of the right, confirming that section 24(a) 'is immediately realisable' here and now,[42] compared with other rights which can be progressively realized over time, through reasonable measures.[43]

The climate crisis is not confined to affecting *only* environmental rights. In fact, it is hard to imagine a human right that is not – and will not increasingly be – negatively affected by climate change. Climate change will serve to exacerbate the deep inequality in South Africa. It has far-reaching impacts for all rights, including the rights to: equality,[44] human dignity,[45] life,[46] access to sufficient food and water[47] and the rights of children (the child's best interests are of paramount importance in every matter concerning the child),[48] which are entrenched in South Africa's Constitution.

In many instances, legislation has been enacted to give effect to these rights. In the case of the environmental right, the National Environmental Management Act 1998[49] (NEMA) serves as the umbrella legislation for environmental management and protection in South Africa. NEMA establishes principles for environmental decision making on matters affecting the environment – the National Environmental Management Principles. These serve, inter alia, as the general framework within which environmental management and implementation plans must be formulated;[50] and serve as guidelines by reference to which any organ of state must exercise any function when taking any decision in terms of the Act or any statutory provision concerning the protection of the environment.[51]

NEMA also recognizes a duty of care. It stipulates that:

> Every person who causes, has caused or may cause significant pollution or degradation of the environment must take reasonable measures to prevent such pollution or degradation from occurring, continuing or

[41] (39724/2019) [2022] ZAGPPHC 208 (18 March 2022).

[42] Paragraph 163.

[43] Examples include rights to: health care, food, water and social security, s. 27(2) of the Constitution; and housing, s. 26(2) of the Constitution.

[44] Section 9.

[45] Section 10.

[46] Section 11.

[47] Section 27.

[48] Section 28(2).

[49] Act 107 of 1998.

[50] Section 2(1)(b).

[51] Section 2(1)(c).

> recurring, or, in so far as such harm to the environment is authorised by law or cannot reasonably be avoided or stopped, to minimise and rectify such pollution or degradation of the environment. (section 28(1))

NEMA includes the framework for environmental impact assessments and authorizations – stipulating that a decision maker must take into account all relevant factors including, inter alia, any pollution, environmental impacts or environmental degradation likely to be caused if an application is approved or refused.[52] The case of *Earthlife Africa Johannesburg v Minister of Environmental Affairs*,[53] which will be discussed in this chapter, deals with the extent to which NEMA's environmental impact assessment provisions require consideration of climate change impacts.

South Africa's government is in the process of adopting climate change legislation. South Africa's long-awaited and much-needed Climate Change Bill has been in the pipeline since 2018, when a first draft was published. Once in effect, this will serve as a critical legal mechanism for regulating climate mitigation in South Africa. For now, and in the absence of dedicated climate change legislation, South Africa's GHG emissions are reported, monitored and regulated, to a limited extent, under South Africa's air quality legislation – the National Environmental Management: Air Quality Act 2004[54] and the Carbon Tax Act 2019.[55] At present, there are no legislated GHG emission limits, which may not be exceeded, in South Africa.

In seeking to litigate on environmental or other issues, NEMA and other applicable legislation should be relied upon to the extent possible, rather than direct reliance on the Constitution, as required by the principle of subsidiarity, endorsed by South Africa's courts.[56]

While South Africa's courts adhere to the principle of subsidiarity and the separation of powers,[57] they recognize their role as the ultimate guardians of the Constitution, and will intervene to prevent or stop a

52 Section 24O(1)(b)(i).

53 (65662/16) [2017] ZAGPPHC 58; [2017] 2 All SA 519 (GP) (8 March 2017).

54 Act 39 of 2004.

55 Act 15 of 2019.

56 The case of *South African National Defence Union v Minister of Defence* 1999 (4) SA 469; 1999 (6) BCLR 615 (26 May 1999) confirms that the principle of subsidiarity requires a litigant to rely on legislation when enforcing a constitutional right rather than circumventing the legislation in favour of direct application of a constitutional provision.

57 South Africa's Constitution is founded on the principle of the separation of powers. Constitutional Principle VI, Sch. 4 Constitutional Principles, Constitution of the Republic of South Africa Act 200 of 1993.

violation of the Constitution.[58] The judgment in *Glenister v President of RSA*[59] confirms this:

> [I]n our constitutional democracy, the courts are the ultimate guardians of the Constitution. They not only have the right to intervene in order to prevent the violation of the Constitution, they also have the duty to do so. It is in the performance of this role that courts are more likely to confront the question of whether to venture into the domain of other branches of government and the extent of such intervention. It is a necessary component of the doctrine of separation of powers that courts have a constitutional obligation to ensure that the exercise of power by other branches of government occurs within constitutional bounds. But even in these circumstances, courts must observe the limits of their powers. (paragraph 33)

Administrative decisions could be subject to judicial review under the terms of section 6 of the Promotion of Administrative Justice Act[60] (PAJA), on bases that include reasonableness (if a decision is so unreasonable that no reasonable person could have so exercised the power or performed the function);[61] that the action was taken because irrelevant considerations were taken into account or relevant considerations were not considered;[62] or irrationality (if the means, including the process of making a decision, are not linked to the purpose or ends).[63]

Any public action that is not administrative action can be challenged under the principle of legality – 'a basis on which to review only those exercises of public power that do not amount to administrative action as "a backstop

[58] *Doctors for Life International v Speaker of the National Assembly* (CCT12/05) [2006] ZACC 11; 2006 (12) BCLR 1399 (CC); 2006 (6) SA 416 (CC) (17 August 2006) at paras 68 and 69.

[59] (CCT 48/10) [2011] ZACC 6; 2011 (3) SA 347 (CC); 2011 (7) BCLR 651 (CC) (17 March 2011).

[60] Act 3 of 2000.

[61] Section 6(2)(h) PAJA. The case of *Bato Star Fishing (Pty) Ltd v Minister of Environmental Affairs and Tourism* confirms that 'factors relevant to determining whether a decision is reasonable or not will include the nature of the decision, the identity and expertise of the decision-maker, the range of factors relevant to the decision, the reasons given for the decision, the nature of the competing interests involved and the impact of the decision on the lives and well-being of those affected' (para. 45).

[62] Section 6(e)(iii) PAJA.

[63] Section 6(f)(ii) PAJA.

or safety net" ... when the [Promotion of Administrative Justice Act] PAJA [is] not of application'.[64]

The control of public power is always a constitutional matter, as confirmed in *Pharmaceutical Manufacturers Association of SA: In Re Ex Parte President of the Republic of South Africa*,[65] and the South African judiciary is a strong defender of the Constitution, subject, of course, to the doctrine of separation of powers.

The case of *Bato Star Fishing (Pty) Ltd v Minister of Environmental Affairs and Tourism*[66] bears relevance. Here the Constitutional Court confirmed that if it is satisfied that a 'reasonable equilibrium' has been struck, taking into account all factors and selecting reasonable means to pursue the identified legislative goal, then it will not intervene in the functions of the executive;[67] at the same time, the court cannot rubber-stamp an unreasonable decision. The court held that:

> Often a power will identify a goal to be achieved, but will not dictate which route should be followed to achieve that goal. In such circumstances a court should pay due respect to the route selected by the decision-maker. This does not mean however that where the decision is one which will not reasonably result in the achievement of the goal, or which is not reasonably supported on the facts or not reasonable in the light of the reasons given for it, a court may not review that decision. A court should not rubber-stamp an unreasonable decision simply because of the complexity of the decision or the identity of the decision-maker.[68]

South Africa's coal litigation

In South Africa, activist groups have for a number of years been challenging the harmful impacts (for air, water, land, ecosystems, the climate, health and social wellbeing) of coal mining and coal-fired power stations, in the face of the government's electricity policies and decisions that call for more, and continued reliance on, coal-fired power. South Africa's Life After Coal

64 M Murcott and W Van der Westhuizen, 'The Ebb and Flow of the Application of the Principle of Subsidiarity – Critical Reflections on Motau and My Vote Counts' (2018) *Constitutional Court Review* 44.

65 2000 (2) SA 674; 2000 (3) BCLR 241 (25 February 2000), para. 33.

66 (CCT 27/03) [2004] ZACC 15; 2004 (4) SA 490 (CC); 2004 (7) BCLR 687 (CC) (12 March 2004).

67 Paragraph 50.

68 Paragraph 48.

Campaign[69] works to discourage the development of new fossil fuels, including coal-fired power stations and mines; reduce emissions from existing coal infrastructure and encourage a coal phase-out; and enable a just transition. It has been at the forefront of a number of the legal challenges against coal power, which are addressed in this chapter.

A large part of the work of the Life After Coal Campaign has entailed challenging – through legal and other strategies – individual proposed new coal plants that would contribute to excessive climate emissions. The campaign also uses the law to challenge government action or inaction that pose threats to human health and the environment and, in doing so, seeks to reduce emissions from coal-fired power and mitigate the effects of climate change. These strategies have been highly effective, in that they have achieved what they set out to do. More detail about these strategic cases follows below.

Cases to stop coal projects in South Africa

Globally, litigation is being used to challenge individual projects for fossil fuel extraction and fossil fuel-based power generation.[70] This is increasingly important in the African context as plans are emerging for fossil fuel projects in other African countries, including Mozambique,[71] Malawi,[72] Zimbabwe[73] and Botswana.[74] Activists in

---

[69] Life After Coal/Impilo Ngaphandle Kwamalahle is a joint campaign by Earthlife Africa Johannesburg, groundWork, and the Centre for Environmental Rights, https://lifeafterc oal.org.za/.

[70] Examples include: *Greenpeace Nordic v Norway* (2021), 34068/21 (Norway); *Wayúu Indigenous Community v Ministry of Environment* (2019), 11001-0324-000-2019-00107-00 (Colombia); *Kang v KSURE and KEXIM* (2022) (South Korea); *Students for Climate Solutions v Minister of Energy and Resources* (2021) (New Zealand).

[71] Mozambique faces more than 2,000 MW of coal power with the proposed Jindal, Chitima, Ncondezi and Benga coal power stations. Ember, in partnership with E3G and Global Energy Monitor 'No New Coal Factbook: Data Insights on Countries that Could Commit to No New Coal' (7 October 2021), Version 1, 27.

[72] Malawi faces 400 MW of coal power (the proposed Kammwamba and Rukuru power plants). Ember, in partnership with E3G and Global Energy Monitor 'No New Coal Factbook: Data Insights on Countries that Could Commit to No New Coal' (7 October 2021), Version 1, 24.

[73] A 2,800 MW coal plant (the Sengwa coal power plant) is proposed for northern Zimbabwe's Gokwe South Rural District, by the Zimbabwean mining company RioZim. Bank Track Project Profile, 3 February 2022, https://www.banktrack.org/project/seng wa_coal_power_plant/pdf, accessed 23 October 2022.

[74] Botswana faces 2,850 MW of proposed coal power projects (Ember, in partnership with E3G and Global Energy Monitor 'No New Coal Factbook: Data Insights on Countries that Could Commit to No New Coal' (7 October 2021), Version 1, 14.

Ghana,[75] Kenya[76] and South Africa,[77] among others, have already succeeded in stopping plans for a new coal plants,[78] while lawyers and activists in these and other African countries have spent a number of years opposing proposed fossil fuel projects.[79] Examples of such cases in South Africa are addressed in this chapter.

Cases to stop the building of new fossil fuel infrastructure and projects, including coal, have the advantage of forming one strong angle in a multitude of setbacks globally facing the fossil fuel sector. Financiers become less willing to fund these projects and they become outcompeted by cheaper renewable alternatives. In other words, even an unsuccessful judgment in this kind of litigation may still result in the project falling away (a win) as the litigation – and delays caused by the litigation – make it less attractive to investors.

On the other hand, these cases, even if successful, may not do enough to reduce GHG emissions in time to avert the most severe impacts of the climate crisis. Further, there is no guarantee that if litigation is successful at getting certain projects quashed, those projects would not simply be replaced by others, or (in the context of coal) replaced by another emission-intensive fossil fuel, such as gas.

The Thabametsi cases are discussed in more detail below as a case study. The strategy this outlines is not the only one being pursued by activists in South Africa, nor are they the only project-specific legal challenges in the country. Nevertheless, these cases serve as a good example of an instance when litigation, used as part of a multi-faceted strategy to challenge a coal project, gave rise to a successful High Court judgment with important knock-on effects, including for other cases in South Africa with climate implications.

---

[75] 350.org, 'From anti-coal campaigners to Ghana's renewable energy champions', 18 June 2020, https://350africa.org/from-anti-coal-campaigners-to-ghanas-renewable-energy-champions/, accessed 23 October 2022.

[76] The Save Lamu (https://www.savelamu.org/) campaign in Kenya and a number of other organizations have worked to stop the proposed 1,050 MW Lamu coal plant proposed in Kenya. See also, Business and Human Rights Resource Centre Story. 'Kenya: Lamu Coal Power Plant', 6 February 2022, https://www.business-humanrights.org/en/latest-news/kenya-lamu-coal-power-plant/, accessed 23 October 2022.

[77] See Thabametsi Case Study.

[78] 350.org, 'From anti-coal campaigners to Ghana's renewable energy champions', 18 June 2020, https://350africa.org/from-anti-coal-campaigners-to-ghanas-renewable-energy-champions/, accessed 23 October 2022.

[79] Activists from the Life After Coal Campaign; Oil Watch Africa; Natural Justice; Justiça Ambiental Mozambique; 350 Africa have worked to oppose oil, gas and coal projects in countries like South Africa, Namibia, Botswana, and Mozambique. Further relevant campaigns include: Stope the East African Crude Oil Pipeline, https://www.stopeacop.net/home, accessed 23 October 2022.

Case study: the Thabametsi coal plant litigation

Earthlife Africa Johannesburg v Minister of Environmental Affairs[80] (*Thabametsi I*) has been hailed as South Africa's first climate change case. It was launched as a judicial review in the North Gauteng High Court, to set aside an environmental authorization issued to Thabametsi Power Company (Pty) Ltd, for a 1,200 megawatt (MW) coal plant to be built in two phases in South Africa's Limpopo province. The Minister of Environment's internal appeal decision to uphold that environmental authorization also fell within the scope of the High Court review.

The Thabametsi coal power project was proposed in the context of South Africa's Coal Baseload Independent Power Producer (IPP) Procurement Programme. The Programme's first bid window called for 1,000 MW of new coal capacity to come from one or more independent coal plants. The preferred bidders announced in 2016 were the Thabametsi (557 MW) and Khanyisa (306 MW) coal plant projects. A number of other coal projects had applied for environmental authorizations with a view to generating power under this or subsequent bidding rounds of the Coal Baseload IPP Procurement Programme.[81]

The applicant in the review, Earthlife Africa, argued that the Minister could not uphold the Thabametsi project authorization in the absence of a comprehensive climate impact assessment, which was required by South Africa's environmental legislation (NEMA and the Environmental Impact Assessment (EIA) Regulations). In short, the applicant argued that climate change was a 'relevant factor'[82] that was required to be considered in deciding whether or not to grant the project an environmental authorization.

In March 2017, South Africa's North Gauteng High Court found in favour of Earthlife Africa.[83] The judgment confirmed that, a plain reading of section 24O(1) of NEMA confirms that climate change impacts are indeed relevant factors that must be considered[84] and that:

---

80 (65662/16) [2017] ZAGPPHC 58; [2017] 2 All SA 519 (GP) (8 March 2017).

81 These projects include: the proposed 600 MW KiPower coal plant proposed for the Mpumalanga province in South Africa; the proposed 1,050 MW Colenso coal power plant proposed for the KwaZulu-Natal province. Details of the legal challenges of the projects can be found online on the website of the Centre for Environmental Rights, https://cer.org.za/.

82 Section 24O(1) of NEMA obliges competent authorities to take account of all relevant factors in deciding on an application for environmental authorization, including any pollution, environmental impacts or environmental degradation likely to be caused if the application is approved or refused.

83 The court issued an order setting aside the Minister's appeal decision (pertaining specifically to the climate change ground of appeal) and remitting the appeal back to the Minister for reconsideration alongside Thabametsi's climate change impact assessment report.

84 Paragraph 78.

> climate change poses a substantial risk to sustainable development in South Africa. The effects of climate change, in the form of rising temperatures, greater water scarcity, and the increasing frequency of natural disasters pose substantial risks. Sustainable development is at the same time integrally linked with the principle of intergenerational justice requiring the state to take reasonable measures to protect the environment 'for the benefit of present and future generations' and hence adequate consideration of climate change. Short term needs must be evaluated and weighed against long-term consequences.[85]

The court acknowledged that a climate change impact assessment requires more than a mere quantification of projected GHG emissions. It also requires an assessment of broader climate change impacts, such as water scarcity, on the project and surrounding area – in alignment with the EIA requirements of NEMA.[86] This goes some way towards reflecting the complex ways in which climate change affects law and policy in South Africa, as already highlighted. The judgment further confirmed that the existence of policy that calls for the establishment of new coal-fired power cannot preclude the need for a climate change impact assessment in the environmental authorization process of specific projects. In other words, electricity policy cannot be treated as a binding administrative decision that overrides project-specific impact assessments and decision making.[87]

The *Thabametsi I* judgment created a welcome basis in confirming the obligation, under South African law, to fully assess climate impacts as part of an EIA process. Staggeringly, as Professor Tracy-Lynn Field has noted, the then Department of Environmental Affairs and the independent practitioner conducting the assessment did not themselves consider or raise the need for an assessment of climate impacts in the EIA for a project as blatantly harmful to the climate as a coal-fired power station.[88] In early 2018, following the *Thabametsi I* judgment, the Minister proceeded to consider the Thabametsi project's climate change impact assessment. The assessment confirmed extremely high (negative) climate impacts. The Minister – in making her appeal decision a second time, this time with an assessment of climate impacts before her – decided to uphold the environmental authorization

85 Paragraph 82.

86 The court acknowledged the relevance of the proposed power station's location in a water-stressed region, thereby 'aggravating the impact of climate change in the region by contributing to water scarcity, raising in turn questions about the viability of the power station over its lifetime', para. 44.

87 Paragraphs 95 and 96.

88 T Field, 'Climate Change Impact Assessment in South Africa Post Earthlife Africa (Thabametsi) (Part 2): A Tale of Two Impact Reports' (2017) *LinkedIn*.

for Thabametsi. The Minister's decision was that the country's then 2010 Integrated Resource Plan for Electricity (IRP 2010) permits the establishment of new coal capacity and that, in calling for new coal capacity, the IRP 2010 concluded that the harmful impacts of the coal plant were outweighed by the benefit to the country of much-needed electricity capacity.

Earthlife Africa and groundWork launched another judicial review (*Thabametsi II*) of the second decision on the basis that, among other things, the Minister unlawfully fettered her discretion by treating an outdated electricity policy (the IRP 2010) as determinative of her decision and considering it in a rigid and inflexible manner.[89] Whereas *Thabametsi I* was much more narrowly focused on the interpretation of environmental legislation, the primary issue in *Thabametsi II* was that, in relying almost exclusively on the IRP 2010, the Minister reached an irrational and unreasonable conclusion that the harms of the project were outweighed by alleged benefits.[90] This rendered her decision challengeable under the grounds for review of administrative action under PAJA as referenced in the Legal Mechanisms section.

In December 2020, Earthlife Africa and groundWork, in the *Thabametsi II* matter, secured a court order by agreement, setting aside the environmental authorization for the Thabametsi project. The project has since been abandoned. The precedent and clarity that the *Thabametsi II* case had hoped to achieve on the rationality and reasonableness of relying almost exclusively on an electricity plan to make a decision on an EIA will, therefore, have to wait for another case.

An important outcome of the *Thabametsi I* decision is that it has opened the door to challenging other proposed coal and gas projects that were approved despite a failure to assess (adequately or at all) climate impacts. Further cases based on the failure to adequately assess climate impacts as part of an EIA and prior to issuing an authorization were instituted in relation to other proposed coal plants, including the proposed, and successful bidder, Khanyisa coal power station.[91] Those cases were all successful in stopping the coal power projects – with the North Gauteng High Court setting the authorizations aside or confirming that the authorizations had since lapsed.

Going forward, a fundamental result of *Thabametsi I* is that there is no longer any doubt that climate change impacts need to be assessed as part of an EIA for projects that could have climate impacts. The days of the cursory climate impact one-liner that 'while quantification of the relative

---

89 Founding Affidavit of Phillipine Lekalakala, 26 March 2018, paras 22 and 109.

90 Founding Affidavit of Phillipine Lekalakala, paras 106, 110.2, 112.

91 *groundWork v Minister of Environmental Affairs* (Khanyisa), case no. 61561/17 and *groundWork v Minister of Environmental Affairs* (KiPower), case no. 54087/17.

contribution … is difficult, the contribution is considered to be relatively small in the national and global context',[92] as was stated in Thabametsi's EIA, are (hopefully) over.

The judgment also paves the way for better policy decisions that include consideration of climate change impacts, especially because South Africa is extremely vulnerable to the effects of climate change.[93] If climate impacts are properly assessed and considered, it should be far more difficult to justify fossil fuel projects, given how significant and generally unavoidable their climate impacts are. In 2021 the Department of Environment published a draft National Guideline for 'Consideration of Climate Change Implications in Applications for Environmental Authorisations, Atmospheric Emission Licences and Waste Management Licences'.[94] These guidelines are intended to provide developers with the minimum required content of a climate change assessment, and are also intended to assist regulatory authorities in their decision making.

Legal challenges of policies or decisions calling for new coal power

In addition to the governmental decisions to authorize individual projects, there are a number of policy and administrative decisions that call for coal power capacity, and thus give rise to increased GHG emissions and climate harms. Examples in South Africa would be the IRP 2019 or ministerial determinations for new fossil fuel capacity issued in terms of the Electricity Regulation Act 2006[95] (ERA) and in reliance on the IRP 2019.

A prevalent opposing argument by project proponents in cases to challenge individual projects is that they are simply responding to government policy by proposing to build these fossil fuel projects.[96] In other words, since government has called for new fossil fuel capacity in its plans and these projects are seeking to fill that alleged need, opposition to these projects should instead be directed at the policies and government decisions that

---

92 Final Environmental Impact Report, Thabametsi Power Station, May 2014, prepared by Savannah Environmental (Pty) Ltd, 144.

93 The *Thabametsi I* precedent has been applied in other contexts too. The case of *Philippi Horticultural Area Food & Farming Campaign v MEC for Local Government, Environmental Affairs and Development Planning: Western Cape* (16779/17) [2020] (3) SA 486 (WCC) (17 February 2020) makes reference to the *Thabametsi* case and the need to consider climate impacts on water availability in relation to authorizations for developments with impacts on farming and livelihoods.

94 GN 559, Gazette no. 44761, 25 June 2021.

95 Act 4 of 2006.

96 *Thabametsi I*, the first respondent's answering affidavit, para. 29 and *Thabametsi II*, fourth respondent's answering affidavit, paras 4, 5, 12.

called for these projects in the first place. An example of such a case in the South African context is that brought by the African Climate Alliance and others against the Minister of Mineral Resources and Energy and others,[97] challenging the Minister's decision for the development of 1,500 MW of new coal power electricity capacity – this is addressed as a case study.

Although removing fossil fuels from electricity plans and policies should provide the impetus and policy direction to develop clean energy urgently, in many ways, litigation to stop fossil fuels should go hand-in-hand with legal challenges and/or advocacy strategies to remove any arbitrary barriers to much-needed, replacement clean energy. Similarly, litigation to stop or phase out fossil fuels must take cognizance of the need for a transition that is just and does not perpetuate – or worsen – existing inequalities and human rights violations.

Case study: the Cancel Coal *case*

South Africa's electricity plan for 2020–2030, the IRP 2019, provides for, inter alia, 1,500 MW of new coal-fired power capacity to be developed between 2023 and 2027.[98] On 25 September 2020, the Minister of Mineral Resources and Energy made a determination, with the concurrence of the National Energy Regulator of South Africa (NERSA), for the IRP-allocated 1,500 MW of new electricity capacity to be generated from coal-fired power in the next decade, and to be procured from independent power producers.

The relationship between the IRP and ministerial determinations is relevant. The IRP is intended to be a 'living plan', which is revised regularly (although it took more than eight years for the IRP 2010 to be replaced with the IRP 2019). The IRP 2019 itself states that it 'is an electricity infrastructure development plan based on least-cost electricity supply and demand balance, taking into account security of supply and the environment (minimize negative emissions and water usage)'.[99] The legislation providing for the IRP, the ERA, provides only very limited detail on what the IRP is, with no stipulated objectives or requirements,[100] and the Regulations

97 *African Climate Alliance, Vukani Environmental Movement and Trustees for the time being of the groundWork Trust v Minister of Mineral Resources and Energy, NERSA, Minister of Environment, Forestry and Fisheries, and the President of RSA,* case no. 56907/21.

98 Table 5, IRP 2019.

99 IRP 2019, 8.

100 Section 1, ERA defines the IRP as 'a resource plan established by the national sphere of government to give effect to national policy'. Note: at the time of drafting, a draft amendment to the ERA proposes a number of provisions setting out more detail on the IRP, including a proposed amendment to definition of the IRP: 'an indicative, forward looking plan [established by the national sphere of government to give effect to] for

for New Generation Capacity under ERA[101] stipulate that 'the integrated resource plan shall (a) be developed by the Minister after consultation with the Regulator; and (b) be published in the Government Gazette by the Minister'.[102]

Ministerial determinations for new generation capacity are provided for in section 34 of the ERA. Section 34 states that the Minister of Energy may, in consultation with NERSA, determine that new generation capacity is needed and the types of energy sources from which electricity must be generated. A ministerial determination is administrative action.[103]

New electricity generation capacity should be established on the basis of, and guided by, the IRP. This is because all new generation capacity must be licensed by NERSA (unless specified exemptions are met[104]) and an application for a NERSA licence must provide evidence of compliance with any IRP applicable at that point in time or provide reasons for any deviation from the IRP, for the approval of the Minister.[105] In other words, all new generation capacity must (unless exempt) be aligned with the IRP, including new capacity called for under a ministerial determination.

The IRP 2019 providing for new coal capacity, and ministerial determinations calling for that capacity from coal, both present factors that would give rise to harmful GHG emissions. These might be decisions that could be challengeable as administrative action under PAJA or under the principle of legality. Furthermore, the IRP and any ministerial determinations for new electricity capacity must be consistent with the Bill of Rights.[106] Administrative action, which materially and adversely affects the rights of

electricity generation, compiled in accordance with section 32A to reflect national policy on electricity planning, which plan specifies the types of energy sources and technologies from which electricity may be generated and indicates the amount of electricity that is to be generated from each of such sources or technologies'. GN 1746, GG 45898 of 10 February 2022.

101 Electricity Regulations on New Generation Capacity, Government Notice R399, Government Gazette 34262 of 4 May 2011. As amended by Government Notice R1366, Government Gazette 40401 of 4 November 2016 and by Government Notice 1093, Government Gazette 43810 of 16 October 2020.

102 Regulation 4(1).

103 The Western Cape High Court in *Earthlife Africa and SAFCEI v the Minister of Energy* (19529/2015) [2017] ZAWCHC 50; [2017] 3 All SA 187 (WCC); 2017 (5) SA 227 (WCC) (26 April 2017) noted that 'it is conceptually difficult to view the sec 34 determination as a whole as anything other than administrative action', para. 40.

104 Schedule 2, Exemption from Obligation to Apply for and Hold a Licence, ERA.

105 Section 10(2)(g), ERA.

106 *President of the RSA v SARFU* 2000 (1) SA 1 (CC) para. 134 confirms that executive decisions can be challenged on the grounds that they do not comply with the Bill of Rights.

the public,[107] would have to meet the requirements of section 4 of PAJA, in addition to being aligned with the Bill of Rights.

In November 2021, environmental and climate justice organizations – including the youth-based African Climate Alliance, community-based Vukani Environmental Justice Movement in Action and groundWork – filed a constitutional challenge in the North Gauteng High Court[108] against the Minister of Mineral Resources and Energy, NERSA, the Minister of Environment and the President of the Republic (the *Cancel Coal* case). The applicants are challenging government's plans to procure 1,500 MW of new coal-fired power capacity, as encompassed in the September 2020 ministerial determination and underlying IRP 2019.[109] The case is proceeding through preliminary stages and the substantive issues have not yet been heard in court.

This application is brought on two legal bases. First, it is a constitutional challenge to the decisions to develop 1,500 MW of new coal power, as they unjustifiably limit basic constitutional rights. Second, it is a review application, based on PAJA, alternatively, the constitutional principle of legality (as discussed in the Legal Mechanisms section).[110]

The applicants seek orders declaring invalid and setting aside the ministerial determination, NERSA's concurrence with that determination, and the 2019 IRP to the extent that they provide for the procurement of 1,500 MW of new coal power capacity. They argue that the procurement of 1,500 MW of new coal-fired power represents a severe threat to the constitutional rights of the people of South Africa, including the section 24 environmental rights, the best interests of the child,[111] and the rights to life,[112] dignity[113] and equality,[114] among other implicated rights. As already mentioned, climate change affects a broad spectrum of human rights, far beyond only environmental rights. These constitutional violations will disproportionately impact the poor and the vulnerable, women, children and young people.

---

[107] *Earthlife Africa Johannesburg and Another v Minister of Energy* (19529/2015) [2017] ZAWCHC 50; [2017] 3 All SA 187 (WCC); 2017 (5) SA 227 (WCC) (26 April 2017), para. 44 confirmed that plans to build 9.6 GW of new nuclear capacity would have far-reaching consequences for the South African public with substantial spending and new infrastructure. The same could be said for plans to build new coal and gas capacity in terms of the IRP 2019 or a Ministerial determination.

[108] *African Climate Alliance, Vukani Environmental Movement and Trustees for the time being of the groundWork Trust v Minister of Mineral Resources and Energy, NERSA, Minister of Environment, Forestry and Fisheries, and the President of RSA*, Case No. 56907/21.

[109] Notice of Motion, Case No. 56907/21, 10 November 2021.

[110] Founding Affidavit of Sarah Robyn Farrell, 3 November 2021, para. 24.

[111] Section 28 of the Constitution of RSA 1996.

[112] Section 11 of the Constitution of RSA 1996.

[113] Section 10 of the Constitution of RSA 1996.

[114] Section 9 of the Constitution of RSA 1996.

The case relies further on the argument that there is no reasonable and justifiable basis for the limitation of constitutional rights resulting from the government's plans for new coal power. This is because cleaner renewable energy, with flexible generation capacity, is both a feasible and cheaper alternative to coal. This has been acknowledged by government. The IRP 2019 recognized that no new coal-fired power stations would be built unless artificial caps were imposed on renewables in the modelling exercise.[115] In other words, the IRP 2019 confirms that a least-cost plan does not include any new coal,[116] yet it calls for 1,500 MW of new coal capacity.

The applicants therefore contend that South Africa has the opportunity to move away from its reliance on polluting fossil fuels *and* to protect constitutional rights.[117] The case is supported by a number of key expert reports and modelling, which demonstrate, inter alia: the incontrovertible harms for climate, human health and wellbeing that would result from proceeding with the development of 1,500 MW of new coal power in South Africa; that these harms cannot be substantially mitigated by proposed coal plant technology (addressing the contention that this coal capacity will be 'clean'); and the availability and feasibility of cheaper, less harmful, clean electricity alternatives.[118] Further, the case is supported by individual testimonies, in the form of affidavits, from children, young people, and parents currently living in the Western Cape, Limpopo and Mpumalanga provinces in South Africa. They describe their experiences of climate change and its impact on their lives, as well as their experiences of living in close proximity to coal-fired power stations.[119]

Success in this legal challenge would draw a strong line in the sand for the development of any new coal power capacity in South Africa, as opposed to blocking specific coal projects as previous campaigns have done. Success would also set an important legal precedent on the constitutionality of plans to develop coal power. This would send a strong signal against *all* new coal power capacity, in circumstances where science and cost-based modelling

---

115 Founding Affidavit, para. 374.2.

116 The IRP 2019 states that 'the system only builds renewables (wind and PV) and gas if unlimited renewable and gas resources are assumed', 41.

117 The Minister and NERSA have given notice of their opposition to the application, and – at the time of writing – further papers have yet to be filed in the main application. The President (the fourth respondent) has given notice that he will not oppose the application and will abide by the decision of the court. An interlocutory application, filed by the applicants against the Minister, is underway, in order to gain access to outstanding records from the Minister in terms of r. 53 of the Uniform Rules of Court.

118 The reports are listed in the Founding Affidavit at para. 27, are referenced throughout and are attached as annexures: FA1 to FA6 of the Founding Affidavit.

119 Founding Affidavit, paras 218–30; and 308–22. See annexures FA69–76 and FA85–8.

make clear that no new coal-fired power should be built. In addition, success in the *Cancel Coal* case would prevent cumulative GHG emissions of 289 megatonnes of carbon dioxide equivalent (Mt CO_2-eq) to 2050,[120] and could save additional costs for the people of South Africa between R23 and 109 billion.[121]

Furthermore, this case could further serve as a valuable foundation for challenges to gas power capacity, with the arguments on climate harms being, to a large extent, replicable in the context of gas. For the same reason that plans for new coal power pose risks of unjustifiable limitations to constitutional rights, the exploitation of gas equally poses an unacceptable threat of harm to fundamental human rights by virtue of high GHG emissions, threats to health and environment, and the availability of less harmful energy alternatives.

Legal challenges to government's failure to act on the harms of coal power

Litigation may also result when the government's failure to act gives rise to high GHG emissions and climate harms. Challenging a failure to take adequate steps on climate mitigation is a current feature of global climate litigation.[122] A local example of a case to challenge government inaction is *Trustees for the Time Being of the groundWork Trust and Vukani Environmental Justice Alliance Movement in Action v Minister of Environmental Affairs*,[123] (the *Deadly Air* case). Here the applicants challenged the failure of the South African government to protect people's constitutional rights to health and wellbeing from toxic levels of ambient air pollution caused predominantly by coal-fired power generation projects in the Highveld priority area, situated in South Africa's Mpumalanga province.

While this case does not focus on climate change or government's failures to take steps to address climate change explicitly, the health and air pollution-focused aspects of the judgment are very relevant for climate-related outcomes. This is because any remedies to reduce the sources of the bulk

---

[120] J Burton, P Lehmann-Grube, B Merven, 'Assessment of New Coal Generation Capacity Targets in South Africa's 2019 Integrated Resource Plan for Electricity' (2021) *Centre for Environmental Rights*, 39–40.

[121] Burton, Lehmann-Grube and Merven (n 120), 4, 5, 38–42. Rate of exchange, as at 23 October 2022, 1 Pound Sterling equals 20.45 South African Rand.

[122] Examples here include: *Urgenda Foundation v State of the Netherlands* HA ZA 13–1396, C/09/456689, ECLI:NL:RBDHA:2015:7145, ILDC 2456 (NL 2015), 24 June 2015; *Ashgar Leghari v Federation of Pakistan* Case No. WP No. 25501/2015; and *Future Generations v Ministry of the Environment (Colombia)* Case No. 11001 22 03 000 2018 00319 00, 5 April 2018.

[123] (39724/2019) [2022] ZAGPPHC 208 (18 March 2022).

of air pollution from coal power inevitably give rise to reductions of GHG emissions. As noted by Bouwer and Field, 'it is more likely that what might be framed or analyzed as climate challenges will be embedded in litigation about localized environmental harm or pollution control, natural resource provision or infrastructure projects. In such cases, the climate policy aspects may be incidental to, or even unmentioned, in the adjudicated dispute.'[124]

Case study: the Deadly Air *case*

The *Deadly Air* case is a landmark constitutional case launched in South Africa in 2019, focused on health and the rights of people living in South Africa's Mpumalanga Highveld, an area where 12 coal-fired power stations, Sasol's coal-to-liquids plant, a refinery, and a number of other polluting industries and mines are located. The applicants sought, inter alia, a declaratory order that the poor air quality in the Highveld Priority Area (HPA) is in breach of residents' section 24(a) constitutional right to an environment that is not harmful to their health and wellbeing; and an order that the Minister prepare regulations under the terms of section 20 of the Air Quality Act 2004,[125] to implement and enforce the existing Air Quality Management Plan for the HPA.

As relevant background to the matter, the Highveld was declared a priority area in 2007,[126] and an Air Quality Management Plan (the Highveld Plan)[127] adopted in 2012. The Highveld Plan sets out the mechanisms and timeframes to control and reduce the various sources of air pollution in the Highveld, including large-scale industrial emitters. The government's overarching goal was to bring the area into compliance with health-based air quality standards by 2020. Despite the priority area status and the Highveld Plan developed to address the unsafe levels of air pollution, government failed to reduce the ambient air pollution in accordance with its own plan and stipulated timeframes.

The applicants argued that the toxic ambient air pollution in the Highveld results in a breach of residents' right to an environment that is not harmful to their health and wellbeing, as enshrined in section 24(a) of the Constitution, with disproportionate impacts on women, children and the elderly. The expert evidence relied on by the applicants, showed that cumulative emissions from just 14 facilities – 12 of which are coal-fired power stations – created

---

124 K Bouwer and T Field, 'Editorial: The Emergence of Climate Litigation in Africa' (2021) 2 *Carbon & Climate Law Review* 125.

125 Act 39 of 2004.

126 GN 1123, Government Gazette 30518, 23 November 2007.

127 GN 144, Government Gazette 35072, 2 March 2012.

acute exposures in 2016 that exceeded the World Health Organization's guidelines for daily or hourly averages for all criteria pollutants.[128] The report, by Dr Andrew Gray, found that despite the hundreds of other sources of air pollution – particularly particulate matter and nitrogen dioxide – in and around the HPA these 14 facilities contribute alarmingly high percentages of national limits.[129] Therefore, the problem was easily reducible by managing their pollution levels. The applicants argued that the pollution problem was largely a result of the government's initial refusal and then unreasonable delay to develop and prescribe implementation regulations (provided for under the Air Quality Act) to enforce the Highveld Plan. The applicants also asserted that the Minister of Forestry, Fisheries and the Environment has a legal duty to prescribe regulations under section 20 of the National Air Quality Act, to implement and enforce the Highveld Plan and that the Minister's failure and/or refusal to do so is unconstitutional, unlawful and invalid.

The government respondents, led by the Minister of Forestry, Fisheries and the Environment, denied that government is failing in its obligations to address the air pollution in the Mpumalanga Highveld. In their opposition, they argued that the applicants are not entitled to rely directly on section 24(a) of the Constitution (referencing the principle of subsidiarity), and that the rights in section 24 are subject to progressive realization and the principle of sustainable development.

The United Nations Special Rapporteur on Human Rights and the Environment intervened in the court application (a first for South Africa) as *amicus curiae*. He made submissions on the South African state's international human rights law obligations, which arise from international treaties ratified by South Africa and other instruments. The Special Rapporteur also provided evidence, based on expert opinion, on the adverse impacts of air pollution on the enjoyment of human rights.

The *Deadly Air* case was heard in the North Gauteng High Court in May 2021 and judgment was handed down on 18 March 2022. The court found in favour of the applicants in a landmark decision, which, for the first time, declares that the South African government is in breach of a constitutional right due to the health impacts of air pollution. The High Court concluded that – in the present matter – the right in section 24(a) is immediately realizable and that, on the evidence presented, the levels of air pollution in the HPA are not consistent with the section 24(a) right to an environment that is not harmful to health or wellbeing. The fact that the air quality in

[128] A Gray, *Air Quality Impacts and Health Effects due to Large Stationary Source Emissions in an Around South Africa's Mpumalanga Highveld Priority Area* (Centre for Environmental Rights 2019) 1.

[129] Gray (n 128), 2.

the Highveld Priority Area fails to meet the National Ambient Air Quality Standards (National Standards), is a prima facie violation of the right. When the failure to meet air quality standards persists over a long period of time, there is a greater likelihood that the health, wellbeing and human rights of the people subjected to that air is being threatened and infringed upon.[130]

On the subsidiarity point raised by the respondents, it was held that the principle of subsidiarity did not preclude direct reliance on section 24(a) of the Constitution in this instance. The available legislation does not provide residents with clear procedures and remedies for ambient air pollution that exceeds the National Standards and where their lives are threatened by poor air quality. Further, the legislation could never have been intended to obstruct affected individuals from accessing the courts in such an instance.[131]

The High Court found that the Minister, by her own concession, had failed to promulgate regulations proposed by her own Department and which her own Department had concluded would save lives. The applicants established an omission on the part of the Minister to promulgate regulations timeously, and the Minister was ordered to promulgate these regulations within 12 months. These regulations are intended to set out requirements for implementing and enforcing air quality management plans, including enforcement measures for non-compliance to apply to the key contributors to poor air quality in relevant regions.[132]

At the time of writing, the Minister has filed an application for leave to appeal the orders that the Minister has a legal duty to prescribe regulations under section 20 of the Air Quality Act; that she has unreasonably delayed in initiating the regulations; that she must prescribe, initiate and prepare regulations within 12 months of the order; and that, in preparing the regulations, the Minister must pay due regard to the considerations listed in the court order.[133] Importantly, the Minister has not sought to appeal the declaratory relief confirming that the poor air quality in the HPA is in breach of residents' section 24(a) constitutional right to an environment that is not harmful to their health and well-being.

Key insights from the coal power cases in South Africa

While this chapter only considers a handful of the legal cases with a climate and/or coal focus to have passed through South Africa's courts, a number

130 *Deadly Air*, para. 10.

131 Paragraphs 169–1843.

132 'Consultation on Proposed Regulations for Implementing and Enforcing Priority Area Air Quality Management Plans', GN R2353. No. 47199.

133 The Minister has filed an application for leave to appeal against paras 241.2–241.5, inclusive, of the order made on 18 March 2022.

of key insights can already be gleaned from these cases and the experience of litigating them.

A key question to be asked – considering the climate focus of this chapter – is the following: although the target has very much been coal, have these cases and legal strategies been effective at addressing broader climate change impacts and issues? If so, what has made them effective? This section therefore looks at the insights gained, with these questions in mind.

The value of multi-faceted legal challenges

The legal challenges of proposed coal plants in South Africa, including Thabametsi, were multi-faceted; with the Life After Coal Campaign opposing every single licence and authorization that the projects would need in order to proceed, and tackling the proposed coal projects from multiple angles.[134] Challenging one coal power project entailed not only litigation, but also community mobilization, advocacy and engagements with the financiers for these projects – with the important result of having the promise of funding successfully withdrawn by local commercial banks.[135]

Since the start of this campaign, none of the 14 coal-fired power stations that were seeking environmental, and other, authorizations in order to proceed under South Africa's First Coal Baseload Independent Power Producer Procurement Programme have been built, nor do any of them have all the authorizations they would need in order to go ahead. Although not all 14 proposed projects were opposed through legal processes, the litigation against the two preferred bidder coal projects (Thabametsi and Khanyisa) under the government's power procurement process, effectively stalled the first bid window of the coal procurement process and made it clear that new coal power projects will face hurdles of litigation and difficulties in accessing finance. Indeed, in the IRP 2019 South Africa's government flagged, as a risk consideration for coal, that '[t]here is risk of 900 MW of coal procured not materializing due to financing and legal challenges. There is also likelihood of future coal to power capacity not being realized due to financing challenges'.[136]

[134] These angles include: litigation to challenge the environmental authorization; appeals and objections to other licences required including the atmospheric emission licence and electricity generation licence; writing objections to the financiers for the projects; and opposition campaigns on the ground, led by communities, in the areas where the projects would be based.

[135] These coal plant legal challenges have also required delving into other areas of law, such as energy and public finance law, and utilizing all available forums for opposition, such as the National Energy Regulator's electricity generation licensing process.

[136] IRP 2019, 51.

The abandonment of the Thabametsi and Khanyisa coal plant projects has meant that 205.7 million tons of CO_2 equivalent will not enter the atmosphere – saving valuable carbon space, and that R19.68 billion has been saved in comparison to a least-cost electricity plan.[137] The inescapable conclusion then is that these legal challenges have indeed been effective at avoiding GHG emissions and climate harms.

As already noted, despite the time and resources taken to challenge one project, having a proposed coal project scrapped may not necessarily result in the needed material GHG emission reductions. There is the risk that a quashed coal project could simply be replaced by others, or replaced by another emission-intensive fossil fuel, such as gas. However, this multi-pronged strategy is now also being relied upon to challenge proposed gas power projects – as a number of gas power projects are applying for, and being granted, required authorizations in the hopes of supplying power under the government's upcoming gas to power procurement process.[138]

Nevertheless, when viewed in the broader context of large-scale policy shifts and economics, stopping and slowing new fossil fuel projects enables clean energy alternatives to step in and, importantly, incentivizes electricity system reforms to switch from the traditional dirty fossil fuel systems, to cleaner, climate-resilient, decentralized models.

The value of strong and clear technical evidence

A notable element for success, particularly in ensuring that a presiding court is alive to all the relevant issues, is having strong technical and scientific backing supporting a case. This is especially true in relation to establishing the causal link between the inaction, or action, from government and the harm being, or to be, suffered as a result.[139]

---

[137] Burton, Lehmann-Grube and Merven (n 120), 4.

[138] Some of these proposed gas to power projects include: Phinda Power Projects (Pty Ltd's 320 MW gas to power project proposed for Richards Bay South Africa; Phakwe Richards Bay Gas Power 3 (Pty) Ltd's proposed 2,000 MW gas to power project proposed for Richards Bay; Richards Bay Gas Power 2 (Pty) Ltd's proposed 400 MW gas to power plant proposed for Richards Bay; the proposed Nseleni Independent Floating Power Plants 8,400 MW, Richards Bay; and three proposed Karpowership gas to power projects proposed for Richards Bay, Nqura and Saldanha.

[139] While attribution science (see the work of the Climate Accountability Institute at https://climateaccountability.org/ and https://www.carbonbrief.org/mapped-how-climate-change-affects-extreme-weather-around-the-world) is now widely accepted and has advanced substantially, a more conservative court may not be as easily convinced, or rather, may prefer a more conservative approach requiring a more direct causal link between GHG emissions and the specific climate impacts (loss and damage) referred to. P Toussaint, 'Loss and Damage and Climate Litigation: The Case for Greater Interlinkage' 30 (2020) *RECIEL* 16.

A crucial component in South Africa's coal project challenges was reliance on credible independent expert reports assessing the costs and climate impacts of building these coal plants, in comparison to a least-cost electricity system. This is a lesson that has applied across the board to all the spectrum of cases, including the *Thabametsi* and *Cancel Coal* cases.

The efficacy of the evidence in the *Cancel Coal* case remains to be seen. However, the independent modelling relied on does show that the proposed 1,500 MW of new coal power capacity (as challenged in the *Cancel Coal* case), is not only unnecessary and anticipated to cause substantial GHG emissions, but would also cost more in comparison to a least-cost electricity system (some R23 billion more by 2030, and R74 billion to R109 billion if South Africa intends to meet its 2021 NDC targets), with 25,000 anticipated job losses economy-wide in 2030.[140] In other words, the result of expanding coal capacity in South Africa would be that people would have to pay more for electricity and jobs will be lost across the economy.

These tangible figures and monetary values have already proven to be useful advocacy tools in the coal-power challenges – gaining substantial media attention in South Africa around concern over higher electricity prices, economic impacts and resultant job losses.[141]

The value of human voices to support a case

Individual testimonies to support litigation are incredibly powerful in lending human voices and experiences to legal cases, which, at their core, are about protecting the lives, health and wellbeing of people.

The *Deadly Air* case referenced supporting affidavits provided by three residents in the Mpumalanga Highveld.[142] They provided testimony of the lived experiences of people living with daily exposures to harmful air

140 Burton, Lehmann-Grube and Merven (n 120); J Burton, G Ireland, 'An Assessment of New Coal Plants in South Africa's Electricity Future: The cost, Emissions, and Supply Security Implications of the Coal IPP programme' (2018) *Energy Systems Economics and Policy group – University of Cape Town.*

141 C Yelland, 'Big Black Holes Emerge in South Africa's Integrated Resource Plan for Electricity – Coal is Not the Answer', *Daily Maveric,* 15 November 2021, https://www.dailymaverick.co.za/article/2021-11-15-big-black-holes-emerge-in-south-africas-integrated-resource-plan-for-electricity-coal-is-not-the-answer/, accessed 23 October 2022; T Phillips, 'The Post COP26 State of Coal, *Mail & Guardian*, 25 November 2021, https://mg.co.za/environment/2021-11-25-the-post-cop26-state-of-coal/, accessed 23 October 2022; M Fourie, B Peek, M Lekalakala, 'SA Saved from the R12.57bn Environmental Disaster That Thabametsi Would Have Been', *Business Day*, 30 November 2020, https://www.businesslive.co.za/bd/opinion/2020-11-30-sa-saved-from-the-r1257bn-environmental-disaster-that-thabametsi-would-have-been/, accessed 23 October 2022.

142 Annexures SP34, SP35 and SP36 to the Founding Affidavit, 512–22.

pollution in the area where coal power is a dominant source of pollution. In her judgment, Collis J noted that:

> Supporting affidavits filed in these proceedings by some residents in the town of Emalahleni falling within the Highveld Priority Area, set out how the state of air pollution in the area has affected them over a period of time. The contents of these affidavits are *undisputed evidence* that have been placed before this court, confirming the contention that *persons living in the Highveld Priority Area are exposed to air pollution that is harmful to their health and wellbeing.*[143]

The *Cancel Coal* case is supported by 12 affidavit testimonies, some of which are from young people, outlining their experiences of life during times of drought or heavy rainfall events, for example, which affect their homes and ability to go to school. The affidavits outline in detail how climate change and living in the shadow of coal-fired power has affected them. This is important not only in providing a human face and experience to litigation, but also to provide people with a platform to share their stories and personal experiences through the litigation.

Challenges of lengthy litigation in the context of urgent climate and health crises

Regardless of victory or loss, one drawback of any litigation can be the long time-lapse before an outcome in a case is reached. Litigating against government in South Africa inevitably means a long and drawn-out process, predominantly due to unresponsive and overburdened state opponents and the State Attorney. In many instances, additional applications have to be instituted to compel action by the government respondents, incurring additional time, effort and costs.[144] There may also be strings of appeals after a judgment of first instance. This is particularly the case where the legal requirements for urgency are not met, meaning the case has to proceed through the court system without an accelerated process.

In the context of a climate emergency where time is always of the essence, lengthy litigation can be counter-productive, unless the litigation is being relied on to stop a proposed harm (such as the development of a new coal power plant) from occurring. Nevertheless, merely launching climate-focused litigation usually results in public and media attention on important climate issues from the outset. High-impact strategic litigation can put the

[143] Paragraph 153, emphasis added.

[144] A portion of the costs are reimbursed if the case succeeds.

wheels in motion for necessary change from government, even prior to a court decision.

Cases need not expressly mention climate change, to have climate-based outcomes

Based on the *Deadly Air* case, it is worth noting that, for purposes of achieving meaningful GHG reductions, litigation need not take on an explicit climate focus. In some instances, more tangible health and other arguments may be as, or more, effective.[145] This is particularly the case in South Africa, where we have a constitutional right to an environment not harmful to health and wellbeing.

The *Deadly Air* relief has far-reaching implications for climate as well as health. Air pollution is the world's largest environmental health risk,[146] and throughout Africa the same sources of the bulk of air pollution are also the main sources of GHG emissions. In South Africa these sources are Eskom and Sasol.[147] Therefore, any successful efforts to accelerate the retirement of facilities or limit the pollution from these sources will also limit their GHG emissions.

It remains to be seen what tangible outcomes will result from the *Deadly Air* case success. A potential substantial climate mitigation win to arise from the *Deadly Air* case would include plans for earlier decommissioning of South Africa's aged coal fleet, due to the facilities' inability to meet the minimum emission standards and their contributions to unconstitutional exceedances of ambient air quality standards in the Highveld. Suffice to say that the victory is a crucial first step in recognizing the threats to rights posed by coal-fired power, and can go a long way to reducing GHG emissions from South Africa's coal fleet.

Opportunities in relying on government's own policies and direct legal obligations

An important tool lies in the fact that the South African government does not dispute the harms and severe risks of climate change for its people. In fact, national policy confirms South Africa's vulnerability to the impacts

[145] This perspective aligns with the views of Bouwer and Field (n 124), 125.

[146] United Nations Economic Commission for Europe, 'Air Pollution and Health', Environmental Policy: Air Pollution, https://unece.org/air-pollution-and-health, accessed 23 October 2022.

[147] P Burkhardt, 'Eskom, Sasol Emit Over Half of S. Africa's Greenhouse Gas', *Bloomberg Africa Edition*, 30 July 2019, https://www.bloomberg.com/news/articles/2019-07-30/eskom-sasol-emit-over-half-of-south-africa-s-greenhouse-gas., accessed 23 October 2022.

of climate change, highlighting in particular the water-scarce nature of the country. The fact that the government has acknowledged these climate harms, which pose direct risk for constitutional rights, renders it difficult for the government to justify decisions that give rise to these harms and consequent rights violations.[148] The development of further fossil fuel capacity seems to fall squarely into this category.

In a number of the discussed cases, the doctrine of separation of powers was frequently relied on by respondents in their opposition.[149] What we have learned from climate cases at home and across the world[150] is that many courts are hesitant, or unwilling, to order governments to undertake stronger mitigation actions. This is because of their concerns of inappropriate judicial interference with the executive's powers. Courts prefer instead to defer to governments on decision-making around the setting and achieving of mitigation targets. The stronger cases tend to be those where the relief being sought is narrow and confined to existing, specific policies, national commitments or legal obligations already entrenched in law,[151] enabling judges to avoid any insinuation of stepping on the toes of the executive. For example, the *Thabametsi I* case simply sought to confirm the interpretation of legal requirements for environmental impact assessments to include climate impacts. In the *Deadly Air* case, the court referenced the exceedances of government's own air quality standards as evidence of the rights breach in question,[152] stating: 'Now it is so that not all air pollution violates the right

[148] The Constitution recognizes and makes provision for limitations of rights (s. 36) 'in terms of law of general application to the extent that the limitation is reasonable and justifiable in an open and democratic society based on human dignity, equality and freedom, taking into account all relevant factors, including – (a) the nature of the right; (b) the importance of the purpose of the limitation; (c) the nature and extent of the limitation; (d) the relation between the limitation and its purpose; and (e) less restrictive means to achieve the purpose'.

[149] First Respondent's Answering Affidavit in the *Deadly Air* case at para. 13 and the Fourth Respondent's Answering Affidavit in *Thabametsi II* at para. 5.

[150] An example is the case of *Family Farmers and Greenpeace Germany v Germany* (2018) 00271/17/R /SP. The court concluded that the government is entitled to wide discretion in deciding how to fulfill its climate obligations, as long as precautionary measures to protect fundamental rights are not wholly unsuitable or wholly inadequate.

[151] For example, in the case of *Urgenda Foundation v State of the Netherlands* the emission reduction ordered by the court (a reduction of at least 25 per cent by 2020) was aligned with reductions that the Dutch government itself had initially agreed to in the context of international negotiations. The Dutch government had initially itself stated that a 25–40 per cent reduction by 2020 was needed to maintain a real (50 per cent) chance to avoid dangerous climate change, and that these reduction goals were both technically and economically feasible. Paragraph 27, Summons in the *Urgenda* case.

[152] *Deadly Air* judgment, at para. 63: 'In this light, it is therefore unsustainable for the Minister to claim that the National Standards have no legal significance for this case. They reflect

to a healthy environment. However, if air quality fails to meet the National Ambient Air Quality Standards [...], it is a prima facie violation of the right'.[153] At the same time, the nature of a climate change challenge will also require courts to be increasingly bold in defending constitutional rights, despite the complexity of the decision or the identity of the decision-maker, as already noted.

There is potential for South African lawyers to move towards more 'systemic' climate change litigation, probably relying on constitutional protections. Given the existence of strong constitutional obligations on the state, and the extensive harmful impacts to South Africa of the climate crisis, there is a strong basis to argue that the obligation to take steps to avoid the harms of climate change and mitigate GHG emissions is a constitutional one. In other words, it is an obligation owed by government (and horizontally by non-state actors as well) to the people of South Africa directly, and not merely to the global community as part of international commitments. This is an important argument that forms the basis of the *Cancel Coal* case.

South Africa's long-awaited (and much-needed) Climate Change Act – legislation to regulate climate change mitigation and adaptation in South Africa – has been delayed and awaiting promulgation for over two years. It is not clear what the final Act will look like. But almost more concerning is that the government is not prioritizing the Climate Change Bill, and it may still face substantial delays before coming into effect. Climate legislation is urgently needed, as a starting point, to set out in more detail the obligations on government to implement mitigation and adaptation measures, and to provide the legislative basis for regulating emission reductions within GHG emitting sectors and by companies.[154] Calling for the prioritization of a robust Climate Change Act has become a key focus area for a number of legal activists.[155]

As already mentioned, there are currently no direct GHG emission limits prescribed by the law. Although we have the obligations, duty of care and

---

the government's own assessment of the content of section 24(a) of the Constitution and there must be accountability for failures to achieve these standards'.

[153] Paragraph 10.

[154] Currently emission reduction plans and GHG emission reporting are regulated under the Air Quality Act 2004. Entities emitting over certain thresholds are obliged to report their GHG emissions and/or prepare pollution prevention plans setting out how they intend to reduce their GHG emissions over a five-year period. There are no prescribed targets or limits that must be met under any of these laws.

[155] See S Bega, 'Climate change bill: One of the most important draft laws to cross the desks of SA's lawmakers', *Mail & Guardian*, 19 May 2022, https://mg.co.za/environment/2022-05-19-climate-change-bill-one-of-the-most-important-draft-laws-to-cross-the-desks-of-sas-lawmakers/, accessed 23 October 2022.

environmental management principles outlined in the Constitution and NEMA, specific and overarching climate change legislation[156] would go a long way to provide the necessary legal certainty and a clearer path for climate action in South Africa.

The important relationship between climate legislation and climate litigation cannot be overlooked. The Climate Change Bill – or Act, once promulgated – presents an opportunity to challenge any provisions that are not sufficiently aligned with the Constitution or Bill of Rights, so as to achieve more ambitious emission reduction targets that are adequately aligned with, and ensure the realization of, the rights in the Bill of Rights. Importantly, once the legislation is promulgated there will be increased opportunities, with potentially strong prospects, to hold government and other entities to account under the legal obligations imposed by it, such as the emission targets and/or limits that would need to be complied with by sectors and emitting entities.

Conclusion

South Africa's coal litigation has played, and continues to play, a vital role in holding back new coal development in South Africa and encouraging a phase-out of existing polluting coal in line with a just transition plan. These strategies are now being broadened to challenge decisions beyond coal – such as the build out of new gas capacity in South Africa – and beyond South Africa's borders.

In considering legal strategies, one must be alive to situational contexts and complexities that may result in sound cases being weakened by competing rights and policy imperatives. Some of the key insights gained from South Africa's coal litigation have been discussed. Having existing legal obligations to rely on is a fundamental element to these cases, and South Africa's Climate Change Act, once promulgated, would have an important role to play in this regard.

As litigation strategies become more ambitious and seek to have broader strategic impact (for example broader policy or administrative decision challenges such as the *Cancel Coal* matter), the project-by-project challenges remain crucial in the struggle to avoid harmful GHG emissions. Now, as African countries are faced with increasing proposed

[156] Some of the climate change-related laws currently in place, include the Carbon Tax Act 2019 as well as the National Greenhouse Gas Reporting Regulations (GN 275, GG 40762) of 3 April 2017 and National Pollution Prevention Plan Regulations (GN 712 GG 40996) of 21 July 2017, under the National Environmental Management: Air Quality Act 2004.

fossil fuel developments, dedicated legal strategies to push back on these contested developments will need to be explored. These strategies are by no means mutually exclusive and the importance and value of employing a wide range of varying, complementary strategies simultaneously cannot be understated.

5

Climate Change Litigation in Civil Law African Countries: An Assessment of Barriers and Potentialities in Cameroon

Daniel Armel Owona Mbarga[1]

Introduction

It seems like a long time ago that there were only a handful of climate lawsuits. Since the first climate lawsuits were filed in the United States in 1990,[2] a myriad of litigation has emerged at the national, regional and global levels. According to the Grantham Research Institute on Climate Change and the Environment, as of May 2021 the databases on climate litigation around the world contained 1,841 cases that were either in progress or had already been decided.[3] This shows the exponential development of the phenomenon through which civil society organizations, public law legal entities and private individuals are trying to establish the responsibility of states and companies in the oil and energy industry in general on the causes and effects of climate change.[4]

However, this phenomenon does not develop in the same way in different geographical areas. While the United States alone has 1,387 climate-related

---

1 The author thanks the editors of this book for their comments that helped improve this chapter. The ideas in this chapter are the responsibility of the author and do not reflect those of the Field Legality Advisory Group (FLAG).

2 Among the first cases *City of Los Angeles v National Highway Transportation Safety Administration et al,* 912 F2d 478 (DC Circ. Court of Appeal) 1990.

3 J Setzer and C Higham (2022), *Global Trends in Climate Change Litigation: 2021 Snapshot* Policy Report, 2022, p. 10.

4 C Cournil and L Varison (eds), *Les procès climatiques. Entre le national et l'international* (Editions A Pedone 2018) 20.

cases,[5] the African continent has only ten recognized climate cases, according to the databases of the Sabin Center for Climate Change Law and the Grantham Research Institute. One is pending before the East African Court of Justice[6] at the sub-regional level, and nine have been tried or are pending in various countries such as South Africa,[7] Nigeria,[8] Kenya[9] or Uganda.[10] Yet Africa is one of the most vulnerable regions in the world to climate change. One would have expected climate litigation to proliferate considerably there, but this is not the case according to the definition of climate litigation that Global North scholars are using.[11] Recent work, including this volume, has sought to track and understand the contribution of climate litigation in Africa and other regions in the Global South.

One point of analysis that reminds underexplored, and which this chapter seeks to address, is the extent to which the litigation recorded to date on the continent has taken place only in countries with common law legal

5 Setzer and Higham (n 3), 10.

6 East African Court of Justice, *Center for Food and Adequate Living Rights v Tanzania and Uganda*, 2020.

7 High Court of South Africa Gauteng Division, Pretoria, *South Durban Community Environmental alliance v Minister of Environment, Forestry and Fisheries,* Founding Affidavit, 2021; High Court of South Africa Gauteng Division, Pretoria, *SDCEA & Groundwork v Minister of Forestry, Fisheries and the Environment,* Founding Affidavit, 2021; High Court of South Africa, Western Cape Division, Cape Town, *Philippi Horticultural Area Food & Farming Campaign v MEC for Local Government, Environmental Affairs and Development Planning: Western Cape,* Judgement, Case No. 16779/17; High Court of South Africa Gauteng Division, Pretoria, *The Trustees for the time being of Groundwork Trust v The Minister of Environmental Affairs*, Case No. 54087/17, 2017; High Court of South Africa Gauteng Division, Pretoria, *The Trustees for the time being of Groundwork Trust v The Minister of Environmental Affairs et al*, Case No. 61561/17, 2017; High Court of South Africa Gauteng Division, Pretoria, *Earthlife Africa Johannesburg v Minister of Environmental Affairs*, Judgement, Case No. 65662/16, 8 March 2017.

8 Federal High Court of Nigeria, *Jonah Gbemre v Shell Petroleum Development Co. of Nigeria Ltd*, FHC/B/CS/53/05, 14 November 2005.

9 National Environmental Tribunal, *Save Lamu v National Environmental Management Authority and Amu Power Co. Ltd*, No. 196, 2016.

10 High Court of Uganda *Holden, Mbabazi v The Attorney General and National Environmental Management Authority*, Civil Suit No. 283 of 2012, 28 August 2015.

11 Several renowned jurists, noting this situation, have also identified possible avenues of litigation on the continent, such as the fuel-based electrical energy sector, the exploitation of oil resources or the phenomenon of land-grabbing. Others think that an adjustment of the 'lens' through which we view climate litigation helps reveal notable case law developments in the Global South including Africa. LJ Kotzé and A Du Plessis, `Putting Africa on the Stand: A bird's eye view of climate litigation on the continent` (2020) 50(3) *Environmental Law* 615–63; J Peel and J Lin, 'Transnational Climate Litigation: The Contribution of The Global South' (2019) 11(4) *The American Journal of International Law* 701; K Bouwer and T-L Field, 'The Emergence of Climate Litigation in Africa' (2021) 15(2) *Carbon & Climate Law Review* 123–8.

systems, influenced to some extent by English law. Indeed, at the time of writing, no African country with a civil law system appears to have registered a climate case; this means that no challenges to climate (or environmental) policy have arisen, but also that climate change has not come up as an issue in court disputes that focus on other matters. The reason for this is not that environmental protection and climate action in civil law countries is already so good that there is no cause for citizens to be concerned; it is also not because members of society are apathetic and do not engage with these issues. So in view of this, it is reasonable to wonder about the causes of the absence of climate disputes in African countries with a civil law system. This chapter intends to show the legal obstacles that prevent the development of climate litigation in countries with the civil law system and the potentialities that exist by focusing on Cameroon. It also shows what civil society actors can do given the means available to them.

African civil law countries have a dynamic and effective environmental civil society. In Cameroon, for example, non-governmental organizations (NGOs) opposed the exploitation of the Ebo forest, whose classification process as a national park was initiated in 2006 because of the importance of the space and the resources found there for the communities and its biodiversity (rare apes).[12] One of their arguments was based on the impact of the exploitation of this forest on Cameroon's international commitments regarding climate and biodiversity. In a letter to the prime minister, they argued that the reclassification process to allow the Ebo forest's exploitation could undermine Cameroon's leadership role in the Congo Basin at the 26th Conference of Parties of the United Nations Framework Convention on Climate Change.[13] Their lobbying led to the withdrawal of one of the decrees classifying the forest and to the temporary suspension of the classification process for the second forest management unit.[14] A climate change dispute that in another context might have resulted in litigation was resolved through civil society activism and political campaigning.[15]

---

[12] E Abwe *et al*, 'Recours pour la suspension du processus de classement de deux unités forestières d'aménagement dans la forêt d'Ebo et l'initiation d'un processus plus inclusif de planification de l'utilisation des terres', *Letter*, 28 April 2020, https://www.globalwildlife.org/wp-content/uploads/2020/04/French_version_Letter_GoC_Ebo_Forest.pdf, accessed 3 September 2022.

[13] Abwe (n 12), 1.

[14] Congo Basin Forest Partnership (CBFP), 'Cameroon cancels logging plan that threatened rare apes-reuters', *CPBF*, https://pfbc-cbfp.org/news-partner/apes-reuters.html, accessed 3 September 2022.

[15] However, the Prime Minister finally proceeded to the classification of a part of the Ebo'o Forest through the decree n° 2023/01630/PM of the 27th April 2023. Even though he added a new article mentioning that studies will be conducted to identify activities to protect the climate, this decree is contested by civil society in Cameroon.

The landscape of climate justice work in African civil law countries has its own distinct character. As we explore in the first two sections of this chapter, civil society organizations (CSOs) have limited access to environmental judges and have prioritized means of action other than litigation in the field of climate change. This is not necessarily a bad thing, as litigation should be the strategy of last resort. It certainly does not mean that there is no engagement with climate justice issues, or that CSOs and activists do not have their own well-developed strategies. But, as we shall explore in the final part of the chapter, there are also some opportunities for developing this activism into climate change litigation.

Cameroonian law and restricted access to justice

Under foreign domination between 1884 (Germany, France and United Kingdom) and 1959, Cameroon has a legal system that is based on both the common law and the civil law systems on the one hand, and on customary law on the other.[16] However, since the reunification of the former western Cameroon under common law and the former eastern Cameroon under civil law in 1961 and the unification of the country in 1972, the country has produced an abundance of legislation that has given common law and customary law less influence, thus showing that Cameroon is increasingly governed by civil law, particularly in environmental matters.[17] There are many Acts, decrees or orders that organize the management of environment and natural resources in Cameroon. However, contrary to African countries where climate litigation has developed, the Cameroonian legal framework limits the access of CSOs and even individuals to the courts in environmental matters. This is brought about by the restrictive conditions for the admissibility of cases, notably concerning the standing and the capacity to act of CSOs and the priority given to legal entities by environmental law for conflicts before the judge to the detriment of natural persons.

Conditional capacity and standing of civil society organizations

Capacity and standing are conditions for the admissibility of legal action. Standing refers to the advantage that the plaintiff would obtain if the judge recognized the validity of his claim.[18] It is concrete, particularized, actual

---

16 JM Tchakoua, 'La question environnementale dans le système juridique du Cameroun' in O Ruppel and E Kam Yogo (eds), *Environmental Law and Policy in Cameroon. Towards Making Africa the Three of Life* (PUCAC 2018) 108.

17 Tchakoua (n 16), 112.

18 S Guinchard and T Debard, *Lexique des termes juridiques 2017–2018* (Dalloz 2017) 25th edn 1051.

or imminent. Capacity refers to the legal title conferring on an individual the power to ask the judge to examine his claim.[19]

In Cameroon, natural or legal persons have an interest in acting in environmental matters.[20] Indeed, constitutional law states that 'Everyone has the right to a healthy environment. The protection of the environment is a duty for all. The State ensures the defense and promotion of the environment'.[21] By this provision, constitutional law confers on individuals and legal persons a right to a healthy environment while conferring them the capacity and the standing in the exercise of their constitutional duty of environmental protection.[22] However, the capacity and standing to act in environmental matters is conditional, in particular for CSOs. Under the Law on the Environment,[23] CSOs must first be approved to exercise the rights recognized for civil parties with regard to the facts constituting an infringement of the provisions of the law and causing direct or indirect damage to the collective interests that they aim to defend.[24] Thus, the admissibility of legal action by an association in environmental matters is conditional on the holding of an approval granted by the ministry in charge of the environment, the Ministry of the Environment, Nature Protection and Sustainable Development (Ministère de l'Environnement, de la Protection de la nature et du Developpement Durable, MINEPDED).

This is what happened in the case of the *Association Club HSE (Hygiène Sécurité Environnement) v State of Cameroon (Ministry of the Environment, Nature Protection and Sustainable Development) and Gaz du Cameroun.*[25] In this case, the administrative judge declared the applicant association's action inadmissible for lack of standing and capacity, basing his decision on article 8(1) and (2) of

19 Guinchard and Debard (n 18), 1530.

20 Preamble of Law No. 96/06 of 18 January 1996 revising the Constitution of 2 June 1972, amended and supplemented by Law No. 2008/001 of 14 April 2008.

21 Preamble of Law No. 96/06.

22 A Nyetam Tamga, 'Les tendances de la jurisprudence administrative camerounaise en matière d'environnement' (2020) 5 *Revue Africaine de Droit de l'Environnement* 185.

23 Section 8(2) of Law No. 96/12 of 5 August 1996, establishing a framework law on environmental management in Cameroon (hereinafter referred to as the Law on the environment).

24 Article 8(2), Law No. 96/12: 'the grassroots communities and the approved associations contributing to any action of the public and semi-public organisms having for object the protection of the environment, can exercise the rights recognized to the civil party as regards the facts constituting an infringement of the provisions of the present law and its texts of application, and causing a direct or indirect damage to the collective interests which they have for object to defend'.

25 Administrative Court of Douala, *Affaire Association club HSE v Etat du Cameroun (MINEPDED) et Gaz du Cameroun,* Annulation du certificat de conformité environnementale, 26 mai 2016 referenced by Nyetam Tamga (n 22), 185.

the Environment Act.[26] The HSE club association sought the cancelation of a decision of the MINEPDED that led to the issuance of a certificate of environmental conformity for the construction of a gas pipeline in Douala by Gaz du Cameroun.[27] According to the plaintiff, MINEPDED had violated, among other things, the rules prescribed by Decree No. 2013/0171/PM of 14 February 2013 establishing the modalities for conducting environmental and social impact studies, particularly those relating to public consultations and public participation[28] prior to a project.[29] However, the administrative judge considered that, not having the status of a public body and not being accredited, the HSE association could not meet the capacity and standing requirements to request the annulment of the administrative act that confers the certificate of environmental conformity on a third party, all the more so as it did not bring proof of the personal prejudice resulting from the act in question.[30]

This discussion highlights the legal rule and its application. But it also raises questions about the extent to which climate litigation in African civil law countries is being recognized. *Association Club HSE* was brought to challenge the potential local environmental problems arising from the proposed gas pipeline, and none of the parties raised climate change as a factor that should be considered in the public consultation or the decision making. However, this is a challenge to the fossil fuel infrastructure, and could be framed as a climate case; but no one has thought to do this. The problems mentioned are more related to the environmental consequences of the project.[31] It would of course be an unsuccessful climate change case as the litigation failed and the pipeline was built,[32] as well as laying down an unhelpful rule for other climate cases.

---

[26] Nyetam Tamga (n 22), 185.

[27] Nyetam Tamga (n 22).

[28] Article 20(2) and (3), Decree No. 2013/0171/PM of 14 February 2013, establishing the modalities for conducting environmental and social impact studies. It states that: '(2) The public consultation consists of meetings during the study, in the localities affected by the project. (3) The public hearing is intended to publicize the study, to record any objections and to allow the population to express its opinion on the conclusions of the study'.

[29] Nyetam Tamga (n 22), 186.

[30] Nyetam Tamga (n 22).

[31] Investir au Cameroun (2014), *Un Collectif demande au Parlement camerounais d'empêcher la construction d'un gazodu de 17 km à Douala*, https://www.investiraucameroun.com/energie/2205-5334-un-collectif-demande-au-parlement-camerounais-d-empecher-la-construction-d-un-gazoduc-de-17-km-a-douala, accessed on 2 May 2023.

[32] In December 2016, Gaz du Cameroun announced the completion of Phase II and III of the Bonaberi pipeline extension programme where a total of 15 km of gas pipeline was laid, including spur lines and metering points. Cf. Gaz du Cameroun, *Bonaberi-Pipeline Extension Case Study*, https://www.gazducameroun.com/case-studies/bonaberi-pipeline-extension-case-study/, accessed on 30 April 2023.

Under these conditions, it is difficult to see the development in Cameroon of successful strategically-brought climate cases such as *Save Lamu* in Kenya, in which the plaintiff, a CSO, sought the cancellation of an authorization for the realization of a project because of the failure to respect public participation procedures.[33] In countries such as South Africa where climate actions have been identified, CSOs have greater scope to act based in the first instance on the Constitution. Section 38 of the South African Constitution mentions that 'anyone listed in this section has the right to approach a competent court alleging that a right in the Bill of Rights has been infringed or threatened, and the court may grant appropriate relief, including a declaration of rights'.[34] Furthermore concerning environmental law, section 32(1) of the National Environmental Management Act in South Africa allows any person or group of persons to take legal action in the event of a breach or threatened breach of any provision of the Act or any other statutory instrument relating to the protection of the environment or the use of natural resources.[35] They may act in their own interest, in the interest of environmental protection or in the context of group actions.

This restriction undoubtedly explains why the majority of cases in environmental matters or concerning given natural resources are brought by the administration in charge of their management, as is the case in forestry and wildlife matters in Cameroon, where the Ministry of Forests and Wildlife (Ministère des Forêts et de La Faune, MINFOF) has the authority to initiate public action and acts as a civil party in the trial.[36] Between 2016 and 2018, 319 court cases in which MINFOF was a party were listed in these matters.[37] This does not mean that there cannot be cases between private

33 National Environmental Tribunal, *Save Lamu v National Environmental Management Authority and Amu Power Co. Ltd*, No. 196, 2016.

34 Constitution of South Africa 1996.

35 'Any person or group of persons may seek appropriate relief in respect of any breach or threatened breach of any provision of this Act. Including a principle contained in Chapter 1, or any other statutory provision concerned with the protection of the environment or the use of natural resources (a) in that person's or group of person's own inters; (b) in the interest of, or on behalf of, a person who is, for practical reasons, unable to institute such proceedings; (c) in the interest of or on behalf of a group or class of persons whose interests are affected; (d) in the public interest; and (e) in the interest of protecting the environment'.

36 Article 147, Law No. 94–01 of 20 January 1994 on the regime of forests, wildlife and fisheries. 'In the absence of a settlement or in the event of non-execution of the settlement, and after prior notice to the offender, public action is initiated within seventy-two (72) hours at the request of the administrations in charge of forests, wildlife and fisheries, as the case may be, which are parties to the proceedings'.

37 N Horline, D Owona and M Feudjeu, *Sommier des infractions forestières et fauniques au Cameroun: Le reflet de la gestion du contentieux forestier et faunique*, Note d'analyse (2021), p. 13.

individuals in forestry or wildlife matters, but they fall under the radar due to the absence of a database tracking them. Unlike countries such as Gabon, where the standing and capacity to act of associations and CSOs in general are recognized without conditions,[38] in Cameroon approval considerably limits their access to judges.

Apart from approval, a reading of article 8(2) of the law on the environment also highlights the obligation of associations to contribute to the actions of public and para-public bodies. In fact, according to this article, only approved associations contributing to the actions of these institutions are entitled to exercise the rights recognized for a civil party concerning environmental offences. However, this obligation is an additional condition that limits even more the access of associations to environmental judges.

Thus, it appears that the activism shown by CSOs elsewhere in the world in environmental or climate matters is difficult to achieve in Cameroon because of procedural barriers related to the capacity and standing to act as defined by the law on the environment. However, this is not the only legal barrier in Cameroon. In environmental law, there is a clear prioritization of legal persons, to the detriment of natural persons, for referral to courts in environmental matters.

Prioritization of legal entities for referral to courts in environmental matters

According to article 8(2) of the Law on the Environment, the entities that are entitled to exercise the rights of the civil party in environmental matters are the grassroots communities and approved associations that contribute to the actions of public and para-public bodies. While it is not difficult to know what associations refer to, it is more complex to determine the entity to which the legislator refers when designating grassroots communities. Indeed, the law on the environment does not define such an entity, but makes it an essential actor in the implementation of the national environmental policy alongside decentralized territorial authorities and environmental protection associations.[39] Apart from the law on the environment, it is difficult to find any mention of such entities. So, there is clearly some recognition that there

---

38 Article 14, Law No. 007/2014 on the protection of the environment in the Gabonese Republic. This article states 'The associations for the defense of the environment, independently of the citizens concerned by certain projects or certain measures, can take legal action against any decision likely to harm the environment. They can also constitute civil party before the repressive jurisdictions'.

39 Article 3 of the framework law on the environment states: 'The President of the Republic defines national environmental policy. Its implementation is the responsibility of the Government, which applies it in concert with the decentralized territorial authorities, the grassroots communities and the environmental protection associations'.

should be a broader range of actors that can exercise rights in this context. What is less clear is exactly who these entities are. Does it include, for example, the peasant forest committees set up within the legal framework of forest protection and that participate and are the spokespersons of the population during the process of classifying a forest?[40] What differentiates a grassroots community from a simple community? What are its constitutive elements? What is its legal personality? These are some questions raised by the mention of a grassroots community, which can lead to the inadmissibility of legal actions brought by communities.

Moreover, the reference to grassroots communities raises the question of the Law's conformity with the Constitution. Indeed, in its preamble, the Constitution gives every person, natural or legal, the duty to protect the environment.[41] On reading it, it does not appear that this duty was to be exercised through other entities, given that the preamble grants everyone the right to a healthy environment. Therefore, since everyone has this right, they are also expected to act to protect the environment. However, the law on the environment obliges individuals to turn to grassroots communities and approved associations to exercise the rights recognized for the civil party. In order to respect constitutional law (that is superior to the law on the environment in terms of the hierarchy of norms) one would have expected that the right to take legal action would also be mentioned as an individual right of any natural person beyond the other entities likely to bring a case before an environmental judge. On reading this provision, the legislator seems to have considered that civil action in environmental matters could be better exercised only by persons grouped in communities and not in an individualized manner. This interpretation limits the access of natural persons to environmental judges. It thus goes against the spirit of the preamble of the Constitution, which seems to give to each person, physical or moral, the duty to act by themselves for the protection of the environment.

Thus, given the conditional capacity and standing of CSOs and the prioritization of legal entities over natural persons for referral to environmental judges, environmental protection actors face considerable constraints that discourage pursuing litigation as a sole strategy for climate justice. As discussed above, there may be more instances of climate litigation in Cameroon that have been recognized (depending on which definition and framing one uses). However, given the poor prospects of such cases, it

40 Procedures for the classification of forests in the permanent forest estate of the Republic of Cameroon, November 1999.

41 Law No. 96/06 of 18 January 1996 revising the Constitution of 2 June 1972, amended and supplemented by Law No. 2008/001 of 14 April 2008.

is clear why environmental justice in general and climate justice in particular is sought by other kinds of political engagement.

Civil society actions for environmental and climate justice in Cameroon

In the context of this chapter, we understand environmental justice as depending on a set of actions carried out by different actors in favour of environmental protection. In terms of climate change, we are talking about actions that contribute to the fight against climate change, such as the reduction of greenhouse gas (GHG) emissions, adaptation to the effects observed or even the capacity building of institutions for adaptation or mitigation actions. As we shall now explore, in general CSOs in Cameroon carry out awareness-raising actions and technical, financial and/or material support to local communities and indigenous populations as well as to law enforcement agencies. Finally, they also carry out advocacy and the monitoring of legality in the exploitation and management of natural resources.

Awareness-raising actions and sharing knowledge

In Cameroon, different groups of actors are not always aware of their rights in terms of natural resource management. This is the case for indigenous populations and local communities whose rights in relation to logging, for example, are not always effectively controlled. This is why organizations such as the Center for Environment and Development (CED) have developed various guides in this regard.[42] In addition, organizations such as the Service d'Appui aux Initiatives Locales de Développement (SAILD), in partnership with the Friedrich Ebert Foundation, initiated training for journalists on international climate negotiations in the run-up to COP 26.[43] This training aimed to provide journalists with the basis for a good understanding of the stakes in the climate negotiations at the international, regional and national levels in order to allow for better media coverage.[44] Finally, as part of the awareness and knowledge-sharing actions, we should also mention the CI4CA organization, which initiated the building of a bridge between

[42] F Same *et al*, *Guide simplifié d'observation externe des forêts à l'usage des communautés,* Guide, https://cedcameroun.org/?project=guide-simplifie-dobservationexterne-des-forets-a-lusagedes-communautes, accessed 1 November 2022.

[43] SAILD, 'Journalists Trained on International Climate Negotiations", *SAILD*, 29 October 2021, https://www.saild.org/en/les-journalistes-a-lecole-des-negociations-internationales-sur-le-climat/, accessed 1 November 2022.

[44] SAILD (n 43).

the traditional knowledge of indigenous populations and students in order to highlight the impact of climate change on forest communities and encourage them to protect the environment.[45]

Technical, financial and/or material support to local communities and law enforcement agencies

As an example of such support, the Forests and Rural Development Association (Forêts et Developpement Rural, FODER) supports communities by providing improved stoves to women living along the Benue National Park. After noticing that the traditional fireplaces used by women in these areas expose them to various health problems, due to smoke and harmful particles, and that they contribute to the abusive cutting of firewood, this organization has set up an improved earthen fireplace that uses wood rationally and produces less smoke.[46] Other organizations such as the Field Legality Advisory Group (FLAG), with support from the World Resources Institute, supports natural resource law enforcement agencies. This is the case with training for forestry administration on the Open Timber Portal (OTP).[47] This is a platform that promotes transparency and legality in the marketing of timber through the provision of various kinds of information, including legal documents regarding exploitation by companies, or CSO denunciations of the illegal operations of a given company. This information is useful to government officials who can easily carry out their powers.

Advocacy

Some organizations are also involved in advocacy on environmental and climate issues. This is, for example, the case with SAILD, which organized a workshop to prepare the advocacy of civil society for its participation in the COP15 of the United Nations Convention to Combat Desertification,

---

45 CI4CA, 'Programme scolaire Green Classes', *Facebook watch*, https://m.facebook.com/ci4ca/videos/472839994119704/?locale=ne_NP, accessed 1 November 2022.

46 FODER, 'Des foyers améliorés pour faciliter la vie des femmes riveraines du Parc National de la Benoué-Région du Nord Cameroun' *FODER*, 6 June 2022, https://forest4dev.org/des-foyers-ameliores-pour-faciliter-la-vie-des-femmes-riveraines-du-parc-nationale-de-la-benoue-region-du-nord-cameroun/, accessed 1 November 2022.

47 FLAG, 'Exploitation forestière illégale: Les étudiants et enseignants de l'ENEF se forment à l'utilisation des plateformes OTP, Forest Watcher et Atlas forestier interactif du Cameroun', *LinkedIn*, 2022, https://www.linkedin.com/posts/flag-cameroon_formation-activity-6981469691772817408-i4td?utm_source=share&utm_medium=member_desktop, accessed 1 November 2022.

which was held in May 2022 in Côte d'Ivoire[48] – in particular promoting agroecology as a solution to desertification. An other organization, Green Development Advocates (GDA), has mobilized civil society to strengthen the development and implementation of actions to combat climate change in Cameroon.[49] Among other things, it is asking the government to integrate the consideration of climate change in the realization of environmental and social impact studies.

Monitor the legality of the exploitation and management of natural resources

For more than 20 years, Cameroonian CSOs have been involved in monitoring the legality of the exploitation and management of natural resources through a mechanism called 'independent monitoring'. Defined as a set of activities to monitor the management of natural resources and the environment conducted by third parties,[50] independent monitoring first developed in the forestry sector. The first experience of independent forest monitoring was in Cambodia and was undertaken by Global Witness, which was responsible for ensuring accurate and timely reporting of forest offences.[51] Despite the positive results of the increased documentation of significant forest crimes and exposure of weak government action, including collusion with illegal logging, the Cambodian government was increasingly reluctant to work with Global Witness.[52] This led to the suspension of the independent observation project in that country. However, this experience was appreciated by donors who wanted independent monitoring to be implemented in Cameroon in the 2000s.[53] This choice was justified by the context of structural adjustment in the country; it had resources, such as forests, the exploitation of which was supposed to bring in revenue, but

48 SAILD, 'Cameroon's Civil Society Prepares Its Advocacy Against Desertification", *SAILD*, 30 March, 2022, https://www.saild.org/en/la-societe-civile-du-cameroun-prepare-son-plaidoyer-contre-la-desertification/, accessed 1 November 2022,

49 GDA, 'Atelier de mobilisation des organisations et réseaux de la société civile pour renforcer l'élaboration et la mise en oeuvre des actions de lutte contre le changement climatique au Cameroun_Communiqué final', *GDA*, 5 November 2021, https://gdacameroon.org/atelier-de-mobilisation-des-organisations-et-reseaux-de-la-societe-civile-pour-renforcer-lelaboration-et-la-mise-en-oeuvre-des-actions-de-lutte-contre-le-changement-climatique-au-cameroun-_/, accessed 1 November 2022.

50 Plateforme africaine d'Observation indépendante, Flyer, https://pa-oi.org/wp-content/uploads/simple-file-list/Finale-version-Plaquette-PA-OI1.pdf, accessed 4 October 2022.

51 Marie Vallée *et al*, 'Independent forest monitoring in the Congo Basin: Taking stock and thinking ahead', *Working Paper*, March 2022, p. 4.

52 Vallée (n 51).

53 Vallée (n 51).

this was considerably undermined by corruption.[54] Thus, Global Witness and other organizations such as Resources Extraction Monitoring and the AGRECO-CEW consortium have succeeded each other from 2000 to 2012 as independent monitors of the legality and exploitation of forests in Cameroon, governed by a memorandum of understanding signed with the administration in charge of forests.[55]

Since then, non-mandated independent forest monitoring has developed as no organization has a mandate from the forest administration in Cameroon. In practice, independent monitors, whether acting on a mandate or not, analyse official documentation related to forests and visit logging sites or timber transport routes to identify potential problems.[56] They publish reports on the facts observed and recommend solutions. In addition, they follow up on observed forestry infractions. In Cameroon, for example, mandated independent monitoring has led to the sanctioning of the Hazim forestry company in 2000 and a fine of nearly €4 million in 2002, the highlighting of the most common illegalities in the sector[57] and even the cancellation of forest titles.[58]

As for independent, non-mandated or so-called external observation, FODER reports have led to seizures of timber, temporary suspensions of logging permits, legal proceedings against companies for unauthorized logging, and even sanctions against agents of the MINFOF.[59] Others, such as FLAG, have highlighted several of MINFOF's shortcomings in the

---

[54] Cameroon ranked last in Transparency International's Corruption Perceptions Index in 1998. Cf. Transparency International, *The Transparency International Corruption Perceptions Index 1999- Framework Document* (October 1999), p. 23.

[55] Vallée (n 51), 4.

[56] Vallée (n 51), 8.

[57] These included non-payment of taxes, geographic relocation of logging titles, logging under the guise of fictitious development projects, off-limit logging, and timber laundering using transport and processing documents. Some of these illegalities are still visible today, notably the geographic relocation of forest titles. Cf. Clarisse Fombana, *Problématique de l'attribution des titres forestiers au Cameroun: la délocalisation géographique des ventes de coupe*, Présentation de l'organisation SAILD, Forum sur la Gouvernance forestière, République du Congo, 2022, https://cidt.org.uk/wp-content/uploads/2022/06/Session-7B-PPT3-Problematique-de-lexploitation-forestiere-illegale-dans-les-forets-du-domaine-nationale-cas-de-la-delocalisation-geographique-des-ventes-de-coupe-Clarisse-Fombaba.pdf; REM, *Evolution du contrôle et des sanctions de l'exploitation forestière illégale au Cameroun*, Rapport, Bilan mars 2005-décembre 2009, p. 2.

[58] The AGRECO-CEW consortium allowed the cancellation of 15 Timber Recovery Permits (TRP) and Timber Removal Permits (TRP) following a mission to ensure the effective termination of activities in these small forest titles. Cf. AGRECO-CEW (2012) *Rapport technique No. 5 du 1er janvier au 30 juin 2012,* Observateur indépendant au contrôle et au suivi des infractions forestières au Cameroun, Report, p. 12.

[59] Vallée (n 51), 14.

management of forestry and wildlife litigation, such as the non-respect for procedural rules for the settlement of forestry disputes, while quantifying the volume of forestry and wildlife litigation in Cameroon.[60] This shows the importance of independent monitoring in the quest for the sustainable management and exploitation of natural resources in Cameroon.

In light of the emergence of new issues, independent monitoring actors are adapting monitoring to the specificities of given sectors. This is how the independent monitoring of mines developed,[61] and is developing for wildlife[62] and REDD+.[63] FLAG contributed to the development of a REDD+ observation methodology in the Democratic Republic of Congo.[64] It resulted in the definition of scopes of application for independent monitoring of REDD (reducing emissions from deforestation and forest degradation) including the legality of REDD+ projects, social and environmental safeguards, grievance redress and benefit distribution mechanisms, as well as the development of a methodology, several diagnostic matrices and checklists comprised of indicators to evaluate performance.[65]

Transparency International has also developed a guide to independent monitoring of REDD+ governance for civil society organizations.[66] This guide aims to provide the latter with an overview of the main steps and

---

60 Law No. 94/01 of 20 January 1994 on the regime of forests, fauna and fisheries stipulates in its art. 147 that in the absence of a transaction and a prior formal notice to the offender, the Ministry of Forests and Fauna shall initiate public action within 72 hours. However, when analysing the Ministry's list of forest and wildlife infractions, which contains the cases in court and the litigation pending at the Ministry for a given period, FLAG found several cases that had already been the subject of a formal notice but that were not followed by legal action after the 72-hour deadline. For more information see Horline, Owona and Feudjeu (n 37), 21.

61 FODER, "Les comités de veille citoyenne dans la gestion des ressources minières se partagent les expériences", *FODER*, 2022, https://forest4dev.org/les-comites-de-veille-citoyenne-cvc-dans-la-gestion-des-ressources-minieres-se-partagent-les-experiences/, accessed 4 October 2022.

62 FLAG has developed an approach for independent monitoring of illegal wildlife exploitation activities by communities bordering protected areas. It consists of training communities living near protected areas on simplified monitoring techniques and methods while relying on their experience and knowledge of the area to promote better wildlife monitoring and contribute to the fight against poaching. Cf. FLAG, 'Surveillance faunique: FLAG aux côtés des riverains de la Réserve de Biosphère du Dja (Sud Cameroun)', *Facebook*, https://web.facebook.com/OngFLAG/?_rdc=1&_rdr,, accessed 4 October 2022.

63 The role of conservation, sustainable management of forests and enhancement of forest carbon stocks in developing countries.

64 EU REDD Facility, *Independent Monitoring in the forest sector: moving beyond law enforcement*, Policy Brief (2021), p. 6.

65 EU REDD Facility (n 64).

66 Transparency International, *Observation indépendante de la gouvernance de la REDD+. Guide à destination des organisations de la société civile*, Guide (2019), p. 2.

considerations in the design and implementation of independent observation systems for REDD+ governance.[67] It is also envisaged to extend the independent monitoring to nationally determined contributions in order to monitor their implementation.[68]

The actions of civil society organizations in Cameroon are therefore considerable despite the obstacles to the development of judicial activism. This makes it possible to envisage ways of achieving climate justice – for instance by ensuring proper safeguards are in place, and that carbon reduction projects are run ethically and fairly – that are not limited to litigation.

The possibilities of developing climate litigation in Cameroon

So far, this chapter has examined both the procedural constraints that limit climate cases in an African civil law country, but also highlighted how well-developed civil society environmental protection work is in this context. Finally, it is necessary to consider what role these might play in growing a climate justice movement using more litigation. Given the legal context in Cameroon, the development of climate litigation requires looking beyond associations to other actors and examining the type of litigation that can be conducted. However, this can only really take place if civil society actions in terms of independent monitoring of climate change issues are intensified.

Identification of claimants and type of litigation

In Cameroon, the judicial organization is based on three jurisdictional branches – judicial, administrative and jurisdictions not attached to a specific order.[69] Within the judicial branch, there are courts, such as the courts of first instance and higher courts, that deal with civil and criminal cases.[70] In the administrative branch, there are jurisdictions such as the administrative courts, which hear in first instance appeals for annulment on the grounds of excess of power, actions for compensation for damage caused by an administrative act, or contractual disputes, with the exception of those concluded even implicitly under private law.[71] Finally, in the branch of jurisdictions not

67 Transparency International (n 54).

68 EU REDD Facility (n 64), 10.

69 YR Kalieu Elongo, 'Organisation judiciaire du Cameroun' in Issa Sayegh Joseph (ed), *Répertoire quinquennal OHADA 2006–2010*, vol. 1 (Association pour l'Unification du Droit en Afrique 2010) 96.

70 Law No. 2006/015 of 29 December 2006 on judicial organization.

71 Article 2(3), Law No. 2006/022 of 29 December 2006 fixing the organization and functioning of the administrative courts: 'Administrative litigation includes: a) appeals for

attached to the judiciary or the administration, we find the Constitutional Council and the High Court of Justice.[72]

In other countries, climate litigation is characterized by the seeking of the annulment of administrative acts that are taken without consideration of the climatic risks.[73] So it is possible to envisage, in Cameroon also, the development of climate litigation before the administrative courts. This might challenge the legality of specific administrative acts or seek compensation for damage caused by an administrative act that contributes to amplifying the harmful consequences of climate change, and be undertaken by actors other than associations, such as natural persons with an interest in acting, that is those directly impacted by the contested administrative act.

Moreover, given the jurisdiction of administrative courts in Cameroon, applications for the annulment of decisions for excess of power can be initiated, as in the case of *Commune de Grande Synthe v France*.[74] In this case, the Commune de Grande Synthe brought proceedings in relation to the inaction kept by the President of the Republic and other governmental authorities on its request for appropriate measures to curb the growth of GHG emissions on the national territory.[75] It was argued that this silence implicitly constituted a rejection of the request. This was based on Cameroon's vulnerability to climate change due to its immediate proximity to the coast and the physical characteristics of its territory.[76]

In Cameroon, cities are decentralized territorial authorities that enjoy administrative and financial autonomy.[77] So, the chief executive of a city is empowered to represent the interests of this entity before the law.[78] Thus, a city that is particularly vulnerable to climate change can validly bring before the administrative judge a request for the annulment of an act of the central

annulment on the grounds of excess of power and, in non-criminal matters, incidental appeals for assessment of legality. The following constitute abuse of power within the meaning of this article – the violation of a legal or regulatory provision; – the misuse of power. b) actions for compensation for damage caused by an administrative act; c) disputes concerning contracts (with the exception of those concluded even implicitly under private law) or public service concessions; d) disputes concerning the public domain; e) disputes concerning law enforcement operations'.

72 Elongo (n 69), 96.

73 For example *Earthlife Africa Johannesburg v Minister of Environmental Affairs*, p. 3.

74 Conseil d'Etat, *Commune de Grande Synthe et autre c/ France*, No. 427301, November 2020.

75 Conseil d'Etat, *Commune de Grande Synthe et autre c/ France*, p. 1.

76 Conseil d'Etat, *Commune de Grande Synthe et autre c/ France*, p. 4.

77 Article 8, Law No. 2019/024 of 24 December 2019 on the general code of decentralized territorial authorities.

78 Article 13(2), Law No. 2019/024 of 24 December 2019 on the general code of decentralized territorial authorities: 'The Head of the Executive represents the Territorial Collectivity in civil life and in justice'.

administration for excess of power. The same applies to the region, which is the second largest decentralized territorial authority in Cameroon.[79]

In addition to the administrative judge, the courts of the judicial branch may also be utilized by individuals. Indeed, the latter generally attempt to establish the responsibility of companies in environmental matters. That was the case in *Atangana v Paterson Zochonis*, in which the plaintiff complained of the nauseating odours emitted by the hide processing company near his home, making his house uninhabitable.[80] Olfactory nuisances are sanctioned by the framework law on the environment in article 61,[81] and the company was ordered to pay in damages a sum of CFAF 8,500,000.[82] So, the civil liability of companies can effectively be engaged in Cameroon in environmental matters by natural persons who are able to demonstrate their interest and capacity to act, where there is also a causal link between the act reproached and the damage caused to the defendant. Therefore, cases like that of Mr Lliuya against the German company RWE could potentially see the light of day in Cameroon. In this case, Lliuya brought an action before the District Court of Essen in Germany to hold RWE responsible for the risk of flooding due to the rise in the level of Lake Palcacocha, which contributed to damage to his home.[83] The court considered that the specific cause of this situation was RWE's GHG emissions, based on provisions relating to neighbourhood disturbance in Germany.[84]

Although interesting and possible in principle, given that Cameroon's environmental litigation already includes cases arising in nuisance, as in the *Atangana* case mentioned above, this may not be enough. It would be difficult to see this type of case develop in Cameroon because of the need for advanced scientific expertise to prove the connection between the

[79] Article 2(1), Law No. 2019/024 of 24 December 2019 on the General Code of decentralized territorial authorities: 'The Territorial Authorities of the Republic are the Regions and the Cities'.

[80] P Oumba, 'L'encadrement du contentieux civil environnemental au Cameroun et en République Démocratique du Congo' (2020) 5 *Revue Africaine de Droit de l'Environnement* 131.

[81] It states that: '(1) The emission of noise and odours which are likely to be injurious to human health, constitute an excessive nuisance to the neighbourhood or harm the environment shall be prohibited. (2) The persons responsible for such emissions shall take all necessary steps to suppress, prevent or limit their spread unnecessarily or through lack of precaution. (3) Where warranted by the urgency of the situation, municipalities shall take all enforceable measures to to stop the disturbance. In case of necessity, they may request the assistance of the public force'.

[82] Oumba (n 80), 135.

[83] District Court Essen, *Saul Ananias Luciano Lliuya v RWE AG*, 2 O 285/15, 15 December 2016, p. 2.

[84] *Saul Ananias Luciano Lliuya*, p. 5.

defendant's conduct and the harm. In this context it could be easier to frame a case on the environmental consequences of companies' exploitation and mention alternatively the link between the exploitation and climate change and its consequences. In Cameroon, cases like this could target carbon major companies listed in Richard Heede's research on GHG emissions among those companies already registered in Cameroon. For example, CIMENCAM is a cement industry company that is the local subsidiary of the Lafarge Holcim group mentioned in the report.[85]

It would be more obvious to look for ways to develop climate litigation from the most prolific environmental litigation within the country, that is forestry and wildlife litigation. Indeed, one could argue that, as argued in the literature, any litigation and activism relating to forestry is part of the African model of climate litigation.[86] Indeed, between 2016 and 2018, 1,036 cases were recorded in forestry and wildlife matters, including 319 cases in court and 717 cases monitored by MINFOF.[87] These cases are being brought by the forestry administration against illegal loggers. First of all, because deforestation contributes to climate change, any legal challenges to logging have the potential to demonstrate a legal challenge to activities that contribute to climate change. So there may already be a category of climate cases in Cameroon arising from this. But also, this indicates a potential on which to build. For example, MINFOF could be supported in legal proceedings involving illegal forest exploitation by a company or a person in order to highlight the consequences of this act on carbon sequestration by the forest as extending carbon retention in harvested wood products. This is considered as a mitigation option by the Intergovernmental Panel on Climate Change.[88] Given the existing problem of deforestation, and the beginnings of litigation about logging, this is the most likely area in which Cameroonian climate litigation might start to develop.

Though access to justice is conditional for CSOs in Cameroon, slight opportunities may have opened following the judgment of the Court of First Instance of Batibo in *FEDEV v China Road and Bridge Corpn*.[89] In this

---

85 R Heede, *Carbon Majors: Accounting for carbon and methane emissions 1854–2010. Methods & Results Report* (2014), p. 9.

86 See, for example, Bouwer and Field (n 11), 123–8.

87 Horline, Owona and Feudjeu (n 37), 13.

88 GJ Nabuurs *et al*, 'Forestry' in B Metz *et al* (eds), *Climate Change 2007: Mitigation. Contribution of Working Group III to the Fourth Assessment Report of the Intergovernmental Panel on Climate Change* (Cambridge University Press 2007) 543.

89 Batibo Court of First Instance, *FEDEV v China Road and Bridge Corpn*, Judgment No CFB/004/09 (unreported). Cf. FJ Achu, 'The Law in Cameroon and the Vexing Problems of Ground Water Pollution' (2019) 2(4) *Scholars International Journal of Law, Crime and Justice* 106.

case, the Foundation for Environment and Development (FEDEV) – an NGO located in Bamenda in Cameroon – brought an action against the respondent because it polluted land along the road it was building.[90] The judge intimated that FEDEV had no locus standi based on section 8(1) and (2) of the environmental law.[91] He argued that the applicant ought to have liaised up with a grassroots organization proximate to the community directly affected by the environmental nuisance.[92] However, the court was reminded that in addressing its mind to section 8, it should focus on the words 'common good', which should be examined alongside public interest.[93] In the court's opinion, any individual or association can bring an action in court on behalf of the public at large if 'public interest' is affected.[94] Therefore, the judge recognized the locus standi of FEDEV. From this case, it appears that CSOs could in future base their arguments on the public interest to avoid the obstacle of approval by the minister in charge of the environment.

Strengthening of civil society actions in terms of independent monitoring of climate change issues

Civil society organizations that monitor play an informative role. They highlight governance problems or indications of illegalities in the natural resource sector. As mentioned earlier, these actions have so far contributed to several changes in the natural resource management sector. But it is not just the case that civil society activities replace formal litigation processes in civil law countries. The reports produced by these organizations can be used as evidence in legal proceedings. In the case of mandated independent monitoring, for example, a report can be cited as evidence because the organization has a collaborative framework with MINFOF. Continuing the example of illegal logging activities referred to above, such a framework would give the CSO access to the logging titles of loggers.

The potential problem with this is that the integrity of the evidence from an independent, non-mandated observation may be questionable, given that CSOs do not always have access to sites. For example, an unauthorized independent observation report highlighting illegal logging and its impact on the climate could be challenged by the perpetrator on the basis that the evidence was not collected with an official mandate. However, in

90 MC Monoji, 'The Judiciary and Compliance and Enforcement of Corporate Environmental Governance in Cameroon: A Critical Appraisal' (2022) 1(2) *Justice and Law Bulletin* 43.

91 Achu (n 89), 106.

92 Achu (n 89).

93 Monoji (n 90), 44.

94 Achu (n 89), 106.

other situations, the productions of independent observers could support claimants' arguments. These could, for example, be reports or analysis notes presenting the administration's failures in the implementation of climate change adaptation measures. It is therefore necessary for CSOs to take an even greater interest in monitoring climate change aspects. For this purpose, training on climate change is essential, as well as the support of donors for the financing of monitoring actions.

Conclusion

The development of climate litigation in Cameroon faces many obstacles, due to limited access to the courts. Apart from the interest and capacity to act of CSOs conditioned by the approval and participation in the activities of public or semi-public bodies, environmental law gives priority to legal entities as entities likely to bring environmental matters before the judge. Despite this context, civil society actors carry out various types of activities to contribute to the protection of the environment and the fight against climate change. This includes advocacy, awareness raising, but also the monitoring of legality in the management of natural resources, especially forestry. Moreover, some openings seem to be possible for the development of climate litigation, such as actions brought by public authorities or civil liability actions initiated by individuals. It may also be that more indirect litigation around the protection of these natural resources becomes – or becomes recognized – as a more typical model of climate litigation in Cameroon.

Either way, in this architecture, the role of CSOs continues to be crucial in that the information they obtain during their investigations can be used as evidence to support given arguments. In such a context, the fight for climate justice appears to be more easily achievable through the actions already implemented by CSOs on the ground.

PART II

Rights-Based Approaches

6

The Prospects and Challenges of Litigating Climate Change Before African Regional Human Rights Bodies

Elsabé Boshoff

Introduction

Climate change has been characterized as a magnifying glass, through which all other struggles are magnified. Therefore, many authors have identified that it is at times challenging to classify something as a 'climate' case. Some cases at the international and also national levels have been brought specifically on climate change (and based their claims on the commitments of states under, for example, the Paris Agreement[1]), and are thus easy to classify as climate cases.[2] Other cases refer to climate impacts as one among many consequences of a violation.[3] Still other cases, that deal with the *consequences*

---

[1] Conference of the Parties, Adoption of the Paris Agreement, Dec. 12, 2015. UN Doc. CCC/CP/2015/L.9/Rev/1 (12 Dec. 2015).

[2] At the national level, see for example the groundbreaking case of *Urgenda Foundation v State of the Netherlands* ECLI:NL:HR:2019:2007, decided by the Hoge Raad of the Netherlands. At the international level, consider the case of Communication 104/2019 *Sacchi et al. v Argentina et al*, before the United Nations Committee (UN) on the Rights of the Child, and the decision of the UN Human Rights Committee in Communication 3624/2019 *Daniel Billy v Australia*, issued on 23 September 2022.

[3] See for example the Kenyan case of *African Centre for Corrective and Preventive Action v Lolldaiga Hills Ltd; Kenya Wildlife Service* [2022] eKLR, and the case before the Indian National Green Tribunal in *Rajiv Dutta v Union of India,* MA No. 122/2019 in Original Application No. 60/2018.

of climate change, such as displacement or damages from extreme weather events, may not even mention climate change.[4] Therefore, when we speak about litigating climate change through a human rights lens, this does not have to refer only to cases regarding mitigation of climate impacts on the environment or a violation of environmental rights, but could also relate to the myriad of other climate impacts, including on life, health, education, food, housing, leisure, property, among many others.

To date, no cases directly focused on climate change have been brought before African regional human rights bodies, namely the African Commission on Human and Peoples' Rights (the Commission), the African Court on Human and Peoples' Rights (the Court) and the African Committee of Experts on the Rights and Welfare of the Child (the Committee).[5] This is likely a reflection of the broader continental context, with only a handful of climate cases having been brought before national courts in Africa on climate change, some of which are ongoing at the time of writing.[6] As discussed below, one of the admissibility requirements of litigating before the regional bodies is exhaustion of domestic remedies. Thus, it is at least partially understandable why there have not been cases on this matter at the regional level, given that national courts have only heard a few cases and that some are ongoing. Another more strategic reason why only a few cases against African states have been brought on climate change is because these states are mostly not the main perpetrators of climate wrongs, that is, most African states are among the lowest contributors to CO_2 and other greenhouse gas (GHG) emissions.

4 See for example the United States case of *Pietrangelo v S & E Customize It Auto Corp.*, SCR 100/13 NY Civ. Ct., which concerned an action for damages incurred to a vehicle stored at repair shop during Hurricane Sandy.

5 This chapter differs from previous work on climate change and the African regional human rights bodies, such as the work by Jegede – see for example Ademola Oluborode Jegede, 'The Protection of Indigenous Peoples' Lands by Domestic Legislation on Climate Change Response Measures: Exploring Potentials in the Regional Human Rights System of Africa' (2017) 24 *International Journal on Minority and Group Rights* 24–56; Ademola Oluborode Jegede, 'Rights Away From Home: Climate Induced Displacement of Indigenous Peoples and the Extraterritorial Application of the Kampala Convention' (2016) 16 *African Human Rights Law Journal* 58–82 – in that it focuses beyond the regional instruments particularly on the emerging regional human rights norms and the prospect of successful litigation before all three human rights bodies. It also has a broader focus than these works in that it does not specifically focus on one vulnerable group.

6 See for example *Kenyan National Environmental Tribunal Save Lamu v National Environmental Management Authority and Amu Power Co. Ltd* [2019] eKLR; *Mbabazi v The Attorney General and National Environmental Management Authority* Civil Suit No. 283 of 2012, in the High Court in Uganda; and *EarthLife Africa Johannesburg v Minister of Environmental Affairs* Case No. 65662/16 (2017) in the South African High Court.

Nevertheless, it is still possible to say something about the prospects and challenges of successful climate litigation before the regional bodies, based on (1) the norms and substantive rights contained in the main African human rights instruments (the African Charter on Human and Peoples' Rights,[7] the Maputo Protocol on the Rights of Women in Africa,[8] and the African Charter on the Rights and Welfare of the Child[9]), (2) the formal criteria for bringing cases before these bodies, (3) previous jurisprudence of these bodies that may shed light on their potential reasoning in climate cases, as well as (4) other ways through which these bodies have communicated on the climate crisis that could demonstrate their receptiveness to climate cases. In particular, this chapter will draw on the case law of the Commission in the cases of *Social and Economic Rights Action Center (SERAC) and Center for Economic and Social Rights (CESR) v Nigeria*[10] (hereafter the *SERAC* case), the *Centre for Minority Rights Development (Kenya) and Minority Rights Group International on behalf of Endorois Welfare Council v Kenya*[11] (hereafter the *Endorois* case), and the more recent case of *African Commission on Human and Peoples' Rights v Republic of Kenya*[12] (hereafter the *Ogiek* case). It relies on these cases to discuss the extent to which they lay the theoretical, doctrinal and remedial groundwork for future climate cases. While many lessons could also be drawn from comparison with climate litigation elsewhere in the world, consideration of these examples are beyond the scope of this chapter, and the focus is on that which is already contained within the African system itself.

This chapter is structured in five parts. Following this introduction, the second section considers some of the core human rights norms underlying the African human rights system, and asks what the implications of these norms are for successful climate litigation. The third section considers the substantive provisions in African human rights instruments that could serve as the basis for bringing climate cases, and further looks at the ways in which the three human rights bodies through jurisprudence and non-jurisprudential developments are putting in place the building blocks for dealing with climate litigation in future. The fourth section looks at the formal requirements for bringing cases before African human rights bodies, namely the admissibility

7 Organization of African Unity (OAU), African Charter on Human and Peoples' Rights, 27 June 1981, entered into force on 21 October 1986.

8 African Union, Protocol to the African Charter on Human and Peoples' Rights on the Rights of Women in Africa, 11 July 2003, entered into force on 25 November 2005.

9 Organization of African Unity (OAU), African Charter on the Rights and Welfare of the Child, 11 July 1990, entered into force on 29 November 1999.

10 ACHPR Communication 155/96, decided at the 30th Ordinary session held in Banjul, The Gambia, 13–27 October 2001.

11 ACHPR Communication 276/2003, decided on 4 February 2010.

12 ACtHPR Application No. 006/2012, decided on 26 May 2017.

criteria that they all share, as well as their respective rules around standing, highlighting the contrast between broad standing before the Commission and Committee and the relatively narrow standing before the Court. The final section draws some general conclusions about the procedural and substantive opportunities and challenges of litigating climate change before the African human rights system.

African human rights norms and climate change

Viljoen and Mutua both speak of an African human rights normative network that spans the different human rights treaties on the continent, that 'to varying degrees reflect a particularly African "fingerprint"'.[13] This section will focus on those norms that may have a particular relevance in the context of climate change litigation. These relate to: (1) the justiciability of all rights, (2) peoples' rights and indigenous people, (3) individual duties, (4) norms around refugees, and (5) the best interest of the child principle.

Justiciability of all rights

The main African human rights instrument, the African Charter, was adopted in 1981. It eschewed the traditional division between the different generations of rights, and the hard line drawn by the adoption of two covenants at the global level between civil and political rights on the one hand and economic, social and cultural rights on the other.[14] The African Charter in its Preamble states that all rights are on the same level in terms of conception and universality, and cannot be dissociated from each other. Viljoen argues that, consequently, all rights in the African Charter are justiciable, and this is also the approach that has been followed by the Commission and Court through their complaints mechanisms.[15] The Commission in the *SERAC* decision introduced the 'four-layered conceptualization of government obligations to "promote", "respect", "protect" and "fulfil" rights' and confirmed that 'there is no right in the African Charter that cannot be made effective'.[16]

---

[13] F Viljoen, *International Human Rights Law in Africa* (Oxford University Press 2012) 2nd edn 213–14; M Wa Mutua, 'The Banjul Charter and the African cultural fingerprint: an evaluation of the language of duties' (1995) 35 *Virginia Journal of International Law* 339.

[14] Viljoen (n 13), 214.

[15] Institute for Human Rights and Development in Africa, 'African Human Rights Case Law Analyser', http://case law.ihrda.org/doc/search/?m=83%3A85, accessed 17 February 2022. Where it is clear that the Commission and Court together have adjudicated cases on all the rights provided in the African Charter.

[16] Viljoen (n 13), 216; *Communication 155/96: Social and Economic Rights Action Center (SERAC) and Center for Economic and Social Rights (CESR) v Nigeria (African Commission on Human and Peoples' Rights)*, para. 68. This case is discussed in further detail below.

When thinking about the four layered obligations of states in the context of climate change in Africa, one has to take account of the fact that most African states are among the lowest contributors to climate change, and the obligation to respect is thus less prominent than in the case of major polluters.[17] Nevertheless, African states do have an obligation to respect human rights in the climate context. National level cases from Uganda and South Africa have shown that litigants in Africa do not limit themselves to holding states accountable for lack of adaptation actions, but also take on African states for not limiting their own contribution to climate change – thus they have argued that states do also have obligations to respect the right to live in a safe climate.[18]

As duty bearers in relation to climate change, arguably the most important obligation on African states is the duty to protect. This entails the obligation on the state 'to protect civilians against violations by non-state actors',[19] which would also extend to non-state actors like corporations that cause climate change through GHG emissions produced through activities on the continent. In one case before the Commission, it held that even if the state is not itself the perpetrator, 'a government cannot absolve itself from the responsibility when it failed to prevent and took no action to investigate",[20] in which case they can be held responsible under human rights law for the actions of non-state actors. The Commission, while speaking about the context of extractive industries, places an obligation on states as part of the duty to protect, that they should "lay down the administrative, civil and criminal liabilities that result from the failure of non-state actors including businesses such as those in extractive industries to comply with [fiscal, environmental, labour, health and human rights observance standards] and any harm or violations arising from such non-compliance'.[21]

African states as human rights duty bearers have obligations not only to respect and protect rights, but also to fulfill and promote them. In the context of climate change this translates to not only an obligation not to cause climate change, but also to put in place adaptive measures and

17 There are exceptions; for example South Africa is ranked among the top 12 CO^2 emitters in the world, see AO Jegede, 'Should a Human Right to a Safe Climate Be Recognized Under the AU Human Rights System?' in M Addaney and AO Jegede (eds), *Human Rights and the Environment Under African Union Law* (Palgrave Macmillan 2020).

18 See cases at n 6.

19 Viljoen (n 13), 216.

20 Viljoen (n 13), 216. ACHPR, Communication 74/92 *Commission Nationale des droits de l'Homme et des libertés v Chad* (decided during the 18th Ordinary Session, Praia, Cape Verde, October 1995), para. 22.

21 African Commission on Human and Peoples' Rights, *State Reporting Guidelines and Principles on Articles 21 and 24 of the African Charter Relating to Extractive Industries, Human Rights and the Environment* (2018) 34.

processes to limit the impacts of climate change on their people.[22] This could include building sea walls to protect low-lying towns from sea level rise and increasing extreme weather events, providing social security nets to farmers who are exposed to more erratic weather patterns and could lose their harvests and livelihoods, investment in new farming techniques, education of society and, in particular, children to be able to adapt to changing weather patterns, among other proactive measures. This of course requires decisions about investment and resource allocation. The African Commission has held that there is a duty on states to make resources available for fulfilling of rights, and states must take 'concrete and targeted steps towards the realization' of rights.[23]

Peoples' rights and indigenous peoples

The African human rights system, particularly through the Charter, affords protections not only for the rights of individuals, but also peoples. The term 'peoples' is not defined in the Charter itself, and Viljoen has urged that 'a search for a single meaning of "people" should be abandoned', but that its meaning would rather depend on the context.[24] The term has been used to apply both to all the people of a country as a collective, as well as to sub-groups within a state.[25] One way in which these sub-groups as peoples can be understood is by equating it with groups (within states), which have a shared 'linguistic, ethic, religious' or other common characteristics.[26] This contextual understanding has been supported by the Commission in its jurisprudence.[27]

The State Reporting Guidelines of the Commission on Articles 21 and 24 of the Charter further holds that a community affected by extractive

---

22 E Boshoff and SG Damtew, 'The Potential of Litigating Children's Rights in the Climate Crisis Before the African Committee of Experts on the Rights and Welfare of the Child' (2022) 22 *African Human Rights Law Journal*), 328.

23 Viljoen (n 13), 217. While these cases related to incarcerated persons to whom the state owes a special duty of care, it can be argued that other groups to which the state owes a special duty of care, for example children, are particularly in need of fulfillment of climate related state obligations. Viljoen further argues there is no reason to 'restrict the duty to fulfil […] to narrow categories of persons'.

24 Viljoen (n 13), 219.

25 Viljoen (n 13), 11–12.

26 Viljoen (n 13), 222.

27 Communication 279/03–296/05 *Sudan Human Rights Organisation & Centre on Housing Rights and Evictions (COHRE) v Sudan (Darfur case)* (African Commission on Human and Peoples' Rights), which clarified in para. 220 that a people may be 'a majority or a minority in a particular State'.

industries activities could be characterized as a people.[28] This clearly goes beyond the usual connotations given to the term people, as the only aspect that identifies them is that they share a geographic locality and are collectively impacted. This flexibility around the different categories that might constitute 'peoples' for purposes of recognition of rights under the African Charter could be positive in the context of climate litigation, in that people do not have to share specific linguistic or other minority group distinction, in order to bring collective climate cases before the African human rights system. Cases could potentially even be brought on behalf of the people of the country as a whole. Furthermore, the African Charter recognizes several rights of peoples including to equality, existence and self-determination, to dispose of their natural resources, to development, to peace, and to a satisfactory environment,[29] most of which are rights that would be directly impacted by the consequences of climate change.

Indigenous people are not explicitly referred to in the Charter, but have through jurisprudence of the Commission and Court been accepted as a specific category of 'peoples' under the African human rights system.[30] Characteristics that define indigenous people under the African human rights system include self-identification, special attachment to land or 'historical dependence for survival on the land and resources', and high level of marginalization and vulnerability.[31] What in particular distinguishes indigenous people from other peoples is the specific connection between their land and heritage, and their way of life, which is linked to the right to culture, religion and their existence as a people. The specific protections that have been afforded to indigenous peoples in Africa, first through their recognition as collective rights holders and secondly in terms of specific substantive rights, means that serious impacts of climate change on their way of life would be eligible for litigation before African human rights bodies.

---

[28] African Commission on Human and Peoples' Rights, *State Reporting Guidelines and Principles on Articles 21 and 24 of the African Charter Relating to Extractive Industries, Human Rights and the Environment*, adopted 30 October 2018, 12.

[29] African Union, *African Charter on Human and Peoples' Rights* (1981), arts 19–24.

[30] See for example para. 112 of the *Ogiek* case, in which the Court recognizes the Ogiek as an indigenous population 'that is part of the Kenyan people having a particular status and deserving special protection deriving from their vulnerability' and the proceeds to find violations of their peoples' rights under the African Charter on that basis. Similarly, the African Commission in the *Endorois* case, para. 162, accepts the Endorois as an 'indigenous community', and 'is satisfied that the Endorois are a "people", a status that entitles them to benefit from provisions of the African Charter that protect collective rights', and in particular that 'the alleged violations of the African Charter are those that go to the heart of indigenous rights – the right to preserve one's identity through identification with ancestral lands'.

[31] Viljoen (n 13), 230–2.

Individual duties

A unique characteristic of the African system – what Mutua calls part of the 'African cultural fingerprint'[32] – is the inclusion in the regional human rights system of individual duties, in addition to rights. Nevertheless, as pointed out by Viljoen, cases have not yet been brought before the African Commission on the basis of individual duties, and the Commission has also not fully elaborated on what individual duties – such as a contribution to 'the harmonious development of the family' and 'to work to the best of his abilities and competence' for society – entail.[33] In recent years, the Commission through soft law has elaborated on some individual human rights duties, focused in particular on how they might apply to corporations. In its State Reporting Guidelines on Articles 21 and 24 of the Charter, in discussing how individual duties may be extended to corporations, the Commission posits that Article 27 of the Charter provides for the duties of individuals, and its sub-provision 2 lays down the obligation to exercise rights 'with due regard to the rights of others'.[34] Clearly, if this obligation can be imposed on individuals, there is an even stronger moral and legal basis for attributing these obligations to corporations and companies.

I have argued elsewhere that situating corporate duties in the context of individual duties 'which limit the exercise of rights and freedoms in that they have to be exercised "with due regard to the right of others, collective security, morality and common interest"', is relevant in the context of climate change.[35] This is because 'climate change impacts not only on the rights of others [...] but also on collective security and common interest, and corporations operating on the continent thus have a duty to exercise their rights within these limits'.[36] Furthermore, many global corporations are significantly larger emitters of GHG emissions than many African states, which means that morally speaking, accountability for climate impacts should attach to them in the context of human rights duties. While to date no corporations have been held accountable before African regional human rights bodies for human rights violations, the Commission has

[32] Mutua (n 13).

[33] Viljoen (n 13), 239.

[34] African Commission on Human and Peoples' Rights, *State Reporting Guidelines and Principles on Articles 21 and 24 of the African Charter Relating to Extractive Industries, Human Rights and the Environment*, 37.

[35] E Boshoff 'The role of human rights soft law instruments in clarifying the obligations of oil and gas companies for climate change related impacts in Africa' in AO Jegede and O Adejonwo (eds), *Climate Change and Human Rights: An African Perspective* (Pretoria University Law Press, 2022).

[36] Boshoff (n 35), 2022.

recognized their complicity in human rights violations. For instance, in the case of *Institute for Human Rights and Development in Africa (IHRDA) v Democratic Republic of the Congo*[37] (the *Kilwa* case) the Commission made recommendations for how corporations should be held accountable.[38] Therefore individual duties[39] and accompanying mechanisms may in future be developed further to particularly apply to corporations whose operations on the continent contribute to climate change.

Refugees and internally displaced persons

Another area in which the African human rights system has developed distinct norms is in relation to the protections extended to refugees and internally displaced persons. According to the latest reports of the Intergovernmental Panel on Climate Change (IPCC), drought resulting from changing climate patterns on the African continent will displace up to 700 million people.[40] Particularly important in the African context is that the Organization of African Unity (former OAU, now AU) Convention Governing the Specific Aspects of Refugee Problems in Africa (1969)[41] expands the definition of refugees beyond the narrow definition of the United Nations Refugee Convention.[42] Unlike the latter, refugees, under the OAU Convention, are not limited to persons fleeing political persecution,[43] but also include persons who are 'compelled to flee a country of residence "owing to […] events seriously disturbing public order"'.[44]

---

[37] ACHPR, Communication 393/10 *IHRDA, RAID and ACIDH v Democratic Republic of Congo* decided in 2016.

[38] ACHPR Working Group on Extractive Industries Environment and Human Rights in Africa, *The Kilwa case: The importance of Communication 373/10: IHRDA v DRC* (African Commission on Human and Peoples' Rights 2018); See also *Communication 155/96: Social and Economic Rights Action Center (SERAC) and Center for Economic and Social Rights (CESR) v Nigeria*.

[39] J Oloka-Onyango, 'Reinforcing Marginalized Rights in an Age of Globalization: International Mechanisms, Non-State Actors, and the Struggle for Peoples' Rights in Africa' (2003) 18 *American University International Law Review* 851.

[40] Working Group II contribution to the Intergovernmental Panel on Climate Change (IPCC) Sixth Assessment Report, ch. 9: Africa, 148.

[41] Organization of African Unity (OAU), Convention Governing the Specific Aspects of Refugee Problems in Africa, 10 September 1969, 1001 UNTS 45, entered into force on 20 June 1974.

[42] UN General Assembly, Convention Relating to the Status of Refugees, 28 July 1951, United Nations, Treaty Series, vol. 189, entered into force on 22 April 1954.

[43] UN Refugee Convention, art. 1(A)(2).

[44] OAU Refugee Convention, art. 1(2). The chapter by Judge Mativo in this volume explores in more depth how the instruments for the protection of refugees might be used in rights-based litigation.

Viljoen argues that this 'allows for more factors to be considered when evaluating refugee status, including serious natural disasters'.[45] This could also be relevant in the context of climate induced displacement across borders, in terms of which climate refugees would be entitled to all the same protections as other refugees in the African human rights system. In relation to the plight of internally displaced persons (IDPs) (those who do not cross international borders) the AU has adopted the Convention for the Protection and Assistance of Internally Displaced Persons in Africa (the Kampala Convention).[46] Similarly to the OAU Refugee Convention, the Kampala Convention in the Preamble recognizes natural disasters as one of the causes of internal displacement that should be addressed, and the definition of an IDP recognizes that displacement may be due to 'natural or human-made disasters'.[47] In terms of states' obligation to protect and assist IDPs, the Kampala Convention explicitly refers to the need for 'measures to protect and assist persons who have been internally displaced due to natural or human made disasters, *including climate change*'.[48] In this regard, Jegede argues that it is 'the first international instrument to link climate change to displacement'.[49] While the Commission's jurisdiction is limited to applying the Charter, it may draw on other international instruments (see discussion below), and the Court has wide jurisdiction in terms of the instruments it is able to adjudicate on, and would be able to directly apply the OAU Refugee Convention and the Kampala Convention.[50]

Best interest of the child

Children, because they have developing minds and bodies that are more seriously affected by environmental changes than most adults, and because

45 Viljoen(n 13), 243.

46 African Union, African Union Convention for the Protection and Assistance of Internally Displaced Persons in Africa ('Kampala Convention'), 23 October 2009, entered into force on 6 December 2012.

47 African Union Convention (n 46), preamble and art. 1.

48 African Union Convention (n 46), art. 5(4). Emphasis added.

49 Jegede (n 5), 74.

50 See arts 60 and 61 of the African Charter, which allows the Commission to draw inspiration from international law on human and peoples' rights and mandates the Commission to 'take into consideration, as subsidiary measures to determine the principles of law, other general or special international conventions' of the AU. See art. 3 of the Protocol to the African Charter on Human and Peoples' Rights on the Establishment of an African Court on Human and Peoples' Rights 10 June 1998, entered into force on 25 January 2004, which sets out the jurisdiction of the Court to include the interpretation of the African Charter, this Protocol and 'any other relevant human rights instrument ratified by the States concerned'.

they will inherit the climate change impacts caused by current GHG emissions, are a group with a specific interest in a safe climate now and in the future. One of the four pillars of the protection of children's rights, both at the international as well as African levels, is the best interest of the child principle. While under the United Nations Convention on the Rights of the Child[51] it should be 'a primary consideration',[52] under the African Children's Charter, the best interest of the child must be *the* primary consideration in all decisions affecting the child.[53] This formulation 'maximises the influence of this principle'.[54] In relation to climate change impacts, it necessitates that 'despite considerations such as economic growth, interest of private sector or any other factor that aims to justify environmental degradation and policy decisions on development, the best interest of the child trumps all'.[55] State actions which go contrary to their climate obligations 'are contrary to the best interest of the child [...], as it affects the survival, health, physical wellbeing and development of the child' and, therefore, despite no specific protection for children to a right to healthy environment in the African Children's Charter, the best interest principle could play a key role as part of arguments on the child rights climate litigation nexus.[56]

This section looked at some of the distinctive characteristics and norms of the African human rights system, and how they relate to potential future climate litigation. From this discussion it can be seen that the regional norms in general open pathways to, rather than hinder, climate litigation in the region, through providing for justiciable socio-economic rights and collective rights, strong obligations on duty bearers to respect, protect, promote and fulfil rights, strong norms for the protection of child rights and the possibility of individual (corporate) duties. The next part considers how these different bodies have engaged with climate change to date, and also how the reasoning in their jurisprudence may be adapted to climate cases.

---

51 UN General Assembly, Convention on the Rights of the Child, 20 November 1989, United Nations, Treaty Series, vol. 1577, entered into force on 2 September 1990.

52 UN Convention on the Rights of the Child, art. 3(1).

53 African Children's Charter, art. IV(1).

54 B Mezmur, 'The African Children's Charter versus the UN Convention on the Rights of the Child: A zero-sum game?' (2008) 23 *SA Public Law* 1, 9.

55 E Boshoff and SG Damtew, 'Children's right to sustainable development under the African human rights framework' (2019) 3 *African Human Rights Yearbook* 119, 134.

56 Boshoff and Damtwe (n 55), 134. Bright Nkrumah's chapter in this volume discusses the role of the principle of intergenerational equity for young people asserting their human rights to be protected from climate change.

Substantive human rights protection and climate litigation

As noted in the introduction to this chapter, climate change impacts can be felt in relation to most, if not all, human rights. It also has different impacts on different vulnerable groups, including children, older persons, persons with disabilities, indigenous peoples/communities and displaced persons or refugees. The focus of this part is on substantive rights in the African human rights instruments, particularly the way in which they have been interpreted by the Court, Commission and Committee in their jurisprudence and other statements of normative value, and that may hold insights for future climate litigation. The cases discussed below do not represent a comprehensive review of all relevant jurisprudence. They merely serve as an illustration of the theoretical, doctrinal and remedial groundwork that existing jurisprudence has put in place for future climate cases, taking account of some of the potential substantive and thematic rights avenues through which cases may be brought.

Jurisprudence with relevance to climate litigation

In considering previous jurisprudence of African human rights bodies that may shed light on their potential reasoning in climate cases, a good point of departure is the right to a healthy environment, because of the potential of arguing that an upsetting of the climatic systems violates the right to a healthy and sustainable environment. To date there has been only one case from the regional system where the right to a healthy environment was found to have been violated, the *SERAC* case.[57] In this case, the Commission elaborated on the content of the right to a healthy environment, formulated in the Charter article 24 as a right to a general satisfactory environment favourable to development. The Commission developed both the substantive and procedural aspects of the right to a healthy environment, including substantive obligations on states to 'desist from directly threatening the health and environment of their citizens', 'to take reasonable measures to prevent pollution and ecological degradation, to promote conservation, and to secure an ecologically sustainable development and use of natural resources'.[58] Procedurally, the decision obligates states to require and publish environmental and social impact assessments, provide 'information to those communities exposed to hazardous materials and activities' and provide

[57] Communication 155/96: *Social and Economic Rights Action Center (SERAC) and Center for Economic and Social Rights (CESR) v Nigeria.*

[58] Communication 155/96 (n 57), para. 52.

'meaningful opportunities for individuals to be heard and to participate in the development decisions affecting their communities'.[59]

In my opinion, these substantive environmental rights have their limitations in the context of climate change. This is because African states have little control over the causes of climate change, and therefore would likely not be able to address climate concerns by desisting from certain action, and cannot without significant mitigation action from developed states secure ecologically sustainable development for their citizens. Nevertheless, all states have obligations to protect their citizens against the impacts of climate change, and thus African states could be held accountable for lack of action in taking concrete and substantive adaptive measures, such as building of sea walls. Furthermore, procedural environmental rights may have more potential in terms of placing obligations on states to regulate corporate activities on the continent that may cause climate change, for example, through the requirement to undertake environmental and social (which increasingly is understood to include climate change) impact assessments before new projects – particularly for fossil fuel extraction – are started.[60]

Despite the extensive development of environmental rights in *SERAC*, the remedies granted by the Commission in this case are limited. It provides for a right to participate in, and benefit from, the development, and provides for safeguards to monitor and (to the extent possible) clean up environmental degradation. One of the key shortcomings is the extent to which the right to participate in decision making is recognized, in that the Commission 'does not challenge the government's right to exploit the oil resources in Ogoniland, irrespective of the wish of the affected people'.[61] While also being critical of the weak implementation measures and recommendations ordered by the Commission to back up these rights, Bouwer nevertheless notes that 'one could argue that such cases lay the jurisprudential groundwork for more focused, human rights-based climate litigation targeting fossil fuel production in African states'.[62]

In terms of collective rights protection, one group that is particularly at risk of the impacts of climate change, is indigenous peoples/communities, because of their reliance on the land for their subsistence as well as cultural

59 Communication 155/96 (n 57), para. 53.

60 This view is supported also by the fact that the lack of climate or environmental impact assessments have been at the core of some of the successful national level climate litigation on the continent.

61 Elsabé Boshoff, 'Rethinking the Premises Underlying the Right to Development in African Human Rights Jurisprudence' (2022) 31 *Review of European, Comparative & International Environmental Law* 27, 32.

62 Kim Bouwer, 'The Influence of Human Rights on Climate Litigation in Africa' (2022) 13 *Journal of Human Rights and the Environment* 157, 169.

and spiritual connections. Two of the most important decisions on the rights of indigenous people in Africa are the Commission case in *Endorois* and the more recent *Ogiek* decision from the Court.[63] The cases are similar in many respects, namely both concerned indigenous groups with grievances over government decisions regarding development of the land on which they had lived for centuries, without appropriately consulting them and without them receiving sufficient benefit from the development projects. The Commission and the Court respectively, in finding a violation of the right to development, relied heavily on the procedural right to participate and be consulted, thereby building on the groundwork established in the *SERAC* case. This is very important also in the context of development projects that rely on fossil fuel extraction, for example coal mining, because of the strong connection between indigenous peoples and the land they live on, and the serious impacts of climate change on their way of life. Because of this strong link, 'both the Court and the Commission decisions, while not directly engaging the environmental degradation concerns, imply in their decisions that compliance with the duty by the State to consult and allow effective participation would prevent the negative social and environmental implications which result from violations of the right to development', and further that 'at least in cases related to indigenous communities, that fulfilling the elements of the right to development would result in sustainable development'.[64]

The *SERAC* case further demonstrates that states may be held liable under the African human rights system for the actions of non-state actors, in this case oil companies. This was further developed in the jurisprudence of the Commission and quoted favourably by the Committee, that 'a State Party is responsible for violation of human rights committed by non-state actors as its obligation to ensure the respect for human rights demand it to take all the necessary measures to ensure that non-state actors also respect the rights of children'.[65] As noted before, most climate change-inducing activities are undertaken by non-state actors, particularly corporations, making this a crucial obligation.

The *SERAC* case is very important for a further reason, and that is in its elaboration and extension of socio-economic rights. As noted above, climate change on the African continent directly impacts on peoples' livelihoods

---

63 See nn 10 and 11.

64 See further Elsabé Boshoff, 'Protecting the African Child in a Changing Climate: Are Our Existing Safeguards Adequate?' (2017) 1 *African Human Rights Yearbook* 23, 33.

65 See for example African Commission Communication *Mouvement Burkinabe des Droits de l'Homme et des Peuples v Burkina Faso*, as quoted in African Children's Rights Committee Decision No. 003/2012 *The Centre for Human Rights (University of Pretoria) and La Rencontre Africaine pour la Defense des Droits de l'Homme (Senegal) v Government of Senegal*, decided 15 April 2014 (*Talibes* case), para. 37.

and ability to survive. The Commission in the *SERAC* case recognized two implied rights in the African Charter, namely the right to food and to shelter.[66] State responsibility to respect, protect, promote and fulfill all rights thus also extend to these two rights which are crucial in the context of climate impacts, such as drought, floods and displacement. In climate litigation before African human rights bodies, claimants could therefore argue that the lack of state action to protect them against the impacts of climate change violated their right to food and shelter. For example if drought, floods or other extreme weather events destroy their crops or houses, and the state failed to take the necessary measures to build sea walls or put in place social protection measures to assist subsistence farmers in times of hardship, this could be a cause for climate litigation.

A further relevant avenue for litigating climate-related human rights violations, as already alluded to, is through children's rights. The African Children's Charter provides strong protections to many children's rights, which are of relevance in climate cases. While no such cases have been brought before the Committee, an example from the European Court of Human Rights on the impact of climate change on the rights of children is illustrative. Arguments were made around children's right to life, right to respect for their private and family lives and right not to be discriminated against, and the Court also raised as pertinent the right not to be subjected to inhuman or degrading treatment, all of which are also rights protected in the African Children's Charter. The best interest of the child, as discussed above, is also core to many of the findings of the Committee, as it 'aims at safeguarding the realization of children's rights effectively and contributing to their holistic development',[67] and it 'implies that all policies and distribution of resources must "be used in a progressive way" to fulfill the best interest of the child "to the maximum extent possible"'.[68] The Committee in the *SOS-Esclaves* case[69] further held that 'considering the multi-sectoral nature of children's rights' states should 'put in place a child rights governance system that ensures the visibility, advancement and realization of all children's rights across the full implementation processes of all role players', and should ensure child-sensitive budgeting.[70] Given the negative consequences of climate change for child rights, the principle of best interest of the child

66 *SERAC* case, paras 60, 65 and 66.

67 African Children's Rights Committee, *Talibes* case, para. 34.

68 M Mauras 'Public Policies and Child Rights: Entering the Third Decade of the Convention on the Rights of the Child' (2011) 633 Annals 53.

69 *Minority Rights Group International and SOS-Esclaves on behalf of Said Ould Salem and Yarg Ould Salem v The Republic of Mauritania* (ACERWC) 2015.

70 *SOS-Esclaves*, para. 50.

therefore requires that states take all measures, ensure cooperation among all stakeholders and use all available resources to ensure that children are protected against the impacts of climate change.[71]

In also recognizing the close link between the environment and socio-economic rights, the Committee in the *Talibés* case found that the right to survival and development in the African Children's Charter places an obligation on states to ensure that children are able to access clean water, and 'the right to live in safe and clean environment'.[72] Furthermore, in the *Nubian Descent* case, the Committee held that because 'a year in the life of a child is almost six percent of his or her childhood [...] the implementation and realization of children's rights in Africa is not a matter to be relegated for tomorrow, but an issue that is in need of proactive immediate attention and action'.[73] This is of particular relevance to the climate context, especially if we also take account of the temporal disjuncture in climate impacts which continue to manifest long after the emissions were released, and which will therefore also continue to have impacts on future generations of children – thereby connecting child rights in this context with the principle of intergenerational justice. This is also in line with the best interest of the child principle, with General Comment 5 on the African Children's Charter providing that:

> The child's best interests include short term, medium term and long term best interests. For this reason, State actions which imperil the enjoyment of the rights of future generations of children (e.g. allowing environmental degradation to take place, or inappropriate exploitation of natural resources) are regarded as violating the best interests of the child standard.[74]

Non-jurisprudential engagements with climate change

While no individual cases directly concerned with climate change have been brought for adjudication before the African human rights system,

---

71 Boshoff (n 64), 31.

72 Communication 001/2012 *Centre for Human Rights (University of Pretoria) and La Rencontre Africaine pour la Défense des Droits de l'Homme (RADDHO) (on behalf of the Talibes) v Senegal*, Decision No. 003/Com/001/2012, para. 42.

73 *Nubian Descent* case, para. 33.

74 ACERWC, 'General Comment 5 on article 1 of the African Children's Charter on "State Party Obligations under the African Charter on the Rights and Welfare of the Child (Article 1) and systems strengthening for child protection"' (2018) https://www.acerwc.africa/wp-content/uploads/2019/09/ACERWC%20General%20Comment%20on%20General%20Measures%20of%20Implementation%20African%20Children's%20Charter.pdf, 4.2.

regional human rights bodies have through other mechanisms at their disposal made statements on the links between climate change and human rights. The Court's mandate to engage outside judicial pronouncements is its most limited of the three bodies, since its mandate is to complement the protection mandate of the Commission. Nevertheless, in recent years, the Court has on occasion noted the importance of the climate rights nexus. For example, in October 2019, the Court, together with the European Court of Human Rights and the Inter-American Court of Human Rights, issued the Kampala Declaration at the First International Human Rights Forum. In this Declaration, the Courts agreed to 'undertake knowledge-sharing through digital platforms, on topical human rights issues, including on [...] environmental hazards, climate change [...] and on the working methods of the three courts'.[75] This opened the door for knowledge exchange and mutual learning within and between the regional systems. It also makes it likely that when climate cases are to come before the Court, they will draw on the precedents that are being set by these other regional courts in ongoing cases. The Court also convened the Fourth African Judicial Dialogue in November 2019, which brought together judges from across the continent. In the Final Communique of the Judicial Dialogue, participants identified what they consider to be 'contemporary human rights issues' and the role of the judiciary in relation to them.[76] Statelessness is identified as one of these issues. Climate change is considered to be one of the main drivers of statelessness, and judiciaries are urged 'to avoid decisions that leave persons in a situation of statelessness'.[77]

The Commission and Committee have much broader mandates, with the Commission tasked to ensure protection and promotion of human rights on the continent. As part of this mandate, the Commission has adopted several resolutions over the years, recognizing the challenges that climate change poses to human rights, and with the first resolution calling on the Commission to undertake a study on the human rights impacts of climate change dating back to 2009.[78] In this and subsequent resolutions, the Working Group on Economic, Social and Cultural Rights and the Working Group

---

75 African Court on Human and Peoples' Rights, 'Kampala Declaration', https://www.african-court.org/wpafc/kampala-declaration/.

76 African Court on Human and Peoples' Rights, Final Communique – Fourth African Judicial Dialogue', https://www.african-court.org/wpafc/final-communique-fourth-african-judicial-dialogue/, para. 1.

77 African Court on Human and Peoples' Rights, 'Final Communique – Fourth African Judicial Dialogue', https://www.african-court.org/wpafc/final-communique-fourth-african-judicial-dialogue/.

78 See, for example, 153 Resolution on Climate Change and Human Rights and the Need to Study its Impact in Africa – ACHPR/Res.153(XLVI)09; 271 Resolution on Climate

on Extractive Industries, Environment and Human Rights were jointly tasked to undertake the Study on Climate Change and Human Rights, an internal draft of which had been prepared at the time of writing. In an unprecedented step, the Commission and the Committee issued a joint Statement on the occasion of the 33rd Assembly of the Heads of State and Government of the African Union, calling on the AU to 'declare 2021 a year for collective action for addressing the threat of climate crisis in Africa to human and peoples' rights'.[79]

The Commission's Working Group on Indigenous Populations/ Communities has also frequently made reference to the impacts of climate change on the rights of indigenous people, the role that traditional knowledge and practices can play in mitigating climate change, as well as the need for indigenous people to be actively involved in decision making on climate change mitigation, adaptation and disaster risk reduction.[80] Other special mechanisms, including the Working Group on the Rights of Older Persons and Persons with Disabilities in Africa,[81] the Special Rapporteur on Refugees, Asylum Seekers, Internally Displaced Persons and Migrants in Africa[82] and the Special Rapporteur on the Rights of Women in Africa[83] have also made mention of the challenges of climate change to these specific groups.

For its part, the Committee went a step further in 2020, through establishing a Working Group on Children's Rights and Climate Change, with the first

Change in Africa – ACHPR/Res.271(LV)2014; 342 Resolution on Climate Change and Human Rights in Africa – ACHPR/Res.342(LVIII)2016; 417 Resolution on the human rights impacts of extreme weather in Eastern and Southern Africa due to climate change – ACHPR/Res. 417(LXIV)2019; 491 Resolution on Climate Change and Forced Displacement in Africa – ACHPR/Res. 491(LXIX)2021.

79 ACHPR, 'Press Statement on the occasion of the 33rd Assembly of the Heads of State and Government of the African Union', https://www.achpr.org/pressrelease/detail?id=476.

80 See for example ACHPR, 'Yaoundé Declaration on the Implementation in Africa of the Outcome Document of the World Conference on Indigenous Peoples', 2015, https://www.achpr.org/news/viewdetail?id=85; 'Final Communiqué on the National Dialogue on the Rights of Indigenous Peoples and Extractive Industries, 27–28 November 2018, Kampala, Uganda', https://www.achpr.org/news/viewdetail?id=5; 'National Dialogue on the Rights of Indigenous Peoples and Extractive Industries, from 7 to 8 October 2019, Nairobi, Kenya', https://www.achpr.org/news/viewdetail?id=203.

81 ACHPR, 'Statement of the Working Group on the Rights of Older Persons and Persons with Disabilities in Africa of the African Commission on Human and Peoples' Rights, on the occasion of the International Day of Persons with Disabilities – 3rd December 2016', https://www.achpr.org/pressrelease/detail?id=106.

82 ACHPR, 'Statement by the Special Rapporteur on Refugees, Asylum Seekers, Internally Displaced Persons and Migrants in Africa on the occasion of International Migrants Day', https://www.achpr.org/pressrelease/detail?id=66.

83 ACHPR, 'Statement by the Special Rapporteur on the Rights of Women in Africa on the Occasion of the International Women's Rights Day 2022', https://www.achpr.org/pressrelease/detail?id=624.

members appointed in 2021. The Resolution establishing the Working Group 'makes a direct link between the impact of climate change and various rights enshrined in the African Children's Charter, including its impact on the rights to survival and development, health and welfare, education, protection from harmful practices, non-discrimination and protection from violence' and indicates that 'this is not an exhaustive list of rights affected, merely an illustrative list indicating the rights that are most at stake'.[84] The 2018 Study of the Committee on Children on the Move also highlighted some of the child rights impacts from climate change for displaced children and the Committee is also in the process of drafting a Continental Study on the Impact of Climate Change on the Rights of Children in Africa.[85]

It is proposed that these normative pronouncements and actions by the human rights bodies engage with, and draw attention to, the serious nature of climate change-induced human rights violations. These offer an important indication that they do take climate change threats seriously, and that cases brought before them that allude to climate would be treated as matters of concern. The next section looks at the procedural component of the regional human rights institutions, to determine how admissibility and standing before these bodies might impact climate litigation.

Jurisdiction and admissibility before African human rights bodies

The jurisdiction of courts and judicial bodies is circumscribed in terms of its material, temporal, personal and territorial scope. Climate cases may be challenging because it is not always easy to show that they fall within the jurisdiction of courts, and cases were, especially in the early days of climate litigation, thrown out based on questions of jurisdiction.[86] The Court, pursuant to rule 49 of its 2020 Rules of Court,[87] must ascertain its jurisdiction, before consideration of the case on admissibility and merits. The Commission and Committee do not have such a separate requirement for consideration of jurisdiction, and questions of scope have been dealt with under the admissibility stage. Thus, before cases are considered on the

[84] ACERWC, 'Resolution on the Establishment of Working Group on Children's Rights and Climate Change' (2020); Boshoff and Damtwe (n 55).

[85] African Committee of Experts on the Rights and Welfare of the Child, 'Mapping Children on the Move Within Africa' (2018), 53.

[86] United Nations Environment Programme, Columbia University and Sabin Center for Climate Change Law, 'The Status of Climate Change Litigation: A Global Review', 2017, https://wedocs.unep.org/handle/20.500.11822/20767, 28–9.

[87] ACtHPR, 'Rules of Court', revised rules adopted on 1 September 2020, https://www.african-court.org/wpafc/wp-content/uploads/2021/04/Rules-Final-Revised-adopted-Rules-eng-April-2021.pdf.

merits, the admissibility stage is used to 'ensure that the supranational body in question is the appropriate venue in which for the case to be heard'.[88] The Charter sets out the admissibility criteria for communications (cases) brought before the Commission by applicants other than states in article 56.[89] Following their establishment, the same admissibility criteria apply also to cases brought before the Court and the Committee.[90] This section discusses the different aspects of jurisdiction and also the other admissibility criteria and how this supports or limits the potential for climate litigation.

Material jurisdiction

In terms of material scope, the Court, pursuant to article 3 of the Protocol to the African Charter on Human and Peoples' Rights on the Establishment of an African Court on Human and Peoples' Rights,[91] has jurisdiction to deal with all cases relating to the Charter, the Protocol 'and any other relevant human rights instrument ratified by the States concerned'. This gives it the widest material jurisdiction of the three bodies, since the material scope of the Commission is limited to the Charter and its various Protocols,[92] and the Committee only has jurisdiction over cases concerning the African Children's Charter. As alluded to in the introduction to this chapter, climate change impacts on most, if not all, human rights, and the fact that jurisdiction is limited to these instruments is thus not in itself a significant limitation to bringing climate cases before these bodies. Furthermore, pursuant to articles 60 and 61 of the Charter, the Commission in interpreting the Charter 'shall draw inspiration from international law on human and peoples' rights' and as a subsidiary means of determining the law shall draw on state practice, custom and 'other general or special international conventions'. This means that, in interpreting state obligations under the Charter, the Commission would be able, and is in fact obliged, to also take account of obligations under, for

88 International Federation for Human Rights, *Admissibility of Complaints Before the African Court: Practical Guide* (IFHR 2016) 8.

89 Cases brought by states against other states are very rare in the African human rights system, and the discussion here is thus limited to those considered to be 'individual" communications/cases.

90 African Union, *Protocol to the African Charter on Human And Peoples' Rights on the Establishment of an African Court on Human and Peoples' Rights, entered into force in 2004* (1998), art. 6; African Committee of Experts on the Rights and Welfare of the Child, *Guidelines for the Consideration of Communications.*

91 African Union (n 90).

92 This jurisdictional matter is dealt with by the African Commission under the admissibility requirement that cases brought before it must be compatible with the AU Charter and African Charter, African Charter, art. 56(2).

example, the Paris Agreement to which all African states are signatories.[93] Additionally, the Commission has 'read in' rights not explicit provided for in the Charter as implied rights,[94] which means that the Charter is a living and flexible instrument, and thus the limited material scope of the Commission is therefore to a large extent mitigated.

Territorial jurisdiction

Issues of territorial jurisdiction arise in relation to potential respondents. As with other treaty bodies, African regional human rights bodies have jurisdiction only over those states that have ratified their respective instruments. Of the 55 African states recognized by the AU, 54 (all with the exception of Morocco) have ratified the Charter, 49 the Children's Charter and only 30 the Court Protocol. In addition, the state parties of these instruments comprise only African states, and developed nations can thus not be held accountable under this system. This is particularly a shortcoming when regarded from the perspective of climate litigation, since climate change is a transboundary challenge, and the main culprits in GHG emissions causing climate change can thus not be held accountable through litigation under the regional human rights system in Africa.

Furthermore, only states are signatories to the treaties, so it could be argued that litigation brought against non-state actors would not succeed before African human rights bodies, despite the impact of many multinational corporations on climate change. Nevertheless, there is a strong counter-argument that corporations can and should be held accountable under this system, including on the basis of the link made by the Commission between duties of individuals and duties on corporations under the Charter, even if the mechanisms for such accountability are not yet fully in place.[95] The challenge in this regard remains that the Commission does not yet have any jurisprudence or extensive elaboration on individual duties and currently only states are being held to account under the Charter. Nevertheless, the *obiter dictum* of the Commission in the *Kilwa* case that a corporation had contributed to the human rights violations, even if no finding of human rights violation by the corporation was made, opens the door to further

[93] See n 1.

[94] Communication 155/96: *Social and Economic Rights Action Center (SERAC) and Center for Economic and Social Rights (CESR) v Nigeria*, discussed above.

[95] Consider for example the obligations of corporations elaborated by the African Commission in African Commission on Human and Peoples' Rights, *State Reporting Guidelines and Principles on Articles 21 and 24 of the African Charter Relating to Extractive Industries, Human Rights and the Environment*; see also the ongoing efforts at UN level towards a binding instrument on business and human rights.

strategic litigation on this issue. Additionally, as noted above, states can, and have, been held accountable for the violations committed by non-state actors, and regional litigation against states in cases where corporations are the main culprits may incentivize stronger regulation at the national level.

Furthermore, it has been argued that the lack of a specific jurisdiction clause in the Charter 'may provide a legal foundation for the extraterritorial extension of the rights of the latter instrument', where signatory states would have obligations towards persons not within their territory.[96] While this is as yet untested and may have far-reaching consequences, it is not clear to whom African states would owe such obligations in the particular context of climate litigation, given the low level of their contribution to overall climate change impacts.[97] Nevertheless, what may also be a possibility is that, while there have to date been very few inter-state communications before the Commission, the inequality between African states in how much they contribute to climate change could also give rise to interstate litigation before African regional bodies on climate change impacts.[98]

Personal jurisdiction

Who has standing in climate cases is a question that has often led to cases in other jurisdictions being dismissed.[99] Contrary to many jurisdictions that have several requirements for standing, standing before the Commission and the Committee is very broad. All persons (natural and juridical) have standing before the Commission as well as the Committee, as long as they can assert a prima facie violation of a right protected in the relevant instruments identified above.[100] Both bodies also allow public interest litigation, where cases are brought on someone else's behalf or in the interest of a group. The far-reaching implications of such broad standing was demonstrated

96 Daniel M Pallangyo and Werner Scholtz, *Africa and Climate Change: Legal Perspectives from the AU* (Edward Elgar Publishing 2015) 61.

97 This would be an area for further elaboration and research.

98 For example, South Africa in 2017 accounted for about 1.3 per cent of global CO^2 emissions, whereas Kenya accounted for 0.05 per cent and Liberia for only 0.003 per cent, Hannah Ritchie and Max Roser, 'CO_2 and Greenhouse Gas Emissions' (2020) OurWorldInData.org accessed 20 April 2021.

99 See, for example, the 2020 Ninth Circuit Court of Appeals decision in *Juliana v United States* No. 18-36082 (9th Cir. 2020), which found lack of standing due to it being unlikely that 'the relief sought be substantially likely to redress the plaintiffs' injuries' http://climatecasechart.com/climate-change-litigation/case/juliana-v-united-states/.

100 One case before the African Commission was dismissed on the basis that the applicant was a judicial person which had been dissolved in the respondent state before they brought the case: see Communication 670/17 *Fadhl Al Mawla Husni Ahmed Ismail (represented by Freedom and Justice Party of Egypt) v Arab Republic of Egypt*, decided 10 September 2020.

in a communication before the Committee, in which a case was brought on behalf of all school girls in Tanzania, even though they could not be individually identified.[101]

This would be relevant also in the context of climate litigation, where the affected persons are often not specific individuals, but rather groups within the population negatively affected by specific climate-related consequences. Because of the serious repercussions for children from the impacts of climate change and the broad standing before the Committee, the Committee is an attractive avenue for submitting cases on climate at the African regional level.[102] Furthermore, the wide standing before these bodies opens up possibilities where national level laws do not provide for *actio popularis*, and cases can thus be brought at national level only by 'individuals who have been directly affected by a violation and any decision will provide remedy only for those litigants, or for those who are directly connected to the case or have "*un interest et qualite pour agir*"'.[103] The broad standing provided at regional level is thus really useful for cases like climate that may be met with technical challenges in national level.

Standing before the Court is much more restrictive. Consequently, only where a state has made a declaration under articles 5(3) and 34(6) of the Protocol may cases be brought directly to the Court by non-governmental organizations or individuals. At the time of writing, only seven African states had made the article 34(6) declaration.[104] In addition, states, African intergovernmental organizations or the Commission may submit cases to the Court. As noted before, interstate cases are very rare in the African human rights system, and exhaustion of domestic remedies requirements also apply in such cases.[105] Additionally, mainly due to capacity constraints and lack of a clear process for doing so, very few cases have been referred to the Court from the Commission. These limitations mean that only individuals from the few states that have made the article 34(6) declaration are likely to bring climate cases directly before the Court. Under rule 84 of its 2010 Rules of Procedure of the African Commission on Human and Peoples'

[101] ACERWC *Legal and Human Rights Center and Center for Reproductive Rights (on behalf of Tanzanian girls) v United Republic of Tanzania* (2020), para. 1.

[102] For a comprehensive discussion of this, see Boshoff and Damtew (n 55).

[103] *Talibes* case, para. 5.

[104] Burkina Faso, Malawi, Mali, Tanzania, Ghana, Cote d'Ivoire and Benin. Tanzania, Benin and Cote d'Ivoire have since moved to withdraw the declaration again. See International Commission of Jurists, 'Withdrawal of States from African Court a blow to access to justice in the region', 1 May 2020, https://www.icj.org/withdrawal-of-states-from-african-court-a-blow-to-access-to-justice-in-the-region/, accessed 12 March 2022.

[105] African Union, *African Charter on Human and Peoples' Rights*, art. 50.

Rights,[106] the Commission had the ability to refer cases to the Court *inter alia* where they relate to a 'situation of serious or massive violation of human rights', which would certainly include climate change. However, with the adoption of the Rules of Procedure of the African Commission on Human and Peoples' Rights of 2020,[107] this reference has been removed, and no specific guidance is provided under the new rule 130 of when there should be referral of cases from the Commission to the Court. This further limits the likelihood of non-governmental organizations indirectly accessing the Court through the Commission, thus at least for the present making the Court an unlikely forum for the hearing of climate cases.

Temporal jurisdiction

Temporal jurisdiction comprises two aspects, first, that the relevant 'treaty cannot be applied retrospectively to situations and circumstances that occurred before its entry into force', or before a state has ratified it.[108] This is a general principle of international law. Second, under the admissibility requirements in article 56 of the Charter, cases must be 'submitted within a reasonable period from the time local remedies are exhausted'. Temporal scope is a challenge in relation to climate litigation, because of the delayed effect between the actions causing climate change, and the repercussions being felt in the form of human rights violations. While some judicial bodies, such as the European Court of Human Rights, have applied a strict requirement of submission within 'four months from the date on which the final decision was taken',[109] African human rights bodies have been more flexible in determining what constitutes a reasonable period, taking account of the specific circumstances of the case. Additionally, the Court has held that where human rights violations started before ratification, but are continuing, these do fall within the temporal scope of the Court.[110] Since

---

[106] ACHPR, '2010 Rules of Procedure of the African Commission on Human and Peoples' Rights', adopted during its 47th Ordinary Session held in Banjul (The Gambia), 12–26 May 2010. These rules have since been replaced with a revised document adopted in 2020.

[107] ACHPR, 'Rules of Procedure of the African Commission on Human and Peoples' Rights of 2020', adopted during its 27th Extra-Ordinary session held in Banjul, The Gambia 19 February–4 March 2020, https://www.achpr.org/public/Document/file/English/Rules%20of%20Procedure%202020_ENG.pdf.

[108] Application No. 006/2012 *African Commission on Human and Peoples' Rights v Republic of Kenya* (*Ogiek* case) (African Court on Human and Peoples' Rights), para. 62.

[109] Article 35 § 1 of the Council of Europe, European Convention for the Protection of Human Rights and Fundamental Freedoms, as amended by Protocols Nos 11 and 14, 4 November 1950, entered into force on 3 September 1953.

[110] Application No. 006/2012 *African Commission on Human and Peoples' Rights v Republic of Kenya* (*Ogiek* case), para. 65.

climate violations would mostly be ongoing, there would most likely not be a danger that communications or cases are submitted out of time. Temporal jurisdiction is also related to the exhaustion of domestic remedies, in that the reasonable time period starts *either* at the time domestic remedies are exhausted, *or* at the time when it becomes clear that domestic remedies will not be exhausted. This is discussed below.

Exhaustion of domestic remedies

According to article 56 of the Charter, communications will be considered if they comply with seven criteria. In addition to the aspects already considered above, other criteria include that it must not be written in disparaging language, not be exclusively based on news media, not have been dealt with before another international body, and must be submitted after exhaustion of local remedies. Most of these are quite straightforward formal requirements and will not be discussed here. The criterion on which most cases are dismissed, however, is the requirement that communications must be submitted after exhaustion of 'local remedies, if any, unless it is obvious that this procedure is unduly prolonged'.[111] The lack of exhaustion of domestic remedies is also the ground on which the first climate case before the UN Children's Rights Committee, *Sacchi v Argentina*,[112] was dismissed. The reason for this criterion is to allow states the opportunity to redress the violation at the national level, thereby enabling the state to 'save its reputation, which would be inevitably tarnished if it were brought before an international jurisdiction'.[113]

To date only a handful of cases have been brought before national courts in Africa regarding the negative consequences of climate change on human rights. Some of them have been successful at the national level and there is no need for further litigation at the regional level. The regional human rights system is therefore complementary to existing national level systems, and only where no remedy is obtained at that level are cases considered at the regional level. However, as noted above, local remedies may be dispensed with, where 'it is obvious that this procedure is unduly prolonged'. The *Mbabazi* case in Uganda is one case that comes to mind, as it has been pending before the national courts since it was filed in 2012.[114] In determining

---

[111] African Union, *African Charter on Human and Peoples' Rights*, art. 56(5).

[112] African Union (n 111).

[113] See ACHPR, Communication 54/91-61/91-96/93-98/93-164/97_196/97-210/98 *Malawi Africa Association, Amnesty International, Ms Sarr Diop, Union interafricaine des droits de l'Homme and RADDHO, Collectif des veuves et ayants Droit, Association mauritanienne des droits de l'Homme v Mauritania*, 11 May 2000, para. 80.

[114] For updates see https://www.ourchildrenstrust.org/uganda.

whether the procedure has become unduly prolonged, the Court has held in its jurisprudence that there must be no justifiable explanation for the delay or the delay must be excessive.[115] In one case before the Commission, a case that had been pending before the Supreme Court for five years was considered to be unduly prolonged.[116] In the case of the Tanzanian school girls discussed above, the Committee found that the case had been unduly prolonged because the 'domestic remedy has taken over 7 years in total and the appeal has taken 2 years without the Court fixing a date for a hearing of the case'.[117] Based on the specific facts and justifications, the *Mbabazi* case could thus arguably be submitted before the regional system. Other exceptions to the exhaustion of domestic remedies requirement exist where domestic remedies are unavailable, ineffective or insufficient.[118]

A further very important exception that has developed in the jurisprudence of the African Commission and has also been applied by the Committee, is in cases of massive or large-scale violations of rights that would '*ipso facto* make local remedies unavailable, ineffective and insufficient'.[119] Following a similar reasoning, the Commission found that where several states are involved, applicants would not have to pursue domestic remedies in all states since it would be impractical and 'would involve seizing the domestic courts in respect of each violation and/or victim, which would in effect unduly prolong the process of exhausting local remedies in such cases'.[120]

This part considered the formal requirements for bringing cases before African human rights bodies, namely the jurisdiction and admissibility criteria before the different bodies. Some of the main barriers that could be an impediment to climate litigation at the regional level, but that can be overcome through justification and reasoning, include the exhaustion of the domestic remedies requirement, the territorial scope and the material scope of the jurisdiction of these bodies. As is clear from the above, cases that relate to large-scale climate impacts, in particular where violations implicate several states, would make it unreasonable to expect the exhaustion of

---

115 ACtHPR App. No. 006/2013 *Wilfred Onyango Nganyi v United Republic of Tanzania*, 18 March 2016, para. 91.

116 ACHPR, Communication 272/03: *Association of Victims of Post Electoral Violence & INTERIGHTS v Cameroon*, 25 November 2009, para. 67.

117 ACERWC, *Legal and Human Rights Center and Center for Reproductive Rights (on Behalf of Tanzanian Girls) v United Republic of Tanzania* (2020), paras 19 and 21.

118 ACHPR, Communication 386/10: *Dr Farouk Mohamed Ibrahim (represented by REDRESS) v Sudan*, 18 October 2013, para. 71.

119 ACHPR, *Sudan Human Rights Organisation & Centre on Housing Rights and Evictions (COHRE) v Sudan*, para. 100.

120 ACHPR, Communication 409/12: *Luke Munyandu Tembani and Benjamin John Freeth (Represented by Norman Tjombe) v Angola*, 30 April 2014, para. 103.

domestic remedies and could be brought before the regional system directly. Cases that have suffered from an undue prolongation at the national level could also be brought before regional level bodies. On the material scope, it would be up to litigants to show how the lack of climate action by states have directly resulted in human rights violations. In this regard it may be easier to hold African states accountable for lack of adaptation measures than for lack of climate mitigation. This is because it would be harder to prove causation between their comparatively small GHG contributions and the consequences suffered by their citizens, but a clear case could be made for the need for African states to take adaptive steps to protect those within their borders against the adverse impacts of climate change. The limited territorial scope of the African Charter and the African Children's Charter would impact on the kinds of remedies that can be expected from climate litigation in Africa, as remedies related to GHG emission reductions, which are usual in litigation in developed states, would likely take a back seat to remedies associated with adaptation and increasing resilience to climate impacts. The personal scope will likely not present challenges in litigation before the Commission or Committee, but may be more challenging in relation to the Court.

Conclusion

The African regional human rights system not only provides a robust system of substantive rights protection, but also provides flexible procedural requirements with broad standing to bring collective and public interest cases, and provides room for justification for lack of strict compliance with admissibility criteria. The African system has also developed unique norms that extend the protections of the human rights of specifically vulnerable groups, including indigenous people, refugees and children, as some of the groups most vulnerable to the impacts of climate change. Regional human rights bodies have also considered the human rights instruments that they have the mandate to interpret as living instruments to which they have given purposive interpretation in ensuring that victims of human rights violations are not denied justice on the basis of too narrow or restrictive interpretations.

Specifically important in terms of potential climate litigation is the strong protection of socio-economic rights, the substantive and procedural aspects of the right to environment and the strong interrelated nature of the various rights of children, with the best interest of the child as a principle underlying all decisions related to children. Beyond judicial decisions, African human rights bodies have through other normative declarations also made it clear that they consider climate change to be a factor that can seriously undermine the realization of human rights on the continent. Therefore litigants before the Court, Commission and Committee will be assured of their cases receiving due attention.

Some of the main limitations of the system include the procedural limitations and barriers in bringing cases directly before the Court, the fact that African states are in most cases not directly responsible for climate change, and can therefore only be held accountable as breaching their duty in that regard. They do, however, retain responsibility related to the actions of non-state actors and in not taking sufficient action in terms of adapting to climate change impacts, such as rising sea levels. Nevertheless, this limits the kinds of remedies that can be ordered against African states and also the potential for satisfaction, if the real perpetrators of the violations ultimately cannot be held accountable before these bodies. Finally, as with other human rights systems, the African human rights system lacks strong enforcement mechanisms and, even where remedies are ordered, there is no guarantee that the respondent states will take the necessary steps to implement them.

In weighing up these considerations, it is likely that certain types of cases would greatly benefit from being heard before these regional bodies, whereas in terms of others there may be less success. Cases that would potentially benefit from a decision from these bodies would include cases regarding lack of effort on the part of African states collectively to take steps to adapt to climate change impacts, or where states fail in their duty to protect their people against the actions of non-state actors, and that consequently has serious human rights repercussions for some of the most vulnerable groups. Some of the remedies that could be asked for in such a case could include orders for legislative reform, for implementation of existing laws and policies, for participation and consultation, as well as for concrete steps, such as the building of sea walls or putting in place social security nets.

7

Climate Change Displacement Litigation in Africa: A Human Rights and Refugee Law-Based Approach

Judge John Mativo

Introduction

In recognition of the urgent need for global action to tackle the challenges posed by climate change, in 1992 the global community adopted the United Nations Framework Convention on Climate Change.[1] Subsequently some parties adopted the Kyoto Protocol,[2] and in 2015 the Paris Agreement was adopted.[3] The Paris Agreement consolidates the international legal framework for tackling climate change. It imposes a range of commitments requiring state actors to put in place measures with the objective of averting average global warming in excess of 1.5°C and 2°C. Such measures typically take the form of legislative instruments.

At municipal level, there are laws and policies in almost every country that address climate change either directly or by implication. Governments are the key actors in implementing obligations created by such laws to address

1 United Nations Framework Convention on Climate Change.(adopted January 20, 1994, entered into force 21 March 1994): resolution 1771 UNTS 107 (UNFCCC).

2 Kyoto Protocol to the United Nations Framework Convention on Climate Change (adopted 11 December 1997, entered into force 16 February 2005) 37 ILM 22 (UNFCCC).

3 Paris Agreement to the United Nations Framework Convention on Climate Change (adopted 12 December 2015 and entered into force on 4 November 2016) N. Doc FCCC/CP/2015/I.9/Rev.1. UNFCCC(2015).

climate change. The advent of global climate protests has shone a spotlight on the inadequacy of government action and required lawyers to think about how else they can use the law to push for change. Litigants have begun to make use of these codified instruments in arguments before courts regarding the adequacy or inadequacy of efforts by governments to protect individual rights vis à vis climate change and its impacts.[4]

These international conventions have created more space to utilize climate change litigation in a quest to use the law to bring about real change.[5] The United Nations Framework Convention on Climate Change (UNFCCC) recognizes the need for states to focus on giving solutions to climate change-induced disasters while protecting the human rights of the affected communities. It encourages states to put in place climate policies that are formulated in a way that places utmost priority on the protection of the human rights of those most vulnerable. Being a global issue, it mandates all countries to put in place measures to protect the human rights of the most vulnerable communities, particularly in developing countries. The Human Rights Council notes that human rights obligations play a big role in the promotion of international and national policy making in the area of climate change.[6] The Paris Agreement has been a crucial tool in encouraging governments to adopt climate-oriented laws and implement them. This is the one international instrument that extensively deals with the problem of coordination of international action on greenhouse gas (GHG) emissions. It aids in the removal of gaps between current policy and the policy needed to achieve mitigation and adaptation objectives by providing constituents with a more effective platform for action.[7]

In addition to these climate treaties, the role of treaties dealing with disaster prevention and management in mitigating against climate-induced displacement and migration of communities cannot be understated. Climate change-induced displacement can lead to such persons becoming refugees

---

4 Paris Agreement, art. 2a. These efforts are documented each year by the LSE, see most recently Joana Setzer and Catherine Higham, *Global Trends in Climate Change Litigation: 2022 Snapshot* (Grantham Research Institute on Climate Change and the Environment and Centre for Climate Change Economics and Policy, London School of Economics and Political Science 2022). Many of the chapters in this collection engage with the potential of domestic law in the climate crisis.

5 I Alogna, 'Climate Change Litigation: Comparative and International Perspective' (2020), p. 4, https://www.biicl.org/documents/88_climate_change_litigation_comparative_and_international_report.pdf, accessed 9 June 2023.

6 Office of the High Commissioner for Human Rights, 'Understanding Human Rights and Climate Change', OCHCR, https://www.ohchr.org/Documents/Issues/ClimateChange/COP21.pdf, accessed 9 July 2020.

7 United Nations Environment Programme (2017), p. 5.

and requiring protection under the refugee treaties.[8] Accordingly, a strong case can be made that for persons adversely affected by climate change – for instance through climate change-induced displacement – the treaty provisions ought to give clear recognition to the dangers they face. This is necessary if they are to achieve climate justice under a convention or treaty.

Against this background, this chapter examines the prevailing international legal frameworks on climate change-induced displacement. Given the absence of adequate protections under the prevailing international refugee law for refugees and other persons displaced by climate change-induced natural disasters, the chapter examines the possible role that litigation, using human rights-based approaches, can play in extending protections to refugees and other persons who suffer displacement on account of climate change-induced disasters. The chapter concludes that for effective protections the Africa region needs to develop and extend the reach of international refugee law using human rights-based approaches in order to make effective climate change displacement strategic litigation.

Climate change and displacement

Climate change causes, and will continue to cause, people to move, to avoid its impacts. Since the 1970s scientific literature has mentioned environmentally-induced or climate-related migration. For example, the Intergovernmental Panel on Climate Change (IPCC) in its first assessment report (AR1) addresses the likely impacts of climate change on human settlement.[9] The UNFCCC considers the implications of climate change on human mobility. The UNFCCC has noted that the increased frequency of human migration can be directly linked to climate change and environmental phenomena such as environmental degradation and natural disasters. The displacement of approximately 17.2 million people worldwide in 2018 can be linked to natural disasters that were primarily related to climate change.[10] Rapid onset events including floods, droughts or other serious weather events, which can often be further exacerbated by climate change, has resulted in forced mass human migration. The number of displaced people may actually be much higher in terms of climate impacts that accumulate slowly (slow-onset events

8 'Explanatory Note – Internal Displacement', https://www.internal-displacement.org/sites/default/files/inline-files/200910-training-KC-Explanatory-Note-Eng.pdf, accessed 9 July 2022.

9 IPCC, First Assessment Report (FAR) (1990) https://www.ipcc.ch/site/assets/uploads/2018/03/ipcc_far_wg_II_full_report.pdf, accessed 6 February 2022.

10 Displacement, 'Bonn Climate Change Conference – Displacement, Human Mobility and Climate Change: UNFCCC and Beyond', *Disaster Displacement*, 24 June 2019, https://disasterdisplacement.org/sb50sideevent, accessed 6 February 2020.

or processes), such as rising sea-levels, desertification, ocean acidification, loss of biodiversity and so on, which force individuals to leave their homes over a period of time. Other secondary effects of climate change, such as human conflict or pressure on (sometimes already scarce) resources, also have a direct impact on increased human displacement.

Environment-induced migration is of increasing and serious concern to many governments across the globe, particularly those in the developing world. The World Bank estimates that by 2050 Latin America, Sub-Saharan Africa and Southeast Asia will produce approximately 143 million more climate migrants.[11] Northwest Africa for example is facing a confluence of climate challenges including sea-level rise, drought and desertification resulting in 'seasonal migrants' who place considerable strain on their countries of origin as well as destination countries, in which they may seek asylum. The present challenge is that there is no legal framework or multilateral treaty that takes into account climate change as a principal factor and driver of forced human migration across borders.

There have, however, been recent international developments that consider this phenomenon. In 2019, the United Nations Commissioner on Human Rights (UNHCR) and the United Nations International Organization on Migration (UN IOM) both recognized climate displaced persons. The Global Compact on Refugees (Refugee Compact),[12] for example, addresses refugee protection and the sharing of obligations whereas the Global Compact for Migration (Migration Compact)[13] details principles on safe, orderly and regular migration. The Migration Compact further encourages states to 'cooperate to identify, develop and strengthen solutions for migrants compelled to leave their countries due to slow-onset natural disasters, the adverse effects of climate change and environmental degradation'.[14] Among other things, governments are encouraged to provide humanitarian visas, private sponsorships as well as the adoption of other initiatives aimed at these individuals.

Though these developments are positive, there remains a lacuna in international refugee law in providing legal protections to climate-displaced migrants. A human rights based approach has therefore been posited as a means of enforcing climate responsibilities.

---

11 KK Rigaud *et al*, 'Groundswell', *Open Knowledge Repository*, 19 March 2018, 2, https://openknowledge.worldbank.org/handle/10986/29461, accessed 6 February 2020.

12 United Nations High Commissioner for Refugees, 'The Global Compact on Refugees', UNHCR, https://www.unhcr.org/the-global-compact-on-refugees.html, accessed 8 July 2020.

13 180711 Final Draft, 'Refugees and Migrants', https://refugeesmigrants.un.org/sites/default/files/180711_final_draft_0.pdf, accessed 8 July 2020.

14 180711 Final Draft (n 13), para. 21(h).

African regional legal frameworks on refugee and displacement

Refugee and internally displaced persons law of the Africa region is made up of the 1981 African Charter on Human and Peoples' Rights, which has near universal ratification, the Kampala Convention[15] and the Revised African Convention on the Conservation of Nature and Natural Resources.[16] The ACHPR also takes into account the 1969 OAU Convention Governing the Specific Aspects of Refugee Problems[17] (1969 OAU Convention).

African Charter on Human and People's Rights

The African Charter on Human and Peoples' Rights (the Banjul Charter) has influenced the drafting of state constitutions throughout the continent. African states provide for the relevant rights under their legislation, constitutions and the African Charter. The inclusion of environmental rights under the Banjul Charter[18] means that it is an ideal avenue for protection from climate change-related adverse impacts. The African Court of Human

---

[15] 'African Union Convention for the Protection and Assistance of Internally Displaced Persons in Africa (Kampala Convention)' (*African Union Convention for the Protection and Assistance of Internally Displaced Persons in Africa (Kampala Convention)/African Union*, 23 October 2009, https://au.int/en/treaties/african-union-convention-protection-and-assistance-internally-displaced-persons-africa, accessed 7 July 2022.

[16] 'African Convention on the Conservation of Nature and Natural Resources' (*African Convention on the Conservation of Nature and Natural Resources / African Union*, 15 September 1968, https://au.int/en/treaties/african-convention-conservation-nature-and-natural-resources, accessed 7 July 2022.

[17] 'OAU Convention Governing the Specific Aspects of Refugee Problems in Africa' (*OAU Convention Governing the Specific Aspects of Refugee Problems in Africa, African Union*, 10 September 1969, https://au.int/en/treaties/oau-convention-governing-specific-aspects-refugee-problems-africa, accessed 7 July 2022. The Organization of African Unity (OAU) was an intergovernmental organization established in 1963. Its key aims included encouraging political and economic integration in Africa, as well as the eradication of colonialism from the Continent. It was disbanded in 2002 and replaced with the African Union.

[18] Organization of African Unity, African Charter on Human and Peoples' Rights(Banjul Charter) (adopted 1 June 1981, entered into force 21 October 1986) CAB/LEG/67/3 rev. 5, 21 ILM 58 (OAU). 'Protocol to the Treaty Establishing the African Economic Community Relating to Free Movement of Persons, Right of Residence and Right of Establishment', *Protocol to the Treaty Establishing the African Economic Community Relating to Free Movement of Persons, Right of Residence and Right of Establishment / African Union*, 29 January 2018, https://au.int/en/treaties/protocol-treaty-establishing-african-economic-community-relating-free-movement-persons, accessed 8 July 2022.

Rights has a contentious and advisory jurisdiction, but no advisory opinion relating to climate displacement has been sought.[19]

State action on climate displacement is addressed by the African Commission in its Resolution on Climate Change and Human Rights in Africa,[20] which urges members to adopt and implement the special measures of protection for vulnerable groups including victims of natural disasters and conflict. This also demonstrates the need for there to be collaboration and cross-pollination across jurisdictions of the Global South and North to determine the best strategy to approach legal challenges relating to climate change.

1969 Organization of African Unity Convention

Both the 1969 OAU Convention and OAU's Refugee Convention and its Protocol provide ways of tackling aspects of the growing refugee crisis in Africa, which is attributable to occurrences specifically within the African continent. These include civil wars, terrorist activities, inter-state conflicts, ethnic conflicts, conflicts caused by socio-economic changes and changes in government and natural disasters. These treaties provide a mechanism for regional action on the refugee problem in Africa.[21]

The OAU Convention starts by highlighting the specific plight of refugees in Africa, as well as the need to solve the problems in Africa within the spirit and context of the African Charter. It then proceeds to define a refugee as a person who, owing to a well-founded fear of persecution on the basis of their race, religion, nationality, membership of a particular social group or political opinion, flees their country of nationality. The Convention thus provides a legal starting point in addressing the problem of displacement and the refugee crisis in Africa.[22]

Refugees, and by implication 'climate refugees', are addressed by the OAU Convention Governing the Specific Aspects of Refugee Problems

---

[19] The jurisdiction of the African Court is discussed in more depth in the preceding chapter by Elsabé Boshoff.

[20] Adopted 20 April 2016, Res.342(LVIII)2016.(ACHPR).

[21] United Nations High Commissioner for Refugees, 'Addis Ababa Declaration of the Continental Commemorative Meeting on the Implementation and Supervision of the 1969 OAU Refugee Convention', *Refworld*, https://www.refworld.org/docid/5f3be7b84.html, accessed 7 July 2020.

[22] United Nations High Commissioner for Refugees, 'Key Legal Considerations on the Standards of Treatment of Refugees Recognized under the 1969 OAU Convention Governing the Specific Aspects of Refugee Problems in Africa', *Refworld*, https://www.refworld.org/docid/5a391d4f4.html, accessed 7 July 2020.

in Africa (1969 AU refugee treaty).[23] This protects not only refugees but also internally displaced persons, which can be a problem arising from or exacerbated by the climate crisis.

Kampala Convention

The problem of displacement and the plight of refugees is also addressed by the African Union Convention for the Protection and Assistance of Internally Displaced Persons in Africa (the Kampala Convention),[24] which was adopted in 2009 and came into force in 2012.

The definition of a refugee under the OAU Convention is broad, but does not specifically extend to certain categories of displaced persons, among them environmental refugees.[25] The Kampala Convention, on the other hand, addresses internal displacement caused by a number of factors including 'violations of human rights or natural or man-made disasters'.[26] Therefore, this is potentially broad enough to encompass climate change-induced disasters, and certainly arguments relating to climate litigation and justice for displaced persons could be made on these grounds.

Other law and policy

African states have thus endeavoured to put in place legal frameworks at the continental level for addressing disaster displacement and how to implement them. The Addis Ababa Declaration of the Continental Commemorative Meeting on the Implementation and Supervision of the 1969 OAU Refugee Convention (2019) provides an example.[27] African states have also developed

---

23 For more important documents/materials on this treaty, see: https://www.refworld.org/topic/50ffbce51b1/50ffbce51ba.html#SRTop11.

24 'Home | African Union', https://au.int/sites/default/files/treaties/36846-treaty-kampala_convention.pdf, accessed 7 July 2020.

25 EO Awuku, 'Refugee Movements in Africa and the OAU Convention on Refugees', 1995, https://heinonline.org/HOL/Page?handle=hein.journals%2Fjaflaw39&id=85&div=10&collection=journals%3E, accessed 4 February 2022.

26 For an in-depth discussion of the potential of the Kampala Convention to extend protections to refugees and other internally displaced persons as a result of climate change see AO Jegede, 'Rights Away From Home: Climate Induced Displacement of Indigenous Peoples and the Extraterritorial Application of the Kampala Convention' (2016) 16(1) *African Human Rights Law Journal* 58–82, https://journals.co.za/doi/abs/10.17159/1996-2096/2016/v16n1a3, accessed 4 February 2022.

27 United Nations High Commissioner for Refugees, 'Addis Ababa Declaration of the Continental Commemorative Meeting on the Implementation and Supervision of the 1969 OAU Refugee Convention', *Refworld*, https://www.refworld.org/topic,50ffbce51b1,50ffbce51ba,5f3be7b84,0,,,.html, accessed 4 February 2022.

standards for treatment of refugees, such as 'Key legal considerations on the standards of treatment of refugees' recognized under the 1969 OAU Convention Governing the Specific Aspects of Refugee Problems in Africa (2017).[28]

From a policy perspective, recent developments, such as the African Unions' Migration Policy Framework for Africa[29] (2018–2030), recognize climate change as one of the major factors driving migration, whereas the Protocol to the Treaty Establishing Free Movement of Persons, Right of Residence and Right of Establishment[30] additionally provides the groundwork for facilitated cross-border migration including for individuals displaced due to slow-onset environmental changes.

In addition to the Migration Compact and the Refugee Compact, soft law such as the 2030 Sustainable Development Goals (SDGs) can also be further implemented by states to supplement the 1969 OAU Convention. SDG 13 on climate action, for example, addresses several targets that directly impact climate refugees, such as the need to strengthen resilience and adaptive capacity to climate-related hazards and natural disasters,[31] the integration of climate change measures into national policies and strategies and planning,[32] and improving education, raising awareness and human and institutional capacity on climate change mitigation, adaptation, impact reduction and early warning.[33] SDG 10.7 in particular addresses migration and calls for signatories to 'facilitate orderly, safe, and responsible migration of people, including through implementation of planned and well-managed policies'.

Effective implementation by governments, however, remains a major challenge hence the growing tendency to look at the potential of litigation through the courts as an enforcement mechanism. Policy developments and

[28] United Nations High Commissioner for Refugees, 'Key Legal Considerations on the Standards of Treatment of Refugees Recognized under the 1969 OAU Convention Governing the Specific Aspects of Refugee Problems in Africa', *Refworld*, https://www.refworld.org/topic,50ffbce51b1,50ffbce51ba,5a391d4f4,0,,,.html, accessed 4 February 2022.

[29] 'Ending Violence against Children – United Nations', https://violenceagainstchildren.un.org/sites/violenceagainstchildren.un.org/files/documents/other_documents/35316-doc-au-mpfa_2018-eng.pdf, accessed 8 July 2022.

[30] 'Protocol to the Treaty Establishing the African Economic Community Relating to Free Movement of Persons, Right of Residence and Right of Establishment', *Protocol to the Treaty Establishing the African Economic Community Relating to Free Movement of Persons, Right of Residence and Right of Establishment / African Union*, 29 January 2018, https://au.int/en/treaties/protocol-treaty-establishing-african-economic-community-relating-free-movement-persons, accessed 8 July 2022.

[31] SDG 13.1.

[32] SDG 13.2.

[33] SDG 13.3.

regional standards, as described above, could foster increased opportunities for climate change displacement litigation. The possibilities of using a human rights approach in climate change litigation is of particular relevance in the Africa region.

Climate change displacement litigation: a human rights and refugee law approach

Most climate change litigation to date has proceeded in courts in Western industrialized countries and not so much in less economically developed countries (LEDCs), including those in Africa, which are home to many vulnerable groups affected by the climate change crisis.[34] However, litigants and courts in the Global South are beginning to make use of burgeoning climate change litigation theories and know how.[35]

There are five main drivers of climate change litigation. Such litigation arises where the litigant is seeking compensation for the costs of adaptation to climate change; challenging climate change-related legislation and policies or their application; seeking to prevent emissions likely to contribute to climate change; requiring governments or regulators to take action to meet national or international commitments; and seeking to put pressure on relevant corporate actors or investors.[36]

For effective litigation the legal framework must provide answers to the following issues:[37]

(1) *Justiciability*. It is imperative to demonstrate that the court has authority to hear and resolve the said claims. Further, the justiciability of the case is decided once it is highlighted that the alleged causal connection between the injury and the action (or inaction) complained of is plausible.
(2) *Sources of climate obligations*. Litigants may draw on various sources of law, including international law, constitutional provisions, statutes, or common law. Plaintiffs identify more than one of these, or a combination

[34] LJ Kotzé and A Plessis, 'Putting Africa on the Stand: A Bird's Eye View of Climate Change Litigation on the Continent', *Semantic Scholar* 2019, p. 2, https://pdfs.semanticscholar.org/da5d/abcb96b26359d1071eb3d8a1d353dde1f72e.pdf?_ga=2.263614661.85126937.1594929994-1039944007.1594929994, accessed 6 July 2020.

[35] United Nations Environment Programme, 'The Status of Climate Change Litigation – A Global Review', 2017, https://wedocs.unep.org/bitstream/handle/20.500.11822/20767/climate-change-%20litigation.pdf?sequence=1, accessed 9 July 2022.

[36] M Clarke and T Hussein, "Climate Change Litigation: A New Class of Action" (*White & Case LLP*, 13 November 2018), p. 1, https://www.whitecase.com/publications/insight/climate-change-litigation-new-class-action, accessed 9 July 2022.

[37] United Nations Environment Programme (n 35).

of them, to support their claims. Litigants may be more successful when a statutory provision expressly talks about climate change mitigation and allows for litigation in case of non-compliance.

(3) *Remedies.* Courts may only grant remedies authorized by the law and so there can be instances of adverse effects in which there are no legally mandated remedies.

Climate change litigation is a fairly new phenomenon, which can be seen as a development of judicial dispute resolution of environmental issues. It has increased following the enactment of laws codifying national and international responses to climate change and creating new rights and duties relating to climate change. Litigation is used to either challenge the validity of these laws or to ensure that they are applied and enforced; to push legislators and policy makers to be more ambitious in their approaches to climate change; and to fill the gaps left by legislative and regulatory inaction. As a result, courts have been adjudicating a growing number of disputes related to climate change mitigation and adaptation efforts. The cost to governments, private actors and communities of dealing with these impacts is significant.[38]

Enforcing constitutional and legal rights through court action presents its own challenges to the litigant. First there is the challenge of a paucity of clear and justiciable rights in international and regional treaty instruments dealing with climate change, refugee law and similar adverse impacts. Where obligations are imposed on states these are often phrased in such a way that they do not lend themselves easily to enforcement by private actors. Of course, climate cases do succeed,[39] but there have been very few successes arising from litigation in the context of climate displacement.[40]

To be able to make out a case, the evidence of climate-induced displacement must be gathered. Being a highly specialized area, gathering such evidence often requires the involvement of technical experts who are not easily available and, if found, come at a cost, which potential litigants may well not be able to afford, particularly when communities are pitted against well-resourced multinational corporations.

Then there is the problem of proof of causation. Under most municipal systems, liability depends on proof of causation, that is linking the damage

[38] United Nations Environment Programme (n 35).

[39] See United Nations Environment Programme (n 35).

[40] J Klaaren, 'Xenophobia-Induced Disaster Displacement in Gauteng, South Africa: A Climate Change Litigation Perspective' (2021) 15 *Carbon & Climate Law Review* 150; also see SM Sterett and LK Mateczun, 'Displacement, Legal Mobilization, and Disasters: Trial Courts and Legal Process' (2020) 11 *Risk, Hazards & Crisis in Public Policy* 348.

suffered to climate change, either as the primary cause or as a significant contributor. When faced with a multi-faceted phenomenon such as climate change, proof of causation can present insurmountable challenges.[41]

Obstacles also arise from strict rules that, to some extent, limit the ability of communities and non-state actors to seek redress in international or regional arbitral fora directly against a state actor for breach of international or regional conventions.[42] This means that, often, the initiative to take enforcement action is in the hands of the nation state, which is unlikely to want to antagonize another sovereign state by initiating adversarial proceedings, except in instances of transgression against the state itself.

Therefore, climate change displacement litigation remains mired in serious challenges given the narrow definition of the refugee enshrined in the 1951 United Nations Convention relating to the Status of Refugees (1951 UN Convention). The 1951 UN Convention requires individuals seeking asylum to meet certain basic minimum criteria in order to be afforded the refugee protections.[43]

Though international human rights law on its part protects individuals affected by hazard events, these individuals are not necessarily entitled to admission or resettlement in the asylum state. The New Zealand courts have affirmed this interpretation. Though individuals fleeing unbearable climactic and environmental conditions resemble refugees, those seeking formal refugee status due to such impacts do not qualify for the legal protections afforded to refugees under the 1951 UN Convention.[44] The term 'environmental' or 'climate' refugee, therefore, has no legal basis in international refugee law, making it difficult to litigate and advocate for this vulnerable group.

The international human rights framework provides surrogate protections for the rights of all people notwithstanding their reasons for migration or movement.[45] The UN Human Rights Committee (HRC) in the landmark ruling in *Teitiota v New Zealand*[46] denied the petitioner's claim of protection on the grounds that he was at imminent risk, thus following the earlier decisions of the New Zealand courts, but affirmed human rights for individuals fleeing the effects of climate change and natural disasters. The

41 See Alogna (n 5).

42 See the discussion in the chapter by Boshoff in this volume.

43 The informal group on Migration/ Displacement and Climate Change of the IASC, 'Climate Change, Migration and Displacement: Who Will Be Affected' (2008) UNHCR.

44 *Genesis Power v Franklin DC* [2005] NRRMA 541(NZ); see also *Meridian Energy Ltd v Wellington City Council* [2007] W031/07 NZEnvC 128 (NZ).

45 See Universal Declaration of Human Rights (adopted 10 December 1948) UNGA res 217 A(III) (UDHR).

46 Adopted 16 December 1966, entered into force 23 March 1976, 999 UNTS 171 (ICCPR).

HRC reasoned that they should not be forced by the asylum state to return to their country of origin if their fundamental human rights would be at risk. The act of *refoulement* or expulsion in this instance would amount to a violation of the right to life enshrined in article 6 of the International Covenant on Civil and Political Rights (ICCPR).[47] Climate change and environmental degradation in this respect was interpreted to pose a serious threat to the human right to life.

From the Africa regional perspective, climate change displacement litigation may prove more successful, given that refugee arrangements at the regional level have a much broader definition of the refugee than was contemplated in the 1951 UN Convention. The 1969 OAU Convention grants the asylum state the discretion to determine refugee status,[48] enshrines the principle of *non-refoulement,*[49] guarantees rights to temporary residence pending resettlement,[50] and also obligates parties to undertake measures to ease the burden on the asylum state.[51]

Notably, refugees within the meaning of the 1969 OAU Convention include those individuals who are compelled to leave their country of origin due to 'events seriously disturbing public order in either part or the whole of his country of origin or nationality'.[52] Though the 1969 OAU Convention does not explicitly refer to those individuals who are forced to leave their respective country of origin or displaced due to environmental factors, the phrase 'events seriously disturbing public order in either part or the whole of his country of origin or nationality' could be interpreted by African courts to extend residual protections to so-called 'climate refugees'. The wider definition in the 1969 OAU Convention may also provide locus standi not only to individuals seeking asylum but to groups or communities of refugees who have been displaced as a result of environmental degradation, climate change or natural disasters. This distinction is of crucial importance, particularly where African courts are faced with claims that consider formal aspects of recognition either on an individual or collective basis.

The 1969 OAU Convention strictly obliges members to 'use their best endeavours consistent with their respective legislations to receive refugees and to secure their settlement'.[53] Given this requirement, climate change displacement litigation within the umbrella of the 1969 OAU Convention

---

47 Organization of African Unity (OAU), *Convention Governing the Specific Aspects of Refugee Problems in Africa* ('OAU Convention'), 10 September 1969, 1001 UNTS 45, art. I-6.

48 OAU Convention, art. I, para. 6.

49 OAU Convention, art. II, para. 3.

50 OAU Convention, art. II, para. 5.

51 OAU Convention, art. II, para. 4.

52 OAU Convention, art. I, para. 2.

53 OAU Convention, art. II, para. 1.

is a possibility provided that the extension of such legal protections are not inconsistent with the asylum state's domestic law.

Notwithstanding such a broad definition under the 1969 OAU Convention, determination of refugee status remains a matter of discretion. Given such state discretion, a human rights-based approach to litigation is imperative for the development of climate change jurisprudence, given that African courts have already generally recognized the importance of human rights. The South African Constitutional Court in *S v Makwanyane*[54] remarked: '[T]he rights to life and dignity are the most important of all human rights, and the source of all other personal rights … [B]y committing ourselves to a society founded on the recognition of human rights we are required to value these two rights above all others'.[55] Article 4 of the Banjul Charter recognizes that human beings are inviolable and are entitled to respect for their lives and integrity of their person. With the decision of the HRC in *Teitiota v New Zealand*, African courts may recognize the right to life in the context of climate change displacement.

Apart from the right to life, the right to development constitutes an important right enshrined in the Banjul Charter. Article 22 of the Banjul Charter further guarantees all peoples 'the right to their economic, social and cultural development with due regard to their freedom and identity and in the equal enjoyment of the common heritage of mankind'. Particular attention is given to the right to development, including the fact that both civil and political rights are inherently linked to economic, social and cultural rights in their conception and universality.[56] This provision thus constitutes grounds for states to grant asylum to climate-displaced persons. Should an individual displaced by climate change be expelled from the asylum state back to their country of origin, this could be a serious violation of the right to development.

In the context of the human rights framework, climate change poses a significant and substantive threat to human rights and could therefore trigger an asylum state's *non-refoulement* obligations under refugee law. This outcome provides fertile ground for climate change displacement litigation through a human rights-based approach.

Features of the 1969 OAU Convention in litigating climate change displacement

On the positive side, the 1969 OAU Convention affords asylum seekers temporary admission pending determination of their individual status. The

54 [1995] ZACC 3.

55 [1995] ZACC 3, para. 4.

56 Preamble, African Charter.

implication therefore is that an asylum request to a member state that may be linked to climate change or some other environmental factor has and retains the immediate refugee protection responsibilities relating to admission even temporarily, including access to fair and efficient asylum procedures. Though the right to seek asylum as enshrined in the 1969 OAU Convention lacks an explicit parallel duty to grant asylum to environmental or climate refugees, in the context of human rights law, member states appear to be bound by the principle of *non-refoulement* which imposes a substantive duty on the contracting asylum state not to turn away asylum seekers facing serious threats to their fundamental human rights.

However, from the perspective of its potential for use in climate change litigation, there are a number of gaps in the 1969 OAU Convention. To start with, there is a lack of specific arrangements to deal with a number of situations. For instance, there are no criteria to distinguish between voluntary and forced movements in hazard disaster settings for individuals who are displaced due to environmental degradation and/or slow onset extreme hazard events. Gaps also arise in other cases, for instance where there is loss of land due to events such as rising sea-levels or desertification, which leads to a state losing its entire territory (a constituent element of statehood). Under such circumstances the state in question may not be recognized by the international community,[57] and by implication its people would be rendered stateless and therefore not fall under the requirements to qualify for asylum under refugee law. Such deficiencies may thus frustrate any efforts to rely on these instruments, but it is also questionable whether they could be successfully litigated in climate change displacement litigation.

Furthermore, from a legal context, notwithstanding the broader definition of the refugee afforded in the 1969 OAU Convention, there is a lack of legal certainty regarding what protections can be extended to such individuals and to what extent they can be litigated. There are no specific individual rights related to climate or environmental related migration under the 1969 OAU Convention and therefore no justiciable guarantees.

The 1969 OAU Convention was drafted with the intent to protect those refugees fleeing persecution based on race, religion, nationality, membership of a particular social group or political opinion. The drivers for human displacement have, however, changed over the past few decades to include forces such as environmental degradation, climate change and unsustainable development. Though the phrase 'events seriously disturbing public order in either part or the whole of his country of origin or nationality' could be interpreted to include individuals displaced by climactic and environmental

57 Climate Change, Migration and Displacement (n 43).

impacts, the interpretation remains a discretion to be exercised by states taking into account their own public policy.

Thus, a purposive approach in the interpretation of the human rights enshrined in the Banjul Charter, such as the right to life and dignity (article 4), the freedom from cruel, inhuman or degrading treatment (article 5) and the right to development (article 22), may circumvent any deficiencies inherent in the 1969 OAU Convention.

Conclusion

The domestication of international and regional law is a fundamental responsibility of the state and is particularly important in areas such as procedures for determination of refugee status of displaced people, where the driving factor is environmental degradation, natural disaster or climate change. Moreover the inextricable link between human rights law and refugee law means that protections afforded to asylum seekers should not be based on the number of persons or individuals seeking asylum. Therefore, such rights should be extended on a collective basis particularly in light of mass migration of communities that is caused by rapid onset of natural disasters or those arising from environmental degradation and/or slow onset extreme hazard events and/or processes. Aside from voluntary repatriation,[58] it is the state's responsibility to make it an initiative to resettle refugees where possible.

The drivers for human displacement have evolved over the past few decades to include forces such as climate change and unsustainable development. Given this, international agreements such as the Paris Agreement – although not making explicit reference to 'climate refugees' – call for the development of recommendations for integrated approaches to avert, minimize and address displacement related to the adverse impacts of climate change.[59] At the regional level, the legal and policy instruments discussed in this chapter may provide qualified protection for people who are displaced due to the impacts of climate change. These developments should provide legal grounds for climate change displacement litigation.

Decisions such as that of the HRC in *Teitiota v New Zealand* illustrate that a human rights-based approach is material in climate change displacement litigation in order to guarantee climate refugees universal protections.

---

[58] OAU Convention, art. V, para. 1.

[59] Paris Agreement (n 3), art. 50.

8

The Vulnerability of African Indigenous Peoples' Traditional Meteorological Knowledge in the Climate Change Debate

Fiona Batt

Introduction

Indigenous peoples of the African continent – although victims of climate change – have accumulated Meteorological Traditional Knowledge (MTK) over generations and are ideally positioned to offer their expert MTK to the scientific community.[1] MTK is a part of the intangible heritage of African indigenous peoples and can contribute to climate change adaptation and mitigation. However, MTK as an emerging sui generis resource is vulnerable to biopiracy and misappropriation; this mirrors generally the experiences indigenous peoples have had when sharing their traditional knowledge.

At the Indigenous Peoples Global Summit in Alaska (2009), the indigenous representatives from the Arctic, North America, Asia, Pacific, Latin America, Africa, Caribbean and Russia, adopted the Anchorage Declaration. The Declaration concluded: 'We offer to share with humanity our TK, innovations, and practices relevant to climate change, provided our fundamental rights as intergenerational guardians of this knowledge are fully recognized and respected'.[2] Additionally the representatives stated

---

1 In 2009 the African Commission passed 153 Resolution on Climate Change and Human Rights and the Need to Study its Impact in Africa 153(XLVI)09.

2 Anchorage Declaration 20–24 April 2009, Alaska, https://unfccc.int/resource/docs/2009/smsn/ngo/168.pdf, accessed 12 November 2022.

the following: 'We call upon the Parties to the UNFCCC to recognize the importance of our TK and practices shared by indigenous peoples in developing strategies to address climate change'.[3] The exchange of MTK can be beneficial to all stakeholders and rights holders, and may be desired by indigenous peoples. However, exchanges carry risks and can lead to cultural harm for indigenous peoples.[4]

The term 'cultural harm' is one increasingly used in discussions surrounding the misappropriation of indigenous peoples' heritage.[5] Presently, there is no clear understanding of what the term means. There exists only one case that uses the term, *George M*, Payunka, Marika v Indofurn Pty Ltd*, where damages were given for cultural harm in relation to intellectual property, though without any real discussion on its meaning.[6] Tsosie has linked the concept of cultural harm to assimilation and the loss of culture.[7]

This chapter seeks to identify legal avenues to preserve and equitably share the MTK of indigenous people in order that it can be used as stated above – to support the development of strategies to tackle climate change – in a manner that will not cause cultural harm to indigenous peoples. The chapter proposes that the profile, vulnerability and value of MTK could be included in customary land rights cases under the African Charter on Human and Peoples Rights (African Charter),[8] before the African Court on Human and Peoples Rights (African Court) and the African Commission of Human and Peoples Rights (African Commission).[9] The

3 Anchorage Declaration (n 2).

4 R Tsosie, 'Cultural Challenges to Biotechnology: Native American Genetic Resources and the Concept of Cultural Harm' (2007) 35 *Journal of Law, Medicine & Ethics* 396.

5 See Commission on Human Rights, Sub-Commission on Prevention of Discrimination and Protection of Minorities, Working Group on Indigenous Populations, Standard Setting Activities: Evolution of Standards Concerning the Rights of Indigenous Peoples: Human Genome Diversity Research and Indigenous Peoples: Note by the Secretariat (4 June 1998) UN Doc. E/CN.4/Sub.2/AC.4/1998/4/Add.1, p. 5, para. 13.

6 See *George Milpurrurru, Banduk Marika, Tim Payunka and the Public Trustee of the Northern Territory v Indofurn Pty Ltd, Brian Alexander Bethune, George Raymond King and Robert James Rylands* (1994) 54 FCR 240 for damages given for cultural harm.

7 R Tsosie, 'Indigenous Peoples' Claims to Cultural Property: A Legal Perspective' (1997) 21 *Museum Anthropology* 5.

8 African Charter on Human and Peoples' Rights 27 June 1981, 1520 UNTS 217 (entered into force 21 October 1981).

9 However the sub regional courts of West and East Africa: The Economic Community of West African States (ECOWAS) Community Court of Justice (CCJ) and the East African Court of Justice could equally hear such cases. See *Socio-Economic Rts & Accountability Project v Nigeria*, No. ECW/CCJ.JUD/18/12, Judgment, The Court of Justice of the Economic Community of West African States [ECOWAS] (12 December 2012), paras 18, 64, 66, 67, 18; Application No. 29 of 2020 (Arising from Reference No. 39 of 2020) *Centre for Food and Adequate Living Rights (CEFROHT) Ltd v Attorney General of the Republic of*

chapter in particular examines the *Endorois* case[10] and the *Ogiek*[11] case to illustrate how MTK could be raised in future customary land rights cases. The *Endorois* case has been viewed as strategic human rights litigation,[12] and the *Ogiek* case has been viewed as a climate litigation case.[13] However, this chapter does not consider them with regards to whether they might be, or might create, avenues for climate litigation.[14] Rather, the chapter is about how the jurisprudence of the court creates legal avenues to preserve and equitably share the MTK of indigenous peoples, so that it can be used to support climate change strategies that will benefit humanity as a whole, but without causing cultural harm. MTK was at risk but this was not a significant legal factor in the cases, and so did not come across strongly in the submissions.[15] In both cases, through the story telling of the Endorois and Ogiek peoples, the significance of MTK and the need to protect it emerge. Strong land tenure would protect the generational meteorological knowledge developed over time and has potential to mitigate climate change.

Furthermore in relation to the sharing of MTK with the scientific community the international principles of Access to Benefit Sharing and Free Prior Informed Consent are included as safeguards against biopiracy, misappropriation and cultural harm.

Uganda, The Attorney General of the United Republic of Tanzania, and The Secretary General of the East African Community.

10 *Centre for Minority Rights Development (Kenya) and Minority Rights Group International on behalf of Endorois Welfare Council v Kenya* Communication No. 276/2003.

11 *African Commission on Human and Peoples' Rights v Republic of Kenya*, ACtHPR, Application No. 006/2012 Judgment (26 May 2017); *The Matter of African Commission on Human and Peoples Rights v Republic of Kenya* Application No. 006/2012 Judgement (Reparations) 23 June 2022.

12 Helen Duffy, *Strategic Human Rights Litigation* (Hart Publishing 2018).

13 See T Morganthau and N Reisch, 'Litigating the Frontlines: Why African Community Rights Cases Are Climate Change Cases' (2020) 25(1) *UCLA Journal of International Law and Foreign Affairs* 85; Panel Discussion, 'The Ogiek Case – a New Paradigm for Conservation in Africa?' The African Commission on Human and Peoples' Rights 73rd Ordinary Session 22 October 2022.

14 As in Elsabé Boshoff's chapter in this volume.

15 African Commission on Human and Peoples Rights, Communication 276/2003 *Centre for Minority Rights Development (Kenya) and Minority Rights Group International on behalf of Endorois Welfare Council v Kenya*, paras 73, 78, 167, 184 and 189; *African Commission on Human and Peoples' Rights v The Republic of Kenya*, Application No. 006/2012, African Commission on Human and Peoples' Rights, 15 March 2013, paras 148, 158, 160,165, 182 and 183.

Indigenous peoples and meteorological traditional knowledge in the African context

Who is 'indigenous' and who are 'peoples' have been contentious issues in relation to accessing human rights for indigenous peoples.[16] However, for those groups who are considered as indigenous peoples the term has been of benefit. Indigenous peoples have been able to articulate their claims based on past and present injustices in domestic, regional and international legal systems successfully and unsuccessfully.[17]

Indigenous peoples are a subject of international law.[18] In particular, the Convention Concerning the Protection and Integration of Indigenous and other Tribal and Semi-Tribal Populations in Independent Countries, No. 107 (Convention 107), the Indigenous and Tribal Peoples Convention 1989 (No. 169) (Convention 169) and the United Nations Declaration on Rights of Indigenous Peoples (UNDRIP),[19] are indigenous peoples' specific international instruments. Indigenous peoples are in an unusual position in international law as they are able to access the rights associated with individuals, minorities and indigenous peoples. In relation to the rights of individuals, although useful, individual rights do not reflect the true nature of the claims of indigenous peoples, as increasingly they are articulated as claims of collectives.[20]

There is no legal definition of indigenous peoples. However, two well-respected, independent United Nations studies in the field of indigenous peoples by Jose Martinez Cobo (Cobo Study) and Dr. Erica-Irene Daes (Daes Study) can serve as a guide on the meaning of 'indigenous peoples'. The Daes Study highlights the following:

(1) priority in time, with respect to the occupation and use of a specific territory;

---

[16] In the discussions around the Declaration on the Rights of Indigenous Peoples the African group had reservations in relation to the fact that the Declaration on Rights of Indigenous Peoples did not define the 'rights holders'. See African Group, Draft Aide-Memoire – United Nations Declaration on the Rights of Indigenous Peoples (9 November 2006).

[17] See *The matter of African Commission on Human and Peoples' Rights v Republic of Kenya* Application No. 006/2012 Judgment (Reparations) 23 June 2022.

[18] R Barsh, 'Indigenous Peoples in the 1990s: From Object to Subject of International Law' (1991) 7 *Harvard Human Rights Journal* 33.

[19] Advisory Opinion of the African Commission on the United Nations Declaration on the Rights of Indigenous Peoples, in which it stated that the Rights enshrines in the UNDRIP were consistent with the African Charter on Human and Peoples' Rights and the jurisprudence of the African Commission.: ACHPR and IWGIA – 2010.

[20] A Xanthaki, *Indigenous Rights and United Nations Standards: Self-Determination, Culture and Land* (Cambridge University Press 2009).

(2) the voluntary perpetuation of cultural distinctiveness, which may include the aspects of language, social organization, religion and spiritual values, modes of production, laws and institutions;
(3) self-identification, as well as recognition by other groups, or by state authorities, as a distinct collectivity; and
(4) an experience of subjugation, marginalization, dispossession, exclusion or discrimination, whether or not these conditions persist.[21]

J Martinez-Cobo, who was Special Rapporteur of the United Nations Sub-Commission on the Prevention of Discrimination and Protection of Minorities, says as follows:

> Indigenous communities, peoples and nations are those which have a historical continuity with pre-invasion and pre-colonial societies that developed on their territories, consider themselves distinct from other sectors of societies now prevailing in those territories, or parts of them. They form at present non-dominant sectors of society and are determined to preserve, develop and transmit to future generations their ancestral territories, and their ethnic identity, as the basis of their continued existence as peoples, in accordance with their cultural patterns, social institutions and legal systems.[22]

Both the Endorois people and the Ogiek people, discussed later under customary land tenure and MTK, would qualify as indigenous peoples according to these definitions. The Endorois and the Ogiek also self-identify as indigenous peoples, in line with the criteria highlighted by Daes.[23]

However the recognition of indigenous peoples as separate from other groups within some African states has been resisted.[24] In Africa, for example, the term 'local communities' is seen as less contentious, and can be found in some legislation.[25] The African Commission has established its own working

[21] EI A Daes, *Working Paper on the Concept of Indigenous People* (10 June 1996) UN Doc. E/CN.4/Sub.2/AC.4/1996/2, para. 69.

[22] See ILO No. 169, Convention Concerning Indigenous and Tribal Peoples in Independent Countries 1989 Article 1 and 2 and United Nations Declaration on the Rights of Indigenous Peoples (2007).

[23] *Ogiek* case, paras 103 and 105; *Endorois* case, para. 157.

[24] Daes (n 21), para. 73.

[25] Convention on Biological Diversity 1992; ARIPO Swakopmund Protocol on the Protection of Traditional Knowledge and Expressions of Folklore within the Framework of the African Regional Intellectual Property Organization 2010; For a full discussion on the term local communities see Secretariat of the Permanent Forum on Indigenous Issues paper, 'Who are Local Communities' UNEP/CBD/WS-CB/LAC/1/INF/5, 16 November 2006.

group on indigenous peoples and has produced an extensive study on the indigenous peoples of the African continent.[26] However, the Working Group's title includes the terms 'indigenous populations/communities'.[27] Within the World Intellectual Property Organization (WIPO), the term 'community' is used to, 'refer broadly to indigenous peoples and traditional, local and other cultural communities'.[28]

This chapter's focus is the MTK of nomadic and semi-nomadic African indigenous peoples. Recommendation 27 of the 5th World Parks Congress describes:

> Mobile indigenous peoples (i.e. nomads, pastoralists, hunter-gatherers, and shifting agriculturalists) as a sub-set of traditional and indigenous peoples whose livelihoods depend on some form of common property use of natural resources, and whose mobility is both a distinctive source of cultural identity and a management strategy for sustainable land use and conservation.[29]

In Africa nomadic and semi-nomadic indigenous peoples include the Pokot of Kenya and Uganda, the Barabaig of Tanzania, the Maasai of Kenya and Tanzania, the Samburu, Turkana, Rendille, Endorois, Ogiek and Borana of Kenya, the Karamojong of Uganda, the Himba of Namibia and the Tuareg, Fulani and Toubou of Mali, Burkina Faso and Niger.[30] Mobility is an essential characteristic of nomadic and semi-nomadic indigenous peoples.

Nomadic and semi-nomadic indigenous peoples have a distinct relationship with their lands and the ecosystems within which they live. They have been said to act as a sentinel, observing changes in the ecosystem.[31] These peoples

---

26 See ACHPR/Res.51(XXVIII)00 Resolution on the Rights of Indigenous Peoples'/Communities in Africa (2000); Report of the African Commission's Working Group of Experts on Indigenous Populations/Communities (2005 ACHPR and IWGIA); African Commission on Human and Peoples' Rights (ACHPR), 'Indigenous Peoples in Africa; The Forgotten Peoples in Africa?' (IWGIA 2006); Advisory Opinion of the African Commission on Human and Peoples' Rights on the United Nations Declaration on the Rights of Indigenous Peoples (2010).

27 African Commission on Human and Peoples Rights Working Group on Indigenous Populations/Communities African Commission on Human and Peoples' Rights Special mechanisms (achpr.org), accessed 12 November 2022.

28 The Protection of Traditional Cultural Expressions: Draft Gap Analysis (11 October 2008) WIPO/GRTKF/IC/13/4(b) Rev.

29 Recommendation 27 of the 5th World Parks Congress (Durban, September 2003), accessed 12 November 2022.

30 IWGIA (n 26).

31 K Galloway Maclean, 'Advance Guard: Climate Change Impacts, Adaptation Mitigation and Indigenous Peoples' (2010) United Nations University. Traditional Knowledge Initiative.

are able to notice and record the slightest changes in the climate and the affects the changes are having on the biodiversity on which they rely for their livelihoods.[32] Methods range from 'examining plants, characteristics and behaviours of animals, observation of patterns of clouds, and knowledge of ecosystems and the rangelands'.[33] The Afar of north-eastern Ethiopia, and Maasai of Kenya and Tanzania observe the flowering Acacia tortillis to forecast the onset of the rainy season.[34] The Maasai from Kenya and Tanzania: '[H]ave a number of techniques for monitoring the onset of rains – the flowering of specific trees, the shape of the moon, special sounds from a particular birds. This indigenous knowledge has proven to be important in matters of wildlife and environmental management and conservation'.[35]

In Uganda, the people of Rakai, who have lived in the same area for many generations, have a collective memory of weather patterns that is representative of MTK and has been termed 'knowledge of climatology'.[36] The authors of 'indigenous climate knowledge in southern Uganda' highlight: 'The specific indigenous and local knowledge that communities use to adapt to climate change comprises knowledge of (a) the seasons; (b) historical storm patterns; (c) the colour of rain-bearing clouds; and (d) wind patterns, including direction and wind types (e.g. wind from the west dries crops and wind from the east is cool and brings rain)'.[37]

There are many articulations of what constitutes traditional knowledge.[38] However, the Convention on Biological Diversity Secretariat understand that

---

[32] EG Kimaro, SM Mor, and JALML Toribio, 'Climate change perception and impacts on cattle production in pastoral communities of northern Tanzania' (2018) 1 *Pastoralism* 8.

[33] Elifuraha Laltaika at the UNESCO Experts Meeting on Indigenous Knowledge and Climate Change in Africa, Nairobi, Kenya, 27–28 June 2018, Report of the UNESCO Expert Meeting on Indigenous Knowledge and Climate Change in Africa, Nairobi, Kenya, 27–28 June 2018 – UNESCO Digital Library, accessed 12 November 2022.

[34] N Kilongozi, Z Kengera and S Leshongo, 'The Utilization of Indigenous Knowledge in Range Management and Forage Plants' FAO of the United Nations, 2005, https://www.fao.org/.../6_Nelson_41.pdf, accessed 12 November 2022.

[35] Report of the UNESCO Expert Meeting on Indigenous Knowledge and Climate Change in Africa, Nairobi, Kenya, 27–28 June 2018, https://unesdoc.unesco.org/ark:/48223/pf0000374999.locale=en, accessed 12 November 2022.

[36] B Orlove, C Roncoli, M Kabugo *et al*, 'Indigenous Climate Knowledge in Southern Uganda: the Multiple Components of a Dynamic Regional System' (2010) *Climatic Change* 24.

[37] Orlove, Roncoli and Kabugo (n 36).

[38] Permanent Forum on Indigenous Issues Sixth session New York Report of the Secretariat on Indigenous Traditional Knowledge (14–25 May 2007) UN Doc. E/C.19/2007/10; Un Doc. E/2004/43; The Report of the Eleventh Session of the Permanent Forum on Indigenous Issues (UNPFII11), New York from 7–18 May 2012 UN Doc. E/2012/43-E/C.19/2012/13; Intergovernmental Committee on Intellectual Property and Genetic Resources, Traditional Knowledge and Folklore The Protection of Traditional

'it is a body of knowledge built by a group of people through generations living in close contact with nature [which includes] a system of classification, a set of empirical observations about the local environment, and a system of self-management that governs resource use'. This articulation somehow straddles an indigenous understanding and a scientific understanding of MTK.[39]

Furthermore, the World Intellectual Property Organization (WIPO) has spent some time examining the protection of traditional knowledge.[40] A new international instrument protecting the traditional knowledge and genetic resources of indigenous peoples is an option. However, after many years of work on a draft legal instrument the process has not come to an end. In contrast the African Regional Intellectual Property Organization (ARIPO), one of the two African intellectual property regional organizations, has been very active in advocating for the protection of traditional knowledge in Africa and recognizes that communities are vulnerable to the misappropriation of their traditional knowledge.[41]

The traditional knowledge in relation to the prediction of the weather of indigenous peoples is increasingly becoming an area of interest to meteorologists.[42] MTK therefore offers an avenue to environmental sustainability and has the potential to monitor and respond to climate change.[43] The N'Djamena Declaration on Adaptation to Climate Change, Indigenous Pastoralism, TK and Meteorology in Africa 2011, stresses that the TK held by these peoples is a valuable resource for monitoring and responding to climate change. The Report of the Plenary of the Intergovernmental Science-Policy Platform on Biodiversity and Ecosystem

Knowledge: Draft Articles Thirty-Fourth Session Geneva, 12–16 June 2017 WIPO Doc. WIPO/GRTKF/IC/34/5.

39 Traditional Knowledge and Biological Diversity, Note by the Executive Secretary, UN Doc. UNEP/CBD/TKBD/1/2 (1997), para. 87.

40 Submission by the African Group: Objectives, principles and elements of an international instrument, or instruments, on intellectual property in relation to genetic resources and on the protection of traditional knowledge and folklore Sixth Session Geneva (15–19 March 2004) WIPO Doc. WIPO/GRTKF/IC/6/12; Intergovernmental Committee on Intellectual Property and Genetic Resources, Traditional Knowledge and Folklore The Protection of Traditional Knowledge: Draft Articles (January 2012) WIPO/GRTKF/IC/21/4.

41 ARIPO Workshop, 'Protection and Utilisation of Traditional Knowledge, Genetic Resources and Expressions of Folklore', The Gambia, July 2014.

42 L Chambers *et al*, 'A Database for Traditional Knowledge of Weather and Climate in the Pacific Meteorological Applications' (2017) 24(3) *Meteorological Applications Science Technology for Weather and Climate* 491.

43 Note further the relationship between MTK and totems; see *Endorois* and *Ogiek* cases.

Services on the work of its fifth session, noted that the indigenous and local knowledge systems is:

> [G]rounded in territory, is highly diverse and is continuously evolving through the interaction of experiences, innovations and various types of knowledge (written, oral, visual, tacit, gendered, practical and scientific). Such knowledge can provide information, methods, theory and practice for sustainable ecosystem management. Many indigenous and local knowledge systems are empirically tested, applied, contested and validated through different means in different contexts.[44]

However the United Nations Food and Agriculture Organization has noted that MTK is not accorded the same recognition as scientific knowledge, which further adds to its vulnerability to biopiracy and misappropriation.[45]

Indigenous peoples, climate change and international law

In general, developed countries are urged to support social groups living in developing countries through the transfer of knowledge and technology in order to strengthen their resilience to the adverse effects of climate change on their livelihoods.[46] The UNFCCC does not discuss indigenous peoples explicitly in relation to climate change, although article 4 is interpreted as describing the urgency that various social groups are facing in relation to climate change.[47] However article 7.5 of the Paris Agreement stresses the importance of including local and indigenous knowledge in understanding climate change and developing relevant actions for adaptation.[48] However indigenous peoples were not able to fully and effectively participate in the development of the UNFCCC, and were not consulted in the development of the framework. Lack of full and meaningful participation in international

---

44 Report of the Plenary of the Intergovernmental Science-Policy Platform on Biodiversity and Ecosystem Services on the work of its fifth session Bonn, Germany, 7–10 March 2017, 6 (a) IPBES/5/15.

45 N Kilongozi, Z Kengera and S Leshongo, 'The Utilization of Indigenous Knowledge in Range Management and Forage Plants' FAO of the United Nations, 2005, http://www.fao.org/home/en/, accessed 12 November 2022.

46 Division for Sustainable Development Goals Sustainable Development: Report of the Second Committee UN Doc. A/70/472.

47 UN Permanent Forum on Indigenous Issues (UNPFII), 2017, 'Report Status of the World's Indigenous Peoples' 101.

48 Paris Agreement to the United Nations Framework Convention on Climate Change, 12 December 2015, TIAS No. 16–1104.

fora is a criticism often raised by indigenous peoples.[49] The UNFCCC 'Local Communities and Indigenous Peoples Platform', a platform for indigenous peoples and local communities, now aims at safeguarding traditional knowledge and facilitating an exchange of traditional knowledge to inform climate change action and policy.[50] Additionally, the International Indigenous Peoples' Forum on Climate Change (IIPFCC) is the joint indigenous caucus in the UNFCCC process, a body that is open to those indigenous activists who wish to engage in the negotiations at any given time.[51] Therefore, the UNFCCC argue indigenous peoples' participation in the climate change debate is increasing.[52]

The implementation of the UNFCCC is facilitated through the Conference of the Parties (COP). All states that are parties to the UNFCCC are represented at the COP.[53] In relation to indigenous peoples, UNFCCC COP 23 operationalized the Local Communities and Indigenous Peoples Platform (LCIPP).[54] The LCIPP is a platform for the exchange of traditional knowledge-based experiences and sharing of best practices on climate change mitigation and adaptation in a holistic and integrated manner.[55] At the UN Climate Change Conference COP26 in Glasgow in November 2021, the Science Panel for the Amazon emphasized the need for indigenous and local knowledge to inform scientific and policy recommendations.[56] Interestingly the United Nations Climate Change website stated that there was direct and 'unprecedented engagement between indigenous peoples, local communities and governments' at COP 26.[57] However there has been

[49] In September 2017 the General Assembly adopted resolution A/RES/71/321 entitled Enhancing the Participation of Indigenous Peoples' Representatives and Institutions in Meetings of Relevant United Nations Bodies on Issues Affecting Them, accessed 12 November 2022.

[50] Local Communities and Indigenous Peoples Platform (unfccc.int).

[51] International Indigenous Peoples Forum on Climate Change (iipfcc.org).

[52] Indigenous Peoples Increasingly Engaging in Climate Action Indigenous Peoples Increasingly Engaging in Climate Action | UNFCCC 9 August 2021.

[53] United Nations Climate Change, https://unfccc.int/process/bodies/supreme-bodies/conference-of-the-parties-cop, accessed 12 November 2022.

[54] See n 50.

[55] K Sena, 'Traditional Knowledge Key in Achieving Africa's Climate Goals', IUCN 2019, https://www.iucn.org/news/commission-environmental-economic-and-social-policy/201901/traditional-knowledge-key-achieving-africas-climate-goals, accessed 12 November 2022.

[56] M Rodrigues, 'Traditional Knowledge is Essential to Sustainability in the Amazon', EOS 2021, https://eos.org/articles/traditional-knowledge-is-essential-to-sustainability-in-the-amazon, accessed 12 November 2022.

[57] UNFCCC, 'COP26 Strengthens Role of Indigenous Experts and Stewardship of Nature', November 2021, https://unfccc.int/news/cop26-strengthens-role-of-indigenous-expe rts-and-stewardship-of-nature, accessed 12 November 2022.

much criticism of COP 26 and the lack of indigenous peoples' participation, particularly from the NGO Cultural Survival.[58] More recently COP 27 came to an agreement on the establishment of the loss and damage fund (Fund), which was welcomed by the IIPFCC.[59] The Fund will provide funding to vulnerable countries and, consequently, climate vulnerable communities, including indigenous peoples.[60] Furthermore, COP 27 recognized that culture could play a crucial role in mitigation and adaption.[61] This recognition of the importance of culture in the climate change debate is supported by this chapter.[62]

In contrast to the UNFCCC, the Convention on Biological Diversity (CBD) was one of the first key environmental treaties enabling indigenous peoples to participate. It is the first broad and legally binding international legal instrument that seeks to protect all ecosystems and all species.[63] The CBD is an example of a legal document more in tune with indigenous knowledge and genetic resources. Indigenous peoples have a special status within the CBD and the Convention recognizes communal ownership. Furthermore, it includes indigenous peoples and local communities. The CBD recognizes the dependence of indigenous and local communities on biological resources, and the desirability of equitable sharing of benefits of the use of traditional knowledge.[64]

Additionally, the United Nations Educational, Scientific and Cultural Organization (UNESCO) operates the Local Indigenous Knowledge Systems (LINKS) programme.[65] LINKS facilitates dialogue between local and indigenous groups and scientists.[66] It includes traditional knowledge

---

58 Cultural Survival, 'States Fail to Adequately Address Climate Change: An Indigenous Peoples' Analysis of COP26 Decisions', November 2021, https://www.culturalsurvival.org/news/states-fail-adequately-address-climate-change-indigenous-peoples-analysis-cop26-decisions, accessed 12 November 2022.

59 International Indigenous Forum on Climate Change iipfcc.orglast, accessed 13 January 2023.

60 'COP27 Reaches Breakthrough Agreement on New "Loss and Damage" Fund for Vulnerable Countries', UNFCCC, 20 November 2022, https://unfccc.int/news/cop27-reaches-breakthrough-agreement-on-new, accessed 13 January 2023.

61 Climate Heritage Network, 'COP 27 Solutions Day: High Level Focus on Culture-based Climate Action', Climate Heritage Network, https://www.climateheritage.org/press/cop-27-solutions-day-high-level, accessed 13 January 2023.

62 See Report of the Special Rapporteur in the field of cultural rights on climate change, culture and cultural rights (A/75/298), 10 August 2020.

63 T Simpson, *Indigenous Heritage and Self-Determination. The Cultural and Intellectual Property Rights of Indigenous Peoples* (IGWA 1997) 92.

64 G Dutfield, 'TRIPS Related Aspects of Traditional Knowledge' (2001) 33 *Case W Res J International Law* 261.

65 Local and Indigenous Knowledge Systems (LINKS) (unesco.org).

66 LINKS (n 65).

on climate change through work with the CCBD, the UNFCCC, the IPCC and the Intergovernmental Platform on Biodiversity and Ecosystem Services (IPBES).[67]

Furthermore, UNDRIP is the most comprehensive legal instrument to date encompassing the rights of indigenous peoples. It is increasingly being acknowledged as a document that can inform environmental policy in relation to the land of indigenous peoples.[68] It includes protective provisions in relation to indigenous resources, which may encompass MTK under the umbrella of traditional knowledge. Article 31(i) includes the right 'to maintain, control, protect and develop their cultural heritage, traditional knowledge and traditional cultural expressions'. Furthermore, article 32 includes the principle of Free Prior Informed Consent (FPIC). The inclusion of these provisions has potential to enable the sharing of valuable MTK in a fair and equitable way. UNDRIP provides a basis for demanding greater and more meaningful participation in international decision-making processes.[69] The African Regional Summit on climate change recognized UNDRIP as 'the instrument for engagement of all indigenous communities in climate change initiatives'.[70]

Regionally, the Indigenous Peoples of Africa Co-coordinating Committee (IPACC) promotes environmental and climate justice with a priority being the promotion of indigenous knowledge systems in National Adaption Plans.[71] The IPACC 2022 theme is,' The Role of Indigenous Women in the Preservation and Transmission of Traditional Knowledge'.[72] Therefore, the relationship women have with their customary lands must not be marginalized in the debate around the protection and preservation of MTK.

Access to benefit sharing and free prior informed consent

Indigenous peoples have offered to share their MTK with the scientific community, provided that their knowledge is respected.[73] In regard to

67 LINKS (n 65).

68 S Duyck and E Lennon *et al*, *Delivering on the Paris Promises: Combating climate change while protecting rights* (IWGIA 2017).

69 See arts 5, 18, 27 and 41.

70 Africa Regional Summit on Indigenous Peoples and Climate Change, Nakuru, Kenya, 5–6 March 2009, Indigenous Knowledge and Climate Change in Africa (unesco.org), accessed 12 November 2012.

71 Environmental and Climate Justice, The Indigenous Peoples of Africa Co-ordinating Committee (ipacc.org.za), accessed 12 November 2022.

72 International Day of The World's Indigenous Peoples 2022, The Indigenous Peoples of Africa Co-ordinating Committee (ipacc.org.za).

73 Respect here is understood to mean an adherence to the principles of ABS and FPIC by states and non-state actors. ABS and FPIC act as safeguards to cultural harm; see Anchorage Declaration adopted at the Indigenous Peoples Global Summit in Alaska.

sharing, the United Nations Study on Cultural and Intellectual Property suggested that 'sharing creates a relationship between the givers and receivers of knowledge. The givers retain the authority to ensure that knowledge is used properly and the receivers continue to recognize and repay the gift'.[74] Central to benefit sharing are the issues of social justice and inequality between resource providers and those who commercialize these resources.[75]

Most of the discussion in relation to access to benefit sharing (ABS) is contextualized in the debate around biodiversity.[76] One of the objectives of the CBD highlighted in article 1 is the fair and equitable sharing of the benefits arising out of the utilization of genetic resources.[77] This concept was further developed in the 2010 Nagoya Protocol on Access to Genetic Resources and the Fair and Equitable Sharing of Benefits Arising from their Utilization to the Convention on Biological Diversity.[78] However, the 2008 WIPO Intergovernmental Committee on Intellectual Property and Genetic Resources, Traditional Knowledge and Folklore: Draft Gap Analysis on the Protection of Traditional Knowledge found gaps in the protection of traditional knowledge in legal mechanisms and highlighted the 'failure to obtain remuneration or other benefits' as one such gap.[79] The Framework principles on human rights and the environment principle 15(d) – which includes the term 'indigenous peoples'– emphasizes that states should ensure 'that they fairly and equitably share the benefits from activities relating to their lands, territories or resources'.[80] In relation to biodiversity, article

[74] EI Daes, 'Study on the Protection of the Cultural and Intellectual Property of Indigenous Peoples, Sub-Commission on Prevention of Discrimination and Protection of Minorities' (28 July 1993) Un Doc. E/CN.4/Sub.2/1993/28.

[75] A Petrov and M Tysiachniouk, 'Benefit Sharing in the Arctic: A Systematic View (2019) 8 *Resources* 155, https://doi.org/10.3390/resources8030155; Emma Wilson, 'What is Benefit Sharing? Respecting Indigenous Rights and Addressing Inequities in Arctic Resource Projects' (2019) 8 *Resources* 74, https://doi.org/10.3390/resources8020074; A Savaresi and K Bouwer, 'Equity and Justice in Climate Change Law and Policy: A Role for Benefit-Sharing' in T Jafry, K Helwig and M Mikulewicz (eds), *Research Handbook on Climate Justice* (Routledge 2018).

[76] The Nagoya Protocol on Access to Genetic Resources and the Fair and Equitable Sharing of Benefits Arising from their Utilization to the Convention on Biological Diversity adopted on 29 October 2010 in Nagoya, Japan and entered into force on 12 October 2014.

[77] Convention on Biodiversity 1992, https://www.cbd.int/Convention/text/default.shtml.

[78] Convention on Biodiversity (n 77).

[79] WIPO Intergovernmental Committee on Intellectual Property and Genetic Resources, Traditional Knowledge and Folklore: Draft Gap Analysis on the Protection of Traditional Knowledge (30 May 2008), WIPO/GRTKF/IC/13/5(b), p. 23, para. 47.

[80] Framework Principles on Human Rights and the Environment, in Report of the Special Rapporteur on the issue of human rights obligations relating to the enjoyment of a safe, clean, healthy and sustainable environment, UN Doc A/HRC/37/59 (24 January 2018), Annex, Framework Principle 15; see also Paris agreement, art. 5.2. 25 Decision 1/CP.16, Cancún Agreements, UN Doc FCCC/CP/2010/7/Add.1, Appendix I, para. 2.

28 UNDRIP contains a right to equitable compensation and has been interpreted in the context of ABS legislation to include compensation for the exploitation of traditional knowledge and genetic resources.[81]

A further safeguard against the misappropriation and/or the inequitable distribution of benefits of MTK is FPIC. FPIC is an important right and permeates UNDRIP through references in articles, 10, 11, 19, 28, 30 and 32. Some states are concerned as to the breadth of the right in UNDRIP, and there has been some academic debate in relation to the status of FPIC following the adoption of the Declaration.[82] However the Permanent Forum on Indigenous Issues has elaborated on the meaning of FPIC.[83] Indigenous peoples have called for consultation and participation in climate change policy and legislative measures, and have stated that the right to participate in decision making and FPIC in line with UNDRIP and principle 10 of the Rio Declaration are crucial in discussions over climate change.[84] Furthermore, in the *Ogiek* case the Court stated that consent must be given in accordance with the Ogiek people's customs and traditions and, in addition, it must be given freely and can be withheld.[85]

Customary land tenure and meteorological traditional knowledge

Customary land tenure, although broadly recognized in the Inter American Court of Human Rights (IACHR),[86] the African Court,[87] the African Commission,[88] some domestic legislation,[89] international

---

81 T Mahop, *Intellectual Property, Community Rights and Human Rights: the Biological and Genetic Resources of Developing Countries'* (Routledge 2010).

82 M Barelli, 'Free, Prior, and Informed Consent in the Aftermath of the UN Declaration on the Rights of Indigenous Peoples: Developments and Challenges Ahead' (2012) 16 *The International Journal of Human Rights* 4.

83 Report of the International Workshop on Methodologies regarding Free, Prior and Informed Consent and Indigenous Peoples (7–19 January 2005) UN Doc. E/C.19/2005/3, para. 46.

84 Report of the Indigenous Peoples' Global Summit on Climate Change, para. 259, 20–24 April 2009, Anchorage, Alaska.

85 *Ogiek* case, p. 12 E iv.

86 Inter-American Court, *Case of Mayagna (Sumo) Awas Tingni Community v Nicaragua*, Judgment of 31 August 2001; I/A Court HR, *Case of the Yakye Axa Indigenous Community v Paraguay*. Judgment of 17 June 2005. Series C No. 125, para. 135.

87 *Ogiek* case.

88 *Endorois* case.

89 For example, Botswana Tribal Land Act 1968; Tanzania Village Land Act (No. 5 of 1999), http://indigenouspeoplesissues.com/index.php?option=com_content&view=article&id=10276:africa-statutory-recognition-of-customary-land-rights-in-africa-an-investigation-into-best-practices-for-law-making-and-implementation&catid=55:africa-indigenous-peoples&Itemid=77, accessed 12 November 2022.

instruments,[90] and jurisprudence,[91] still remains vulnerable to misappropriation by the state and non-state actors.[92] In reality, this means that an indigenous group who have managed their traditional lands since time immemorial can be removed from their traditional lands by the state.[93] By severing the linkage between indigenous peoples and their land, MTK is lost forever.

The loss of land and MTK gives rise to cultural harm. The nature of the cultural harm that arises is said to vary according to the community context.[94] The loss of indigenous lands in the American and Australian context has led to severe intergenerational trauma and cultural harm, evidenced in the high rates of drug and alcohol abuse and incarcerations.[95] Tsosie, an American Indigenous Navajo scholar, has linked the concept of cultural harm to assimilation and the loss of culture.[96] Exactly the meaning of cultural harm in the African indigenous peoples context the author – as a non-indigenous person – is unable to comment.

The importance of a particular geographical location to indigenous peoples stems from the fact that indigenous peoples rely on traditional lands and natural resources for their livelihood and economic sustenance, as well as their religious and cultural life.[97] Furthermore, in the light of climate change

90 See the International Labour Organization (ILO) Convention 169, art. 13 which recognizes the complex and special relationship indigenous peoples have with their land. ILO 169, art. 14 equates ownership and possession with traditional occupation. Furthermore, art. 26 UNDRIP includes the right to indigenous lands based on traditional ownership; The African Commission's Resolution on the Recognition and Protection of the Right of Participation, Governance and Use of Natural Resources by Indigenous and Local Populations in Africa – ACHPR/Res. 489 (LXIX)2021 tasks the Working Group through the African Commission, 'to support indigenous communities and minorities with respect to their rights to natural resources in the territories that they live'.

91 *Western Sahara case*, Advisory Opinion of 16 October 1975; *Mabo v Queensland* [1992] 2 ALR 1 244.

92 *Olosokwan Village Council v Attorney General of the United Republic of Tanzania* Reference No. 10 of 2017.

93 See *Endorois* and *Ogiek* cases.

94 Tsosie (n 7).

95 For more on intergenerational trauma and American indigenous peoples, see 'What is Trauma' Trauma – Healing – Australian Indigenous HealthInfoNet, https://healthinfonet.ecu.edu.au/learn/health-topics/healing/trauma, accessed 12 January 2023; SM Shepherd, B Spivak and LJ Ashford *et al.*, 'Closing the (incarceration) gap: assessing the socio-economic and clinical indicators of indigenous males by lifetime incarceration status' (2020) 20 *BMC Public Health* 710 .

96 Tsosie (n 7).

97 See E Daes, 'Study on Indigenous People and their Relationship to Land', UN Doc. E/CN.4/Sub.2/1999/18 (3 June 1999), para.18; James Anaya, *Indigenous Peoples in International Law: New* (Oxford University Press 2004) 141; J Asiema and F Situma., 'Indigenous Peoples and the Environment: The Case of the Pastoral Maasai of Kenya' (1994) 5 *Journal of International Environmental Law and Policy* 149.

concerns traditional lands are recognized as essential in adaptation and mitigation measures. Therefore, the IPCC has recognized the importance of the customary land tenure of indigenous peoples and local communities in relation to the vulnerability of such communities to climate change.[98]

Regionally, there are two significant human rights fora – the African Commission and the African Court. The Commission is viewed as a quasi-judicial body and its decisions are not legally binding. Anyone may bring a complaint to the attention of the African Commission alleging that a state party to the African Charter has violated one or more of the rights included in the Charter.[99] The African Court in contrast is a judicial forum and decisions are legally binding against signatories to the Protocol to the African Charter on the Establishment of the African Court of Human and Peoples Rights. Article 5 states who can bring a case before the Court, which includes the African Commission.

In 2003 the African Commission had to consider a case between a semi-nomadic indigenous community, the Endorois, and the state of Kenya, in the *Centre for Minority Rights Development (Kenya) and Minority Rights Group International on behalf of Endorois Welfare Council v Kenya* (the *Endorois* case).[100] The case concerned the evictions of the Endorois people from their ancestral lands due to the creation of a game reserve. The Endorois people alleged that the government's decision to gazette Endorois traditional land as a game reserve, which in turn denied the Endorois access to the area, had jeopardized the community's pastoral enterprise and imperiled its cultural integrity.[101] The Endorois peoples cited their continuing presence on the land and customary use of the land as evidence of ownership. The Endorois community had always understood the land in question to be 'Endorois' land, belonging to the community as a whole and used by it for habitation, cattle, beekeeping, and religious and cultural practices. Other communities would, for instance, ask permission to bring their animals to the area.[102] The Endorois argued that Lake Bogoria is also the centre of the community's religious and traditional practices: around the Lake are found the community's historical prayer sites, the places for circumcision rituals, and other cultural ceremonies.[103] The African Commission found that the Kenyan government had violated the following rights included in the African Charter: article

[98] Intergovernmental Panel on Climate Change (IPCC), Special Report: Climate Change and Land, https://www.ipcc.ch/srccl/.

[99] https://www.achpr.org/communications.

[100] 1276/2003 *The Centre for Minority Rights Development (Kenya) and Minority Rights Group International on behalf of Endorois Welfare Council v Kenya.*

[101] *Endorois* case, para. 19.

[102] *Endorois* case, para. 72.

[103] *Endorois* case, para. 73.

8 (the right to practice religion), article 14 (the right to property), article 17(2) and (3) (the right to culture), article 21 (the rights to free disposition of natural resources), and article 22 (the right to development).[104]

Up until now the Kenyan government has not implemented the Commission's decision. However, as a consequence of the case the Endorois Welfare Council and non-governmental organizations drew up the 'Endorois Peoples' Biocultural Protocol: Sustainable Biodiversity Resource Management For Access and Benefit Sharing and Protection from Threats to Culture'.[105] It is a comprehensive document that outlines the protection of resources and details procedures, principles and access in relation to engagement with their resources. This Protocol lays out the terms of engagement in relation to the access to resources when the community is dealing with outside researchers. It is highly likely that MTK will now fall under the Protocol.[106] The Protocol includes monetary and non-monetary benefit sharing.[107]

Furthermore, the Endorois community is actively engaging in climate change mitigation and adaptation, and the Protocol makes reference to this.[108] According to Walter Leal Filho *et al*, the Endorois people have turned to climate-smart agroecological production systems, such as the cultivation of drought-tolerant cereals, tubers and vegetables. This shift in production systems has led to more sustainable land management, minimized water usage, reduced human–wildlife conflict, and enhanced food security among the Endorois.[109] Owing to their close cultural connection to their environment, the Endorois have also embraced nature-based ecotourism enterprises, including medical, cultural and geotourism, in response to the climate-change-induced negative effects on their livelihoods. Other adaptations to climate-change effects among the Endorois people include livestock and crop diversification, herd adjustment by class, livestock destocking, and supplementary feeding of livestock.[110] Even though the state of Kenya has not implemented the Commission's decision, the Protocol is

[104] *Endorois* case, para. 22.

[105] 'Endorois Welfare Council, Endorois Biocultural Protocol Sustainable Biodiversity Resource Management for Access and Benefit Sharing and protection from Threats to Culture' (2019), www.abs-initiative.info/fileadmin//media/Knowledge_Center/Publications/BCPs/Endorois-Peoples-Biocultural-Protocol.pdf, accessed 12 November 2022.

[106] Endorois Welfare Council (n 105), 19.

[107] Endorois Welfare Council (n 105), 28.

[108] Endorois Welfare Council (n 105), 26.

[109] W Leal Filho, W Matandirotya, NR Lütz *et al*, ' Impacts of Climate Change to African Indigenous Communities and Examples of Adaptation Responses' (2021) 12 *Nature Communications* 6224.

[110] Filho *at al* (n 109).

an example of the 'ripple' effect that can occur due to strategic human rights litigation,[111] and the litigation has indirectly led to enhanced protection for traditional knowledge.

The *Ogiek* case in the African Court concerned the Ogiek people's access to the Mau Forest.[112] The Mau Forest is the Ogiek people's spiritual home and is central to the practice of their religion. It is where they bury the dead according to their traditional rituals and is additionally where certain types of trees are found for worship.[113] The forest further provides food and shelter.[114] In reference to the discussion on MTK, the story told by the Ogiek in the submission was one of the preservation of biodiversity flowing from the respect of sacred places. This is not uncommon in the stories that indigenous peoples tell in relation to their environment.[115] Indigenous peoples draw on biodiversity to support their MTK and in turn their MTK maintains their biodiversity. The African Court found that the Kenyan government had violated the following African Charter rights: article 1,[116] article 2,[117] article 4,[118] article 8,[119] article 14,[120] article 17(2) and (3),[121] article 21[122] and article 22.[123]

---

111 Duffy (n 12).

112 *African Commission on Human and Peoples' Rights v Republic of Kenya*, ACtHPR, Application No. 006/2012 (2017).

113 *African Commission on Human and Peoples' Rights v Republic of Kenya*, ACtHP, paras 6, 45.

114 *Ogiek* case, para. 43.

115 *Ogiek* case, para. 43 B and C.

116 'The Member States of the Organisation of African Unity, parties to the present Charter shall recognise the rights, duties and freedoms enshrined in the Charter and shall undertake to adopt legislative or other measures to give effect to them.'

117 'Every individual shall be entitled to the enjoyment of the rights and freedoms recognized and guaranteed in the present Charter without distinction of any kind such as race, ethnic group, colour, sex, language, religion, political or any other opinion, national and social origin, fortune, birth or any status.'

118 'Human beings are inviolable. Every human being shall be entitled to respect for his life and the integrity of his person. No one may be arbitrarily deprived of this right.'

119 'Freedom of conscience, the profession and free practice of religion shall be guaranteed. No one may, subject to law and order, be submitted to measures restricting the exercise of these freedoms.'

120 'The right to property shall be guaranteed. It may only be encroached upon in the interest of public need or in the general interest of the community and in accordance with the provisions of appropriate laws.'

121 '2. Every individual may freely take part in the cultural life of his community. 3. The promotion and protection of morals and traditional values recognized by the community shall be the duty of the State.'

122 '1. All peoples shall freely dispose of their wealth and natural resources. This right shall be exercised in the exclusive interest of the people. In no case shall a people be deprived of it.'

123 '1. All peoples shall have the right to their economic, social and cultural development with due regard to their freedom and identity and in the equal enjoyment of the common

Due to the holistic nature of indigenous peoples resources,[124] all these rights referred to by the African Commission and the African Court are relevant in relation to MTK. However, three rights are worthy of further discussion: article 17(2) and (3) (the right to culture), article 8 (the right to practise religion) and article 22 (the right to development).

In relation to the right to culture, Xanthaki argues that cultural claims should be placed within a cultural rights framework.[125] The right to culture has been highlighted in a number of international instruments and United Nations reports; however, there is no international legal definition of its meaning.[126] Regional human rights courts, however, have been crucial in developing the meaning of cultural rights relating to indigenous peoples.[127] Additionally, the Report of the former Special Rapporteur in the field of cultural rights, Karima Bennoune, stresses that climate change and cultural rights share a clear nexus. She argues: 'Culture is closely connected to ecosystems, especially for indigenous peoples, rural and "traditional" populations. Both cultures and the environment are often place-based'.[128] In her recommendations, she includes that states and other relevant actors should 'Advocate for strong property rights for women and indigenous peoples in line with relevant international standards'.[129]

With reference to article 8, which includes the right to practise a religion, the United Nations Human Rights Committee commenting on article 18 of the ICCPR stated: 'The terms "belief" and "religion" are to be broadly

heritage of mankind. 2. States shall have the duty, individually or collectively, to ensure the exercise of the right to development.'

124 Daes (n 97), paras 31 and 164.

125 Xanthaki (n 20).

126 Article 27 International Covenant on Cultural and Political Rights (ICCPR) and art. 15 International Covenant on Economic, Social and Cultural Rights (ICESCR); Farida Shaheed, Independent Expert in the Field of Cultural Rights Report, 'The Right to Access to and Enjoyment of Cultural Heritage as a Human Right', UN Doc. A/ HRC/17/38; UN; Human Rights Council. Resolution 37/17: Cultural Rights and the Protection of Cultural Heritage (22 March 2018) UN Doc A/HRC/RES/37/17; Committee on Economic, Social and Cultural Rights (CESCR), General Comment No. 21, Right of everyone to take part in cultural life (Art. 15, para. 1a of the Covenant on Economic, Social and Cultural Rights), 21 December 2009, UN Doc. E/C.12/GC/21, para. 11; General Comment No. 25 (2020) on Science and Economic, Social and Cultural Rights, art. 15(1)(b), (2), (3) and (4) of the International Covenant on Economic, Social and Cultural Rights UN Doc. E/C.12/GC/21, para. 39; African Union 2006 Charter for African Cultural Renaissance.

127 *Endorois* case, para. 239 and *Ogiek* case, para. 176.

128 K Bennoune, Special Rapporteur in the Field of Cultural Rights, 'Report on Climate Change, Culture and Cultural Rights', UN Doc. A/75/298, para. 18.

129 Bennoune (n 128), Recommendations B 81 (t).

construed'.[130] In the *Endorois* case, it was stated: 'cultural practices constituted a religion under international law'.[131] With reference to the central land claim in both cases, the importance of the spiritual relationship that indigenous peoples have with land has been articulated in the IACHR, and in the African Commission and the African Court.[132]

In relation to the right to development, article 2(3) UN Declaration on the Right to Development specifically includes 'active, free and meaningful participation in development'. Further, article 23 UNDRIP includes indigenous peoples in the administration of development through their own institutions.[133] Additionally, the African Court stated in regard to section 10(2) of the Kenyan Constitution in the *Ogiek* case:

> [I]t is not a matter of whether or not these instruments provide for the right to development, but rather whether the Respondent has discharged its obligation to protect the Ogieks' right to development. According to the Applicant, this would be by establishing a framework which provides for the realization of this right in its procedural and substantive processes, including consultation and participation.[134]

The African Commission in the *Endorois* case further stated that 'the result of development should be empowerment of the Endorois community'.[135]

Conclusion

Indigenous peoples have been hit thrice. They are negatively impacted by climate change, they contribute the least to climate change, and their MTK is vulnerable to misappropriation. As of yet the MTK of indigenous peoples has not explicitly appeared in the jurisprudence of international, regional or domestic legal fora. However, this chapter argues that MTK is yet another indigenous resource vulnerable to misappropriation. The

130 Human Rights Committee, General Comment 22, art. 18 (48th session, 1993), Compilation of General Comments and General Recommendations Adopted by Human Rights Treaty Bodies, UN Doc. HRI\ GEN\1\ Rev.1 (1994), 35 para. 2.

131 *Endorois* case, paras 283 and 173.

132 *Comunidad Indígena Yakye Axa v Paraguay (Judgment)* (2005); *Mayagna (Sumo) Awas Tingni Community v Nicaragua*, 31 August 2001, Inter-Am Ct HR, reprinted in 'The Case of the Mayagna (Sumo) Awas Tingni Community v Nicaragua' (2002), 19 *Arizona Journal of International and Comparative Law* 148–9.

133 Special Rapporteur Saad Alfarargi on the right to development A/HRC/39/5120, July 2018, para. 19.

134 *Ogiek* case, para. 203.

135 *Endorois* case, para. 283.

preservation and recognition of indigenous peoples' customary land tenure is essential to the preservation of MTK for present and future generations. Additionally the implementation of African Court and Commission decisions by states is crucial to the preservation of MTK. In relation to the sharing of MTK, the right to development, along with the international principles of ABS and FPIC, has the potential to allow MTK to be shared with the scientific community equitably. The principles of ABS and FPIC act as 'back stops' to prevent further cultural harm caused by the exploitation of indigenous peoples' resources, as exemplified by the Endorois Peoples' Biocultural Protocol.

9

Rights-Based Climate Change Litigation Against Private Actors

Pia Rebelo and Xavier Rebelo

Introduction

While the majority of strategic climate litigation cases (around 76 per cent) have targeted governments,[1] an increasing number of private actors are being cited as defendants.[2] Although initial attempts at suing private entities for climate-related harm were largely unsuccessful, scientific advances in quantifying the carbon contributions of polluters has sparked more recent developments of private climate litigation by potentially overcoming problems of causation.[3] Suing private entities as a litigation strategy is driven by the realization that non-state actors have become more powerful than states, particularly in transnational industrial sectors.[4] Despite this recognition, there are still insufficient international law instruments that impose environmental standards on these actors and, where such instruments do exist, the problem

---

1. Climate change litigation refers to those claims brought before international or national tribunals that raise issues of fact or law relating to climate change mitigation or adaptation; see M Burger and J Gundlach, *The Status of Climate Change Litigation: A Global Review. UN Environment Programme* (Sabin Center for Climate Change Law, Columbia University, 2017).
2. J Setzer and C Higham, *Global Trends in Climate Change Litigation: 2021 Snapshot* (Grantham Research Institute on Climate Change and the Environment and Centre for Climate Change Economics and Policy, London School of Economics and Political Science 2021) 12. This number refers to those cases outside the United States.
3. G Ganguly, J Setzer and V Heyvaert, 'If at First You Don't Succeed: Suing Corporations for Climate Change' (2018) 38 *Oxford Journal of Legal Studies* 841.
4. D M Chirwa, 'The Horizontal Application of Constitutional Rights in a Comparative Perspective' (2006) 10(2) *Law, Democracy & Development* 21.

of implementation and enforcement is prevalent. Strategic climate litigants are therefore having to pave new ways to hold private companies accountable for their contribution to climate change.

As early as 2016, an Australian report entitled 'Climate Change and Directors' Liability', found it conceivable that directors who neglect duly to consider pertinent climate change risks may attract liability for breaching their duty of care and diligence.[5] This cognizance has gained momentum and has influenced the latest strategic approach to corporate climate change litigation. Companies are increasingly being accused of 'greenwashing' – a misrepresentation of the sustainable performance of a company or its alignment with reported green targets.[6] Consumer interests in exercising lifestyle choices that are 'green' and aligned with decarbonization targets are hampered by such misinformation, thus preventing such choices from having the desired sustainability impact.[7] As corporate governance decisions respond to growing consumer demand for tackling climate change, private law mechanisms will be creatively engaged with to impose liability on private entities.[8] These efforts should be supported by a constitutional mandate that allows for the recognition of green obligations to be imposed on private actors, and also provides a normative mandate for interpreting the way in which business activities should be performed.

In this regard, the power of constitutionally entrenched environmental and related socio-economic rights cannot be overstated. African states are placed at a unique advantage in respect of private environmental disputes as certain post-colonial constitutions on the continent specifically enshrine a

[5] N Hutley SC and S H Davis, 'Climate Change and Directors' Duties' (2019) *Supplementary Memorandum of Opinion*, https://cpd.org.au/2019/03/directors-duties-2019/, accessed 25 July 2020; subsequently, the Centre for Policy Development in Australia augmented the 2016 opinion by emphasizing five material developments since 2016 that have further elevated the need for directors to engage in board-level governance and duly consider climate risks.

[6] Competition and Markets Authority, Green Claims Code, 20 September 2021, https://www.gov.uk/government/publications/green-claims-code-making-environmental-claims, accessed 21 December 2021. Green taxonomy initiatives and ESG are also opening up the possibility of competition and consumer rights litigation.

[7] In May 2022, KLM was sued for greenwashing by allegedly creating a false impression that their flights are environmentally 'responsible'. See D Gayle, 'Climate Group Sues Dutch airline KLM over "Greenwashing" Adverts', *The Guardian*, 24 May 2022, https://www.theguardian.com/business/2022/may/24/climate-group-sues-dutch-airline-klm-over-adverts, accessed 7 July 2022.

[8] By way of example, this could include the implication of green terms and the interpretation of consumer rights in contracts, or a firm recognition of environmental rights in the public policy underpinnings of determining a tort. See P Rebelo, 'Sustainable Supply Chain Finance: The Incorporation of Green Principles into SCF Agreements' (2020) 26(4) *International Trade Law & Regulation* 262.

right to a healthy environment.[9] South Africa, having a particularly developed environmental law framework, is a good place for climate change disputes arising from private actor conduct. The transformative character of South Africa's 1996 Constitution also views socio-economic rights as conduits for change. Karl Klare has described transformative constitutionalism as connoting an 'enterprise of inducing large-scale change through non-violent political processes grounded in law'.[10] In order for the Constitution to serve as a tool for social justice, it has been argued that environmental protection must be pursued, hence 'transformative environmental constitutionalism' also forms part of South Africa's constitutional jurisprudence.[11] South Africa therefore offers a powerful constitutional framework for overcoming all forms of dominance, even interspecies injustice and the challenges posed by the Anthropocene; thus calling for a 'greening' of judicial interpretation and application of the law.[12]

This chapter is confined to an analysis of one strategy of private climate litigation – rights-based private climate litigation, and its promising prospects within an African context. 'Rights-based litigation' is used broadly to encompass cases that are founded on fundamental rights, as well as those that use rights as a reflexive interpretative tool. The latter considers human rights as part of the 'extra-statutory context' taken into account by the court.[13] The predominant focus of this chapter will be on the latter as it calls for environmental rights, and related socio-economic rights, to guide the interpretation and performance of obligations between private entities. This chapter argues that African constitutions, in particular South Africa's 1996 Constitution, offers significant advantages in providing a legal framework for greening private law, thus enabling new ways of pursuing private actor accountability for climate change. As a specific exemplar, it explores the nascent judicial practice of interpreting the nature and scope of directors' common law and statutory duties through the prism of the Bill of Rights. It is postulated that this reflexive interpretive approach to the horizontal application of the Bill of Rights presents litigants with an additional angle

---

[9] The relatively recent constitutions of South Africa, Mali, and the Democratic Republic of Congo proffer clear articulation of an environmental right.

[10] K Klare, 'Legal Culture and Transformative Constitutionalism' (1998) 14 *South African Journal on Human Rights* 146.

[11] M Murcott, 'Transformative Environmental Constitutionalism's Response to the Setting Aside of South Africa's Moratorium on Rhino Horn Trade' (2017) 6 *Humanities* 84.

[12] D Bilchitz, 'Does Transformative Constitutionalism Require the Recognition of Animal Rights?' (2010) 25 *Southern African Public Law* 267–300.

[13] J Peel and HM Osofsky, 'A Rights Turn in Climate Change Litigation?' (2018) 7 *Transnational Environmental Law* 37.

through which to pursue private climate litigation in South Africa, one that has not yet been attempted.

The influence of a rights-based approach on private climate change litigation

A rights-based approach to suing private actors has emerged from climate litigation against public bodies, focusing on a vertical application of human rights and their interconnectedness with surrounding environmental conditions.[14] Climate litigation trends are moving towards a creative engagement with rights-based arguments with a diversification of defendants – both public and private.[15] This section evaluates how rights-based arguments have gained traction against public bodies and how these can be similarly directed at private defendants. Rights-based arguments against private actors must also necessarily consider the prospect of horizontality – something that has begun to emerge, sometimes implicitly, in some of the cases set out below.

As a starting point, two cases are noteworthy in illustrating a receptiveness to an emerging rights-based jurisprudence – these are the *Leghari* and *Urgenda* cases, based in Pakistan and the Netherlands respectively. Both of these cases illustrate a willingness on the parts of litigants to employ rights-based arguments in the context of climate change to challenge government climate policy and corporate action.[16] The *Leghari* case was significant for rights-based arguments in that it recognized that fundamental rights under the Constitution, 'read with the constitutional values of political, economic and social justice provide the necessary judicial toolkit to address and monitor the Government's response to climate change'.[17] The High Court acknowledged the normative concept of 'climate justice' as a construct which must transform its predecessor, 'environmental justice'. The court in the *Leghari* case stated that its environmental jurisprudence has 'weaved [its] constitutional values and fundamental rights with the international

---

14 See, for example, *Juliana v United States*, 339 F Supp 3d 1062 (D Or 2018).

15 Although this approach is not always mutually exclusive from a rights-based one. See *Massachusetts v Environmental Protection Agency (EPA)* 549 US 497 (2007) generally considered a landmark lawsuit, considered and interpreted the Clean Air Act and whether the US EPA had wrongfully decided to not regulate greenhouse gas emissions.

16 Prior to these judgments, the traditional rights-based approach struggled with the obstacle of attributing human rights violations to GHG emissions, especially where such harm is merely *predicted* or whether rights protections need to be applied *extraterritorially*. See Peel and Osofsky (n 13), 46.

17 *Ashgar Leghari v Federation of Pakistan* (WP No. 25501/2015), Lahore High Court Green Bench, Orders of 4 September 2015, para. 7.

environmental principles';[18] and that: 'Climate Justice links human rights and development to achieve a human-centred approach, safeguarding the rights of the most vulnerable people and sharing the burdens and benefits of climate change and its impacts equitably and fairly. [...] Who is to be penalised and who is to be restrained'.[19]

As a result, the High Court held that the Federal Government of Pakistan and Regional Government of Punjab's delay in implementing climate change policy and its implementing framework had offended fundamental rights. Various government ministries, departments and authorities were ordered to ensure the due implementation of such.[20]

Similar rights violations arguments were employed in the *Urgenda* case, although not initially recognized by the court of first instance. However, the finding of the Hague District court still remains important for the development of rights-based arguments in so far as they apply to private law. The District Court used human rights reflexively to interpret the open standard of a duty of care in negligence, supporting an order that government must cut its greenhouse gas emissions (GHGs) by at least 25 per cent by the end of 2020 compared to 1990 levels. The environmental non-governmental organization (NGO), Urgenda, and around 900 Dutch citizens successfully argued that the Dutch government owed a duty of care to the plaintiffs and larger society and that this duty was breached by the government's unsatisfactory climate change mitigation policy.[21] The District Court specifically stated that international obligations and principles have a 'reflex effect' in national law;[22] and that courts may take international law obligations and principles into account when they interpret open standards in national laws. However, the District Court would not find any direct rights violations.

The Dutch government appealed in 2018,[23] and the Court of Appeal built its reasoning almost entirely on the right to life and the right to private and family life under articles 2 and 8 of the European Convention on Human Rights (ECHR).[24] Although the Appeal Court affirmed that District Court's

---

18 *Ashgar Leghari v Federation of Pakistan* (WP No. 25501/2015), Lahore High Court Green Bench, Orders of 4 September and 14 September 2015, para. 20.

19 *Ashgar Leghari*, para. 21.

20 *Ashgar Leghari*, para. 25.

21 The District Court based this order on the doctrine of hazardous negligence which is stated in the Dutch Civil Code as being tortious behaviour if it unnecessarily creates danger and thus is contrary to what 'according to unwritten law is deemed fit in societal interrelations' (art. 6:162).

22 *Urgenda Foundation v The Netherlands* [2015] HAZA C/09/00456689, para. 4.43.

23 *The State of the Netherlands v Urgenda Foundation*, The Hague Court of Appeal (9 October 2018), Case 200.178.245/01 (English translation).

24 *Urgenda Foundation*, para. 43.

interpretive approach of using rights to inform an understanding of the Dutch state's duty of care in torts, it also took the opportunity to review the District Court's determination that Urgenda could not directly invoke articles 2 and 8.[25] On 20 December 2019, the Dutch government failed in a second appeal to the Supreme Court of the Netherlands, which upheld the decision of the Court of Appeal under articles 2 and 8 of the ECHR.[26] This is significant as the Supreme Court affirmed that climate change is undeniably a human rights issue as it poses risks in the form of sea level rise, heat stress, deteriorated air quality, increasing spread of infectious diseases, excessive rainfall and disruption of food production and drinking water supply. On the other hand, the Appeal Court and the Supreme Court's affirmation of rights informing open standards in national law, like the law of torts, provides a firm recognition of the relevance of rights-based arguments for the private law.

The *Urgenda* and *Leghari* cases heralded a turn in climate change litigation against states, one specifically based on human rights, which led to the emergence of similar cases being brought in various other jurisdictions.[27] However, *Urgenda*'s approach of holding a government accountable for inaction on climate change mitigation is not to be seen as a gold standard. In fact, the *Urgenda* approach has led some courts decline to adjudicate on such matters or to employ a strict separation of powers in allowing the legislature to exercise discretion.[28] Maxwell, Mead, and van Berkel argue that there is a 'a concern on the part of national courts about a perceived lack of standards against which to assess the legality of a State's mitigation'.[29] Nevertheless, these state-directed challenges have undoubtedly contributed to a global impetus to hold *all* contributors to climate change responsible.[30] The success

25 S Roy and E Woerdman, 'Situating *Urgenda v the Netherlands* within Comparative Climate Change Litigation' (2016) 34 *Journal of Energy & Natural Resources Law* 172.

26 Supreme Court of the Netherlands ECLI:NL:HR:2019:2007. The *Urgenda* case is discussed further and from a comparative perspective in the chapter by Sanita van Wyk in this volume.

27 For example: *Juliana v United States* (n 14); *Third Runway at Vienna International Airport case*, Case No. W109 2000179-1/291E, Federal Administrative Court, Austria, 2 February 2017; and *Earthlife Africa Johannesburg v Minister of Environmental Affairs* [2017] ZAGPPHC 58 (hereafter *Earthlife* case), Judgment of High Court of South Africa, Gauteng Division, Pretoria (South Africa), 8 March 2017.

28 L Maxwell, S Mead and D van Berkel, 'Standards for Adjudicating the Next Generation of Urgenda-Style Climate Cases' (2022) 13(1) *Journal of Human Rights and the Environment* 35–63, 37.

29 Maxwell, Mead and van Berkel (n 28), 26.

30 Setzer and Benjamin argue that the success of recent rights-based arguments is also largely supported by two factors: (1) access to justice in conjunction with climate or environmental rights; and (2) judicial activism. See J Setzer and L Benjamin, 'Climate Litigation in the Global South: Constraints and Innovations' (2020) 9 *Transnational Environmental Law* 80.

of these cases also undeniably paved the way for the *Milieudefensie* case,[31] instituted by the same legal team that brought *Urgenda*,[32] which has inspired action against private entities. Non-state actors have also been targeted in the Peruvian case of *Luciano Lliuya v RWE AG*[33] in Germany, and the National Enquiry on Climate Change by the Commission on Human Rights of the Philippines (CHRP).[34]

Although *Luciano Lliuya v RWE AG* was brought in German civil law, which meant a certain standard of causation applied, it was asserted on appeal that any criteria applied to the relevance of partially causal contributions to climate change,

> must be oriented toward the legally protected rights in question. If, as in this case, life and health, the flood protection of the general public, and the property of the appellant are affected, then this must be taken into account in a legal assessment of the criteria for relevance; the result based on the criteria cannot be that the appellant is left ultimately without rights.[35]

This case was brought in Germany by a Peruvian farmer called Saul Luciano Lliuya, with the support of Greenwatch (a German NGO), against the German energy company RWE.[36] Luciano's home city in the Andes, Huaraz, is situated just below the Palcacocha glacial lake. Due to global warming, the volume of the lake has increased along with the risk of dangerous glacial ice avalanches. Avalanches of this kind could cause outburst floods from the lake, which would not only flood the plaintiff's land, but would cause destruction and loss of life.[37] As an affected landowner, the plaintiff based his claim on § 1004 of the German Civil Code.[38] To base a claim on § 1004 of

---

31 *Milieudefensie v Royal Dutch Shell plc*, Hague District Court, Judgment of 26 May 2021.

32 The legal team for both Urgenda Foundation and Milieudefensie was Roger Cox, a partner at the Dutch law firm Paulussen Advocaten.

33 Case No. 2 O 285/15 Essen Regional Court.

34 Commission on Human Rights of the Philippines, National Enquiry on Climate Change (2022). The final report is available at http://climatecasechart.com/wp-content/uploads/sites/16/non-us-case-documents/2022/20220506_Case-No.-CHR-NI-2016-0001_judgment-1.pdf.

35 Unofficial translation, provided by Germanwatch e.V. of the Appeal against the judgment of the District Court of Essen, Az. 2 O 285/15, of 15 December 2016 (02/23/2017) 27.

36 Case No. 2 O 285/15 Essen District Court (15 December 2016).

37 Unofficial English transcript of decision of the Essen District Court (15 December 2016) http://climatecasechart.com/wp-content/uploads/sites/16/non-us-case-documents/2016/20161215_Case-No.-2-O-28515-Essen-Regional-Court_decision-1.pdf, accessed 26 October 2022.

38 Bürgerliches Gesetzbuch (BGB, Civil Code) (2002) Bundesgesetzblatt, Part I, No. 2, 42–341.

the Civil Code, a legally relevant causal link has to be established between the activity of the defendant and the nuisance suffered by the complainant. The test for causality in German Civil Law is the *conditio sine qua non* rule – causality is established if a certain consequence had not occurred fully or partially 'but for' the said activity.[39] The principle of adequacy also has to be fulfilled, 'that the event must have increased, to a not insignificant degree, the probability of an outcome of the kind that occurred'.[40] The District Court of Essen dismissed the claim on the basis that no linear causal chain could be established between Luciano Lliuya's account of the melting of mountain glaciers near his home town of Huaraz and the GHG emissions of the German electricity supplier.[41]

However, the plaintiff successfully argued in an appeal heard by the Higher Regional Court of Hamm, North Rhine-Westphalia, that there is a scientifically provable causal chain between RWE's CO_2 emissions and flood risk to his property.[42] In respect of adequacy, the claimant asserted that RWE, as the largest emitter in Europe, had made a significant enough contribution. The plaintiff also argued that on the issue of relevance, that even small or partial contributions are legally causal where there are infringements of rights.[43] This decision is important as it marks the first time a private company was recognized as capable of being legally responsible for its pro rata contribution to climate change. The appeal court accepted the plaintiff's legal arguments, and the case has now moved into its evidentiary phase where the court will hear expert testimony on whether:[44]

(1) there is a serious threat to the defendant's property due to the increase in volume of the lake in which the glacier is melting into;
(2) the defendant's power plants are contributing to global GHG emissions, resulting in co-causation of the glacier melting.[45]

---

39 W Frank, C Bals and J Grimm, 'The Case of Huaraz: First Climate Lawsuit on Loss and Damage Against an Energy Company Before German Courts' in R Mechler *et al* (eds), *Loss and Damage from Climate Change. Climate Risk Management, Policy and Governance* (Springer, Cham 2018) 477.

40 Frank, Bals and Grimm (n 39), 479.

41 Frank, Bals and Grimm (n 39).

42 Frank, Bals and Grimm (n 39).

43 The plaintiff cited a case involving vaccine damage which had infringed legal rights concerning life.

44 Order to parties to submit evidence (unofficial English translation) 1-5 U 15/17 2 0 285/15 Landgericht Essen, http://climatecasechart.com/wp-content/uploads/sites/16/non-us-case-documents/2017/20171211_Case-No.-2-O-28515-Essen-Regional-Court_order-1.pdf, accessed 26 October 2022.

45 The site visit of the Higher Regional Court of Hamm was delayed due to Covid-19, but has since been conducted in 2022 with a view as to whether the plaintiff's land is actually under threat from flooding.

This case is momentous in terms of its potential to establish the climate change liability of big energy companies.[46] Although not a rights-based case *per se*, it used the impact of climate change on property rights to interpret and apply civil law standards of causation. Recognizing the contribution of a big CO_2 emitter as capable of being a legal cause of climate change sets a monumental precedent that could lead towards holding private entities accountable.[47] Litigation against big carbon emitters, known as the 'carbon majors', has only garnered momentum in recent years, with the Commission on Human Rights of the Philippines announcing in a press release at the end of 2019 that 47 investor-owned corporations, including ExxonMobil, Chevron, Shell, BP, Total, Sasol and Repsol, can be found to be both legally and morally liable for a number of human rights violations against the Filipinos resulting from climate-related disasters.[48] The Commission's Final Report was released on 3 May 2022 and includes some key recommendations to the Philippine government, after concluding that the government exhibited 'mediocre actions' to meet the Paris Agreement on Climate Change and that, to date, there are no 'Philippine laws, policies, or jurisprudence on the intersectionality between business and Human rights, on the one hand, and climate change, on the other'.[49]

The Commission was petitioned in 2015 to conduct an inquiry into the impacts of climate change, as caused by the so-called 'carbon majors', on the human rights of the Filipino people.[50] There are also a number of cases brought around the world that involve a variety of legal arguments under different theories of responsibility or liability, also against the carbon majors.[51] While many of these cases are still ongoing or have reached differing results, there is a need to establish judicial consensus on the responsibility of carbon majors for climate change. Non-judicial mechanisms to achieve this are also

46 Frank, Bals and Grimm (n 39).

47 The Higher Regional Court of Hamm also accepted arguments of legal causation from foreign jurisdictions, including the UK case of *Bonnington Castings Ltd v Wardlaw* [1956] AC 613, [1956] UKHL 1 and the Australian case of *March v E & MH Stramare Pty Ltd* (1991) 171 CLR 506.

48 CHR Philippines, 'CHR Concluded Landmark Inquiry on the Effects of Climate Change to Human Rights; Expects to Set the Precedent in Seeking Climate Justice', Press Release, 13 December 2018, http://chr.gov.ph/chr-concluded-landmark-inquiry-on-the-effects-of-climate-change-to-human-rights-expects-to-set-the-precedent-in-seeking-climate-justice/, accessed 9 April 2022.

49 Commission on Human Rights of the Philippines, *National Enquiry on Climate Change Report* (2022) 152.

50 *National Enquiry on Climate Change Report* (n 49), 1. The Carbon Majors cases are based on the research by R Heede, 'Tracing Anthropogenic Carbon Dioxide and Methane Emissions to Fossil Fuel and Cement Producers, 1854–2010' (2014) 122 *Climatic Change* 229.

51 *National Enquiry on Climate Change Report* (n 49), 2.

being explored, such as framing climate change as a human rights issue and filing a petition before a human rights institution. Given the rising number of typhoons that have ravaged the Philippines in recent years, including the worst typhoon on record in 2013,[52] the people of the Philippines continue to suffer from climate-change related extreme weather events. The Commission recognized that the petition filed had no established legal precedent and that it did not have the resources to undergo such an extensive investigation.[53] Nevertheless, Panel Chairman Commissioner Roberto Cadiz, stated that national human rights institutions have a role to play in testing boundaries and creating new paths: 'to be bold and creative, instead of timid and docile; to be more idealistic, and less pragmatic; to promote soft laws into becoming hard laws; to be able to see beyond legal technicalities and establish guiding principles that can later become binding treaties'.

Although the approach of the Commission was dialogical rather than adversarial, the Commission recognized that the results of the inquiry could be relied upon by rights-holders as a foundation for filing claims for punitive damages at a later stage. The Commission found that climate change has an adverse effect on a number of basic human rights, including: the right to life, the right to health, the right to food security, the right to water and sanitation, the right to livelihood, the right to adequate housing, the right to preservation of culture, and even the rights to non-discrimination for minority groups such as women, children, LGBTQ+, indigenous people, the elderly, and those living in poverty.[54] In addition to declaring the responsibility of states to protect and promote such rights by responding to climate change, the Commission said that business enterprises must equally respect such rights through, inter alia, appropriate policies, disclosure and reporting, human rights due diligence processes, and processes to enable remediation when there are adverse impacts on human rights.[55] The most groundbreaking finding of this report were a number of affirmations that the carbon majors had early awareness of their adverse climate impacts, that they had engaged in willful obfuscation and obstruction to prevent meaningful climate action, and that they had misled shareholders and consumers. The Commission enunciated on a number of civil liability avenues for holding carbon majors accountable.

Globally, there are a number of recent cases seeking to hold carbon majors liable for their climate change contributions. The United States saw a wave

52 Typhoon Hiayan (Yolanda).

53 This was coupled with fervent opposition from the Carbon Majors who argued for dismissal of the petition and argued that the Commission was strictly confined to matters of civil and political rights. See *National Enquiry on Climate Change Report* (n 49), 4.

54 *National Enquiry on Climate Change Report* (n 49), 56–65.

55 *National Enquiry on Climate Change Report* (n 49), 88–98.

of climate lawsuits targeted against fossil fuel companies in the summer of 2020, including a number of 'firsts' in respect of legal arguments – such as the disgorgement of corporate profits and the targeting of a US oil and gas lobbyist group.[56] In March 2022, a milestone was reached when a state judge in Honolulu, Hawaii, issued two final rulings in favour of the City and County of Honolulu and the Board of Water Supply against large oil corporations for their misrepresentations regarding the scale and severity of the adverse climate impacts caused by their fossil fuel products.[57] Although Honolulu was the 13th jurisdiction in the United Staes to file this sort of case, it was the first to move into trial phase.

In extending rights-based arguments to private entities, the most significant development has been the success of the environmental group Milieudefensie and its co-plaintiffs in the Hague District Court in May 2021. The court order required that:

> [Royal Dutch Shell], both directly and via the companies and legal entities it commonly includes in its consolidated annual accounts and with which it jointly forms the Shell group, to limit or cause to be limited the aggregate annual volume of all CO_2 emissions into the atmosphere (Scope 1, 2 and 3) due to the business operations and sold energy-carrying products of the Shell group to such an extent that this volume will have reduced by at least net 45% at end 2030, relative to 2019 levels.[58]

This case concerned a private law matter, wherein Milieudefensie argued that Royal Dutch Shell (' RDS') has an obligation as per the unwritten standard of care under the Dutch Civil Code,[59] to assist efforts to prevent climate change through its corporate policy, which applies across the Shell group.[60] The unwritten standard of care is to be interpreted by the *Kelderluik* criteria[61]

---

56 *Charleston, City of v Brabham Oil Company Inc* 2:20-cv-03579; *State v American Petroleum Institute* 0:20-cv-01636; *State of Delaware v BP America Inc.* 1:20-cv-01429; *City of Hoboken v Exxon Mobil Corp.*, 20-cv-14243; *Baltimore v BP PLC,* 4th Cir., No. 19-1644.

57 *City & County of Honolulu and BWS v Sunoco, LP* Civ. No. 1CCV-20-0000380 (First Circuit Court, State of Hawai'i).

58 *Milieudefensie v Royal Dutch Shell plc.*, ECLI:NL:RBDHA:2021:5339, Hague District Court, Judgment of 26 May 2021.

59 Book 6 s. 162 Dutch Civil Code.

60 *Milieudefensie v Royal Dutch Shell plc* (n 58), para. 3.2.

61 Supreme Court, 5 November 1965, ECLI:NL:HR:1965:AB7079 (*Kelderluik*): 'The Dutch Supreme Court has held variations on the Kelderluik judgment to be applicable to a wide variety of risk situations, such as workplace accidents, toxic torts in the workplace, product liability and governmental liability'; see Ivo Giesen, Elbert de Jong and Marlou Overheul, 'How Dutch Law Responds to Risks' in M Dyson (ed), *Regulating Risks through Private Law* (Intersentia, 2018), 165.

for risk assessment, as well as human rights. Milieudefensie particularly highlighted the right to life and the right to respect for private and family life, as well as soft law instruments such as the UN Guiding Principles on Business and Human Rights, the UN Global Compact and the OECD Guidelines for Multinational Enterprises.[62]

In its judgment, the District Court relied quite heavily on the UN Guiding Principles (UNGP) as, 'an authoritative and internationally endorsed "soft law" instrument, which set out the responsibilities of states and businesses in relation to human rights'.[63] The court found it to be irrelevant whether or not RDS had committed itself to the UNGP, as they are universally endorsed.[64] It was found that Milieudefensie *et al* could not directly invoke the right to life and the right to respect for private and family life (of Dutch residents and the inhabitants of the Wadden region) with respect to RDS, as these rights only apply directly to relationships between states and citizens in Dutch law.[65] However, due to the 'fundamental interest of human rights and the value for society as a whole they embody', the court would factor these in to its interpretation of the unwritten standard of care.[66] The *Milieudefensie* case was helpful in stating that there is: 'a global standard of expected conduct for all business enterprises wherever they operate. It exists independently of States' abilities and/or willingness to fulfil their own human rights obligations, and does not diminish those obligations. And it exists over and above compliance with national laws and regulations protecting human rights'.[67]

There is thus a very clear judicial mandate for Dutch courts to interpret private law using human rights, and consequently to consider the impacts of climate change on such rights.[68] However, the horizontal application of human rights in a European context remains indirect, and environmental or climate change claims have centred on rights to life, property, and a private and family life – not a right to a healthy environment. A climate case invoking a specific environmental right is yet to be tested as the ECHR does not

62 *Milieudefensie v Royal Dutch Shell plc* (n 58), para. 3.2.

63 *Milieudefensie v Royal Dutch Shell plc* (n 58), para. 4.4.11.

64 Nevertheless, RDS had committed itself to the UNGP as advertised on its website.

65 These rights enshrined in arts 2 and 8 of the European Convention for the Protection of Human Rights and Fundamental Freedoms (ECHR) and arts 6 and 17 of the International Covenant on Civil Political Rights (ICCPR).

66 *Milieudefensie v Royal Dutch Shell plc* (n 58), para. 4.4.9.

67 *Milieudefensie v Royal Dutch Shell plc* (n 58), para. 4.4.13.

68 It is also important to note that the court still required that the class action represent the similar interests of affected Dutch residents and the inhabitants of the Wadden Sea area; other collective claims representing the 'interest of the entire world population in curbing dangerous climate change caused by CO2 emissions' were not allowable (*Milieudefensie v Royal Dutch Shell plc* (n 58), para. 4.2.4.).

contain an explicit right to a clean and healthy environment.[69] Arguably, certain African constitutions can achieve more in respect of rights-based arguments as they not only recognize a right to a healthy environment, but permit direct horizontality in addition to indirect horizontality – that is invoking rights adversely impacted by climate change directly against private parties, as well as using rights to interpret private law. The next section explores how the African continent has already made progressive inroads in applying environmental rights horizontally and how climate considerations are increasingly explored in a rights context against private entities. We also discuss how this progressive reading of rights means that African courts have potential to go even further than the groundbreaking cases already discussed. The next section provides a brief trend analysis of how cases in Africa have achieved such inroads in respect of rights-based environmental and climate change litigation.

The horizontal application of rights in an African context

Despite having a 'distinctive and progressive regional human rights architecture', Africa has few climate litigation cases and even fewer instances of climate litigation where both climate change and human rights are critically examined for their interconnectedness.[70] Furthermore, most cases bringing the issue of climate change before African courts have been targeted at government bodies for failing to consider climate change in respect of administrative procedures. Most of this litigation has been in the South African courts, the most recognized of which is the *Thabametsi* case.[71] Almost all of the South African cases have involved challenges to environmental authorizations granted under the National Environmental Management Act 107 of 1998 (NEMA), for reasons including a failure to adequately consider climate change factors in environmental impact authorization (EIA) procedures.[72] Other, recent cases have questioned government action

[69] Similarly, the UK's Human Rights Act 1998 makes no explicit mention of the environment, although a broad interpretation of art. 8 protecting the 'right to respect for … private and family life [and] home' has necessarily incorporated environmental factors.

[70] K Bouwer, 'The Influence of Human Rights on Climate Litigation in Africa' (2022) 13(1) *Journal of Human Rights and the Environment* 157–77, 158.

[71] *Earthlife* case (n 27); see also T-L Humby, 'The Thabametsi Case: Case No. 65662/16 *Earthlife Africa Johannesburg v Minister of Environmental Affairs*' (2018) 30(1) *Journal of Environmental Law* 145–55; L Kotze and A du Plessis, 'Putting Africa on the Stand: A Bird's Eye View of Climate Change Litigation on the Continent' (2020) *Environmental Law* 615–63.

[72] The other three include: *Philippi Horticultural Area Food & Farming Campaign v MEC for Local Government, Environmental Affairs and Development Planning: Western Cape* (16779/17)

in relation to the decision of the Minister of Mineral Resources and Energy to procure a coal power station;[73] whether the consent of the Minster was necessary to approve the purchase of renewable energy from an independent power producer (IPP) by the City of Cape Town;[74] and a challenge of the government's approval of oil and gas exploration.[75]

The *Thabametsi* case was ground-breaking as it was the first instance of 'climate litigation' in South Africa. Although typically aligned with procedural law arguments, this case was significant in connecting climate change issues with human rights.[76] The claimants in this case argued that the Minster of Environmental Affairs had failed to consider GHG emissions and pollution in accordance with section 24 of NEMA and its regulation for the carrying out an EIA. It was also argued that the acceptance of the defective EIA contravened the Promotion of Administrative Justice Act (PAJA).[77] Although such arguments are seemingly rooted in administrative law, it is important to note that the procedural rights and provisions in NEMA were enacted to protect the right to healthy environment and its related socio-economic rights.[78] The court also relied on the constitutional right to a healthy environment to order that a climate change impact assessment report be conducted.[79] Given the robust interpretive rights framework of the South African Constitution, it was easy for the court to move on from a brief discussion of South Africa's constitutional right to a healthy environment to deal with the administrative grounds of argument. The court was concise on the fact that sustainable development is mandated by section 24(b)(iii) of the Constitution. This section provides that the environment will be protected by securing ecologically sustainable development while promoting justifiable economic and social development, and that climate change poses a substantial risk to sustainable development in South Africa.[80]

[2020] ZAWCHC 8; 2020 (3) SA 486 (WCC) (17 February 2020); *Trustees for the Time Being of the GroundWork Trust v Minister of Environmental Affairs, KiPower (Pty) Ltd* (filing date 2017) Case No. 54087/17 (still pending); *GroundWork v Minister of Environmental Affairs and the President* (filing date 2019) Case No. 24571/19 (still pending).

73 *Africa Climate Alliance v Minister of Mineral Resources & Energy* (still pending, Case No. 56907/21).

74 *City of Cape Town v National Energy Regulator of South Africa* (51765/17) [2020] ZAGPPHC 800 (11 August 2020).

75 *South Durban Community Environmental Alliance v Minister of Environment* (still pending).

76 Bouwer (n 70), 157–77, 174.

77 Another argument in this case included contraventions of National Environment Management: Air Quality Act 39 of 2004.

78 Bouwer (n 70).

79 *Earthlife* case (n 27), para. 126.

80 *Earthlife* case (n 27), para. 82.

Kenya's climate change litigation has also centred entirely on government action. Its main climate change case was a challenge to the EIA process behind a licence to Amu Power Company to proceed with a coal-fired power plant project in the County of Lamu. In the *Save Lamu v Amu Power Co. Ltd,* the National Environmental Tribunal found that the respondents' EIA had failed to fully consider the project's contribution to climate change, and was never subjected to proper and effective public participation.[81]

South Africa and Kenya both enjoy a constitutionally-enshrined right to a healthy environment,[82] which is implemented and given effect in national laws through their respective EIA procedures and legislative frameworks, while Kenya also boasts a Climate Change Act.[83] The South African and Kenyan judgments therefore have powerful resonating effects in so far as affirming that EIA procedures must consider climate change risks in order to give effect to environmental rights. However, these cases do not provide much in the way of developing an understanding of the enforcement of environmental rights against private parties. Direct horizontal application of environmental and related rights remains rare; however, a Nigerian court could have been said to have read rights horizontally as early as 2005.

The Nigerian case of *Gbemre v Shell Petroleum* was pioneering in its attempt to declare the activities of oil companies as unconstitutional.[84] Mr Jonah Gbembre, acting on behalf of himself and the Iwherekan community in the Delta State, Nigeria, applied for an order securing or enforcing their fundamental rights to life and dignity of the human person as provided by the Constitution of the Federal Republic of Nigeria,[85] as well as the African Charter on Human and Peoples Rights. The applicants in the appeal decision, being Mr Gbemre and members of the community, stated that the activities of the defendants (two of whom were private parties – Shell and its Nigerian subsidiary)[86] in continuing to flare gas as part of their oil exploration presents a rights violation by polluting the air, causing respiratory disease, and endangering and impairing health.

---

81 *Save Lamu v National Environmental Management Authority and Amu Power Co. Ltd.* Tribunal Appeal No. Net 196 of 2016.

82 Section 24 of the Constitution of the Republic of South Africa, Act 108 of 1996; and arts 42 and 70 of the Constitution of Kenya 2010.

83 Whilst Kenya has a Climate Change Act 11 of 2016, South Africa is in the process of adopting climate legislation and only has a Climate Change Bill [B 9—2022] at present.

84 *Gbemre v Shell Petroleum Development Co.*, Suit No. FHC/CS/B/153/2005 (hereinafter *Gbemre*).

85 Specifically ss 33(1) and 34(1).

86 Shell Petroleum Development Company Nigeria Ltd and the Nigerian National Petroleum Corpn.

The Federal High Court in Nigeria provided useful insights in terms of substantive engagement with human rights, albeit not involving a specific environmental right – but rather the incorporation of environmental factors into other rights. In a stark horizontal application of recognized rights owed by private companies to members of the community, the Federal High Court held that the practice of gas flaring in the Niger Delta is unconstitutional and violates the fundamental rights of life and dignity as provided for in the Constitution of Federal Republic of Nigeria and the African Charter on Human and Peoples Rights.[87] The right to life was expansively interpreted to include the right to a healthy and clean environment – an interpretation that also upholds the right to a satisfactory environment in the African Charter on Human and Peoples' Rights as incorporated into Nigerian domestic law.[88]

Although this case is not widely heralded as an instance of direct horizontal application of human rights (and their correlation to the environment) between private actors, it marks an important judicial willingness to adopting a human rights approach in deciding a case of environmental damage, against private actors. The plaintiffs also argued that the practice of gas flaring leads to the emitting of GHGs, which contributes to climate change and could lead to further rights violations. The court did not make any specific finding on this point, but its declaration on direct rights violations by the defendants is significant in signalling a very early judicial receptiveness to tackling private parties' contribution to climate change with a robust rights-based agenda.[89]

No other African countries have produced a similarly radical judgment, particularly of a direct horizontal application of human and environmental rights. However, constitutional jurisprudence appears to be developing in a way that is opening up avenues for private entities to be held legally accountable for climate change and environmental issues. This is indicative of its new post-2010 constitutional era, which does not consider rights as exclusively concerned with the relationship between the state and individuals.[90] Although not strictly a climate change case, as it deals with land

[87] *Gbemre* (n 84), 29–30.

[88] KSA Ebeku, 'Constitutional Right to a Healthy Environment and Human Rights Approaches to Environmental Protection in Nigeria: *Gbemre v Shell Revisited*' (2007) 16(3) *RECIEL* 312.

[89] Unfortunately, this ruling faced various issues of implementation: HM Osofsky, 'Climate Change and Environmental Justice: Reflections on Litigation over Oil Extraction and Rights Violations in Nigeria' (2010) 1 *Journal of Human Rights and the Environment* 189. Ebeku (n 88) also argues that this case has a lot of weaknesses, including simply accepting the applicants affidavit, lacking in legal authority, not inviting amicus curiae, as well as constitutional rights claims' procedural issues under Nigerian law.

[90] B Sang, 'Horizontal Application of Constitutional Rights in Kenya: A Comparative Critique of the Emerging Jurisprudence' (2018) 26 *African Journal of International and Comparative Law* 1.

use and wetland protection, Kenya readily accepted a horizontal application of constitutional environmental rights as early as 2010, in the case of *Abdalla Rhova Hiribae v Attorney General.*[91] It should be noted, however, that wetlands (such as the Tana Delta, which forms the site of the disputed activities in this case) have immense benefits for mitigating climate change and extreme weather events; therefore, this case could have been considered a climate case and probably would be if heard by a court today.[92] This case concerned the serious threats to livelihood and the infringement of basic human rights of the indigenous communities around the Tana Delta. The petitioning members of the community challenged the approval of several projects, including agricultural projects, shrimp farming, and titanium mining. Although the petition was brought against a number of government officials and agencies, the seventh respondent was the Mumias Sugar Company Ltd, while others were state corporations. Some of the respondents therefore argued a misjoinder of parties and said it was a matter for the Attorney General only (the first respondent).[93]

It was alleged that the respondents failed to develop a comprehensive master plan for guiding land use, development, livelihood and biodiversity/ecological protection and, in failing to do so, they had violated the petitioners' rights to life and a healthy environment.[94] The National Environmental Management Authority opposed the matter on the ground that joinder of all respondents was inappropriate as 'only the state can guarantee fundamental rights' and therefore the court has no jurisdiction to entertain the petition.[95] It argued that 'there is only vertical application of human rights, no horizontal', saying that thus the petition is devoid of merit.[96] The court explained that the new constitutional dispensation in general and the Bill of Rights in particular:

> applies to and binds all persons [and] represents a radical departure from the position under the former Constitution where only the state could be held liable for violation or infringement of constitutional rights. In my view, where the facts so demonstrate, an individual or corporate person . . . can be held to have violated another person's constitutional rights, and appropriate orders or declarations issued.[97]

---

91 HCC No. 14 of 2010.

92 See the definitional and categorization discussion of the editors in the introductory chapter to this volume.

93 HCC No. 14 of 2010, para. 45.

94 HCC No. 14 of 2010, para. 3.

95 HCC No. 14 of 2010, para. 20.

96 HCC No. 14 of 2010.

97 HCC No. 14 of 2010, paras 46–7.

This is aligned with an understanding of article 20(2) of the Kenyan Constitution, which supports a case-by-case approach in determining whether constitutional rights apply horizontally. Article 20 states that the 'Bill of Rights applies to all law and binds all state organs and all persons' and that '[e]very person shall enjoy the rights and fundamental freedoms in the Bill of Rights to the greatest extent consistent with the nature of the right or fundamental freedom'.[98]

Similarly, South African constitutional jurisprudence, coupled with the environmental right framed in section 24 of the Constitution, means that it is possible in South Africa to apply human rights horizontally. However, the horizontal application of those rights enshrined in the Bill of Rights has not always been a straightforward matter. Section 8(2) of the Constitution declares that the Bill of Rights is binding for natural and juristic persons, 'if and to the extent that, it is applicable, taking into account the nature of the right and the nature of any duty imposed by the right'. The interpretation afforded by the *Du Plessis* judgment[99] of the Interim Constitution's correlating section 7(1) is that the Bill of Rights, 'shall bind all legislative and executive organs of state at all levels of government', and therefore constitutional rights merely enjoy indirect effect in private relationships between private entities.[100] However, this is probably no longer the case and the direct application of rights under the 1996 Constitution now seems to be possible. This viewpoint appears to be supported by Judge Dennis Davis who clarifies the application of the Bill of Rights to private parties in *McCarthy v Constantia Property Owners Association*.[101] Judge Davis granted locus standi to those who 'have come to court to protect the environmental fabric of their suburb'.[102] He also clarified that section 8(2) provides that the Bill of Rights binds juristic person:

> [W]hatever the interpretation of this opaque phrase, it is clear that its intention was to extend the scope of application of the Bill of Rights. In short, the Bill of Rights was not only designed to introduce the culture of justification in respect of public law but intended to ensure that the exercise of private power should similarly be justified. Accordingly the carefully constructed but artificial divide between public and private law which might have dominated our law prior to the constitutional

[98] Article 20(1) and (2) of the Constitution of Kenya 2010.

[99] *Du Plessis v De Klerk* 1996 (5) BCLR 658 (CC), 1996 SACLR LEXIS 1 (15 May 1996).

[100] *Du Plessis v De Klerk* 1996, para. 41: the Court based its reasoning on German constitutional law doctrine.

[101] 1999 (4) SA 847 (C).

[102] 1999 (4) SA at 855F.

> enterprise can no longer be sustained in an uncritical fashion and hence unquestioned application.[103]

Kotzé and du Plessis interpret this to mean that in the current South African constitutional rights context, a wide net of duties also rests on the private sector including in the environmental context.[104] This means that environmental rights are also enforceable against companies, and there exists an obligation on companies 'to run their business in a way that would not compromise the protection advanced by section 24'.[105]

This raises the question of whether the horizontality of section 24 requires a negative obligation not to violate environmental rights or a positive obligation to act in accordance with, or to promote, environmental rights. While section 24(a) comprising a right to an 'environment that is not harmful to their health or well-being' has been interpreted of having horizontal effect; this is less clear in relation to section 24(b) to 'have the environment protected, for the benefit of present and future generations, through reasonable legislative and other measures'.[106] Section 8(2) of the Constitution requires that the 'nature of the duty' entailed in a right must be considered in determining whether or not it is capable of horizontality.[107] The duties of the section 24 right seem to lie in section 24(b). Professor Kidd has argued that these duties apply to states as 'other measures' are measures that are necessary to implement legislative measures, including policies and programmes.[108] *BP*

---

[103] 1999 (4) SA at 855C–E; see also MI Kidd, 'Suburban Aesthetics and the Environment Right. *McCarthy v Constantia Property Owners Association* 1999 (4) SA 847 (C)' (1999) 6 *South African Journal of Environmental Law and Policy* 257.

[104] LJ Kotzé and A du Plessis, 'A Gold Rush to Nowhere? The Rights-based Approach to Environmental Governance in South Africa's Mining Sector in Question' (2014) 47(4) *Verfassung und Recht in Übersee/Law and Politics in Africa, Asia and Latin America* 447–81, 457.

[105] Kotzé and du Plessis (n 104).

[106] There have been contrasting views on the nature of the duties contained in this right with differing outcomes for horizontality. Commentators have arrived at differing conclusions that s. 24 comprises: (1) a right and directive principle; (2) two rights; and (3) a single right with two aims. See *HTF Developers (Pty) Ltd v The Minister of Environmental Affairs and Tourism* 2006 5 SA 512 (T); Kotze and Du Plessis, 'Some Brief Observations on Fifteen Years of Environmental Rights Jurisprudence in South Africa' (2011) 3(1) *Journal of Court Innovation* 101, 166; L Feris, 'The Socio-Economic Nature of Section 24(b) of the Constitution – Some Thoughts on *HTF Developers (Pty) Ltd v Minister of Environmental Affairs and Tourism (HTF)*' (2008) 23 SAPR/PL; L Feris and D Tladi, 'Environment Rights' in D Brand and C Heyns (eds), *Socio Economic Rights in South Africa* (Pretoria University Law Press 2005) 257.

[107] *Khumalo v Holomisa* 2002 (5) SA 401 (CC) provided a three-stage process for questions that should be asked in relation to the application of s. 24 to private parties.

[108] M Kidd, *Environmental Law* (Juta 2011) 2nd ed 24.

Southern Africa v MEC for Agriculture, Conservation & Land Affairs supports this interpretation of 'other measures' as interpreting section 24(b) to expressly oblige the state to take reasonable legislative and other measures to protect the environment.[109] On the other hand, Feris and Kotze write that it is the 'the constitutional responsibility of private actors to implement "reasonable other measures"'.[110] Kotze also argues that there is a duty on non-state entities to safeguard health and wellbeing.[111]

However, the court stated in *Governing Body of the Juma Musjid Primary School v Essay* that 'the purpose of section 8(2) of the Constitution is not to obstruct private autonomy or to impose on a private party the duties of the state in protecting the Bill of Rights. It is [...] to require private parties not to interfere with or diminish the enjoyment of the right'.[112] On this interpretation, although it may be difficult to comprehensively impose the rights contained in section 24(b) on private actors, it could certainly be argued that private parties should not interfere with those rights enjoyed by others under section 24(b).

The next question is then whether section 24 can be invoked directly against private entities or if it must be secured through legislative mechanisms. It would appear that on a reading of section 8(3) of the Constitution, legislation must give effect to the rights laid out in the Bill of Rights. Where legislation does not, the common law must be developed to give effect to the right. This marks a difference from the Nigerian *Gbemre* case or the Dutch *Urgenda* case where human rights against the defendants were directly invoked. South Africa's horizontal application of rights is more reflexive, as comparable with *Milieudefensie*, whereby rights must be given effect through legislation and the common law. That is not to say that reflexive rights-based approaches are any less effective. The South African Supreme Court of Appeal has shown a willingness to apply thick environmental constitutionalism in relation to litigation grounded in access to information and related procedural rights. Thick environmental constitutionalism employs

109 (03/16337) [2004] ZAGPHC 38.

110 L Ferris and L Kotzé, 'The Regulation of Acid Mine Drainage in South Africa: Law and Governance Perspectives' (2015) *Potchefstroom Electronic Law Journal/Potchefstroomse Elektroniese Regsblad* 17. 2104. 10.4314/pelj.v17i5.07.

111 L Kotzé, 'The South African Environmental Right: a 20 Year Retrospective' (3rd Yale/UNITAR Conference on Human Rights, Environmental Sustainability, Post-2015 Development, and the Future Climate Regime Yale New Haven, September 2014). In calling for a global environmental constitution, Kotzé also argues for an innovative provision that would apply duties horizontally to non-state entities: 'A Global Environmental Constitution for the Anthropocene?' (2018) 8(1) *Transnational Environmental Law* 11–33.

112 *Governing Body of the Juma Musjid Primary School v Essay NO* (2011) 8 BCLR 761, paras 54–8.

a rights-based approach to environmental governance by treating procedural rights and the substantive environmental right as 'interrelated and mutually reinforcing in a number of ways'.[113]

How the horizontal application of the environmental right contained in section 24 can be achieved through non-environmental legislation is best illustrated by *Company Secretary of Arcelormittal South Africa v Vaal Environmental Justice Alliance*,[114] which reaffirmed that under South Africa's constitutional dispensation, 'there is no room for secrecy and that constitutional values will be enforced' against juristic persons.[115] *Arcelormittal* concerns litigation by a non-governmental environmental advocacy organization, the Vaal Environmental Justice Alliance (VEJA), against South Africa's largest steel producer, Arcelormittal South Africa Ltd.[116] In 2011, VEJA initiated a campaign to access environmental information from Arcelormittal, specifically the company's Environmental Master Plan pertaining to the rehabilitation of the Vanderbijlpark site.[117] The information sought by VEJA would reflect whether or not Arcelormittal had complied with its own environmental strategy as well as with the requirements of the licences issued by various governmental departments under environmental legislation. VEJA asserted that it had a right to access Arcelormittal's records under the Promotion of Access to Information Act (PAIA).[118]

The PAIA allows for the horizontal enforcement of the right to information in cases 'where information is required for the protection of any rights'.[119] In its request, VEJA claimed that the requested records were necessary for the protection of the environmental right, which is also a horizontally enforceable right.[120] Navsa ADP, giving the judgment of the Supreme Court of Appeal (SCA), rejected Arcelormittal's arguments through the application of thick environmental constitutionalism and a rights-based approach to environmental litigation. The Supreme Court of Appeal (SCA) upheld the earlier order of the High Court and directed Arcelormittal to deliver the requested records to VEJA within 14 days. Murcott analyses the judgment

113 M Murcott, 'The Procedural Right of Access to Information as a Means of Implementing Environmental Constitutionalism in South Africa' in Erin Daly and James May (eds) *Implementing Environmental Constitutionalism: Current Global Challenges* (Cambridge University Press 2018) 196.

114 *Company Secretary of Arcelormittal South Africa v Vaal Environmental Justice Alliance* (69/2014) [2014] ZASCA 184; 2015 (1) SA 515 (SCA); [2015] 1 All SA 261 (SCA) (26 November 2014) (hereinafter *Arcelormital*).

115 *Arcelormital* (n 114), para. 82.

116 *Arcelormital* (n 114), para. 2.

117 *Arcelormital* (n 114), para. 8.

118 Promotion of Access to Information Act 2 of 2000.

119 See s. 50(1)(a) of the PAIA.

120 *Arcelormittal* (n 114), paras 8–9.

of Navsa ADP as implementing environmental constitutionalism by, 'by traversing a number of provisions in South African environmental legislation that pursue social justice and explicitly connect questions of participation and transparency to environmental protection'.[121] This environmental constitutionalism takes cognizance of the fact that, in certain instances, private abuses of human rights may be as noxious as those committed by the state.[122]

Of particular relevance, the court affirmed the potential for the horizontal application of section 2(4)(k) of NEMA, which mandates that environmental decisions 'must be taken in an open and transparent manner, and access to information must be provided in accordance with the law'.[123] This is a pioneering judicial development as, although it is uncontroversial that the provisions of PAIA may apply to corporations, prior to the *Arcelormittal* judgment the horizontal application of the principles of NEMA was debatable.[124] It was held that although section 2(4)(k) of NEMA principally applies to the state, it 'must, in principle, apply to corporate decisions and activities that impact on the environment and thus implicate the public interest, particularly when their activities require regulatory approval'.[125] This development is consistent with the emerging acceptance that corporations must respect human rights, particularly those related to the environment.[126] In reinforcing Arcelormittal's environmental corporate accountability, Navsa ADP rejected Arcelormittal's refusal to disclose the documents requested by VEJA.

Although *Arcelormittal* sets an example for rights-based approaches in relation to administrative law challenges targeting private entities, the substantive content of the section 24 right and what it means for corporate responsibility is not yet fully explored. The South African Constitution enshrines a comprehensive and widely-celebrated substantive environmental right, which is capable of both vertical and horizontal application.[127]

---

121 Murcott (n 113), 207.

122 Iain Currie and Johan de Waal, *The Bill of Rights Handbook* (Juta 2000) 41.

123 *Arcelormittal* (n 114), para. 66.

124 See s. 2(1) of the NEMA, which reads: 'The principles set out in this section apply throughout the Republic *to the actions of all organs of state* that may significantly affect the environment' (emphasis added).

125 *Arcelormittal* (n 114), para. 66.

126 J Nolan, 'With Power Comes Responsibility: Human Rights and Corporate Accountability' (2004) 28 *University of New South Wales Law Journal* 581.

127 A du Plessis, 'South Africa's Constitutional Environmental Right and the Pursuit of a Country where "Well-being" Thrives' in UN Environment, *New Frontiers in Environmental Constitutionalism* (UN Environment 2017) 249; L Feris, 'The Public Trust Doctrine and Liability for Historic Water Pollution in South Africa' (2012) 8 *Law Environment and Development Journal* 17.

Despite the existence of a fully-fledged environmental right, environmental constitutionalism in South Africa is generally exercised through the utilization of procedural rights in the narrow sense.[128]

Therefore, the substantive environmental right is 'underutilized' in litigation that seeks to protect the environment.[129] As noted by Feris, 'when one examines South African jurisprudence, there seems to be a marked dearth of cases where the environmental right has been fully utilized and clearly interpreted'.[130] However, developments in disclosure and reporting are marking a decisive break from this pattern and exhibit a wholesome understanding of the interdependency of rights and the horizontal application of the environmental right. Similarly, South African company law, strengthened by the underpinnings of socio-economic rights, allows for litigants to act 'in the public interest'.[131] The next section looks at how the horizontal application of human rights in South Africa is enabling an interpretive renaissance of the common law and statutory duties of company directors in South Africa, providing a richer palette of options for private climate litigation in South Africa.

Corporate responsibility and the horizontal application of rights

The *Arcelormittal* case confirms that, within a South African context, the notion of corporate social responsibility (CSR) must be directed towards social justice as informed by a constitutional environmental mandate – that is, through the horizontal application of rights. Despite the apparent ubiquity of the ethos of CSR and stakeholder theory in South African company law,[132] little attention has been paid to how these concepts may facilitate private climate litigation in South Africa. Particularly, the implications of these paradigms on the nature and direction of directors' duties and responsibilities in a changing world has largely evaded scholarly

[128] Murcott (n 113), 196. It has been noted by Savaresi and Setzer that as climate litigation expands, complaints based on procedural rights are likely to become more widespread; see A Savaresi and J Setzer, 'Rights-Based Litigation in the Climate Emergency: Mapping the Landscape and New Knowledge Frontiers' (2022) 13 *Journal of Human Rights and the Environment* 28.

[129] L Feris, 'Constitutional Environmental Rights: An Under-Utilised Resource' (2008) 24 *South African Journal on Human Rights* at 29; see also M Kidd, 'Greening the Judiciary' (2006) 9 *Potchefstroom Electronic Review* 72.

[130] Feris (n 129), 29.

[131] Section 157(1)(d) of the Companies Act 71 of 2008.

[132] C Mitchell and T Hill, 'Corporate Social and Environmental Reporting and the Impact of Internal Environmental Policy in South Africa' (2009) 16 *Corporate Social Responsibility and Environmental Management* 48–60.

attention. However, the increasing focus on good corporate governance has culminated in a reinvigorated interest in the duties of directors. As company directors personify the companies they serve, it is no surprise that much of company law is directed at the regulation of those directors at the helm of the corporate ship.[133]

In the context of climate change, the importance of holding directors personally liable for environmental transgressions cannot be overstated. Indeed, natural persons are more likely to be deterred by punishment than companies,[134] many of which perceive imposed fines and penalties as 'licence fees for illegitimate corporate business operations'[135] or a necessary 'cost of doing business'.[136] The following sections indicate that the use of human rights as a reflexive interpretive tool is broadening the scope and extent of directors' duties under South African company law. These developments may render directors personally liable for contributions to climate change and environmental degradation, and failure to take account of climate risks, presenting litigants with an additional and potent angle to approach private climate litigation in South Africa.

Companies Act and the Bill of Rights

South Africa's Companies Act[137] (the Act) entwines company law with human rights considerations. The Act is underpinned by the express intention of resituating company law within the constitutional matrix.[138] Section 7 delineates the purposes of the Act, first to 'promote compliance with the Bill of Rights, as provided for in the Constitution, in the application of Company law'. As Katzew contends, 'human rights concerns are placed at the centre of policy making within the company and should be embedded

133 HH Stoop-Koornhof, 'The Role of Voluntary Corporate Governance Codes in the Interpretation and Application of the Statutory and Common Law Duties of the Company Director: A South African Perspective' Durham theses, Durham University (2020), available at Durham E-Theses, http://etheses.dur.ac.uk/13493/, at 3.

134 K Van der Linde, 'The Personal Liability of Directors for Corporate Fault – An Exploration' (2008) 20 *Potchefstroom Electronic Law Journal/Potchefstroomse Elektroniese Regsblad South African Mercantile Law Journal* 454.

135 *S v Coetzee* 1997 (3) SA 527 (CC) 567D.

136 S Wolf, 'Finding an Environmental Felon Under the Corporate Veil: The Responsible Corporate Officer Doctrine and RCRA' (1993) 9 *Journal of Land Use and Environmental Law* 1–2.

137 Act 71 of 2008.

138 M Gwanyanya, 'The South African Companies Act and the Realisation of Corporate Human Rights Responsibilities' (2015) 18 *Potchefstroom Electronic Law Journal* 1.

in the holistic functioning of the company'.[139] Accordingly, the Act has effectively located human rights within the realm of company law.[140]

This is augmented by section 39(2) of the Constitution, which necessitates that any Act of Parliament must be interpreted in a manner that promotes the 'spirit, purport and objects' of the Bill of Rights. Moreover, section 158 of the Act obliges the courts to interpret the Act in a manner that gives optimal realization to the Bill of Rights, while section 5 requires that the Act be interpreted and applied in a manner that gives expression to the Bill of Rights.[141] South African courts have demonstrated an acceptance of these provisions and have asserted that the Act must be interpreted 'through the prism of the Constitution'.[142] Certainly, it is abundantly clear that corporate law must now be interpreted in a 'constitutional setting',[143] providing a rich substrate in which to germinate litigation premised on an indirect application of the Bill of Rights.

Personal liability for directors under the constitutional paradigm

Although the Companies Act is intended to align company law with the Bill of Rights, the possibility of holding company directors personally liable for breaches of their fiduciary duties in cases where their acts or omissions impede the realization of human rights is not readily apparent from a plain reading of the Act. As discussed below, although the Act provides an account of directors' duties, the relevant provisions have been drafted with a high level of abstraction, denoting broad and nebulous standards. The resultant uncertainty pertaining to the nature and scope of directors' duties under South African company law has, traditionally, made holding directors liable in their personal capacity an unattractive option. This would also apply in climate change litigation in South Africa.

Under section 76 of the Act, a director of a company is required to exercise their powers and perform their functions in good faith and for a proper purpose 'in the best interests of the company'.[144] However, the legislature neglected to define the phrase 'best interests of the company'. Numerous

[139] J Katzew, 'Crossing the Divide Between the Business of the Corporation and the Imperatives of Human Rights – the Impact of Section 7 of the Companies Act 71 of 2008' (2011) 128 *South Africa Law Journal* 686.

[140] Gwanyanya (n 138); Katzew (n 139).

[141] Section 5 read with s. 7(a).

[142] *Booysen v Jonkheer Boerewynmakery (Pty) Ltd* [2017] 1 All SA 862 (WCC), para. 41.

[143] *Nedbank Ltd v Bestvest 153 (Pty) Ltd; Essa v Bestvest 153* (Pty) Ltd 2012 (5) SA 497 (WCC) (21857/2011, 2106/2012) [2012] ZAWCHC 139, para. [21].

[144] Section 76(3)(b).

scholars have sought to define the term;[145] however, uncertainty lingers. Traditionally, directors were expected to manage the company in the best interest of shareholders, and it was only to this group to whom their fiduciary duties were owed.[146] Thus, the threshold for meeting these standards has been myopically construed in line with fulfilling shareholder expectations only.[147] This orthodox conception presents significant challenges to litigants who allege that directors have breached their fiduciary duties by violating the rights of others through contributing to climate change.

However, companies are 'now situated within a constitutional framework, and so in considering the "best interests" it is imperative that directors give preference to the values of the Constitution and the Bill of Rights'.[148] In *Bester v Wright*[149] the High Court found that a director will breach fiduciary duties if they fail to comply with a legal rule, whether it be in terms of the Companies Act, or and other law. It may, therefore, be argued that directors may be found to have breached their fiduciary duties if, in the exercise of such duties, they act contrary to the Bill of Rights.[150] The underlying tenor of the court's sentiments in *Bester* parallels recent judicial developments, drawing a connection between the provisions of the King Report and Code on Corporate Governance[151] (King IV Report) and directors' duties under South African company law. This may serve to establish more concrete and objective parameters to enforce environmental compliance and unlatch the door for indirect applications of the Bill of Rights in holding directors personally liable for breaches of their duties.

Although other stakeholder interests are not formally recognized in the Companies Act, South Africa has adopted the King IV Report, which

145 I Esser and JJ Du Plessis, 'The Stakeholder Debate and Directors' Fiduciary Duties' (2007) 19 *South African Mercantile Law Journal* 346; Michael Spisto, 'Unitary Board or Two-tiered Board for the New South Africa?' (2005) 1 *International Review of Business Research Papers* 84–99; T Mongalo, 'The Emergence of Corporate Governance as A Fundamental Research Topic in South Africa' (2003) 120 *South African Law Journal* 173–91; M Haveng, 'Directors' Fiduciary Duties under Our Future Company-Law Regime' (1997) 9 *South African Mercantile Law Journal* 310–23.

146 Gwanyanya (n 137), 3110; S Luiz and Z Taljaard, 'Mass Resignation of the Board and Social Responsibility of the Company: *Minister of Water Affairs and Forestry v Stilfontein Gold Mining Co. Ltd*: Case Comments' (2009) 21 *South African Mercantile Law Journal* 424.

147 *South African Fabrics Ltd v Millman* 1972 4 SA 592 (A).

148 Katzew (n 139), 705.

149 *Bester v Wright* 2011 2 All SA 75 (WCC).

150 Section 8(2) of the Constitution provides that 'a provision of the Bill of Rights binds a natural person or a juristic person if, and to the extent that, it is applicable, taking into account the nature of the right and the nature of any duty imposed by the right'.

151 Institute of Directors, *King IV; Report on Corporate Governance in South Africa* (South Africa, 2016).

comprises a code of good practice and delineates principles pertaining to corporate citizenship, stakeholder protection and investment decision making. The Code introduces the notion of 'corporate citizenship', which necessitates that directors 'adopt a stakeholder-inclusive approach that balances the needs, interests and expectations of material stakeholders in the best interests of the organisation over time'.[152] It is evident that the recommendations in the King IV Report encourage directors to consider a broader array of stakeholders in exercising their duties than those contained in the Act. It is, however, important to note that King IV constitutes a voluntary code and is not binding. Moreover, scant mention of the King Report and Code can be located in the Companies Act.[153]

Despite this, the King Code has been used by South African courts to interpret the scope of directors' statutory duties.[154] This recent judicial trend of interpreting the statutory duties of directors to comply with the provisions of the King Code intimates that the Code may well constitute more than a self-regulatory, voluntary code; and is, at the very least, persuasive in informing the nature of directors' duties under South African company law.[155] In *Minister of Water Affairs and Forestry v Stilfontein Gold Mining Co*[156] the board of a listed mining company resigned en masse in order to evade liability for failing to comply with previous environmental directives. In deciding whether the mass resignation was undertaken in good faith and in the best interests of company, the court utilized the provisions of the King Code to augment the relevant provisions of the Companies Act. In finding the directors personally liable, the court recognized the centrality of social responsibility in corporate governance. It used the provisions of the King Code to inform its interpretation of the directors' fiduciary duties in terms of the Companies Act.

Although the court recognized that directors only owe their duties to the shareholders of the company, it adopted an 'enlightened shareholder value' approach in considering what the best interests of shareholders entail under South Africa's constitutional dispensation.[157] Drawing on the notion of corporate citizenship in the King Code, the court found that it is in the best interests of the company to act in a socially responsible manner. In this

[152] Part 5.5: Principle 16.

[153] Barring reg. 54.

[154] *Minister of Water Affairs and Forestry v Stilfontein Gold Mining Company* (2006) 5 SA 333 (W).

[155] P Delport and I Esser, 'The Duty of Care, Skill and Diligence: The King Report and the 2008 Companies Act' (2011) 74 *Journal of Contemporary Roman-Dutch Law* 449.

[156] *Stilfontein Gold Mining Co.* (n 154).

[157] JL van Tonder, 'An Analysis of the Directors' Duty to Act in the Best Interest of the Company, Through the Lens of the Business Judgement Rule' (2015) 36 *Obiter* 702–24.

regard, the court recited the Code with approval: 'A good corporate citizen is increasingly seen as one that is non-discriminatory, non-exploitative, and responsible with regard to environmental and human rights issues. A company is likely to experience indirect economic benefits such as improved productivity and corporate reputation by taking those factors into consideration.'[158] Most notably, the court substantiates its stance on the basis of constitutional values and declared that allowing the directors to resign and avoid responsibility for environmental degradation 'simply cannot be permitted in a constitutional democracy which recognizes the right of all of its citizens to be protected from the effects of pollution and degradation'.[159] Thus, analogous to the reflexive interpretational approach adopted in *Arcelormittal*, the court in *Stilfontein* used the Bill of Rights with the recommendations in the King IV Report, to inform the scope of directors' statutory duties.

Accordingly, South African courts have intimated that the King Code may be applied indirectly in the interpretation of directors' duties in terms of statute and the common law.[160] This decision may be the final nail in the coffin for shareholder-centric interpretations of directors' duties under South African company law. This shift may be instrumental in construing the nature and extent of directors' duties in accordance with the Bill of Rights. The question then is whether this could facilitate indirect applications of the Bill of Rights as a means to hold directors personally liable for a company's contribution to climate change, or for failures to consider, disclose or appropriately respond to climate change risks. This does not suggest that section 7(a) expands directors' fiduciary duties, but rather that it affirms that the duty of directors has always been to act within the parameters of the law, and that a failure to do so may attract liability.[161] The implications of such reasoning entails that directors are bound to exercise their duties in the interests of a broader array of stakeholders, beyond mere shareholders. This development would certainly parallel international developments regarding directors' liability for breaching duties of care and diligence.[162]

Indeed, the indirect application of the Bill of Rights has proven to be a central approach among plaintiffs in climate litigation cases in South Africa.

---

158 Para. 16.9.

159 Para. 16.9.

160 See *Stilfontein Gold Mining Co.* (n 154); *Levenstein v S* [2013] 4 All SA 528 (SCA); *Kalahari Resources (pty) Ltd v Arcelormittal SA* [2012] 3 All SA 555 (GSJ); *Council for Medical Schemes v Selfmed Medical Scheme* [2011] ZASCA 207; *South African Broadcasting Corpn Ltd v Mpofu* [2009] 4 All SA 169 (GSJ).

161 Gwanyanya (n 138).

162 See 'Climate Change and Directors' Liability' report as discussed in the first section of this chapter.

As the *Earthlife* case indicates, human rights compose an integral part of the 'extra-statutory context' that must be considered by courts when interpreting legislative provisions.[163] Therefore, indirect applications of the Bill of Rights can be used to broaden the statutory scope of directors' duties, consistently with the South African judiciary's commitment to transformative constitutionalism. This entails 'the influence of the overarching values of the Constitution on the legal culture of interpretation to align it with the normative value system'.[164]

The liberal standing afforded to South African litigants in upholding constitutional rights, coupled with the broad standing afforded to 'any person' in the Companies Act, suggests that these constitutionally-compatible interpretations of directors' duties by South African courts may present an avenue for private climate litigation, particularly in cases where it can be shown that a director has breached their fiduciary duties, as interpreted in line with the Bill of Rights. The increased vulnerability of developing nations, like South Africa, to the impacts of climate change makes clear the centrality of a healthy environment to the realization of citizens' fundamental socio-economic rights in the Bill of Rights. Consequently, in light of South Africa's transformative constitutional agenda, alleging that a director has breached their fiduciary duties through acts or omissions that contribute to climate change and environmental degradation may present a nascent, yet fruitful, avenue for private climate litigation.

Conclusion

Although rights-based arguments in the context of climate litigation are emerging as successful strategies in a public law context, their potential against private actors is yet to be fully explored. There are strong legal and moral obligations for private polluters to be held directly responsible for their climate change contributions; however, the jurisprudence that might enable this is still developing. This chapter has presented the strength of a constitutionally enshrined environmental right and related socio-economic rights in achieving both climate and environmental justice. The horizontal application of an environmental right lays the groundwork for pursuing multiple pathways to combat climate change through a constitutional interpretation of private law duties. Given the recognition of an environmental right in many African constitutions, Africa still has much to contribute to the growing body of rights-based climate litigation.

---

[163] *Earthlife* case (n 27) m para. 91.

[164] B Mupantgavanhu, ' Impact of the Constitution's Normative Framework on the Interpretation of Provisions of the Companies Act 71 of 2008' (2019) 22 *Potchefstroom Electronic Review/ Potchefstroomse Elektroniese Regsblad* 1–24.

South African courts have exhibited a willingness to employ human rights as part of the 'extra-statutory' context when interpreting legislation. The recent judicial practice of using the King Code as an interpretive aid to expand the nature and scope of directors' common law and statutory duties in South Africa evidences how the horizontal application of the Bill of Rights may be employed to exploit previously untapped possibilities for climate litigation against private parties. This is particularly salient in light of South Africa's commitment to transformative constitutionalism, which renders indirect applications of the Bill of Rights a powerful mechanism for both reinforcing existing and unlocking new opportunities to pursue climate action in the pursuit of the realization of human rights.

10

Different Roads to the Same Destination: Climate Change Litigation in South Africa and the Netherlands and the Role of Human Rights in the Mitigation of Climate Change

Sanita van Wyk

Introduction

This chapter considers climate change litigation in South Africa and the Netherlands, and considers if two different judicial approaches, set in two different national contexts, can ultimately lead to the same outcome, namely human rights-based climate change litigation to mitigate climate change. More specifically, this chapter investigates how a court decision in a South African climate change case might differ from the climate change decision of the Supreme Court of the Netherlands in *Urgenda Foundation v The Kingdom of the Netherlands* (*Urgenda*).[1] In doing so, underlying

1 *Urgenda Foundation v Kingdom of the Netherlands (Ministry of Infrastructure and the Environment)* 2019 19/00135 (Hoge Raad) (English translation). The *Urgenda* case was first heard in the District Court of the Hague on 14 April 2015, after the suit was instituted against the Dutch State by the Urgenda Foundation and 886 Dutch citizens (collectively referred to as 'Urgenda'). The initial decision, in favour of Urgenda, was delivered by the court a quo in 2015 and reaffirmed by the Hague Court of Appeal in 2018. Ultimately, the Supreme Court of the Netherlands confirmed the aforementioned two decisions on 20 December 2019, and it is this final decision of the Supreme Court which forms the focus of this chapter.

complexities are explored, including the role of national and international law in climate change litigation, as well as the role of administrative law and human rights.

This chapter is able to identify two different approaches to climate change litigation, namely a Dutch approach, where climate change is framed as a central issue in the litigation, and a South African approach where climate change is arguably framed as a peripheral or secondary issue in the litigation. In practice this means that the Dutch approach, as illustrated by the *Urgenda* case, can be thought of as a 'systemic mitigation case', wherein the 'overall efforts of a State to mitigate climate change is challenged'.[2] The South African approach, where comparably less systemic mitigation cases can be identified to date than in the Netherlands, means the focus is on a 'specific project or initiative'[3] that has greenhouse gas (GHG) emission implications, such as the construction of a coal-fired power plant. However, the most recent case law in South Africa is also systemic.

The chapter does not suggest that one approach should be preferred over the other, or that one jurisdiction should emulate another. Instead, the chapter highlights the difference in approaches of the two selected jurisdictions located respectively in the Global North and the Global South. It does this in order to ascertain the value in the different responses, and to determine if both approaches ultimately reach the same destination, namely human rights-based climate change litigation in order to mitigate climate change.

In order to structure the analysis in this chapter, the chapter will focus on two questions related to climate change litigation within both the Dutch and South African legal contexts. Firstly, how severe is the danger of climate change considered to be in the Netherlands and in South Africa, and what emissions reductions are required by the respective states in order to prevent the danger?[4] Secondly, do both states have a legal obligation to make *more* extensive GHG reductions in view of the danger of climate change and, if so, what is the role of human rights?[5]

---

2 L Maxwell, S Mead and D van Berkel, 'Standards for Adjudicating the Next Generation of Urgenda-Style Climate Cases' (2022) 12(1) *Journal of Human Rights and the Environment* 35, 38.

3 Maxwell, Mead and van Berkel (n 2), 38–9.

4 These questions are based on Roger Cox, 'A Climate Change Litigation Precedent: Urgenda Foundation v The State of the Netherlands', *CIGI Paper Series No. 79,* 4 November 2015, https://www.cigionline.org/publications/climate-change-litigation-precedent-urgenda-foundation-v-state-netherlands/, accessed 13 November 2022.

5 Cox (n 4).

Comparative methodology

In order not to overburden the chapter with technical complexity related to the employed comparative legal methodology, the methodological arrangement and rationale will be limited to this part of the chapter.

In a traditional understanding of the functional method of legal comparison it is submitted that, while legal rules might differ, societies tend to solve legal problems in a similar way.[6] In terms of this method of comparative law the basic principle of functionality is prominent, meaning that, as explained by Kötz, 'in law the only things which are comparable are those which fulfil the same function'.[7] As further stipulated by Kötz, 'the legal system of every society faces essentially the same problems, and solves these problems by quite different means though very often with similar results' or through means that fulfil the same function. In this chapter, this means the function of mitigating climate change.[8]

It is important to acknowledge that the method itself as well as Kötz's submissions have attracted criticism, a full discussion of which falls outside the ambit of this chapter.[9] However, it is crucial to acknowledge that there are indeed different functional methods and it is pivotal to explain which functional method is employed in this chapter. The different functional methods of comparative law are distinguished by their aims.[10] According to Michaels, these are: to understand legal rules and institutions; to achieve comparability; to emphasize similarity; to achieve system building; to determine which law is better; to harmonize or unify law; and to provide tools for the critique of law.[11] Therefore, the type of research question,

[6] M Graziadei, 'The Functionalist Heritage' in Pierre Legrand and Roderick Munday (eds), *Comparative Legal Studies: Traditions and Transitions* 100 (Cambridge University Press 2003); R Michaels, 'The Functional Method of Comparative Law', in Mathias Reimann and Reinhard Zimmermann (eds), *The Oxford Handbook of Comparative Law* (Oxford University Press 2019) 2nd ed 341; H Kötz, 'Comparative Law in Germany Today' (1999) 51(4) *Revue Internationale de Droit Comparé* 753–8, 755; M van Hoecke, 'Methodology of Comparative Legal Research' (2015) *Law and Method* 1–35.

[7] Kötz (n 6), 755.

[8] Kötz (n 6), 755.

[9] van Hoecke (n 6). Van Hoecke (n 6), 9, submits that Kötz 'never seem to have elaborated, or even applied' the functional method himself. Michaels, in his analysis of the functional method, remarks that the functional method of comparative research is a 'triple misnomer' for the following reasons: there is more than one functional method; not all functional methods are indeed 'functional'; and generally articles claiming to have employed the functional method do not necessarily follow 'a method' which can be recognized: Michaels (n 6).

[10] Michaels (n 6), 341, 364–80.

[11] Michaels (n 6); van Hoecke (n 6), 9.

linked to the aim of the research, determines which functional method is employed.[12]

Within the context of this chapter, the comparison between the Netherlands and South Africa is employed to emphasize similarity. This chapter considers climate change litigation in the Netherlands and South Africa, and considers if two different judicial approaches, set in two different national contexts, can ultimately lead to a similar outcome, namely human rights-based climate change litigation in order to mitigate climate change. The chapter does not set out to achieve other aims of the functional method, such as determining which law is better, or setting out how the law can be harmonized. Instead, the chapter highlights the difference in approach within the two selected jurisdictions located respectively in the Global North and the Global South, in order to ascertain the value in the different responses, and to determine if both approaches ultimately reach the same destination. Accordingly, this chapter employs the functional method in order to emphasize similarity.

However, this chapter also employs additional, harmonious methods of legal comparison. This is because this functional method advocates a focus on the comparison of common legal problems and solutions of selected jurisdictions without the incorporation of contextual considerations.[13] It can be argued that the functional method traditionally asks 'what are the legal rules of the solution' and not 'how do the legal rules solve the problem', thereby limiting its incorporation of societal context to a significant extent.[14] Thus, at the core of the functional method, in a traditional understanding thereof, lies the assumption that the problem is the same in multiple jurisdictions.[15] While the problem of climate change is indeed global, the impacts of climate change will be different in different jurisdictions, and will be the demands this places on different states, as discussed below in relation to the differing national approaches in determining fair share. Accordingly, the differing national contexts necessitate an expansion of the traditional application of the functional method in this chapter to make more room for the incorporation of context. Therefore, the chapter will not employ the functional method and compare solutions by disassociating problems completely from context, specifically doctrinal legal context, historical background (in particular related to the fair share approach in international climate change law) and socio-economic context.[16] The law-in-context method has a definite historical

[12] van Hoecke (n 6), 9.

[13] van Hoecke (n 6), 8.

[14] van Hoecke (n 6), 10.

[15] van Hoecke (n 6), 10.

[16] For a discussion on the meaning of doctrinal legal context, historical background and socio-economic context, see van Hoecke (n 6), 10.

dimension but also places focus on the law's modern societal context, to a degree that is accepted to be much wider than within the traditional understanding of the functional method.[17] The law-in-context method also requires a consideration of the practical functionality of the law, and thus requires the consideration of case law,[18] as employed in this chapter.

Another key method of comparison employed in this chapter, in addition to the functional method and the law-in-context method, is the common-core method. This sets out to find a common-core among legal systems in specific jurisdictions,[19] and also aims to emphasize similarity (in the same way as the functional method). The development of the common-core method stems from the ambition to determine 'how the different legal systems [are] solving cases rather than on their legal rules and concepts'.[20] In applying the common-core method within this chapter, similarities and differences in the Dutch and South African legal approaches are identified, within the context of human rights-based climate change litigation. So, this chapter employs the following three harmonious comparative methods: the functional method, the law-in-context method and the common-core method.

Applying the above methods of comparison and tracing a parallel legal development in the context of human rights-based climate change litigation in the Netherlands and South Africa is risky if the law is considered in isolation to its practical manifestation.[21] For this reason, this chapter relies on case law to illustrate the theoretical and practical manifestation of the law. Therefore, it is imperative that this chapter starts off with an analysis of the *Urgenda* case, which explains the practical manifestation of Dutch law in the context of the mitigation of climate change based on human rights grounds, in order for this manifestation of Dutch law to stand in contrast to the practical legal developments in South Africa within this context.

Climate change litigation in the Netherlands and the *Urgenda* decision

The severity of the danger of climate change in the Netherlands and the preventative state action required to reduce it

This section will consider the first question within the Dutch context, which can be divided into two components: firstly, how severe is the alleged danger

---

17 van Hoecke (n 6), 16.

18 van Hoecke (n 6), 16.

19 van Hoecke (n 6), 19.

20 van Hoecke (n 6), 8.

21 For a detailed discussion of this conundrum, see van Hoecke (n 6), 1–35.

of climate change and, secondly, what reductions are required in order to prevent dangerous climate change?

The severity of the danger of climate change was not at issue in the *Urgenda* case. Specifically concerning the severity of the problem of climate change in the Netherlands, the District Court found that 'dangerous climate change has severe consequences on a global and local level' and that the 2°C threshold is vital to prevent irreversible climate change.[22] The District and Supreme Court also specified the dangers that climate change holds for the Netherlands in particular, including higher average temperatures, changing precipitation patterns, sea-level rise and a decreased supply of water in the summer, which could lead to making the country partly uninhabitable.[23] The Supreme Court further described the numerous consequences of climate change as 'hazardous', and the materialization of it as 'dangerous climate change'.[24]

Two further Intergovernmental Panel on Climate Change (IPCC) reports have been published since the decision of the Dutch Supreme Court was delivered in the *Urgenda* case, namely the IPCC's Special Report of Global Warming of 1.5°C,[25] and the IPCC's Sixth Assessment Report.[26] This means that the severity of the situation is even clearer.

Having established that the danger of climate change can be classified as 'severe', the next step is to consider what reductions were required. The District Court found that a minimum reduction of 25 per cent, compared to 1990 levels, is required in order to prevent the threat of dangerous climate change exceeding the 2°C threshold. The Supreme Court affirmed this decision, reiterating that climate change does represent a danger and serious risk to the citizens of the Netherlands,[27] and that the above reduction would be the minimum amount required in order to offer Dutch citizens the legal protection to which they are entitled.[28]

---

[22] *Urgenda Foundation v The Kingdom of the Netherlands (Ministry of Infrastructure and the Environment)* 2015 C/09/456689/HA ZA 13-1396 (Rechtbank Den Haag) (English Translation) (*Urgenda Foundation*), 4.16; R Cox 'The Liability of European States for Climate Change' (2014) *Utrecht Journal of International and European Law* 126.

[23] *Urgenda Foundation v The Kingdom of the Netherlands (Ministry of Infrastructure and the Environment)* 2015 C/09/456689/HA ZA 13-1396 (Rechtbank Den Haag) (English Translation), 4.17; *Urgenda Foundation v The Kingdom of the Netherlands (Ministry of Infrastructure and the Environment)* 2019 19/00135 (Hoge Raad) (English translation), 5.6.2.

[24] *Urgenda Foundation* 19/00135 (n 23), 4.2–4.3.

[25] IPCC, 'Special Report, Global Warming of 1.5°C', IPCC, https://www.ipcc.ch/sr15/, accessed 29 July 2022.

[26] IPCC, 'IPCC Sixth Assessment Report', IPCC, https://www.ipcc.ch/report/ar6/wg1/, accessed 29 July 2022.

[27] *Urgenda Foundation* 19/00135 (n 23), 2, 3, 11, 14, 16, 19.

[28] *Urgenda Foundation* 19/00135 (n 23), 16; Du Perron 2019, https://www.youtube.com/watch?v=hCFcyNcYklQ&feature=emb_logo.

Legal obligation of the Dutch state to make more extensive greenhouse gas emissions reductions in view of the danger of climate change

National and international law and the legal obligation of the Dutch state to reduce emissions

This section outlines the national and international framework of the *Urgenda* case. The decision of the District Court was based mainly on tort law and the doctrine of hazardous negligence contained in the Dutch Civil Code,[29] even though Urgenda also based their initial arguments on article 2 (the right to life) and article 8 (the right to respect for private and family life) of the European Convention on Human Rights (ECHR). Urgenda further relied on article 21 of the Dutch Constitution as well as international law in the form of the 'no-harm principle', the United Nations Framework Convention on Climate Change (UNFCCC), and the Treaty on the Functioning of the European Union (TFEU) in supporting their arguments.[30]

In terms of this legal framework, Urgenda argued that the Dutch state has a responsibility to reduce GHG emissions in order to prevent dangerous climate change.[31] Urgenda argued that the Dutch state is acting unlawfully since climate change mitigation action by the state is insufficient when measured against mitigation action described by national objectives, international agreements, and current scientific knowledge at the time.[32] More specifically, Urgenda argued that the state is acting unlawfully by not taking sufficient mitigation action, which endangers the living climate and the health of both man and the living environment, and accordingly that the state is breaching its duty of care.[33] Compliance with the duty of care meant a reduction in GHG emissions by 2020 of between 25 per cent and 40 per cent compared to 1990 levels.[34] This duty of care arose from article 21 of the Dutch Constitution and book 6, section 162 of the Dutch Civil Code (whether or not in combination with book 5, section 37 of the Dutch Civil Code).

Article 21 of the Dutch Constitution stipulates that '[i]t shall be the concern of the authorities to keep the country habitable and to protect and

[29] A Nollkaemper and L Burgers, 'A New Classic in Climate Change Litigation: The Dutch Supreme Court Decision in the Urgenda Case', EJIL: Talk!, 6 January 2020, https://www.ejiltalk.org/a-new-classic-in-climate-change-litigation-the-dutch-supreme-court-decision-in-the-urgenda-case/, accessed on 13 November 2022.

[30] Nollkaemper and Burgers (n 29).

[31] Cox (n 4).

[32] *Urgenda Foundation* C/09/456689 (n 23), 4.35.

[33] *Urgenda Foundation* C/09/456689 (n 23), 4.35.

[34] Cox (n 4).

improve the environment'. The District Court stipulates that the manner in which this duty of care, contained in article 21, is to be implemented is left by the court within the discretion of the Dutch state and would pertain to attending to water defences, water management and the living environment.[35] Accordingly, it found that the legal obligation of the state towards Urgenda *cannot* be imposed by article 21 of the Dutch Constitution.[36] Book 6, section 162 of the Dutch Civil Code deals with a so-called 'tortious act' and was found by the court a quo to be applicable to the *Urgenda* case,[37] even though the state disagreed that section 162 called for a more stringent limitation of GHG emissions than was currently being implemented by the state. The District Court also found that the interpretation of section 162 needed to be informed by the ECHR,[38] which will be discussed in greater detail below.

The District Court set out the international law and principles that inform the interpretation of the duty of care within the context of this case. In regard to the application of international law, the District Court found the state to be 'bound' by the UNFCCC, the Kyoto Protocol and the no-harm principle of international law.[39] The District Court also considered the international law principles of sustainable development, the precautionary principle and the principle of fairness particularly noteworthy within this context.[40] It further found that although the UNFCCC, the Kyoto Protocol and the no-harm principle could be relied upon directly by Urgenda, the state is considered to 'want to meet its international law obligations'.[41] Furthermore, the court emphasized a certain general rule within the Dutch legal system: 'when applying and interpreting national law open standards and concepts, including social proprietary, reasonableness and propriety, the general interest or certain legal principles, the court takes onto account such international-law obligations'.[42] Accordingly, these international law obligations and principles have a 'reflex effect' in the national law of the Netherlands,[43] and therefore were relevant in determining the general duty of care in relation to climate change.[44]

---

35 *Urgenda Foundation* C/09/456689 (n 23), 4.36.

36 *Urgenda Foundation* 19/00135 (n 23), 2.3.1.

37 *Urgenda Foundation* C/09/456689 (n 23), 4.46.

38 *Urgenda Foundation* C/09/456689 (n 23), 4.46.

39 *Urgenda Foundation* C/09/456689 (n 23), 4.42.

40 *Urgenda Foundation* C/09/456689 (n 23), 4.8, 4.76.

41 *Urgenda Foundation* C/09/456689 (n 23), 4.43.

42 *Urgenda Foundation* 19/00135 (n 23), 4.43.

43 *Urgenda Foundation* 19/00135 (n 23), 4.43. Also see E Stein and AG Castermans, 'Case Comment – Urgenda v. the State of the Netherlands: The "Reflex Effect" – Climate Change, Human Rights, and the Expanding Definitions of the Duty of Care' (2017) *McGill Journal of Sustainable Development Law* 303–24.

44 Cox (n 4).

The Supreme Court went further and also considered the Netherlands' legal obligation to reduce GHG emissions within the context of common but differentiated responsibilities. The Supreme Court found that it is clear that the reduction of GHG emissions by a minimum of 25 per cent before the end of 2020 is only a small fraction of action required to combat international climate change, but is nevertheless required by international agreements. It found that the Dutch state's efforts are not to be measured against any other state's efforts and that the state's responsibility to reduce emissions is based on the fact that all emissions contribute to global climate change.[45] The Netherlands could not evade its duty by arguing that other states are not adhering to a similar or a comparable duty. The District Court unequivocally dismissed the argument that the contribution of the Netherlands to global GHG emissions is negligible, providing that it must 'implement the reduction measures to the fullest extent as possible'.[46] The Supreme Court stated that 'every emission of greenhouse gases leads to an increase'.[47] In particular, the Supreme Court considered the Netherlands obligated, under articles 2 and 8 of the ECHR, the UNFCCC, and the no-harm principle of international law, to do their part in preventing dangerous climate change.[48] These findings by the Dutch courts also frame the responsibility of any state (and not just the Netherlands) to mitigate climate change, regardless of the actual collective international response to climate change mitigation. This Dutch fair share approach is contrasted with the South African approach in a subsequent section of the chapter.

The discussion of common but differentiated responsibility is further developed by the Dutch District Court in its consideration of future generations when explaining the term 'sustainable society'.[49] In defining the concept of sustainable development, the court described a sustainable society as containing an intergenerational dimension.[50] In addition, it stipulated that the principle of fairness dictates 'the policy should not only start from what is most beneficial to the current generation at this moment, but also what this means for future generations, so that future generations are not exclusively and disproportionally burdened with the consequences

45 *Urgenda Foundation* C/09/456689 (n 23), 4.78–9.

46 *Urgenda Foundation* C/09/456689 (n 23), 4.79.

47 *Urgenda Foundation* 19/00135 (n 23), 4.6.

48 *Urgenda Foundation* 19/00135 (n 23), 5.7.1–5.7.9.

49 *Urgenda Foundation* C/09/456689 (n 23), 4.8, 4.76; World Commission on Environment and Development, *Our Common Future* (Oxford 1987) 43.

50 Sustainable development is described as 'development that meets the needs of the present without compromising the ability of future generations to meet their own needs': *Urgenda Foundation* C/09/456689 (n 23), 4.8, 4.76; World Commission on Environment and Development (n 49), 43.

of climate change'.[51] The Supreme Court continued this discussion by stipulating that 'the mere existence of a sufficiently genuine possibility that this risk will materialize means that suitable measures must be taken', irrespective of the fact that the risks associated with climate change may only materialize in a few decades.[52]

It is noteworthy that the Dutch District Court found that article 2 and article 8 of the ECHR could, in fact, not be relied upon by Urgenda.[53] However, as mentioned, it did find that these articles of the ECHR are relevant to the interpretation of the national Dutch law pertaining to the duty of care.[54] In this respect it differs from the decision of the Supreme Court, which will now be set out.

Dutch climate change litigation as a matter of human rights

The Supreme Court in the *Urgenda* case found that the Netherlands did have a duty to reduce emissions based on human rights. According to Urgenda, the obligation of the Dutch state to reduce emissions is inter alia based on the legal duty of the Netherlands to respect human rights.[55] Urgenda argued that the state has a positive obligation to take 'protective measures' against climate change in terms of the ECHR, specifically article 2 (containing the right to life) and article 8 (containing the right to respect for private and family life).

As the impacts of climate change are clearly a threat to life, citizens of the Netherlands are able to ask for a reduction in the emissions that cause it. The Supreme Court stated that article 2 can be and has been applied to matters concerning natural or environmental disasters, and that the protection afforded by article 2 also covers risks that may only materialize in the future.[56] Accordingly, the Supreme Court found that article 2 of the ECHR obliges the Dutch state take the appropriate steps as required to safeguard the right to life of everyone within the jurisdiction of the Netherlands.[57] The Dutch Supreme Court further stated that article 8 of the ECHR applies to 'environmental issues'.[58] Accordingly, the Supreme Court derived protection for the living environment from article 8 in the event where an environmental

---

51 *Urgenda Foundation* C/09/456689 (n 23), 4.57.

52 *Urgenda Foundation* 19/00135 (n 23), 5.6.2.

53 Cox (n 4).

54 *Urgenda Foundation* C/09/456689 (n 23), 4.46; Cox (n 4).

55 Du Perron, 'Uitspraak in de klimaatzaak Urgenda', *Youtube*, 2019, https://www.youtube.com/watch?v=hCFcyNcYklQ&feature=emb_logo, accessed 13 November 2022.

56 *Urgenda Foundation* 19/00135 (n 23), 5.2.2.

57 *Urgenda Foundation* 19/00135 (n 23), 5.2.2.

58 *Urgenda Foundation* 19/00135 (n 23), 5.2.3.

hazard (such as dangerous climate change) holds a direct consequence for the private life of a person and if the environmental hazard is sufficiently serious.[59] Article 8 affords a positive obligation to take reasonable appropriate action to protect persons against possible serious environmental damage,[60] which entails an effect on the wellbeing of individuals, preventing individuals from enjoying their homes, or impacting the private life and family life of individuals adversely.[61] Effects do not have to be immediate, and can include long-term risks, which is in line with the precautionary principle contained in international environmental law.[62] Accordingly, the Supreme Court found that article 8 of the ECHR also obliges the Netherlands to take the appropriate steps as required to safeguard this right of everyone within its jurisdiction.[63]

The Supreme Court specifically stated that the fact that the risk associated with climate change will impact large parts of the population, opposed to specific persons, does not invalidate the application of article 2 and 8 of the ECHR to the matter.[64] Finally, article 13 of the ECHR, which deals with the right to an effective remedy, is also considered relevant by the Supreme Court to the interpretation of articles 2 and 8 of the ECHR.[65] In regard to article 13, the Supreme Court of Appeal stated that national states are required to provide remedies that can 'effectively prevent more serious violations' of the rights and freedoms contained in the ECHR.[66] In accordance with articles 93 and 94 of the Dutch Constitution, the Supreme Court held that Dutch courts are obliged to apply every provision of the ECHR that is binding on all persons,[67] and notes that the Netherlands falls within the jurisdiction of the European Court of Human Rights (ECtHR), in accordance with article 34 of the ECHR.[68] Therefore, Dutch courts must interpret provisions and standards of the ECHR in the same way as the ECtHR would, and this has been done by the Dutch Supreme Court in the application of article 2 and article 8 to the *Urgenda* case.[69] Therefore, the Supreme Court found: 'no other conclusion can be drawn but that the State is required pursuant to articles 2 and 8 [of the] ECHR to take measures to counter the genuine threat of dangerous climate change'.[70]

59 *Urgenda Foundation* 19/00135 (n 23), 5.2.3.
60 *Urgenda Foundation*19/00135 (n 23), 5.2.3.
61 *Urgenda Foundation* 19/00135 (n 23), 5.2.3.
62 *Urgenda Foundation* 19/00135 (n 23), 5.2.3, 5.3.2, 5.6.2.
63 *Urgenda Foundation* 19/00135 (n 23), 5.2.2.
64 *Urgenda Foundation* 19/00135 (n 23), 5.6.2.
65 *Urgenda Foundation* 19/00135 (n 23), 5.5.2.
66 *Urgenda Foundation* 19/00135 (n 23), 5.5.2–5.5.3.
67 *Urgenda Foundation* 19/00135 (n 23), 5.6.1.
68 *Urgenda Foundation* 19/00135 (n 23), 5.6.1.
69 *Urgenda Foundation* 19/00135 (n 23), 5.6.1.
70 *Urgenda Foundation*19/00135 (n 23), 5.6.2.

This section has set out the basis for the Dutch Supreme Court's decision in the *Urgenda* case. To illustrate the difference in the national approaches and highlight underlying complexities in the national systems of the Netherlands and South Africa, the section below will frame climate change litigation in South Africa.

Climate change litigation in South Africa

The severity of the danger of climate change in South Africa and the preventative state action required to reduce it

This section will consider the first question within the South African context, which can be divided into two components: firstly, how severe is the alleged danger of climate change and, secondly, what reductions are required in order to prevent dangerous climate change?

The impacts of climate change within South Africa are well recognized by the government and include increased temperatures throughout the country, changes to precipitation patterns and wind, sea-level rise, and an increased prevalence of drought.[71] In addition, the South African economy is highly dependent on sectors such as agriculture, forestry and tourism, which are all highly sensitive to the impacts of climate change.[72] These serious impacts have been recognized by the South African courts, predominantly within the context of the importance of sustainable development. In *Earthlife Africa Johannesburg v Minister of Environmental Affairs* (*Earthlife Africa*),[73] the High Court of South Africa noted that climate change poses a substantial risk to sustainable development in South Africa. The state must, the court found, take steps to protect the environment for the benefit of present and future generations.[74]

The second part of the question concerns what this means in terms of the actual reductions that are required in order to prevent dangerous climate change. The answer to this question in the Netherlands and South Africa is not the same. This can be seen in the approach taken by the courts. The Dutch Supreme Court is able to answer the question of actual reductions definitively

---

71 UNDP, 'South Africa', https://www.adaptation-undp.org/explore/southern-africa/south-africa, accessed 31 January 2020; MT Hoffman, PJ Carrick and L Gillson, 'Drought, Climate Change and Vegetation Response in the Succulent Karoo, South Africa' (2009) 105 *South African Journal of Science* 54–60, 54; Sanita van Wyk, 'Climate Change Law and Policy in South Africa and Mauritius: Adaptation and Mitigation Strategies in Terms of the Paris Agreement' (2022) 30(1) *African Journal of International and Comparative Law* 1–24.

72 UNDP (n 71); van Wyk (n 71).

73 *Earthlife Africa Johannesburg v Minister of Environmental Affairs*, 8 March 2017, Case No. 65662/16, Gauteng High Court Pretoria (South Africa).

74 *Earthlife Africa* (n 73), para. 82.

by stating that the Netherlands must ensure a reduction of 25 per cent by 2020, compared to the 1990 level.[75] However, the South African approach to actual reduction in GHG emissions is less clear-cut. The South African courts thus far have not provided a definitive answer as to what specific emission reduction would be acceptable. As mentioned, the *Urgenda* case can be called a 'systemic mitigation case' wherein 'overall efforts of a State to mitigate climate change is challenged' by the claimants.[76] However, the South African approach has typically featured more targeting of a 'specific project or initiative'[77] that has GHG emission implications, such as the construction of a coal-fired power plant. Accordingly, a South African climate change case does not tend to challenge overall mitigation ambition and, as such, no South African court has made a ruling comparable to *Urgenda* regarding the exact and actual GHG emissions reduction required. However, a recent South African report issued by the University of Cape Town's Energy Systems Research Group (ESRG) has determined that the South African state would have to reduce its GHG emissions by more than 20 per cent by 2030, from 2021 levels, in order to be on the pathway to avoid temperature increases by 1.5°C.[78]

This section serves to set out the South African climate change litigation strategy in order to juxtapose it against the systemic litigation illustrated by the *Urgenda* case in the Netherlands. The next step in this comparative exercise is to discuss the legal obligations of the South African state to make more extensive emission reductions in view of dangerous climate change.

Legal obligation of the South African state to make more extensive greenhouse gas emission reductions in view of the danger of climate change

International law and the legal obligation of the South African state to reduce emissions

This section serves to frame South Africa's international law obligations to reduce GHG emissions under the UNFCCC and the Paris Agreement. Therefore, it is necessary to outline the importance and relevance of

75 Whether or not this approach and reduction percentage is an appropriate response in order to successfully mitigate climate change falls outside the bounds of this chapter.

76 Maxwell, Mead and van Berkel (n 2), 38.

77 Maxwell, Mead and van Berkel (n 2), 38–9.

78 B Merven, J Burton and P Lehmann-Grube, 'Assessment of New Coal Generation Capacity Targets in South Africa's 2019 Integrated Resource Plan for Electricity', ESRG, 2021, https://cer.org.za/wp-content/uploads/2021/11/ESRG_New-coal-plants-South-Africa_021121.pdf, accessed 31 July 2022; R Pejan, 'South Africa's Youth Take on Coal and the Climate Crises', *Earthjustice*, 2021, https://earthjustice.org/from-the-experts/2021-december/south-africas-youth-take-on-coal-and-the-climate-crisis, accessed 31 July 2022.

international law within the national framework of the South African legal system, as dictated by the South African Constitution. Under section 39 of the South African Constitution courts 'must consider international law' and 'may consider foreign law' when adjudicating a matter, including a climate change matter. This approach is practically well-illustrated by the determinations of the High Court of South Africa in the *Deadly Air* case, detailed below, wherein the court specifically mentioned that the 'legal submissions made by the Special Rapporteur relate to aspects of international law which this Court is enjoined by section 39 of the Constitution to take into consideration.'[79] The court in *Deadly Air* further stated that it 'may benefit from the comparative foreign jurisprudence, where courts in other jurisdictions have had to determine similar issues which this Court is required to decide'.[80]

In addition, section 233 of the Constitution further directs South African courts to 'prefer any reasonable interpretation of the legislation that is consistent with international law over any alternative interpretation that is inconsistent with international law'. While section 233 does give substantial weight to international law within South Africa, the court will still ultimately decide whether the application of international climate change law is in accordance with the South African Bill of Rights. Finally, in determining the weight that a South African court may assign to international law in a climate change case, section 232 of the Constitution provides that '[c]ustomary international law is law in the Republic unless it is inconsistent with the Constitution or an Act of Parliament'. Accordingly, South African courts must consider international law within the context of climate change litigation and in determining the legal obligation of the South African state to reduce GHG emissions and mitigate climate change.

Similarly to the Netherlands, South Africa is a party to the UNFCCC and the Paris Agreement. In an international context, South Africa's contribution to climate change mitigation warrants what is called a 'fair share' approach, meaning that South Africa's response to climate change is dictated by its current national capacity and historic responsibility for the climate change problem.[81] In this regard, the Netherlands and South Africa do not have identical international law obligations concerning their respective climate change action. The historic responsibility and current capacity of South

[79] *Trustees for the Time Being of Groundwork Trust & Vukani Environmental Justice Alliance Movement in Action v Minister of Environmental Affairs, et al, and The United Nations Special Rapporteur on Human Rights and the Environment (as amicus curiae)* 2022, Case No. 39724/2019, High Court of South Africa (Gauteng Division Pretoria), para. 6.

[80] *Groundwork Trust* (n 79), para. 6.

[81] Pejan (n 78); Maxwell, Mead and van Berkel (n 2), 53–60.

Africa is very different to the historic responsibility and current capacity of the Netherlands.

Nevertheless, a fair share approach does not mean that South Africa is 'off the hook' when it comes to mitigating climate change. It is within this context that South Africa's reliance on coal-fired power, despite feasible and economically viable renewable energy options being available, can be strongly criticized.[82] By perpetuating a reliance on coal-fired power in the country, South Africa can scarcely be seen to be doing their fair share to combat GHG emissions.[83] As discussed, in *Urgenda* the District Court unequivocally dismissed the argument of the Netherlands that its contribution to global GHG emissions is negligible and ordered that it should 'implement the reduction measures to the fullest extent as possible'.[84] A subsequent report has also found that a fair share approach in the Netherlands would mean 'getting domestically as close to zero as possible and as fast as possible, and substantially supporting other countries' mitigation action'.[85]

The greatest difference in the applied fair share approach of the Netherlands and South Africa is the extent of international consideration; the Netherlands looks inward and then outward in applying the fair share approach, while South Africa, as a developing country, employs an overwhelmingly inward or national lens to its application of the fair share approach. The Dutch Supreme Court further emphasizes these submissions in stating that 'every emission of greenhouse gases leads to an increase'.[86] In particular, the Dutch Supreme Court considers the Netherlands obligated, in terms of article 2 and 8 of the ECHR, the UNFCCC, and the no-harm principle of international law, to do their part in preventing dangerous climate change.[87] These findings of the Dutch Court highlight any state's (including South Africa's) national responsibility to mitigate climate change in terms of international agreements regardless of the collective international response to climate change mitigation and considerations related to the fair share approach.

Nonetheless, the standard starting point under international law, supporting the contention that the Netherlands and South Africa do not have identical international law obligations concerning climate change action, is the Paris Agreement's preamble, which refers to the 'specific needs and special circumstances of developing country parties, especially those that are

[82] van Wyk (n 71), 1–24. Also see Nicole Loser's chapter in this volume.

[83] van Wyk (n 71), 1–24.

[84] *Urgenda Foundation* C/09/456689 (n 23), 4.79.

[85] H Fekete, N Höhne and S Smit 'What is a Fair Share Emissions Budget for the Netherlands?', New Climate Institute, 2022, https://newclimate.org/sites/default/files/2022-08/afairshareforthenetherlands_newclimate_20220829.pdf, accessed 15 April 2023.

[86] *Urgenda Foundation* 19/00135 (n 23), 4.6.

[87] *Urgenda Foundation* 19/00135 (n 23), 5.7.1–5.7.9.

particularly vulnerable to the adverse effects of climate change'.[88] Article 4 of the Paris Agreement further illustrates the differentiation between developed and developing countries in article 4(1),[89] which stipulates that the peaking of GHG emissions 'will take longer for developing country Parties'. In addition, article 4(4) of the Paris Agreement stipulates that developed countries 'should continue taking the lead' in reducing GHG emissions.

A further, very clear indication that the Netherlands and South Africa do not have identical international law obligations concerning climate change arises in the context of the Paris Agreement's nationally determined contributions (NDCs) mechanism. A key characteristic of the Paris Agreement is the NDC system it employs. The system of NDCs provide flexibility to each state to customize its NDC with due consideration for its unique development agenda.[90] Article 4(3) of the Paris Agreement specifically provides that NDCs must represent a state's 'highest possible ambition', while reflecting 'respective capabilities, in the light of different national circumstances' – a clear reference to the principle of common but differentiated responsibility.[91] Although the discussion of NDCs is relevant to both the Dutch and South African contexts, NDCs are discussed here in the South African context, since the unique national circumstances in South Africa place a greater emphasis on the voluntary nature of the mitigation ambitions contained in its NDC.

In submitting its NDC, South Africa stipulated that their response to climate change will be impacted by the country's national circumstances and specifically its principal goals of eliminating poverty and reducing inequality, as set out in South Africa's National Development Plan.[92] The economic or financial burden required to ensure a reduction in GHG emissions in South Africa will dictate – both in policy approaches and also litigation – a very different approach to that which was evident in the *Urgenda* case. In

---

[88] S van Wyk, *The Impact of Climate Change Law on the Principle of Sovereignty over Natural Resources* (Nomos 2017) 149.

[89] van Wyk (n 88), 149.

[90] WP Pauw, P Castro, J Pickering and S Bhasin, 'Conditional Nationally Determined Contributions in the Paris Agreement: Foothold for Equity or Achilles Heel?' (2019) 20(4) *Climate Policy* 468–84, 469; Peggy Schoeman, 'South Africa's Climate Change Legal Regime' (2019) *Without Prejudice – Spotlight on Environmental Law* 10–11, 10. Also take note of arts 2(2) and 4(3) of the Paris Agreement.

[91] van Wyk (n 88), 149.

[92] SA Government, 'South Africa's Intended Nationally Determined Contribution (INDC)', SA Government, https://www4.unfccc.int/sites/submissions/INDC/Published%20Documents/South%20Africa/1/South%20Africa.pdf, accessed 4 February 2020 2; SA Government, 'National Development Plan 2030', SA Government, https://www.gov.za/sites/default/files/Executive%20Summary-NDP%202030%20-%20Our%20future%20-%20make%20it%20work.pdf, accessed 5 June 2020.

the *Urgenda* case it was not a substantial point of contention whether or not the ordered reduction in emissions would be economically or financially viable for the Netherlands.[93] However, a South African court is expected to measure the economic or financial burden of reducing GHG emissions more carefully than any Dutch court. While South Africa is expected to prioritize the elimination of poverty and the reduction of inequality in responding to climate change more obviously than the Netherlands, it is however worthwhile to bear in mind that economic development and climate change action need not be mutually exclusive, even for a developing nation such as South Africa. This contention is supported by David Boyd, in his capacity as the United Nations Special Rapporteur for Human Rights and the Environment and *amicus curiae* in the case of *Trustees for the Time Being of Groundwork Trust v Minister of Environmental Affairs* (*Deadly Air* case),[94] which was recently heard in South Africa:

> The principle of sustainable development further requires that measures put in place to achieve economic development should not sacrifice the environment and human life and wellbeing and it must be that a balance should be struck. Where one trumps the other, it cannot be said the right of section 24(a) [of the South African Constitution] has been achieved.[95]

The extent of the consideration of international law, as located in key international agreements such as the UNFCCC and the Paris Agreement, is evident in climate change litigation in South Africa, as explained in the following sections.

National law and the legal obligation of the South African state to reduce emissions

South Africa's national climate change policy is contained in the National Climate Change Response White Paper (NCCRWP), which aims to ensure a decrease in GHG emissions within the country.[96] This policy informs the

---

93 *Urgenda Foundation* 19/00135 (English translation; Du Perron, 'Uitspraak in de klimaatzaak Urgenda', *Youtube*, 2019, https://www.youtube.com/watch?v=hCFcyNcYklQ&feature=emb_logo, accessed 13 November 2022, 14–15; Cox (n 4).

94 *Groundwork Trust* (n 79).

95 *Groundwork Trust* (n 79), para. 175.

96 Schoeman, (n 90), 10–11, 11; SA Government, 'National Development Plan 2030', https://www.gov.za/sites/default/files/Executive%20Summary-NDP%202030%20-%20Our%20future%20-%20make%20it%20work.pdf, accessed 5 June 2020.

legislative responses to climate change in South Africa, and the legislative foundations that are used to bring a climate change matter to court in South Africa.[97] The discussion that follows will focus on the national legislative, specifically constitutional, grounds for climate litigation in South Africa.

It is in the judicial approach to the constitutional grounds of argument that the most significant doctrinal difference can be observed. In the Netherlands, the legal obligation of the state could not be imposed by article 21 of the Dutch Constitution.[98] In other words, the *Urgenda* decision did not depend on a constitutional legislative basis. Conversely, in the South African context, the Constitution plays a key role in directing the judicial interpretation of legislation in climate change litigation.[99] Section 39(2) of the South African Constitution requires a court to 'promote the spirit, purport and objects of the Bill of Rights' (which includes, in section 24, the right to a healthy environment) when interpreting any legislation. This forms the basis of the most important difference between the Dutch and South African approach to climate change litigation, namely that climate change litigation in South Africa is overwhelmingly framed as a matter of administrative law.

In South Africa, current climate change litigation is fundamentally usually an environmental dispute that was brought to court on a primary basis related to land use, environmental conservation or environmental protection.[100] In addition to decided South African cases – to which the chapter shortly turns – all current pending climate change cases at the time of writing deal with climate change in the context of environmental impact assessment (EIA) and environmental permits.[101] This means that the further

97 Further relevant national legislation includes the Carbon Tax Act 15 of 2019, which commenced on 1 June 2019. Furthermore, in February 2022, the Climate Change Bill of 2018 was introduced to Parliament by the South African Department of Forestry, Fisheries and the Environment (DFFE), and is yet to enter into force.

98 *Urgenda Foundation* 19/00135 (n 23), 2.3.1. I discuss this in more depth above.

99 T-L Humby, 'The Thabametsi Case: Case No. 65662/16 Earthlife Africa Johannesburg v. Minister of Environmental Affairs' (2018) 30 *Journal of Environmental Law* 145, 146.

100 S Adelman in I Alogna, C Bakker and JP Gauci (eds), 'Climate Change Litigation: Global Perspectives' (2021) as referenced in M Burianski, M Clarke, FP Kuhnke and G Wackwitz, 'Climate Change Litigation in Africa, Current Status and Future Development', *White & Case,* 2021, https://www.whitecase.com/publications/insight/africa-focus-autumn-2021/climate-change-litigation-africa accessed 13 November 2022. Also see the chapter of Nicole Loser in this volume.

101 For example: *Sustaining the Wild Coast NPC v Minister of Mineral Resources and Energy* 2021 Case No. 3497/2021 High Court of South Africa; *Africa Climate Alliance v Minister of Mineral Resources & Energy* 2021 Case No. 56907/21 High Court of South Africa; *The City of Cape Town v National Energy Regulator of South Africa and Minister of Energy* 2017 Case No. 51765/17 High Court of South Africa; *South Durban Community Environmental Alliance v Minister of Environment* 2021 Case No. unknown High Court of South Africa; *SDCEA & Groundwork v Minister of Forestry, Fisheries, and the Environment* 2021 Case

legislation underlying these cases is usually comprised of provisions contained in National Environmental Management Act 107 of 1998 (NEMA). This approach, wherein a failure to consider climate change impacts can result in an unacceptable EIA and a matter being designated as a climate change case, is a fairly typical strategic approach to climate change litigation in South Africa and also in the broader Global South context.[102]

Administrative law and human rights as legal basis for South African climate change litigation

Earthlife Africa Johannesburg v Minister of Environmental Affairs (*Earthlife Africa*)[103] is the most prominent climate change case in South Africa. It was 'a watershed decision in South African environmental law', which 'filled an important gap in the South African environmental impact assessment regulatory framework'.[104] In the *Earthlife Africa* case, the High Court of South Africa considered climate change in the context of an EIA, which is required for the construction of a coal-burning power station.[105] NEMA played a key role in the *Earthlife Africa* judgment. The High Court found that the climate change impacts of a proposed coal-fired power station are relevant factors to be taken into consideration under NEMA,[106] stating:[107]

> [A]n assessment of climate change impacts and mitigating measures will be relevant factors in the environmental authorisation process, and […] consideration of such will best be accomplished by means of a professionally researched climate change impact report. For all these reasons, I find that the text, purpose, ethos and intra- and extra-statutory context of section 24O(1) of NEMA support the

---

No. unknown High Court of South Africa; *Trustees for the Time Being of the GroundWork Trust v Minister of Environmental Affairs, KiPower (Pty) Ltd* 2017 Case No. 54087/17 High Court of South Africa; *Trustees for the Time Being of GroundWork v Minister of Environmental Affairs, ACWA Power Khanyisa Thermal Power Station RF (Pty) Ltd* 2017 Case No. 61561/17 High Court of South Africa.

[102] J Peel and J Lin, 'Transnational Climate Litigation: The Contribution of the Global South' (2019) 113 *American Journal of International Law* 679. The first African case to use this approach, wherein a failure to consider climate change impacts results in an unacceptable EIA, was *Jonah Gbemre v Shell Petroleum Development Co. of Nigeria Ltd* (2005) FHC/B/CS/53/05. However, this case is not discussed as the chapter focuses on the jurisdictions of South Africa and the Netherlands.

[103] *Earthlife Africa Johannesburg v Minister of Environmental Affairs*, 8 March 2017, Case No. 65662/16, Gauteng High Court Pretoria (South Africa).

[104] Humby (n 99), 155; Burianski, Clarke, Kuhnke and Wackwitz (n 100).

[105] Burianski, Clarke, Kuhnke and Wackwitz (n 100).

[106] Schoeman (n 90), 10–11, 11; *Earthlife Africa* Case No. 65662/16.

[107] *Earthlife Africa* Case No. 65662/16.

conclusion that climate change impacts of coal-fired power stations are relevant factors that must be considered before granting environmental authorisation.[108]

While it can be stated that both the *Earthlife Africa* and *Urgenda* judgments ultimately served to mitigate climate change, a notable difference is observed between the approach taken to climate change in the reasoning of the respective courts. The South African court (and parties before the court) framed climate change mitigation as a periphery or secondary issue of the case and not the core of the matter, as was done by the court (and parties before the court) in the *Urgenda* case.[109] More specifically, the *Earthlife Africa* case, at its core, dealt with the considerations in the EIA that ought to precede the construction of a coal-fired power plant, and the court did not consider the South African state's legal obligation (as a rights-based obligation) to reduce GHG emissions, as was done in *Urgenda*. Human rights were also peripheral to the decision making, in that there was no direct application of the environmental rights contained in section 24 of the Constitution of South Africa in the *Earthlife Africa* case.[110] Even though a party in *Earthlife Africa* submitted that the court's interpretation of the requirements stipulated in NEMA should be influenced by the rights contained specifically in section 24 of the Constitution, the High Court did not provide an in-depth analysis of the relevance of the constitutional environmental right to its decision,[111] in the same detail as the constitutional discussion contained in the *Urgenda* judgement. It was, nevertheless, at least arguable that human rights protections and particularly section 24 of the Constitution influenced the court's decision making.[112]

While general administrative law has provided the best vehicle for climate change litigation in South Africa,[113] it is also possible to examine these judgments under a human rights lens. The discussion that follows serves to expand on the relevance of section 24 of the South African Constitution in

[108] *Earthlife Africa* Case No. 65662/16, para. 91.

[109] Adelman (n 100).

[110] J Peel and HM Osofsky, 'A Rights Turn in Climate Change Litigation' (2017) *Transnational Environmental Law* 1–31, 24.

[111] The discussion of the Court dealing sustainable development, within the context of s. 24 of the Constitution of South Africa, is the only relevant discussion of the secondary rights-based approach found within the *Earthlife Africa* case. See *Earthlife Africa* Case No. 65662/16, Gauteng High Court Pretoria (South Africa), para. 82. Also see: K Bouwer, 'The Influence of Human Rights on Climate Litigation in Africa' (2022) 13(1) *Journal of Human Rights and the Environment* 157–77.

[112] Bouwer (n 111), 157.

[113] O Rumble and A Gilder, 'Climate Litigation on the African Continent' (2021) KAS, https://www.kas.de/documents/282730/0/Climate_Litigation_Africa.pdf/1450e939-d100-a70e-8a9d-315161f96024, accessed 13 November 2022.

climate change litigation in South Africa, and investigates if some common ground can be found in a human rights context between the *Urgenda* case of the Netherlands and the *Philippi Horticultural Area Food & Farming Campaign v MEC for Local Government, Environmental Affairs and Development Planning: Western Cape (Philippi* case*)*, *Deadly Air* case and *Africa Climate Alliance v Minister of Mineral Resources & Energy (Cancel Coal* case*)* cases of South Africa. In doing so, this section will illustrate that although the Netherlands and South Africa follow different roads within the climate change litigation journey, when viewed through a human rights lens these different roads lead to the same destination, namely the mitigation of climate change.

As Bouwer explains, NEMA and its accompanying regulations 'were enacted to give effect to rights – including the right to a healthy environment – in the post-apartheid Constitution' of South Africa.[114] This is most clearly evidenced by the following South African cases: the *Philippi* case,[115] the *Deadly Air* case[116] and the *Cancel Coal* case.[117]

The *Philippi* case was concerned with an EIA and an environmental permit, and the applicants in the case argued that the administrative decision in the case must consider climate change.[118] *Philippi* was convincingly based on administrative law, similar to the *Earthlife Africa* case. In *Philippi*, the High Court of South Africa determined, in terms of NEMA, that the decision-maker did indeed not consider a 'key relevant factor' that a development would have on a certain aquifer, namely the 'impact on climate change and water scarcity'.[119]

The key difference, though, between *Earthlife Africa* and *Philippi* was that, in the *Philippi* case, the interpretation of NEMA was explicitly framed as a 'legislative instrument which gives effect to the environmental rights contained in [section] 24 of the Constitution'.[120] The High Court held:

> In relation to the aquifer, an assessment of the impact of development on it, having regard to the rights set out in s 24 of the Constitution and the provisions of [the National Environmental Management Act 107 of 1998] and its regulations, required consideration of the impact of the rezoning and subdivision sought in relation to the aquifer as a large underground

114 Bouwer (n 111), 157–77, 173.

115 *Philippi Horticultural Area Food & Farming Campaign v MEC for Local Government, Environmental Affairs and Development Planning: Western Cape* 2019 Case No. 16779/17 High Court of South Africa.

116 *Groundwork Trust* (n 79).

117 *Africa Climate Alliance v Minister of Mineral Resources & Energy et al* (Pending) filed 2021, High Court of South Africa.

118 *Philippi Horticultural* (n 115), para. 80.4.

119 *Philippi Horticultural* (n 115), para. 102.

120 *Philippi Horticultural* (n 115), para. 71.

natural resource, its state, future and impact on issues related to water scarcity and climate change.[121]

Accordingly, *in Philippi* the court's reasoning expressly recognizes the impact that human rights can have on climate change litigation in South Africa.[122]

An even more direct statement of the connection between human rights and climate change, and the importance of human rights for climate change litigation in South Africa, is the recent *Deadly Air* case.[123] This case concerned high levels of air pollution in an area of South Africa known as the Mpumalanga Highveld, an area in which 15 coal-powered power stations are situated (12 of which are owned by Eskom, a company branded by the Centre for Research on Energy and Clean Air as 'the world's most polluting power company').[124] The applicants in the *Deadly Air* case contended that the high levels of air pollution and the resulting poor air quality in the Mpumalanga Highveld constituted an infringement on the realization of environmental rights contained in section 24 of the South African Constitution.

In the High Court's ruling in *Deadly Air*, it found that not all air pollution constituted a violation of section 24 of the Constitution.[125] However, the court submitted that if the air quality does not meet the National Ambient Air Quality Standards for a determined period of time, as was the case in the Mpumalanga Highveld area, it constituted a prima facie violation of section 24.[126] On this basis, along with a consideration of international law and additional comparative jurisprudence, the High Court found a violation of section 24 of the South African Constitution, which included inter alia the human right to an environment that is not harmful to health or wellbeing.[127]

---

[121] *Philippi Horticultural* (n 115), para. 130.

[122] Bouwer (n 111), 157–77, 177.

[123] *Groundwork Trust* (n 79).

[124] Business & Human Rights Resource Centre, 'S Africa: Landmark "Deadly Air" Pollution Case Against the Government Finally Gets to be Heard in Court', (2021) Business & Human Rights Resource Centre, https://www.business-humanrights.org/en/latest-news/s-africa-landmark-deadly-air-pollution-case-against-the-government-finally-gets-to-be-heard-in-court/, accessed 31 July 2022; L Myllyvirta, 'Eskom is Now the World's Most Polluting Power Company' (2021) CREA, https://energyandcleanair.org/wp/wp-content/uploads/2021/10/Eskom-is-now-the-worlds-most-polluting-power-company.pdf, accessed 31 July 2022; van Wyk (n 71), 1–24.

[125] *Groundwork Trust* (n 79), para. 10.

[126] *Groundwork Trust* (n 79), para. 10.

[127] Centre for Environmental Rights (CER), 'Analysis: Why the #DeadlyAir High Court judgment matters', (2022) CER, https://cer.org.za/news/analysis-why-the-deadlyair-high-court-judgment-matters accessed 21 July 2022; K Rigg, 'Landmark Dutch Lawsuit Puts Governments Around the World on Notice' (2015) Huffington Post, http://www.huffingtonpost.com/kelly-rigg/landmark-dutch-lawsuit-pu_b_7025126.html, accessed 31 July 2022.

Strategically, the impact of the campaign and litigation was always understood to have climate change benefits. The case therefore can be framed as a climate change case that greatly advances the connection between climate change and human rights. The United Nations Special Rapporteur on Human Rights and the Environment, David Boyd, joined the proceedings in the *Deadly Air* case as an *amicus curiae*, providing expert evidence on the connection between air pollution and the fulfilment of human rights.[128] Even though the legal basis for preventing air pollution and climate change are not the same, judicial action to mitigate either air pollution or climate change can be considered to be a valuable interconnected action that ultimately serves to mitigate both. To support this contention, the interconnection between air pollution and climate change is well-framed by the European Commission as follows:

> [A]ir pollution and climate change influence each other through complex interactions in the atmosphere. Increasing levels of GHGs alter the energy balance between the atmosphere and the Earth's surface which, in turn, can lead to temperature changes that change the chemical composition of the atmosphere. Direct emissions of air pollutants (eg black carbon), or those formed from emissions such as sulfate and ozone, can also influence this energy balance. Thus, climate change and air pollution management have consequences for each other.[129]

Therefore, the judicial action observed in the *Deadly Air* case, in linking air pollution to human rights, is seen as crucial to the argument that advocates for the consideration of climate change litigation in South Africa through a human rights lens.

The decision in *Deadly Air* can already be compared to the *Urgenda* decision. *Deadly Air* and *Urgenda* share a great similarity in that both cases are heralded as 'landmark'[130] decisions for the application of human rights in the context of climate change litigation – the *Deadly Air* case for its application of section 24 of the South African Constitution and the *Urgenda* case for its application of article 2 and article 8 of the ECHR – indicating that both roads lead to the same destination, regardless of the differing underlying complexities.

---

[128] Business & Human Rights Resource Centre (n 124).

[129] European Commission, 'Combined Policies for Better Tackling of Climate Change and Air Pollution' (2010) 24 *Science for Environment Policy, Special Issue, Air Pollution and Climate Change*, https://ec.europa.eu/environment/integration/research/newsalert/pdf/24si_en.pdf, accessed 31 July 2022.

[130] CER (n 127); Rigg (n 127).

However, in addition to an increased reliance on human rights grounds in climate cases, South Africa is also moving towards 'systemic' approaches in its climate litigation strategy. A current pending matter in the High Court of South Africa, which presents a progression from the *Deadly Air* case, is the *Cancel Coal* case, which was instituted in 2021.[131] The core objective of *Cancel Coal* is to determine whether or not the South African state's decision to procure new coal-fired power is constitutional or not.[132] The applicants argue that the construction of a new coal-fired power plant would be an unjustifiable infringement of section 24 of the Constitution, containing the human right to an environment that is not harmful to health or wellbeing, considering that renewable energy generation is a feasible and less costly alternative to coal-fired power generation.[133] Therefore, like the applicants in the *Deadly Air* case, the applicants are seeking to rely directly on human rights protections. In this context, it is also predicted that the appointment in 2022 of a United Nations Special Rapporteur on the Promotion and Protection of Human Rights in the Context of Climate Change (namely, Ian Fry) might play a significant role in climate change litigation on the African continent, including South Africa, and in cementing the link between human rights and climate change litigation in the years to come.[134]

Conclusion: different roads to the same destination

The discussion in this chapter aimed to answer the following questions in a Dutch and South African context. Firstly, how severe is the alleged danger of climate change and what reductions are required in order to prevent the danger? Secondly, does the state have a legal obligation to make more extensive GHG reductions in view of the danger of climate change?

The *Urgenda* case, although set in a Global North context, signals an important new era in climate change litigation globally.[135] The decision of

[131] *Africa Climate Alliance v Minister of Mineral Resources & Energy* (Pending) filed 2021, High Court of South Africa.

[132] Grantham Research Institute on Climate Change and the Environment, 'Climate Change Laws of the World' Grantham Research Institute on Climate Change and the Environment, https://climate-laws.org/geographies/south-africa/litigation_cases/africa-climate-alliance-et-al-v-minister-of-mineral-resources-energy-et-al-cancelcoal-case, accessed 31 July 2022.

[133] Life after coal / *Impilo Ngaphandle Kwamalahle,* 'Youth-led #CancelCoal Climate Case Launched Against Government's Plans for New Coal-Fired Power' (2021) Life after coal / *Impilo Ngaphandle Kwamalahle*, https://lifeaftercoal.org.za/media/youth-led-cancelcoal-climate-case-launched-against-governments-plans-for-new-coal-fired-power, accessed 31 July 2022.

[134] CER (n 127); OHCHR, 'Special Rapporteur on climate change', 2022, https://www.ohchr.org/en/specialprocedures/sr-climate-change, accessed 31 July 2022.

[135] van Wyk (n 88), 328–33; Maxwell, Mead and van Berkel (n 2), 61.

the Supreme Court of the Netherlands in that case clearly demarcated a movement towards human rights-based climate litigation, evidenced by the Supreme Court's detailing of the impact of human rights, as contained in the ECHR, on the final decision. Specifically, the Dutch Court found that article 2 and article 8 of the ECHR is violated where the Netherlands does not adhere to the reduction of GHG emissions by 25 per cent in 2020 compared to 1990 levels. In ordering the Dutch state to reduce GHG emissions based inter alia on the ECHR, the Supreme Court cemented human rights-based climate change litigation in order to mitigate the impact of climate change.

On the other side of the globe, climate change litigation in South Africa, specifically when referring to the prominent *Earthlife Africa* case, is arguably primarily based on aspects related to administrative law, such as EIAs and environmental permits required in terms of NEMA, and not directly on violations of human rights. *Earthlife Africa* in particular cannot be earmarked as a quintessential illustration of climate change litigation succeeding on human rights grounds, in a manner similar to *Urgenda*. It also focused very much on the overall implications of coal projects, rather than taking a 'systemic' approach to South Africa's climate policy as a whole. Taking only the decision of the *Earthlife Africa* case into consideration, the future of rights-based climate litigation in South Africa leaves ample room for 'novel argumentation'[136] that is not necessarily based on NEMA. This is already emerging as the decision in the *Deadly Air* case is directly based on section 24 of the South African Constitution; the pending *Cancel Coal* case might lead to a similar outcome. The decided *Deadly Air* case in particular has changed the South African climate change litigation landscape, making it more comparable to the Dutch landscape when it comes to rights-based climate change litigation.[137]

The decision of the South African High Court in *Deadly Air* has reimagined the potential impact of human rights on climate change litigation in South Africa,[138] specifically the human right to an environment that is not harmful to health or wellbeing, as contained in section 24 of the South African Constitution. When the approach of the *Deadly Air* case is studied, it reveals a similarity to the Dutch approach in the *Urgenda* case, since both jurisdictions illustrate a rights-based approach to climate change litigation, in which 'a State's obligations to protect the human rights of people within its jurisdiction [is enforced], whether under a constitution or pursuant to regional or international human rights law'.[139] In *Urgenda* this occurred in

[136] Peel and Osofsky (n 110), 26.

[137] Peel and Osofsky (n 110), 26.

[138] Bouwer (n 111), 157–77, 175.

[139] Maxwell, Mead and van Berkel (n 2), 39.

terms of article 2 and article 8 of the ECHR, and in *Deadly Air* this occurred in terms of section 24 of the South African Constitution.

Even though the Dutch approach is based on human rights contained in the ECHR and the South African approach is based on human rights contained in the Constitution, it can be concluded that the two different jurisdictional approaches do reveal different roads leading to the same destination, namely human rights-based climate change litigation in order to mitigate the impact of climate change. Although the same outcome is arguably reached in the Netherlands and South Africa, the underlying complexities in each jurisdiction, in particular including the considerations related to a fair share approach, remain quite different. This is undoubtedly why South Africa's move to more systemic litigation has been slow. Even so, this means that, within both jurisdictions, human rights are employed to make a considerable impact on either the public law or tort law bases underlying climate change litigation. In addition, this chapter shows how different contextual considerations in the Netherlands and South Africa do not preclude a common-core approach to human rights-based climate change litigation in order to mitigate the impact of climate change.

PART III

Justice, Equity and Activism

11

Climate Change and Multinationals in Nigeria: A Case for Climate Justice

Eghosa O Ekhator and Edward O Okumagba

Introduction

Climate change, which has led to a plethora of negative impacts on the world, remains a raging issue globally. The destructive effects of climate change can be discerned in the short term via natural hazards including drought, flooding, landslides, storms and tidal waves; and in the long term via the continuing destruction of the environment.[1] Furthermore, the Intergovernmental Panel on Climate Change (IPCC) report in 2021 has highlighted the various threats climate change poses to the survival of the planet.[2] The report evidences that there has been a big rise in global warming and the greenhouse gas (GHG) emissions, which are having negative impacts on the planet and on billions of people.[3] No part of the world is left out from climate change impacts. This has led to droughts, heatwaves, heavy rainfall and cyclones occurring in different parts of the world.[4] Africa is one of the

1 T Kompas, Van Ha Pham and T Nhu Che, 'The Effects of Climate Change on GDP by Country and the Global Economic Gains from Complying with the Paris climate accord' (2018) 6(8) *Earth's Future* 1153–73.

2 United Nations, Climate Change 2021: The Physical Basis (Intergovernmental Panel on Climate Change IPCC, 2021) https://www.unep.org/resources/report/climate-change-2021-physical-science-basis-working-group-i-contribution-sixth; U Afinotan, 'How Serious is Nigeria About Climate Change Mitigation Through Gas Flaring Regulation in the Niger Delta?' (2022) 24(4) *Environmental Law Review* 288–304.

3 IPCC Report 2021 (n 2).

4 IPCC Report 2021 (n 2); Afinotan (n 2).

places bearing the brunt of climate change. According to the IPCC, 'Africa is one of the most vulnerable continents to climate variability and change'.[5]

The impacts of climate change will have negative consequences on the human rights and wellbeing of its victims in Nigeria (especially the Niger Delta).[6] In Nigeria, climate change has led, among other things, to increased and frequent flooding, rising sea levels and droughts.[7] For example, the flooding that took place in late 2022 in Nigeria affected more than 2.5 million people and led to the widespread destruction of farmland in the country.[8] Nigeria is one of the ten countries categorized by the International Rescue Committee (IRC) as highly vulnerable to climate change impacts.[9] This has been exacerbated by a plethora of factors not limited to poverty, the activities of multinational companies (MNCs) and endemic environmental injustice issues in many parts of the country (especially the Niger Delta, wherein the oil and gas industry is located).

The activities of MNCs in the Nigerian oil and gas industry also have negative impacts on the climate.[10] Gas flaring is a regular occurrence in the Niger Delta region of Nigeria (where the oil and sector is predominantly

---

5 Intergovernmental Panel on Climate Change (IPCC), 'Special Report on the Regional Impacts of Climate Change: An Assessment of Vulnerability', (2007), https://www.grida.no/climate/ipcc/regional/index.htm , accessed 25 May 2023. Furthermore, a plethora of reports have highlighted that Africa is overly impacted by climate disasters. For example, rising sea levels and temperature, extreme weather conditions and unpredictable rain patterns are having negative impacts on health, water and food security and development in African countries. Generally, see World Meteorological Organization (WMO), 'State of the Climate in Africa 2019 (WMO-No.1253) 2020', https://library.wmo.int/index.php?lvl=notice_display&id=21778#.X5giydPsYiR, accessed 25 May 2023.

6 M Addaney, E Boshoff and B Olutola, 'The Climate Change and Human Rights Nexus in Africa' (2017) 9(3) *Amsterdam Law Forum* 5–28.

7 Climate Knowledge Portal for Development Practitioners and Policy Makers, 'Nigeria', https://climateknowledgeportal.worldbank.org/country/nigeria/vulnerability accessed 25 May 2023.

8 International Rescue Committee (IRC), '10 Countries at Risk of Climate Disaster', 25 May 2023, https://www.rescue.org/article/10-countries-risk-climate-disaster accessed 25 May 2023.

9 IRC (n 8).

10 In Nigeria, many MNCs, including Shell, Chevron and Agip, have always had subsidiaries that operated in the oil and gas industry in Nigeria. For example, Shell Petroleum Development Company of Nigeria (SPDC), a Royal Dutch Shell (RDS) subsidiary, is one of Nigeria's oldest oil firms and the first company to export oil from Nigeria has led the field in the oil and gas sector in the country. Generally, see JG Frynas, MP Beck and K Mellahi, 'Maintaining Corporate Dominance After Decolonization: the "First Mover Advantage' of Shell-BP in Nigeria" (2000) 27(85) *Review of African Political Economy* 407–25. RDS is now called Shell plc.

located).[11] Gas flaring occurs 'when oil is pumped out of the ground, the gas produced is separated and, in Nigeria, most of it is burnt as waste in massive flares'.[12] Therefore, in the process of refining, the natural gas, otherwise called 'associated gas', is removed from the crude oil being refined.[13] Notwithstanding a plethora of laws and regulations, the Nigerian government has been unable to tackle the menace of gas flaring in the country.[14] Nigeria is one of the 'top ten flaring countries [that] accounted for 75 percent of all gas flaring and 50 percent of global oil production in 2021'.[15] Nigeria's significant economic reliance on the oil and gas industry has limited its ability to address the human rights and climate-related issues emanating from gas flaring.

This chapter relies on the concept of climate justice as its analytical lens. Climate justice – which is a variant of the environmental justice paradigm – can be used as a means to evaluate strategies to improve access to justice and protect climate change victims in Nigeria. This chapter also examines the potential of climate change litigation in Nigeria as one of the strategies in ventilating climate justice issues in the country. There are many definitions and understandings of climate change litigation.[16] The use of climate change litigation is soaring globally, and it has become a key slant of the emergent transnational litigation.[17] According to scholars, climate change litigation is still in its infancy in Nigeria.[18] This chapter

[11] Generally, see I Aye and EO Wingate, 'Nigeria's Flare Gas (Prevention of Waste & Pollution) Regulations 2018' (2019) 21(2) *Environmental Law Review* 119–27.

[12] Amnesty International, 'Nigeria: Petroleum, Pollution and Poverty in the Niger Delta', (2009) 18 https://www.amnesty.org/en/documents/afr44/018/2009/en/, accessed 25 May 2023.

[13] M Ishisone, 'Gas Flaring in the Niger delta: The Potential Benefits of Its Reduction on the Local Economy and Environment', http://nature.berkeley.edu/classes/es196/projects/2004final/Ishone.pdf, accessed 25 May 2023.

[14] Generally, see KO Mrabure and BO Ohimor, 'Unabated Gas Flaring Menace in Nigeria. The Need for Proper Gas Utilization and Strict Enforcement of Applicable Laws' (2020) 46(4) *Commonwealth Law Bulletin* 753–79; Aye and Wingate (n 11).

[15] World Bank, '2022 Global Gas Flaring Tracker Report', 2022, https://www.worldbank.org/en/programs/gasflaringreduction/publication/2022-global-gas-flaring-tracker-report, accessed 25 May 2023.

[16] J Setzer and LC Vanhala, 'Climate Change Litigation: A Review of Research on Courts and Litigants in Climate Governance' (2019) 10 *Wiley Interdisciplinary Reviews: Climate Change* e580. Also see the discussion about definitions and conceptualizations of this by the editors in the introductory chapter to this volume.

[17] P Obani and E Ekhator, 'Transnational Litigation and Climate Change in Nigeria' in *Symposium: Nigeria and International Law: Past, Present and the Future* (AfronomicsLaw Blog 2021), https://www.afronomicslaw.org/category/analysis/transnational-litigation-and-climate-change-nigeria, accessed 25 May 2023.

[18] U Etemire, 'The Future of Climate Change Litigation in Nigeria: COPW v NNPC in the Spotlight' (2021) 2 *Carbon & Climate Law Review* 158; PK Oniemola, 'A Proposal

explores how it might expand in future and considers its potential to improve climate justice in the country.

This chapter is divided into five further parts. The first part discusses the role of MNCs in climate change-related activities. This part of the chapter also focuses on how their role is addressed in the 2015 Paris Agreement on Climate Change, which was adopted in December 2015. Part two of the chapter focuses on climate justice. The third part of the chapter discusses how climate litigation can be a tool or strategy to promote climate justice. The fourth part focuses on the potential of climate litigation in Nigeria against the backdrop of recent judicial and legislative developments. The fifth part of the chapter is the conclusion.

Multinationals and climate change

MNCs are said to be the major contributors to climate change in the world today.[19] Fossil fuel companies have been singled out as needing to take responsibility for climate change.[20] In the Carbon Majors Report published in 2017, it was confirmed that 'Just 100 companies have been the source of more than 70% of the world's greenhouse gas emissions since 1988'.[21] Unquestionably, activities in the global energy industry, especially those associated with energy production and consumption, continue to be major sources of GHG emissions, thus resulting in extensive climate change.[22] A report by Zhang *et al* avers that a fifth of CO_2 emissions come from MNCs' global supply chains.[23] Since the publication of the Carbon Majors Report

for Transnational Litigation Against Climate Change Violations in Africa' (2021) 38 *Wisconsin International Law Journal* 301; E Okumagba, 'Examining Global Court Practices in Reducing Climate Change Impacts Through litigation: Lessons for Nigeria' in EO Ekhator, S Miller and E Igbinosa, (eds) *Implementing the Sustainable Development Goals in Nigeria: Barriers, Prospects and Strategies* (Routledge 2021).

19 M Rumpf, 'Climate Change Litigation and the Private Sector – Assessing the Liability Risk for Multinational Corporations and the Way Forward for Strategic Litigation' in OC Ruppel, T Markus, E Schulev-Steindi and H Müllerova (eds), *Climate Change, Responsibility and Liability* (Nomos Verlagsgesellschaft mbH & Co. KG 2022) 441–90.

20 R Heede, 'Tracing Anthropogenic Carbon Dioxide and Methane Emissions to Fossil Fuel and Cement Producers, 1854–2010' (2014) 122(1) *Climatic Change* 229–41.

21 T Riley, 'Just 100 Companies Responsible for 71% of Global Emissions, Study Says', *The Guardian*, 10 July 2017, https://www.theguardian.com/sustainable-business/2017/jul/10/100-fossil-fuel-companies-investors-responsible-71-global-emissions-cdp-study-climate-change, accessed 25 May 2023.

22 NA Obeng-Darko, 'Editorial' OGEL Special Issue on 'Energy Transitions' (2021) 19(1) *Oil, Gas & Energy Law.*

23 Z Zhang *et al*, 'Embodied Carbon Emissions in the Supply Chains of Multinational Enterprises' (2020) 10(12) *Nature Climate Change* 1096–101.

2017, many MNCs have been progressively subject to climate change-based litigation by different actors.[24] MNCs are also now at the driving force behind the new markets for what has been termed 'green' goods and services in different parts of the world.[25] Therefore, MNCs are at the forefront of developing and embedding GHG targets as one of the strategies to combat the effects of climate change.[26] It should be noted that many of the changes espoused by MNCs have come about because of pressure from relevant stakeholders, including non-governmental organizations (NGOs), government and investors, among others.[27]

The 1992 United Nations Framework Convention on Climate Change (UNFCCC) is said to have established a climate change architecture or framework.[28] The Paris Climate Change Agreement of 2015 (Paris Agreement) is a key element of the global climate governance architecture.[29] COP21 to the UNFCCC witnessed over 196 parties voluntarily pledging to a treaty in furtherance of mitigation strategies for climate change,[30] where in signing the Paris Agreement countries came together to agree a route on how to reduce GHG emissions and ensure that global warming remains 'well below 2°C'.[31] The Glasgow Climate Pact was agreed to by 197 countries during the COP 26 that took place in 2021.[32] This is said to be the first

[24] See Rumpf (n 19).

[25] J Pinkse and A Kolk, 'Multinational Enterprises and Climate Change: Exploring Institutional Failures and Embeddedness' (2012) 43(3) *Journal of International Business Studies* 332–41.

[26] D Wang and T Sueyoshi, 'Climate Change Mitigation Targets Set by Global Firms: Overview and Implications for Renewable Energy' (2018) 94 *Renewable and Sustainable Energy Reviews* 386–98.

[27] R Sullivan and A Gouldson. 'The Governance of Corporate Responses to Climate Change: An International Comparison' (2017) 26(4) *Business Strategy and the Environment* 413–25.

[28] S Hori and S Syugyo, 'The Function of International Business Frameworks for Governing Companies' Climate Change-Related Actions Toward the 2050 Goals' (2020) 20(3) *International Environmental Agreements: Politics, Law and Economics* 541–57.

[29] L Wegener, 'Can the Paris Agreement Help Climate Change Litigation and Vice Versa?' (2020) 9(1) *Transnational Environmental Law* 17–36.

[30] A Savaresi, 'The Paris Agreement: A New Beginning?' (2016) 34(1) *Journal of Energy & Natural Resources Law* 16–26.

[31] B Comyns, 'Climate Change Reporting and Multinational Companies: Insights from Institutional Theory and International Business' (2018) 42(1) *Accounting Forum* 65–77.

[32] UNFCC, 'The Glasgow Climate Pact – Key Outcomes from COP26', https://unfccc.int/process-and-meetings/the-paris-agreement/the-glasgow-climate-pact-key-outcomes-from-cop26?gclid=Cj0KCQiA7bucBhCeARIsAIOwr-8ys8neosn3oP2CKvo3Vy-TXDNdKEzeyWx9Szgbun3erXRzSRG4U0UaAhHDEALw_wcB, accessed 25 May 2023; Afinotan (n 2).

international climate agreement to expressly mention fossil fuels.[33] However, the provision referring to fossil fuels that eventually appeared is said to be a highly watered-down or diluted version, due to compromises between negotiators at the conference.[34]

Irrespective of express mentions, the crux of Paris Agreement is for individual countries to start transitioning from an economy largely based on fossil fuels to a decarbonized economy.[35] It sets a target to reduce emissions enough to restrict the rise in the global average temperature to well below 2°C, the scientifically-advised limit of safety, with an aspiration not to go below 1.5°C above pre-industrial levels.[36] Arguably, current climate plans and targets are still inadequate to meet the Paris Agreement climate goals, and countries will be compelled to re-evaluate their reliance on fossil fuels. Already, this has led to an increase in renewable energy development initiatives in different parts of the world.[37]

In 2016, during the COP22, member states discussed the role and utility of companies in helping in the implementation and effectiveness of climate change mechanisms.[38] As stated above, the Paris Agreement is said to be the most important international treaty to be reached by the global community in recent years.[39] Although companies were not explicitly involved in the Paris negotiations, more than 500 signalled their support by agreeing to the Paris Pledge for Action.[40] 'By signing this pledge, companies agree to implement and even exceed commitments made by governments under the Paris Agreement.'[41] The role of MNCs in facilitating climate change places

[33] M Gagen, 'Glasgow Climate Pact: Where Do all the Words and Numbers We Heard at COP26 Leave Us?', The Conversation, 2021, https://theconversation.com/glasgow-climate-pact-where-do-all-the-words-and-numbers-we-heard-at-cop26-leave-us-171704.

[34] Gagen (n 33).

[35] Generally, see EG Pereira, Alberto José Fossa and Eghosa O Ekhator *et al*, 'Fossil Fuel and the Global Energy Transition: Regulation and Standardisation as Panacea for a More Sustainable World Energy Order' (2022) 8(5) *Brazilian Journal of Development* 39838–65.

[36] F Harvey, 'The Paris Agreement Five Years On: Is It Strong Enough to Avert Climate Catastrophe?', *The Guardian*, 8 December 2020, https://www.theguardian.com/environment/2020/dec/08/the-paris-agreement-five-years-on-is-it-strong-enough-to-avert-climate-catastrophe, accessed 25 May 2023.

[37] A Balthasar *et al*, 'Energy Transition in Europe and the United States: Policy Entrepreneurs and Veto Players in Federalist Systems' (2020) 29 (1) *The Journal of Environment & Development* 3–25.

[38] Hori and Syugyo (n 28).

[39] J Vidal and A Vaughan, 'Paris Climate Agreement "may signal end of fossil fuel era"', *The Guardian*, 13 December 2015, https://www.theguardian.com/environment/2015/dec/13/paris-climate-agreement-signal-end-of-fossil-fuel-era, accessed 25 May 2023.

[40] Comyns (n 31).

[41] Comyns (n 31), 65.

an obligation (at least a moral one) on them to be at the forefront of efforts aimed at addressing climate change.

An important pre-requirement for MNCs and private sector adaptation is the ability or capacity to adapt. Adaptation and mitigation policies are expensive ventures and increases economic costs for companies.[42] Perhaps only rich and wealthy firms (especially MNCs) are in the position to engage in such measures. Adaptive capacity affects the extent to which a business or firm is cognizant of its 'vulnerability, and can evaluate, make decisions about and implement adaptation measures, whether in anticipation or in response to climate change impacts'.[43]

However, not all companies or MNCs have adequate capacity to deliver adaptation to climate change for their operations or the communities in which they operate. Also, some companies might claim that, due to government policies, regulations and laws, they are unable to do more to deliver adaptation and mitigation measures. Arguably, this is what is occurring in the Niger Delta region of Nigeria. Here, some MNCs are pulling out of some parts of the extractive industry after decades of economic activities that have exacerbated the environmental crisis in the Niger Delta region. However, even though some MNCs are divesting from onshore oil and gas operations in Nigeria, MNCs still have an obligation to finance environmental remediation/restoration activities, decommission disused facilities, and pay just compensation for other damages, 'whilst ensuring proper consultation and thorough consideration of community needs throughout this process'.[44]

Mitigation is the duty to reduce climate-producing endeavours.[45] Policies or measures 'to mitigate global climate change entail significant economic costs. Yet a growing number of firms lobby in favour of regulation to mitigate carbon emissions'.[46] Thus, notwithstanding the costs of adaptation and mitigation responses by MNCs to climate change, and the opposition of some MNCs to these measures, there appears to be universal approval by a

---

[42] A Kennard, 'The Enemy of My Enemy: When Firms Support Climate Change Regulation' (2020) *International Organization* 187–221.

[43] A Averchenkova *et al*, 'Multinational Corporations and Climate Adaptation – Are We Asking the Right Questions? A Review of Current Knowledge and a New Research Perspective' (2015) Grantham Research Institute on Climate Change and the Environment Working Paper 183, 2.

[44] Stakeholder Democracy Network (SDN), 'Divesting from the Delta: Implications for the Niger Delta as International Oil Companies Exit Onshore Production', 2021, https://www.stakeholderdemocracy.org/report-divestment/, accessed 25 May 2023.

[45] GAS Edwards, 'Climate Justice' in B Coolsaet (ed), *Environmental Justice: Key Issues* (Routledge 2021) 148–60.

[46] Kennard (n 42), 187.

plethora of MNCs.[47] Thus, it can be argued that there is a business case for MNCs to engage in adaptation and mitigation activities that will invariably enhance or contribute to profit maximization.[48]

Therefore, the extent of the climate challenge has led to a growing recognition at global and national levels of the need to engage the private sector, especially MNCs, in climate change governance.[49] However, some stakeholders and academics have argued that major MNCs are not meeting their net-zero climate change pledges.[50] For example, the Corporate Climate Responsibility Monitor Report 2022 suggests that many MNCs fall short of the targets set in the globally agreed goals of the Paris Agreement and that were developed to avoid the serious impacts of climate change.[51]

Reliance on the concept of climate justice can be one of the strategies that can used to protect and promote the rights of Nigerians in climate actions. The most vulnerable in society tend to be the major victims of the negative impacts of climate change in different parts of the world. Climate justice is commonly referred to as the inequitable 'distribution of costs and burdens of climate change'.[52] The concept of climate justice is a framework that has been developed to help in addressing the injustices or inequities inherent in the global climate regime.[53]

Arguably, the concept of climate justice is implicit and explicit in some of the existing international frameworks on climate change (for example, the Paris Agreement and UNFCCC). Hence the next section focuses on the concept of climate justice and its implications for climate change governance.

Overview of climate justice

There is a plethora of definitions or connotations of climate justice; there is no universally accepted definition.[54] For example, climate justice is premised on the need for international law to protect the rights of the most vulnerable

---

47 Kennard (n 42), 187.

48 Sullivan and Gouldson (n 27).

49 Obani and Ekhator (n 17).

50 S Meredith, 'World's Biggest Companies Accused of Exaggerating Their Climate Actions', CNBC, 7 February 2022, https://www.cnbc.com/2022/02/07/study-worlds-biggest-firms-seen-exaggerating-their-climate-actions.html, accessed 25 May 2023.

51 Meredith (n 50).

52 P Kashwan, 'Climate Justice in the Global North: An Introduction' (2021) 5(1) *Case Studies in the Environment* 1–13, 4.

53 F Sultana, 'Critical Climate Justice' (2022) 188(1) *The Geographical Journal* 118–24.

54 T Jafry, K Helwig and M Mikulewicz (eds), *Routledge Handbook of Climate Justice* (Routledge 2018).

from the unequal negative impacts of climate change.[55] However, this chapter favours the definition of climate (change) justice as proffered by the Task Force on Climate Change Justice and Human Rights of the International Bar Association (the IBA Task Force). The IBA Task Force defines climate justice as follows:

> To ensure communities, individuals and governments have substantive legal and procedural rights relating to the enjoyment of a safe, clean, healthy and sustainable environment and the means to take or cause measures to be taken within their national legislative and judicial systems and, where necessary, at regional and international levels, to mitigate sources of climate change and provide for adaptation to its effects in a manner that respects human rights.[56]

Thus, climate justice is a concept or framework that acknowledges that climate change will unduly affect people or communities who are less capable in preventing, adapting or being able to respond to its negative impacts, such as the now common extreme weather occurrences, rising sea levels and new resource limitations.[57] In essence, climate justice embeds the explicit recognition of the development inequities accentuated by climate change.[58]

Climate justice is an offshoot of environmental justice, and environmental justice is also a movement and concept.[59] For example, there is close connection between the struggles for environmental justice and climate justice in the Niger Delta. Thus, there is an explicit link between the grassroots struggles of people suffering from pollution to broader concerns about the climate change impact of MNCs – mostly because of the same conduct by the same MNCs. They pollute locally, and globally, with the effects being felt even more locally due to vulnerabilities in the Niger Delta.[60]

[55] DS Olawuyi, 'Advancing Climate Justice in International Law: An Evaluation of the United Nations Human Rights-Based Approach' (2015) 11 *Florida A & M University Law Review* 103–25.

[56] International Bar Association (IBA), 'Achieving Justice and Human Rights in an Era of Climate Disruption', (2014) 2 https://www.ibanet.org/MediaHandler?id=0f8cee12-ee56-4452-bf43-cfcab196cc04, accessed 25 May 2023.

[57] IBA (n 56); Sultana (n 53).

[58] IBA (n 56); Edwards (n 45).

[59] For example, K Jenkins, 'Setting Energy Justice Apart from the Crowd: Lessons from Environmental and Climate Justice' (2018) 39 *Energy Research & Social Science* 117–21, 117 defines environmental justice 'as the distribution of environmental hazards and access to all natural resources; it includes equal protection from burdens, meaningful involvement in decisions, and fair treatment in access to benefits'.

[60] Also, see K Bouwer, 'The influence of human rights on climate litigation in Africa' (2022) 13 (1) *Journal of Human Rights and the Environment* 157–77, 158.

Hence, notable environmental justice NGOs such as the Environmental Rights Action (ERA) have been at the forefront of promoting climate justice action in Nigeria.[61]

Environmental justice has an indelible impact on how climate justice has been conceptualized and developed as a scholarly construct.[62] On the other hand, Edwards suggests that 'climate justice' as an idea or a concept emerged concurrently in scholarly circles and civil society when climate change issues rose to prominence and public consciousness in the 1990s.[63] Like environmental justice, climate justice is rooted in anti-establishment social movements. Schlosberg and Collins suggests that one of the conceptualizations of climate justice is that it is rooted in grassroots movements.[64] At the international level, climate justice is also a transnational movement encompassing a coalition of groups that mobilized during successive climate change conferences.[65] This is exemplified in the development of the Bali Principles of Climate Justice, which, according to Gonzalez, is 'the first major articulation of the idea of climate justice by a transnational social movement'.[66]

Notwithstanding that the concepts of climate justice and environmental justice originated as theories in the Global North, this terminology has diffused to other parts of the world.[67] In the Global South, climate justice has become a popular mobilizing narrative used by various stakeholders to formulate strategies to hold different actors (including government and non-state actors) accountable for their actions, omissions and commitments under various climate change frameworks (both domestic and global).[68] Arguably,

61 Generally, see DN Pellow, 'Global Environmental and Climate Justice Movements' in É Laurent and K Zwickl (eds), *The Routledge Handbook of the Political Economy of the Environment* (Routledge 2021).

62 D Schlosberg and LB Collins, 'From environmental to climate justice: climate change and the discourse of environmental justice' (2014) 5(3) *Wiley Interdisciplinary Reviews: Climate Change* 359–74.

63 Edwards (n 45), 149. Also, see RD Bullard, *Dumping in Dixie: Race, Class, and Environmental Quality* (Westview 1990).

64 Schlosberg and Collins (n 62).

65 CG Gonzalez, 'Climate Justice and Climate Displacement: Evaluating the Emerging Legal and Policy Responses' (2018) 36 *Wisconsin International Law Journal* 366–96.

66 Gonzalez (n 65), 371.

67 Generally, see PC Pezzullo, 'Environmental Justice and Climate Justice' in M Grasso and M Giugni (eds), *The Routledge Handbook of Environmental Movements* (Routledge 2022) 229–44. However, some scholars and activists suggest that concept of climate justice originated in the Global South. Generally, see Carbon Brief, 'In-depth Q&A: What is "climate justice"?', 4 October 2021, https://www.carbonbrief.org/in-depth-qa-what-is-climate-justice/, accessed 25 May 2023.

68 S Fisher, 'The Emerging Geographies of Climate Justice' (2015) 181(1) *The Geographical Journal* 73–82.

the character of climate justice might be distinct in the Global South. For example, Pezzullo suggests that in some parts of the Global South climate justice is characterized by reliance on ancient or indigenous knowledge and already existing environmental justice mobilization movements.[69] Hence, some scholars and activists suggest that Global South and Global North countries contributed equally to the development of environmental justice and climate justice paradigms.[70]

Akin to environmental justice, which is underpinned by distributional, procedural and recognitional justice dimensions, among others; climate justice is also underpinned by similar justice dimensions. Therefore, the three recurrent themes of environmental justice (and climate justice) consist of distributive, procedural and recognition elements and these are sometimes referred to as the 'three concepts of justice'.[71] Also, the IPCC, via its Intergovernmental Panel on Climate Change Working Group III in a report in 2022, states that the climate justice concept consists of distributional, procedural and recognition principles.[72]

The distributional dimension of climate justice focuses on the 'fair distribution of costs and burdens of climate change and the societal responses to climate change'.[73] In many parts of the world, people are not protected equally from the vagaries of climate change and the most vulnerable in society tend to bear the worst effects of climate change. This means that poorer countries suffer disproportionately and that more vulnerable communities within both less and relatively affluent nations experience or are subject to environmental and climate injustice. One conceptualization of this distributive dimension is via the North/South divide.[74] Gonzalez and Atapattu have noted that developed countries are responsible for climate change damage, 'accounting for seventy four per cent of global economic activity since 1950, though such nations comprise only eighteen per cent

[69] Pezzullo (n 67).

[70] LSE Grantham Research Institute on Climate Change and the Environment, 'What Is Meant by "Climate Justice"?', 7 June 2022, https://www.lse.ac.uk/granthaminstitute/explainers/what-is-meant-by-climate-justice/#:~:text=More%20generally%2C%20climate%20justice%20highlights,their%20higher%20per%2Dcapita%20emissions., accessed 25 May 2023.

[71] G Walker, *Environmental Justice: Concepts, Evidence and politics* (Routledge 2012). On the other hand, according to D Schlosberg, *Defining Environmental Justice: Theories, Movements, and Nature* (OUP 2007), the four dimensions of environmental justice are distribution, recognition, participation and capabilities.

[72] Climate Change 2022: Impacts, Adaptation and Vulnerability, www.ipcc.ch/report/ar6/wg2/, accessed 25 May 2023.

[73] Kashwan (n 52), 4.

[74] CG Gonzalez and S Atapattu, 'International Environmental Law, Environmental Justice, and the Global South' (2016) 26 *Transnational Law & Contemporary Problems* 229–42.

of the planet's population'.[75] Notwithstanding their lesser contribution to climate change, several countries and marginalized societies or communities in the Global South bear an unequal share of the negative impacts of climate change due to their vulnerable physical locations and inadequate resources for climate change actions.[76]

In the Global North, (for example, in the United States), ethnic minorities and poorer people in society, who are already facing environmental injustices, bear the worst of climate change.[77] In the Global South, already vulnerable communities and individuals face the brunt of environmental injustices exacerbated by the impacts of climate change.[78] The Niger Delta is said to be among the least developed parts of Nigeria, and has a high incidence of poverty and inadequate infrastructure or amenities.[79] Due to the more than six decades of oil exploration production activities, the Niger Delta is also one of the areas in Nigeria most impacted by climate change and the industries that cause it, especially with the rise in global warming and the impacts of gas flaring and allied activities.[80] Unless concerted efforts are made by the relevant stakeholders to develop climate actions, the Niger Delta will continue to bear the brunt of the negative impacts of climate change and the industries that have caused it.

Another dimension of climate justice is procedural justice, 'which refers to whether and how the groups most affected by climate change have meaningful opportunities to participate in brainstorming, designing, and implementing climate responses'.[81] In Nigeria, very few laws encourage public participation and consultation in environmental and climate-based issues. Furthermore, there is a plethora of challenges associated with procedural justice in Nigeria (especially in oil and gas, where the bulk of environmental injustices takes place), including the limited resources of

75 Gonzalez and Atapattu (n 74), 230.

76 Gonzalez (2018) (n 65).

77 Kashwan (n 52).

78 R Ako, *Environmental Justice in Developing Countries: Perspectives from Africa and Asia-Pacific* (Routledge 2013).

79 E Emeseh, 'Limitations of Law in Promoting Synergy Between Environment and Development Policies in Developing Countries: a Case Study of the Petroleum Industry in Nigeria' (2006) 24 *Journal of Energy and Natural Resources Law* 574–606.

80 HP Faga and U Uchechukwu, 'Oil Exploration, Environmental Degradation, and Future Generations in the Niger Delta: Options for Enforcement of Intergenerational Rights and Sustainable Development Through Legal and Judicial Activism' (2019) 34 *Journal of Environmental Law & Litigation* 185–218.

81 Kashwan (n 52), 5. Also, Kashwan argues that in the United States, ethnic minorities have been underrepresented in environmental (including) climate movements and environmental law-making process.

litigants and delays in judicial proceedings, among others.[82] These factors have hampered access to environmental justice in Nigeria and arguably will also have negative impacts on climate justice. Fortunately, activists, NGOs (local and foreign), oil communities, individuals and other relevant stakeholders have relied on national, sub-regional and regional litigation to improve access to environmental justice in Nigeria, and this has implications for climate justice in Nigeria.[83] Litigation is one of the strategies that can be used to enhance the procedural justice dimension of climate justice.

The next dimension of climate justice is recognitional justice. Chu and Michael,[84] relying on Miranda Fricker's work,[85] define recognitional justice as the 'explicit forms of unfair treatment of experiences, understandings, and participation in communicative or decision-making practices'. Many relevant actors or stakeholders from different social groups are not always recognized as legitimate actors, whose awareness of the problems and interests (or priorities) 'should inform the design and implementation of policies and programs'.[86] Furthermore, some marginalized or vulnerable groups can also be misrecognized which, according to Fraser, is how some policies or actions lead to the situation whereby relevant stakeholders are seen as 'less than full members of society' and prevented from participating as equals.[87]

One of the major causes of the intractable conflicts in Niger Delta is the lack of recognition and participation of the people of the Niger Delta in the governance framework.[88] Thus, laws that encourage public participation and consultation with the people in environmental and climate-based issues should be enacted in Nigeria. In the context of the Niger Delta,

---

82 EO Ekhator, 'Improving Access to Environmental Justice Under the African Charter on Human and Peoples' Rights: The Roles of NGOs in Nigeria' (2014) 22(1) *African Journal of International and Comparative Law* 63–79.

83 Obani and Ekhator (n 17).

84 E Chu and K Michael, 'Recognition in Urban Climate Justice: Marginality and Exclusion of Migrants in Indian Cities' (2019) 31(1) *Environment and Urbanization* 139–56, 142.

85 M Fricker, *Epistemic Injustice: Power and the Ethics of Knowing* (Oxford University Press 2007).

86 Kashwan (n 52), 6.

87 N Fraser, 'Rethinking Recognition' (2002) 3 *New Left Review* 107–20, 114. Also, some scholars have argued that in the United States, government policies and responses have prioritized richer parts of the United States rather than the areas with ethnic minorities and poorer citizens. Generally, see Kashwan (n 52) and P McKenna, 'What's Happening in Puerto Rico Is Environmental Injustice,' SLATE, 27 September 2017, https://slate.com/technology/2017/09/puerto-rico-is-experiencing-a-crisis-created-by-environmental-injustice.html, accessed 25 May 2023.

88 R Ako, P Okonmah and T Ogunleye, 'The Niger Delta Crisis: A Social Justice Approach to the Analysis of Two Conflict Eras' (2009) 11(2) *Journal of African Development* 105–22.

oil-producing or host communities should be recognized by the government and MNCs as important stakeholders in environmental governance.[89]

However, it should be noted that reliance on justice principles in the climate justice paradigm has been criticized by some scholars. One reason given is that the emphasis on justice diminishes rather than enhances climate policy and regulation.[90] Furthermore, the notion of justice or injustice can be subject to different understandings and interpretations. The concept of climate justice is also understood and subject to a wide range of understandings (and interpretations) in its usage, and this is said to be one of its major weaknesses.[91]

Another major criticism is that the concept or principles of climate justice have already been integrated partially in the current climate change regime.[92] This is exemplified by the implicit recognition of climate justice in the preamble to the Paris Agreement.[93] This does not mean that climate justice has been achieved. A major weakness of the inclusion of the concept of climate justice (including human rights) in the Paris Agreement is that the preamble is not enforceable.[94] Some of the global mechanisms promoting climate justice remain generally out of the reach of many of the individuals who are seeking or pursuing climate justice.[95]

Notwithstanding the criticisms of climate justice, it remains a valid and useful framework to analyse injustices in the global climate regime. Also, the concept of climate justice is one of the strategies that have been relied upon by activists, NGOs, communities, and other relevant stakeholders in different parts of the world (including in developing countries) in mitigating the negative impacts of climate change on the most vulnerable in society and helping to hold MNCs and government accountable for their climate action commitments.

Climate litigation is on the rise globally. The next section focuses on how climate litigation can be used as one of the strategies to promote climate justice.

---

89 Ako, Okonmah and Ogunleye (n 88).

90 Edwards (n 45).

91 Jenkins (n 59).

92 CG Gonzalez, 'Racial Capitalism, Climate Justice, and Climate Displacement' (2021) 11(1) *Oñati Socio-Legal Series, Symposium on Climate Justice in the Anthropocene* 108–47.

93 JR May and E Daly, 'Global Climate Constitutionalism and Justice in the Courts' in Jordi Jaria-Manzano and Susana Borrás (eds), *Research Handbook on Global Climate Constitutionalism* (Edward Elgar Publishing 2019).

94 A Boyle, 'Climate Change, the Paris Agreement and Human Rights' (2018) 67(4) *International & Comparative Law Quarterly* 759–77.

95 May and Daly (n 93).

Climate litigation to promote climate justice

Arguably, due to the weaknesses in the global climate change framework (including the Paris Agreement), other strategies, including litigation, have evolved to seek justice or redress for past and future harm arising from climate change.[96] It has also been contended that the Paris Agreement has positively impacted the rising number of climate-related cases in different parts of the world.[97] Furthermore, the role of climate litigation in impacting climate governance has been recognized by a plethora of international agencies, including the UNEP and IPCC.[98]

Climate litigation is now a global phenomenon challenging governments and corporations (including MNCs) for their climate change response.[99] Furthermore, there is perceived slowness in Global South countries, but the character of climate litigation in those countries may be different, including a close connection with environmental justice cases.[100] Notwithstanding the disproportionate impact of climate change on Africa, some scholars posit that there have been very few cases in Africa.[101] There will be a rise in climate litigation cases in Africa soon. One plausible reason for this assertion, is that the regional African Human Rights system which is well-grounded and has been at the forefront of innovative treaties and judicial decisions. Also, previous environmental rights or environmental justice decisions of national, sub-regional, and regional courts in Africa can be reconceptualized from a

---

96 C Beauregard *et al*, 'Climate Justice and Rights-Based Litigation in a Post-Paris World' 21(5) *Climate Policy* 652–65.

97 Generally, see J Peel and J Lin, 'Transnational Climate Litigation: The Contribution of the Global South' 113(4) *American Journal of International Law* 679–726; J Setzer and C Higham, 'Global Trends in Climate Change Litigation: 2022 Snapshot' (Grantham Research Institute on Climate Change and the Environment and Centre for Climate Change Economics and Policy, London School of Economics and Political Science 2022).

98 Generally, see UNEP, 'The Status of Climate Litigation: A Global Review', 2017, https://wedocs.unep.org/handle/20.500.11822/20767. 'Climate Change 2022: Mitigation of Climate Change', Contribution of Working Group III to the Sixth Assessment Report of the Intergovernmental Panel on Climate Change https://www.ipcc.ch/report/ar6/wg3/, accessed 25 May 2023.

99 G Ganguly, J Setzer and V Heyvaert, 'If at First You Don't Succeed: Suing Corporations for Climate Change' (2018) 38 *Oxford Journal of Legal Studies* 841.

100 Peel and Lin (n 97); C Rodríguez-Garavito, 'Human Rights: The Global South's Route to Climate Litigation' (2020) 114 *American Journal of International Law* 40–4.

101 LJ Kotzé and A du Plessis, 'Putting Africa on the Stand: A Bird's Eye View of Climate Change Litigation on the Continent' 50(3) *Environmental Law* 615–63.

climate justice or climate protection lens.[102] This will have implications for climate litigation in Africa in the future.[103]

This chapter relies on a broader definition or conceptualization of climate litigation – that existing environmental rights/justice cases can be reconceptualized as climate litigation whether they have peripheral or central connections with climate change issues.[104] Thus, in the context of climate litigation in Nigeria, Niger Delta environmental justice cases are arguably the model of climate litigation in the country.[105] This chapter analyses or reconceptualizes *Gbemre v Shell* and *Centre for Oil Pollution Watch v Nigerian National Petroleum Corpn*[106] as climate litigation case law or jurisprudence. The reasons for focusing specifically on these two cases is because they are internationally recognized as expressly being climate cases,[107] and environmental justice and climate justice issues are close in those cases.[108]

The next section focuses on the potential of climate litigation in Nigeria.

Climate change litigation in Nigeria

Before discussing climate litigation in Nigeria, this section will briefly highlight the climate change regime in Nigeria. The Nigerian government has always actively engaged with international climate conferences and negotiations.[109] African states are expected to enact substantive climate change laws due to their international obligations under international (including African Union) instruments.[110] However, the Nigerian Constitution does

---

[102] Also see T Morgenthau and N Reisch, 'Litigating the Frontlines: Why African Community Rights Cases Are Climate Change Cases' (2020) 25 *UCLA Journal of International Law & Foreign Affairs* 85.

[103] SJ Adelman, 'Climate Change Litigation in the African System' in I Alogna, C Bakker and J-P Gauci (eds), *Climate Change Litigation: Global Perspectives* (Brill 2021).

[104] Bouwer (n 60).

[105] Also, see Bouwer (n 60); Etemire (n 18).

[106] *Gbemre v Shell*, Suit No. FHC/B/CS/153/05; *Centre for Oil Pollution Watch v Nigerian National Petroleum Corpn* [2019] 5 NWLR 518.

[107] For example, the University of Columbia climate chart website lists *Gbemre* and *COPW* as climate litigation cases from Nigeria, http://climatecasechart.com/non-us-jurisdiction/nigeria/, accessed 25 May 2023.

[108] However, see M Adigun and AO Jegede, 'A Human Rights Approach to Climate Litigation in Nigeria: Potentialities and Agamben's State of Exception Theory' (2023) 16(3) *Carbon & Climate Law Review* 179–91, who analysed climate litigation in Nigeria from human rights-centred approach.

[109] OF Oluduro, 'Combating Climate Change in Nigeria: An Appraisal of Constitutional and Legal Frameworks' (2020) 38 *Wisconsin International Law Journal* 269–300.

[110] For example, the Africa Union's Climate Change and Resilient Development Strategy and Action Plan (2022–2032) 4 states that 'the Strategy provides a robust framework for ensuring climate justice for Africa through inclusive and equitable participation in climate action and climate-resilient development pathways'.

not explicitly provide for measures by the state and its citizens to adequately tackle the scourge of climate change in Nigeria.[111] Until November 2021, when President Buhari signed into law Nigeria's Climate Change Act 2021,[112] there was no standalone or specific climate change legislation in Nigeria.[113] Arguably, the enactment of the Climate Change Act is a fulfilment of Nigeria's commitments to the ideals of the global climate regime, including the Paris Agreement.

Notwithstanding the absence of climate change law in Nigeria until November 2021, a plethora of laws, policies and guidelines have been used as means of regulating climate change issues in Nigeria.[114] Furthermore, the new climate change law in Nigeria has been applauded by scholars and other relevant stakeholders for its mechanisms, such as the establishment of the National Council on Climate Change.[115] Some of the other key innovations of the Nigerian Climate Change Act include the following: it provides a framework for achieving low GHG emissions and embedding climate action into national programmes; the possibility of the development of the Climate Change Fund (including for carbon taxes); and the law is applicable to both private and public companies, and government agencies and bodies.[116] The National Council on Climate Change has been established and the first Director General of its Secretariat was appointed in July 2022.[117] These recent developments shows that the Nigerian government is committed to the successful implementation of the Climate Change Act in the country.

---

[111] Oluduro (n 109).

[112] A copy of the Nigerian Climate Change Act 2021 is available online at https://climate-laws.org/document/nigeria-s-climate-change-act_5ef7, accessed 25 May 2023.

[113] Generally, see MA Ayoade, 'Bridging the Gap Between Climate Change and Energy Policy Options: What Next for Nigeria?' in P Kameri-Mbote *et al* (eds), *Law | Environment | Africa* (Nomos Verlagsgesellschaft mbH & Co. KG 2019).

[114] Some of the laws and policies include the Nigerian Constitution 1999, the National Environmental Standards and Regulations Enforcement Agency (NESREA) (Establishment) Act 2007), the 2011 National Adaptation Strategy and Plan of Action on Climate Change for Nigeria (NASPA-CCN) and the 2012 Nigeria Climate Change Policy Response and Strategy, among others. Generally, see OO Olashore, 'Implementation of the International Legal Framework Regarding Climate Change in Developing Countries; A Review of Nigeria, Kenya, and Botswana's Environmental Provisions Governing Climate Change' (2019) 21(3) *Environmental Law Review* 189–209.

[115] PwC Nigeria, 'Nigeria's Climate Change Act – Things to Know and Prepare for', 18 January 2022, https://www.pwc.com/ng/en/publications/nigeria-climate-change-act-things-to-know.html, accessed 25 May 2023. Also see the chapter by Ademola Jegede in this volume.

[116] PwC Nigeria (n 115).

[117] Z Abubakar, 'President Buhari Appoints DG National Council on Climate Change', Voice of Nigeria (VON), 29 July 2022, https://von.gov.ng/president-buhari-appoints-pioneer-dg-national-council-on-climate-change/, accessed 25 May 2023.

However, there are weaknesses.[118] Section 15(1)(e) of the Nigerian Climate Change Act stipulates for a carbon tax in the country. Arguably, one of the major strengths of carbon tax regime under the Nigerian Climate Change Act is that, if it is well implemented, it might help reduce climate pollution by internalizing its economic costs and disincentivizing emissions,[119] if properly applied. On the other hand, some argue that, due to the antecedents of governmental agencies and activities of MNCs in the Nigerian oil and sector, carbon taxes will not have the desired impacts in Nigeria. One major criticism is that the development of carbon taxes without adequate consultation with the relevant stakeholders might be unsuccessful and could lead to additional burdens on taxpayers in Nigeria.[120] Notwithstanding the criticisms of carbon tax regime in Nigeria, it is a step in the right direction for climate justice in the country. It should be said that, despite the new legislation, and notwithstanding that the Nigerian government has promised to end gas flaring in country by 2030,[121] continuous gas flaring in the Niger Delta will continue in the meantime, worsening environmental and climate change harms in Nigeria.[122]

Arguably the enactment of the Climate Change Act will have positive implications for climate change litigation in Nigeria. For example, section 34 of the Climate Change Act states:

> (1) A person, or private or public entity that acts in a manner that negatively affects efforts towards mitigation and adaptation measures made under this Act commits an offence and is liable to a penalty to be determined by the Council.

---

[118] PwC (n 115). Also see Adigun and Jegede (n 108).

[119] Generally, see A Mojeed, 'Climate Change: FG to Unveil Carbon Tax System in Nigeria', Premium Times, 13 February 2023, https://www.premiumtimesng.com/news/more-news/581752-climate-change-fg-to-unveil-carbon-tax-system-for-nigeria.html, accessed 25 May 2023. For the utility of the carbon tax regime in South Africa, see M Nemavhidi and AO Jegede, 'Carbon Tax as a Climate Intervention in South Africa: A Potential Aid or Hindrance to Human Rights?' (2023) 25(1) *Environmental Law Review* 11–27.

[120] PwC (n 115). However, on the other hand, the new Petroleum Industry Act 2021 has just reduced taxes on petroleum activities; perhaps there is space for additional tax burdens for MNCs in Nigeria. Arguably, if MNCs and other emitters are charged carbon taxes, such taxes can be used to address some of the climate-related impacts of the oil and gas industry.

[121] J Lo, 'Nigeria to End Gas Flaring by 2030, Under National Climate Plan', Climate Home News, 13 August 2021, https://climatechangenews.com/2021/08/13/nigeria-end-gas-flaring-2030-national-climate-plan/#:~:text=The%20Nigerian%20government%20has%20pledged,huge%20part%20of%20Nigeria's%20emissions, accessed 25 May 2023.

[122] Furthermore, the Nigerian government is in the process of awarding contracts to capture flared gas in the country, https://www.reuters.com/world/africa/nigeria-award-flare-gas-contracts-by-end-december-2022-10-04/, accessed 25 May 2023.

(2) A Court, before which a suit regarding climate change or environmental matters is instituted, may make an order –

(a) to prevent, stop or discontinue the performance of any act that is harmful to the environment;

(b) compelling any public official to act in order to prevent or stop the performance of any act that is harmful to the environment;

(c) compensation to the victim directly affected by the acts that are harmful to the environment.

Furthermore, the possible imposition of climate obligations on public and private entities, under section 23 and 24 of the Act, could form the basis of a cause of action against them in climate litigation. Also, section 26 provides for climate change education. This can both boost climate awareness but also lead to litigation in Nigeria if the provisions of the section are not met. Thus, the new legislation will not only hopefully improve climate action in Nigeria, but also create avenues for legal challenges if its promises are not fulfilled. There are clear legislative duties to reduce harm and a failure to meet these can be challenged in the courts.[123]

As highlighted in the previous section, one strategy for enhancing the procedural justice dimension of climate justice is via climate litigation. Akin to environmental justice, climate justice is also based on the realization of human rights, including the right to health, the right to life, the right to healthy environment, the right to information, access to justice and participation, among others.[124] Enforceable human rights provisions in national constitutions can be 'greened' to enhance climate justice in countries.[125] The Nigerian Constitution does not provide for justiciable and enforceable socio-economic rights,[126] and the overarching view is that there has been no justiciable or enforceable right to the environment *per se*.[127] Arguably, this is no longer the case. By virtue of the Supreme Court judgment

123 Also, see MT Ladan, 'Nigeria's Climate Change Act and Policy 2021 and the Future of Climate Litigation', SSRN, 2022, https://ssrn.com/abstract=4019698 or http://dx.doi.org/10.2139/ssrn.4019698, accessed 25 May 2023.

124 Gonzalez (n 65); Gonzalez (n 92).

125 BE Ugochukwu, 'Climate Change and Human Rights: How? Where? When?' (2015) CIGI Papers, No. 82, November 2015, Osgoode Legal Studies Research Paper No. 45/2016 SSRN, https://ssrn.com/abstract=2760399.

126 O Enabulele and E O Ekhator, 'Improving Environmental Protection in Nigeria: a Reassessment of the Role of Informal Institutions' (2022) 13(1) *Journal of Sustainable Development Law and Policy* 162–99.

127 On the other hand, Nigeria is a signatory to the African Charter on Human and Peoples' Rights ('African Charter'). The African Charter was domesticated into Nigerian law via the African Charter on Human and Peoples' Rights (Enforcement and Ratification)

in the *Centre for Oil Pollution Watch v Nigerian National Petroleum Corpn* (the *COPW* case),[128] the right to environment is now justiciable and enforceable in Nigeria. In Nigeria, a strategy or route on how climate litigation can be relied upon in Nigeria is via the right to environment litigation that plays an important role in environmental protection in Nigeria. The right to a healthy and clean environment under domestic law and international human rights law can be the basis of climate change litigation[129] and enhancing climate justice in Nigeria. Also, the enactment of the Climate Change Act 2021 provides an opportunity for public participation in the burgeoning climate change framework in Nigeria. Furthermore, litigation premised on the Climate Change Act will arguably promote public awareness and advocacy by relevant stakeholders in the country.

The next part discusses two cases in Nigeria that are key to climate litigation in the country. The cases are *Gbemre v Shell* and the *COPW case*.[130] The first case to be discussed is the Gbemre's case.

Gbemre case

One of the first climate change cases in the world is *Gbemre v Shell Petroleum Development Nigeria Ltd* (the *Gbemre* case). According to Varvastian and Kalunga, *Gbemre* was the 'very first case to raise the issue of climate change in an African court'.[131] Hence, the *Gbemre* case is internationally recognized or seen as a 'climate case'.[132] In *Gbemre*, the plaintiff (on behalf of himself and his community) filed a suit against Shell (SPDC), the Attorney General and the Nigerian National Petroleum Corporation (NNPC) to end the practice of gas flaring. The plaintiff argued that the gas flaring laws that permitted gas flaring subject to ministerial approval contravenes the plaintiff's right to a healthy and clean environment. The court held that the gas flaring laws were 'inconsistent with the Applicant's right to life and/or

---

Act 1983. Article 24 of the African Charter provides the rights of the African people to a healthy environment, and, by domestication, Nigeria has localized the rights which are also enforceable in Nigeria. Arguably, the African Charter in tandem with relevant Nigerian laws can also be the basis of climate litigation in Nigeria.

128 *Gbemre v Shell*, Suit No. FHC/B/CS/153/05; *Centre for Oil Pollution Watch v Nigerian National Petroleum Corpn* [2019] 5 NWLR 518.

129 S Varvastian, 'The Human Right to a Clean and Healthy Environment in Climate Change Litigation' *Max Planck Institute for Comparative Public Law & International Law (MPIL) Research Paper* (2019–09).

130 *Gbemre v Shell* (n 128).

131 S Varvastian and F Kalunga, 'Transnational Corporate Liability for Environmental Damage and Climate Change: Reassessing Access to Justice after Vedanta v. Lungowe' (2020) 9(2) *Transnational Environmental Law* 323–45, 332.

132 Generally, see Bouwer (n 60), 166.

dignity of human person' as enshrined in the Nigerian Constitution and the African Charter.[133]

The court also held that the failure of SPDC and NNPC to undertake an environmental impact assessment (EIA) exercise in the Iwherekan community concerning the impacts of their gas flaring activities was in violation of section 2(2) of the Environmental Impact Assessment Act of 1992. This has implications for procedural and recognition dimensions of environmental (and climate) justice in the Niger Delta. The EIA Act is one of the few Nigerian laws explicitly promoting the participation and consultation of Nigerian citizens and other relevant stakeholders in environmental governance.[134] Here, the actions of SPDC and NNPC had negative impacts on the participation and recognition of Nigerian citizens in the EIA process, thereby worsening access to environmental justice (and climate justice) in Nigeria. This is arguably because some MNCs and governmental agencies in Nigeria regularly ignore the provisions of the Act regarding EIA exercises.[135]

The *Gbemre* case was the first Nigerian judicial decision where the court adopted 'constitutional human rights approach to environmental protection with respect to climate unfriendly activities in the oil and gas sector'.[136] In its decision, the court alluded to and reiterated the plaintiffs' claims in their affidavit that 'gas flaring leads to the emission of carbon dioxide, the main greenhouse gas' and 'contributes to adverse climate change'.[137] From the distributive dimension of the climate justice paradigm, *Gbemre* shows how the negative consequences of climate change has more adverse impacts on the already poor and vulnerable in the Niger Delta. For example, uneven consequences of gas flaring are faced by the Niger Delta people, and most of the flare sites are located close to the oil-producing communities, and away from the more prosperous parts of the country. Thus, the environmental (and climate) injustices as exemplified by gas flares are unevenly distributed in Nigeria to the detriment of already vulnerable members of society (especially those living in the Niger Delta).

This judgment has been criticized and has not been enforced, so it has not had any impacts.[138] However, despite this, in 2021 SPDC instituted an appeal

---

[133] *Gbemre v Shell* (n 128), 30.

[134] Ekhator (n 82).

[135] Generally, see Ekhator (n 82).

[136] Etemire (n 18), 414.

[137] *Gbemre v Shell* (n 128), 4 and 5. Also see Etemire (n 18), 162–3.

[138] Generally, see B Faturoti, G Agbaitoro and O Onya, 'Environmental Protection in the Nigerian Oil and Gas Industry and Jonah Gbemre v. Shell PDC Nigeria Limited: Let the Plunder Continue?' (2019) 27(2) *African Journal of International and Comparative Law* 225–45.

at the Court of Appeal against the decision in *Gbemre*.[139] The appeal was heard on 18 January 2023. This appeal will arguably create an opportunity for the Nigerian judiciary to provide more clarity on the implications of the *Gbemre* case for environmental justice (including climate justice) in the country. At the time of writing, a decision is still awaited.

However, some scholars have questioned whether *Gbemre* is a climate case.[140] For example, Bouwer suggests that that the extent to which *Gbemre* is more of a climate case than other litigation against MNCs in Nigeria is questionable, because the judge just mentions climate change in passing.[141] Thus, it is not any more material to the reasoning than in other case filed against oil MNCs in Nigeria. The argument of this chapter is that the climate change identity of *Gbemre* is better understood because of the closeness or connection between climate justice and environmental justice in this context.[142] Furthermore, the large amount of litigation or cases filed against oil MNCs in Nigeria has to some extent improved the business activities of MNCs.[143] Arguably, *Gbemre* alone did not do much to improve climate justice in Nigeria, but it is recognized as a climate change case. Also, the utility or relevance of *Gbemre* can be juxtaposed with less well-known local litigation (in Nigeria) that has done a lot more to improve conditions in the Niger Delta.[144]

The next part of this chapter focuses on a recent Nigerian Supreme Court decision, the *COPW* case, and its implications for climate justice and climate litigation in the country.

---

139 E Addeh, 'Shell Challenges Judgement Ordering Halt to Gas Flaring in N'Delta Community', Thisday, 26 December 2021, https://www.thisdaylive.com/index.php/2021/12/29/shell-challenges-judgement-ordering-halt-to-gas-flaring-in-ndelta-community, accessed 25 May 2023.

140 Etemire (n 18); PE Oamen and EO Erhagbe, 'The impact of climate change on economic and social rights realisation in Nigeria: International cooperation and assistance to the rescue?' (2021) 21 (2) *African Human Rights Law Journal* 1080–1111, Bouwer (n 60).

141 Bouwer (n 60).

142 Also see Bouwer (n 60). Another justification for reconceptualizing *Gbemre* as a climate litigation case, is that the judge in the case engaged with climate change issues. This formulation can be premised on the definition of climate litigation by Ganguly *et al* (n 99).

143 Generally, see Ekhator (n 82).

144 For examples of successful lawsuits instituted against oil companies operating in Nigeria, see Centre for Environment, Human Rights and Development (CEHRD), 'After Bodo: Effective Remedy & Recourse Options for Victims of Environmental Degradation Related to Oil Extraction in Nigeria', 2015, https://www.bebor.org/wp-content/uploads/2016/03/CEHRD-After-Bodo-Report.pdf, accessed 25 May 2023.

Centre for Oil Pollution Watch case

Prior to the recent decision of the Supreme Court in *Centre for Oil Pollution Watch v Nigerian National Petroleum Corpn*, NGO involvement in public interest litigation in Nigeria was seriously hindered by the doctrine of locus standi. Nigerian courts were reluctant to rule that NGOs had the requisite legal standing to institute court cases especially in human rights and environmental issues.[145] However, in *COPW*, some of the justices in explicitly referred to sections 20 and 30 of the Nigerian Constitution, section 17(4) of the Oil Pipelines Act and article 24 of the African Charter to hold that the right to a clean and healthy environment is recognized under Nigerian law.[146] The Supreme Court held that environmental NGOs have the locus standi (legal standing) to institute environmental cases in Nigeria.[147] This case has liberalized the locus standi of NGOs in environmental matters in Nigeria, thereby improving access to environmental justice and promoting sustainable development for those wishing to bring action to protect the environment in Nigeria.[148]

The *COPW* case has implications for climate change litigation in Nigeria[149] and, as such, the promotion of climate justice. Arguably, the *COPW* case promotes the three dimensions of environmental justice and climate justice – distributive, procedural and recognition. For example, the court stated:

> every person, including NGOs, who bona fide seek in the law court the due performance of statutory provisions or public laws, especially laws

[145] Also, see EP Amechi, and A Ihua-Maduenyi, 'Greening the Judiciary in Nigeria: Centre For Oil Pollution Watch v. NNPC in Perspectives' (2022) 1(2) *African Journal of Law and Justice System* 39–60; MC Anozie, and EO Wingate, 'NGO Standing in Petroleum Pollution Litigation in Nigeria – Centre for Oil Pollution Watch v Nigerian National Petroleum Corporation' (2020) 13(5–6) *The Journal of World Energy Law & Business* 490–7.

[146] However, 'it should be noted that these comments by the Supreme Court's justices on right to environment were made *obiter* and right to environment was not an issue directly before the court. On the other hand, this decision can serve as a launchpad to further develop the evolving jurisprudence around economic and social rights (ESR) in Nigeria'. See E Ekhator, 'Sustainable Development and the African Union Legal Order' in O Amao, M Olivier and K Magliveras (eds), *The Emergent African Union Law: Conceptualization, Delimitation, and Application* (Oxford University Press 2021) 335–58, 353.

[147] *COPW* 571.

[148] However, TN Alatise, 'The Future of "Standing to Sue" in Environment and Climate Change Litigations in Nigeria' (2022) 13(1) *Nnamdi Azikiwe University Journal of International Law and Jurisprudence* 28–39, 37 argues that there 'is the need to translate this judicial breakthrough into a substantive legislative provision in order to remove it from the vagaries of judicial interpretations'.

[149] Oamen and Erhagbe (n 140); Etemire (n 18).

> designed to protect human lives, public health and the environment, should be regarded as proper persons clothed with in law to request adjudication on such issues of public nuisance that are injurious to human lives, public health and environment.[150]

Arguably, this can be applied to climate action in Nigerian courts.

Furthermore, from a distributive justice dimension, one possible implication of the *COPW* case is that oil communities and individuals suffering from the negative impacts of the activities of oil MNCs will be able sue such companies successfully notwithstanding the lack of explicit environmental rights provisions in the Nigerian Constitution. Thus, this might act as a restriction on the oil companies engaging in egregious activities that will worsen environmental injustices in Nigeria.

From a procedural justice dimension, *COPW* arguably improves or enhances access to environmental justice (including climate justice) in Nigeria for individuals, communities and environmental injustice victims. For example, NGOs can now sue on behalf of communities or individuals in environmental justice litigation. Many environmental injustice victims in the Niger Delta are poor and do not have the financial resources and technical expertise to take on oil companies in Nigeria. Thus, the broadening of the legal standing of environmental NGOs will enable NGOs (acting in the public good via public interest litigation) to sue on behalf of environmental injustice victims. With proper engagement, this will improve the participation of individuals and communities in environmental justice in Nigeria. Environmental public interest litigation takes more prominence in Nigeria because many of the government agencies that are responsible for environmental protection and remediation do not live up to that legal responsibility. Thus, litigation by public-spirited individuals and NGOs or pressure groups can be a strategy to ensure that governmental agencies live up to their environmental protection responsibility in Nigeria.[151]

From a recognition justice dimension, everyone in Nigeria (and not just the government and MNCs) by virtue of the *COPW* case is now seen as a relevant stakeholder in the promotion of environmental justice in the country. The court stated that no specific person or individual owns the environment, and the 'environment is a public good'.[152] Thus, arguably by virtue of *COPW*, every Nigerian (including public-spirited taxpayers and NGOs) are recognized stakeholders in environmental justice (including climate justice) promotion in Nigeria.

---

[150] *COPW* 595.

[151] Also see, *COPW* 591–2.

[152] Also see Etemire (n 18), 166; *COPW* 590–1, 597–8.

The Supreme Court in *COPW* specifically referred to climate-related issues and used climate-related terminologies in the judgment.[153] According to Etemire, this 'serves as a clear indication by the apex court of the challenges of climate change and global warming, and the fact that the courts have a key role to play in tackling these challenges for the benefit of present and future generations'.[154] Thus, the Supreme Court is currently in tune with matters relating to climate change. Furthermore, Oamen and Erhagbe suggest that the decision has undoubtedly improved the prospects of climate litigation in Nigeria.[155] For example, NGOs are no longer constrained by rigid rules of standing in environmental adjudication in Nigeria.[156] Hence, based on the *COPW* case, NGOs, climate injustice victims, individuals, and communities, can institute cases in Nigeria to ventilate their rights in climate-related environmental justice cases, or more direct climate litigation.[157]

Another innovation from the *COPW* case is that the Supreme Court recognized that courts in Nigeria – under sections 16 (2), 17 (2)(d)(3), and 20 of the 1999 Constitution, section 17(4) of the Oil Pipelines Act and the Oil and Gas Regulations – are 'under a duty to protect the environment, in appropriate cases, and would fail in that duty if they do not facilitate the protection these laws have put in place'.[158] This has implications for climate litigation jurisprudence in Nigeria, and this is arguably a clear directive from the apex court to the relevant stakeholders in environmental protection regime in the country . Taking this approach will allow' the existing human rights provisions of the Constitution and existing laws to be used as means for enforcing climate justice in Nigeria.

The view of this chapter is that the jurisprudence of the two cases (*Gbemre* and *COPW*) analysed is paving the way for improved environmental and climate justice in Nigeria. The cases 'are noteworthy for recognizing the right to a clean and healthy environment and for establishing a range of

153 Per Aka'ahs J, 580.

154 Etemire (n 18), 167–8.

155 Oamen and Erhagbe (n 140).

156 However, see TN Ogboru, 'The Sufficient Interest Requirement for Locus Standi in Environmental Litigation: A Case Review of Centre for Oil Pollution Watch v Nigerian National Petroleum Corporation (NNPC) [2019] 5 NWLR (PT 1666) 518' (2020/2021) 20(1) *University of Benin Law Journal* 29–56, who is very critical of the *COPW* judgment.

157 This argument is premised on the definition or formulation of climate litigation by Bouwer. Bouwer argues that climate litigation in the Global South has its unique characteristics and existing environment rights/justice (and relevant human rights) cases can be reconceptualized as climate litigation whether they have peripheral or central connections with climate change issues, see Bouwer (n 60). Also, relying on Ganguly, Setzer and Heyvaert (n 99) definition or conceptualization of climate litigation, the *COPW* can be seen as climate case because climate change was expressly referred in the judgment.

158 *COPW* 577.

qualitative human rights standards that Nigeria must observe in order to protect her citizens. Such elaborate human rights standards can be extended to climate change issues/litigation'.[159]

Conclusion

Climate litigation is one of the strategies that can used in attaining climate justice, especially in Global South countries. Arguably, there is going to be a rise in climate change litigation in Africa due to the adverse impacts of climate change and the broadening or reworking of existing legal frameworks (including the use of municipal, sub-regional and regional courts) in Africa to encapsulate such cases. Furthermore, the potential of climate litigation in holding MNCs accountable for their alleged human rights abuses and environmental degradation is also a factor that might aid the rise of climate change litigation on the continent.[160]

This chapter has argued that some existing relevant environmental justice cases (for example, *Gbemre* and *COPW*) in Nigeria can be reconceptualized as climate litigation cases, even though they have peripheral connections to climate change as the litigation was brought to address other environmental problems. This fits within the existing jurisprudence of environmental justice litigation in Nigeria, and the Global South, where frequently climate change arguments are introduced (or implicit) along with claims about other environmental problems. In Nigeria, the connection is particularly pronounced, because the harm caused by MNCs, particularly in the Niger Delta, is closely associated with the same activities of those MNCs that cause climate change. The destruction in the Niger Delta also makes those communities more vulnerable to climate change impacts. Notwithstanding that scholars have argued that climate litigation is in its infancy in Nigeria, on this understanding it is very well developed, and there is significant potential for the prospects in such cases to improve.

The decisions in *Gbemre*, and especially *COPW*, arguably signify a fundamental move by Nigerian courts to improve access to environmental justice (including climate justice) and environmental rights in Nigeria. By the liberalization of the locus standi rule, and the recognition that the right to the environment is justiciable and enforceable in Nigeria, the courts are promoting environmental justice (and climate justice) in the country. This will enhance the ability of the victims of environmental injustice and climate

[159] Ladan (n 123), 10. Furthermore, the two cases can be seen as climate cases because they expressly mention climate change issues in the judgments.

[160] O Rumble and A Gilder, *Climate Litigation on the African Continent* (Konrad Adenauer Stiftung 2021).

change to rely on the courts to enhance access to justice for vulnerable individuals and communities in Nigeria – thus, arguably, promoting the three dimensions of environmental justice and climate justice – distributive, procedural and recognition.

The position of this chapter is that climate litigation is one of the strategies that can be used to promote climate justice in Nigeria. There are other strategies, including an activist judiciary (as represented by the views of the some of the judges in *CPOW* and the judge in *Gbemre*), a vibrant civil society, the political will of the government to enact new laws (as seen in the recently enacted Climate Change Act 2021) and the enforcement of laws and regulations. Climate litigation should also be seen as complementary to regulatory process or frameworks and not the sole panacea for tackling the negative impacts of climate change in Nigeria.

12

Law and Climate Change in North African Countries: Morocco as a Case Study

Riyad Fakhri and Youness Lazrak Hassouni

Introduction

The Mediterranean and North Africa are among the areas that are severely affected by climate change, including reduced rainfall and rising temperatures (with more frequent heat waves) and increased instances of flooding.[1] These climate fluctuations clearly threaten ecosystems and the entire development process. Consequently, Mediterranean and North African countries have been obliged to review environmental protection laws and to include climate change as a new dimension.[2] Morocco has been a leader among these countries, by reviewing its public environmental policies and incorporating climate change, in order to combat global warming and contribute to climate heat mitigation or adaptation.[3]

Law No. 99.12 (2014), the Framework Law for a National Charter for Environment and Sustainable Development, is one of Morocco's most

1 The World Bank Group, 'Climate Risk Country Profile: Morocco, 2021'.

2 The Arab Maghreb States are aware of the importance of environmental protection. Morocco, Mauritania, Libya, Tunisia and Algeria have signed the Maghreb Charter on Environmental Protection and Sustainable Development as an important step, given the similarity of environmental issues in the Maghreb countries: http://www.moqatel.com/openshare/Wthaek/Molhak/MalahekMag/AMalahekMagrab38_2-1.htm_cvt.htm, accessed 10 September 2022.

3 The official website of the Government Authority for the Environment, contain a series of official reports on Morocco's national environmental protection policies: http://www.environnement.gov.ma/en/.

important legal texts on the environment, and is the cornerstone of its climate change public policy.[4] Article 1 sets out the objectives and principles, which include promoting actions to mitigate and adapt to climate change and combat desertification. Law 99.12 further requires state actors to incorporate sustainable development into sectorial public policies, and harmonize the national legal framework with international conventions and standards relevant to environmental protection and sustainable development. Pursuant to this framework, Morocco developed a climate change policy in 2014,[5] a national greenhouse gas (GHG) inventory system in 2014,[6] and a national sustainable development strategy in 2017.[7] The climate change policy and sustainable development strategy agree on the need to strengthen the legal and institutional framework to meet the requirements of the United Nations Framework Convention on Climate Change (UNFCC), the Kyoto Protocol, and the Paris Agreement.

However, although Morocco has begun to incorporate climate change into its legal system, climate litigation has not evolved to the degree observed in the Global North, and some African countries such as Nigeria, Kenya and Uganda.[8] As far as we know, no climate change disputes have been brought before the Moroccan judiciary. This chapter considers the reasons for the absence of cases relating to climate in Morocco, and whether it is notwithstanding or due to Morocco's strengthening of its climate change legal and institutional framework.

The IPCC has highlighted the detrimental impacts of climate change on water resources, air and forests in the region[9] In this chapter, we accordingly place particular emphasis on how the Moroccan legal system has dealt with climate change in water law and laws dealing with air.[10] Our study will

---

[4] Dahir No. 1.14.09 issued on 6 March 2014 implementing the Framework Law No. 99.12 as a National Charter for Environment and Sustainable Development – Official Bulletin No. 6240 on 20 March 2014, p. 3194.

[5] Morocco Climate Change Policy, https://www.umi.ac.ma/wp-content/uploads/2020/11/ODD-13-A9-politique_du_changement_climatique_au_maroc.pdf, accessed 11 September 2022.

[6] Decree No. 2.18.74 of 21 March 2019, Official Bulletin No. 6766 of 4 April 2019, p. 1791.

[7] National Sustainable Development Strategy, https://www.environnement.gov.ma/images/AR/SNDD_AR_3010_1.pdf, accessed 10 September 2022.

[8] United Nations environment programme, 'Global Climate Litigation Report 2020 Status Review'.

[9] This is what emerges from the latest report of the Intergovernmental Panel on Climate Change (IPCC), 'Climate Change 22: Impacts, Adaptation and Vulnerability', p. 558. In addition, the 2020 edition of the United Nations World Water Development Report (UN WWDR 2020) entitled 'Water and Climate Change'.

[10] Dahir No. 1.03.61 of 12 May 2003, implementing Act No. 13.03 on combating air pollution, Official Bulletin No. 5118 of 19 June 2003, 1912.

necessarily take into account the general provisions of the Framework Law and the Environmental Assessment Law.

Firstly the legal requirements relating to climate change are discussed, before we turn to the institutions entrusted with the enforcement of the provisions. Finally, we turn to the difficulties that prevent the development of climate litigation in Morocco.

Legal texts on climate change

Morocco's legal system is a constitutional, democratic, parliamentary and social monarchy. It is based on civil law, with Islamic law governing areas like inheritance and family law. The judiciary is divided into three types of courts: general jurisdiction courts, specialized courts, and special courts. The Constitution proclaims the independence of the judiciary from legislative and executive authority.

In theory, Morocco attaches great importance to the protection of the environment, including the section on the legislative handling of climate and its changes. This is reflected in the large number of legal texts dealing with the issue and the number of institutions in charge of the implementation of public climate policies.

The Moroccan legislative system has been very dynamic in recent years in response to the call for a rapid response to the effects of climate change. Morocco is located in one of the regions most vulnerable to adverse climate impacts. Since the early 2000s, the Moroccan legislature has addressed climate risk by developing two types of legislative regulation. The first type is concerned with distinct areas in the field of the environment – there are specific legal texts relating to, among others, water, air and renewable energies. The second type of legislative instrument is more generic texts, addressing fundamental principles of environmental protection, including the need to deal with climate change and its impacts.

Climate-relevant legislation enacted prior to the Framework Law

Morocco made great strides at the beginning of the twenty-first century to renew legal texts related to the environment, which had become obsolete due to technological and industrial development. None of these texts, however, explicitly addressed climate change or facilitated climate litigation. To clarify this, we will briefly discuss the contents of the law related to Environmental Protection and Rehabilitation Law, the law on renewable energies, and the law on air pollution.

At the time of the promulgation of the Environmental Protection and Rehabilitation Law No. 11.03 of 12 May 2003, the Moroccan legislature was the most modern in this area compared with those in other North African countries.[11] This Law defines a set of basic principles for the protection of the environment. Although the Law does not contain a chapter on climate change, article 30 relates to the protection of the air from all forms of pollution that contribute to a deterioration in quality, global warming and the weakening of the ozone layer. Article 31 of the same law prohibits the emission into the air of any contaminated substances, especially smoke, dust and toxic, corrosive or radioactive gases, beyond the limits provided for in the legislative and regulatory texts.

In 2010, Morocco promulgated Law No. 13.09 on renewable energies.[12] In the preamble of this law, it clearly states that the most important focus of the national energy policy is renewable energies in order to preserve the environment and rely on clean energy techniques to reduce GHG emissions. This legal text plays an important role in environmental protection, by stipulating the preparation of an environmental impact study for the licensing of energy business units. This preventive dimension will minimize the negative impacts of projects on the environment and climate.

Furthermore, article 2 of the law, related to air pollution, stipulates that it aims to regulate the prevention and reduction of emissions of air pollutants that can harm human, animal, soil and climate health. Air is given importance in the legal text because any changes in its physical or chemical properties would cause serious damage to organisms, ecosystems and the environment in general. Regardless of the nature of the emissions in the air, they inevitably affect human beings, the environment and the climate. Article 4 accordingly prohibits the use, release or disposal of any contaminated substances into the air.

Article 12 of this Law states that any individual who has suffered harm to their health or property as a result of the emission, release, or disposal of pollutants into the atmosphere has the right, within 90 days of the damage being assessed, to request the authority to conduct an investigation that must be accompanied by appropriate medical or technical expertise. The results of the investigation and the actions taken are communicated to the requester within 60 days. There are a series of administrative penalties, such as partial or total suspension of the activity in question, and an order can be made for work to be done that reduces the pollution. In the event of its failure to do so, the person responsible for the damage who refused to carry out the work likely to reduce the pollution may be subject to criminal penalties, mainly financial fines.

---

11 Dahir No. 1.03.59 of 12 May 2003 implementing Law No. 11.03 on the Protection and Restoration of the Environment – Official Bulletin No. 5118 of 19 June 2003, p. 1900.

12 Dahir Sharif No. 1.10.16 of 11 February 2010 implementing Law No. 13.09 on Renewable Energies, Official Bulletin No. 5822 of 18 March 2010, p. 1118.

To prevent air pollution, stimulate the use of renewable energies and rationalize the use of contaminated energies and materials, the Law refers to the possibility of establishing a system of financial stimulus and tax exemptions. Financial assistance and partial or total exemptions from customs and penal duties can be granted too (Art. 23).[13]

Law 13.03 does not directly address the relationship of air pollution to global warming and climate change. Furthermore, it does not specify the way global warming and climate change should be curtailed, when defined as emissions, projectiles, air quality standards or others. This is evident in all the legislation in force prior to the enactment of the Environment and Sustainable Development Framework Law. The legislature therefore had to intervene in order to harmonize the contents of the air law with Morocco's international obligations.

Basic principles in the Framework Law

The new approach of the Moroccan legislator with regard to the environment is based on three major principles.[14] Firstly, it takes into consideration climate change when planning environmental public policies. Secondly, it ensures the reinforcement of environmental protection measures in order to limit the emission of GHGs. Finally, it maintains that the achievement of these objectives is not only the responsibility of the government, but also of citizens and economic actors.

In this context, Law No. 99.12 (2014), the Framework Law for a National Charter for Environment and Sustainable Development, entrenches the country's approach to the environment. Article 6 of the law establishes the principle of the nation's shared ownership of natural resources, ecosystems and historical and cultural heritage. Article 7 adds that legislative and institutional measures are meant to promote sustainable and economical use of water resources and combating pollution of water resources. They are also meant to revise water legislation in order to adapt it to the requirements of sustainable development, to deal with the issues raised by the repercussions of desertification, climate change and air pollution. Indeed, Morocco's legislature has enacted a new water law that takes into account climate change and sustainable development, as outlined below.[15]

13 For example, electric vehicles are exempted from the annual vehicle tax (art. 260 of the General Tax Code).

14 In addition to some other principles stipulated in arts 1 and 2 of Framework Law No. 99.12.

15 Dahir No. 1.16.113, issued pursuant to Law No. 36.15 on water, Official Bulletin No. 6494 of 25 August 2016, p. 6305.

As part of the legislator's attempt to raise the level of legal protection of the environment, article 34 of the Framework Law refers to the development of a legal system of environmental liability that includes mechanisms for repairing damage, restoring the situation to the previous situation and compensating for damage to the environment. In addition, article 35 establishes the Environment Police;[16] this article aims to strengthen the authority of the relevant departments in the area of prevention, control and inspection.[17]

Climate-relevant legislation enacted pursuant to the Framework Law

The Moroccan legislature has demonstrated a growing commitment to handling climate change by passing a number of laws pursuant to the Framework Law. These include the Water Law (2016) and the Law of Environmental Assessment (2020). These laws demonstrate the priority given to climate change and promoting sustainable development in Morocco.

Water Law

Pursuant to the Framework Law, in 2016 Morocco enacted a new Water Law. Law 15.36 incorporates climate change at several levels.[18] It not only deals with immediate water-related environmental damage, but also incorporates strategic water planning to deal with climate change and its impact on water resources, in addition to creating the governance mechanisms and institutions necessary to implement its content. Article 1 explicitly states that the most important principles of water resources are rational and sustainable use of water, and water planning that takes into account climate change with a view to adapt to it. This aspect is further reinforced in article 2, which emphasizes the incorporation of climate change adaptation into water planning and management at every level.

Environmental Assessment Law

Reflecting the importance of the preventive approach in dealing with environmental issues and enshrining sustainable development, Moroccan law makers recently promulgated Law No. 49.17 on Environmental Assessment.[19]

---

[16] Article 1 of Decree No. 2.14.782 of 19 May 2015 on the organization and conduct of environmental police; Official Bulletin No. 6366 of 4 June 2015, p. 5581.

[17] Dahir Sharif serves as Law No. 1.75.291 of 8 October 1977 on inspection measures in terms of safety and quality for living animals and animal materials or animal origin; Official Bulletin No. 3388 bis 10 October 1977, p. 2857.

[18] The Water Law No. 15.36.

[19] Dahir No. 1.20.78 issued on 8 August 2020 implementing Law No. 49.17 on Environmental Assessment. Official Bulletin No. 6908 of 13 August 2020, p. 4346.

This Environmental Assessment Law replaces the Environmental Impact Study Law No. 12.03 of 2003. The Environmental Assessment Law is considered a qualitative leap in the policy of strengthening legal and institutional governance in the field of the environment by expanding the study of the impact on the environment and opening new areas to it.

One of the greatest advantages of this Law is that the state and public institutions must prepare an environmental impact study (EIS) for all strategies, public policies and programmes (article 2). This assessment aims to determine the compatibility of public policies, strategies and programmes with the requirements of environmental protection and sustainable development as referred to in article 27 of the Framework Law. The state is thus obliged to commit itself and other subjects of public law to comply equally with the duties imposed on private people with regard to the proactive protection of the environment.

The Environmental Assessment Law is not limited to this obligation, but explicitly stipulates that strategies, public policies and programmes prepared by the state and public institutions prior to the Law's entry into force shall be subject to environmental strategic assessment on its interim assessment. Since most public policies are long and medium-term, they are evaluated after a certain period in order to ascertain what has been achieved, and thus provide an opportunity to assess the extent to which the environmental dimension has been evoked.

Since the EIS is of a technical nature and is entrusted to specialized study offices in this area, the Environmental Assessment Law regulates the interaction with these offices: first, through the establishment of a list of offices accredited by the Department, which requires the development of objective criteria for work in this area; second, article 27 allows for sanctions to be given to offices that do not respect these obligations, by preventing the owner of the Office of Studies from carrying out EISs for a period of five years.[20]

The Law also obliges entrepreneurs to provide environmental consent (article 8) or environmental conformity (article 19). Furthermore, entrepreneurs must prepare a contract book setting out the measures to be taken to mitigate or offset the project's adverse impacts on the environment, the population and public health, as well as the ways in which such measures

[20] Article 27 of the Environmental Assessment Act states: 'Anyone who exploits an industrial unit or engages in an activity subject to an environmental impact study shall be liable to a fine of 10,000–100,000 Dhs, but not to the environmental approval decision referred to in article 15 of this Act. The same fine is also imposed on any school office that has provided false information. The fine shall be doubled in the case of the first return, the credit shall be withdrawn in the case of the second return, and the owner of the Office of Studies shall be prevented from conducting environmental impact studies for five years'.

are implemented. Thus, the study of the impact on the environment goes from a purely technical document to a contract with legal implications with which the entrepreneur must comply, under the relevant administrative and criminal penalties. The Law contains a detailed set of such penalties – including a suspension order and a series of fines. The organs entrusted with examining and reviewing violations and monitoring the implementation of the obligations contained in the ledgers annexed to the Environmental Approval Decision or the Environmental Conformity Decision are judicial police officers and environmental police inspectors. In contrast to the Environmental Impact Study Law No. 12.03 of 2003, which assigns jury officers appointed by the local public authorities to this task, this exception certainly increases the professional nature of enforcement.

Despite the various advantages of the Environmental Assessment Law, there are points of criticism, particularly with regard to the fact that entrepreneurs must fund the EIS. In this respect, while this Act allows the concerned population to make observations and suggestions on the potential effects of the project on the environment, it does not impose any compulsion with regard to the results of this research. Technical studies undertaken by the concerned offices pose an issue of objectivity, since it is the entrepreneur who selects and pays for the office's fees. This raises doubts about the impartiality and objectivity of the office, especially because of the difficulty, given its cost, in conducting a counter-expertise study.

The Court of Cassation confirmed this in a case that dealt with the extent to which the EIS of a quarry within a forest was objective. In this case, the entrepreneur was able to obtain a licence for a quarry within a nature reserve based on an EIS. There was no need for substantial technical expertise to ascertain the obvious and possible effects of this activity on the forest. The local authority village council refused to renew the licence because of the damage caused by this activity.[21]

Institutions charged to react to the impact of climate change

To fulfill all environmental protection requirements in general and climate changes in particular, a range of bodies and institutions mandated to monitor and track the implementation of these provisions were created. These institutions and bodies are committed to ensuring that economic actors and individuals adhere to environmental protection laws in general. Other bodies

[21] Decision of the Court of Cassation No. 177 dated 29 March 2012 in Administrative File No. 775/4/2/2011 (published in the Cassation Court's Real Estate Files Journal 'Water and Forest Cases', No. 4, 2014, p. 139).

have a specialized role in dealing with climate change in particular. Institutions involved in this area can be classified as follows: horizontal bodies (Ministries, Economic, Social and Environmental Council, police; judiciary, and so on); and sectorial bodies (Water Basin Agency, National Water and Forestry Agency; High Water and Climate Council, Environmental Police, and so on).

Some of these bodies only play a consultative role, whereas others have decision-making authority.

Consultative bodies

Morocco's institutional interest in the environment dates back to the 1980s. It first created the National Council for the Conservation of the Environment and then Regional Councils for the Environment in 1980.[22] All these councils have a consultative role only. They track studies and propose legislative drafts and regulatory texts related to the environment. They also raise awareness of the importance of preserving the environment and its components. The Economic, Social and Environmental Council is a constitutional institution mandated to prepare studies and proposals to promote sustainable development at all levels.

The new Water Law gives climate change the importance it deserves through its own provisions as well as through the organs it has created. The Supreme Council for Water and Climate (article 78) has been updated and mandated to examine and express its opinion on the general directions of national water and climate policy; in particular, the National Strategy for Improving Knowledge of Climate, its changes and their effects on water resources and the national water programmes. The legislator has also indicated that the Supreme Council has the right to express an opinion on each issue related to water and climate.

The attention to climate is also evident through the membership of the Supreme Council for Water and Climate, chaired by the head of government (article 79), as well as a group of members representing all relevant government bodies in the sector. The Council is open to the participation of civil society through representatives of associations working in the field of water, climate and environment, and representatives of institutions of higher education and scientific research working in the field of water and climate. In addition, it has four distinguished Moroccan experts, with scientific competence and professional experience, specialized in the field of water, environment and climate.

22 Decree No. 2.79.247 of 12 May 1980 on the reorganization and improvement of the institutions responsible for the protection of the environment. Official Bulletin No. 3527 of 4 June 1980, p. 719.

Decision-making bodies

To ensure the alignment of government environmental programmes, it is essential that there is one single body to head a programme or policy. Nevertheless, it can borrow some environmental competencies from other ministries in charge of other government sectors, which intersect in one way or another with the protection of the environment, such as the ministries of the interior, higher education, scientific research, economy and finance, and others.[23]

To implement public environmental policy, the country has established the necessary reporting bodies with the capacity to take measures to protect the environment and punish environmental offenders. Among these bodies is the National Agency for Water and Forestry, which is primarily responsible for protecting forest, ensuring its development, and managing various forest-related areas and the water basin agencies.

The publication of the Framework Law marked an important turning point in the Moroccan approach towards environmental problems, that is, a shift from a purely therapeutic approach to a preventive proactive approach, with the inclusion of the climate changes dimension in public policies directed at the environment.

In this context, the Environmental Assessment Law has established the National Environmental Assessment Commission, which is entrusted with examining EISs and expressing its opinion on environmental approval of projects of a national nature (article 20). Affirming the competence of the Regional Unified Investment Committees set out in Law No. 47.18, article 29(1) of the Environmental Assessment Law empowers these committees to make an economic, environmental and physical assessment of the projects submitted to it. A Regional Unified Investment Committee also examines EISs and expresses its opinion on the environmental approval of the investment projects.[24]

The distinction between the competence of the National Environmental Assessment Commission and the Unified Regional Investment Commission is a positive one – the principle of good governance through the grouping of bodies with common functions. Good governance will have a positive impact on the simplification of procedures and the rationality of work. In addition,

[23] R Fakhri and YL Hassouni, 'The Enforcement of the Environmental Laws in Morocco', unpublished article subject of a communication in The 3rd ASSELLMU Conference and Workshop was held on 1–5 November 2021 at the College of Law, Hamad Bin Khalifa University, Doha, Qatar.

[24] Decree No. 1.19.18 of 13 February, implementing Act No. 47.18 on the reform of regional investment centers and the establishment of unified regional investment committees. Official Bulletin No. 6754 of 21 February 2019, p. 834.

the Standing Regional Committee on Investment is the closest to preserving natural resources from pollution and other risks. Therefore, it is competent to examine the EIS in order to achieve sustainable development that will ensure the preservation of environmental elements and take into account the environmental dimension and climate change in the execution of projects.

In addition to the advisory role of the Supreme Council for Water and Climate, the Water Law confers a range of competencies on the Water Basin Agency (article 80), which had been created by the previous Act No. 95–10, for Morocco's 12 regions. One of the tasks of the Water Basin Agency is to complete measurements, research, and carry out the necessary studies to assess and track the development of water resources at the quantitative and quality levels. It also carries out studies on water planning, management, conservation and prevention of the impact of extreme weather events, particularly floods and droughts. Furthermore, it prepares a blueprint for the integrated development and implementation of water resources, local water management schemes and a blueprint for the management of water failure in the event of drought.

Within the framework of the regional approach, the Act establishes the Water Basin Council (article 88), which is mandated to examine and express its opinion on issues related to the management and planning of water, in particular the guideline for the integrated development of water resources and local water management schemes. Regarding the National Water Scheme, article 90 stipulates that the plan shall be developed by the administration in coordination with the relevant actors at the national level in a participatory approach. It shall be submitted for the opinion of the Supreme Water and Climate Council as the reference framework for the National Water Policy and approved by a decree published in the *Official Bulletin.*

It is noted from the foregoing that the country and its organs are in charge of legislating and establishing bodies responsible for the environment and climate. But in the absence of coordination between the organs and institutions entrusted with these functions, there will be a problem with the effectiveness of the government's programmes in this area. The government has recognized this weakness.[25]

Challenges preventing the development of climate litigation in Morocco

Ensuring access to justice regarding climate change mitigation and adaptation is central to resolving climate-related disputes. Moreover, within this

[25] Morocco Climate Change Policy (n 5), p. 20.

framework, it is essential to encompass proactive measures aimed at reducing environmental harm, fostering sustainable development, and upholding the right to a healthy environment.[26]

To the best of our knowledge, no cases falling within the scope of the aforementioned definition have been presented to the Moroccan judiciary. In this section, we will try to outline the reasons behind the limited progress of climate litigation in Morocco. At the outset, it should be noted that the absence of climate litigation might be attributed to a lack of collective awareness of this legal avenue, as well as the peculiarities of Moroccan's legal system, which is deeply rooted in civil law traditions.

Lack of awareness

In Morocco there are many civil society associations and non-governmental organizations (NGOs), which are active in the field of environmental protection. They are considered an essential partner in preserving the environment's wealth. This role is reflected in their contribution to the development and monitoring of government programmes at all levels. The National Strategy for Environment and Sustainable Development gives priority to civil society associations by strengthening their capacities. A series of annual activities have been organized since 2014, with the objective of pushing NGOs towards professionalism and transparency in environmental work.[27] One successful example of civil society associations' role in environmental protection is the Mohammed VI Foundation for Environmental Protection. This Foundation works under a well-defined strategy aimed primarily at fostering environmental education, sustainable tourism and rising awareness of the need to improve air quality and reduce GHG emissions.[28]

The Mohammed VI Foundation also participates in efforts to combat climate change. Since 2013 it has developed the Carbon Footprint Tool, which allows Moroccan actors to calculate their GHG emissions and support them in their low carbon transition. In addition, since 2022 the Foundation

---

[26] J Peel and HM Osofsky, 'Climate Change Litigation' (2020)16(1) *Annual Review of Law and Social Science* 21–38; United Nations Environment Programme, 'Global Climate Litigation Report 2020 Status Review', p. 6.

[27] In this context, 12 training workshops are organized annually at the level of each Morocco's entities for some 360 collective frameworks on; inter alia, local action to combat climate change and societal action. For more information on the work to promote the role of environmental protection associations, see the following associations: Renforcement-des-capacites.pdf (environnement.gov.ma) Appui-au-financement-des-projets-associatifs-ar-link.pdf (environnement.gov.ma), accessed 19 September 2022.

[28] For more information about the Mohammed VI Foundation for Environmental Protection, https://www.fm6e.org/ar.html, accessed 19 September 2022.

has launched a series of regional meetings to support Moroccan companies in the decarbonization of their activities, in order to best prepare for the EU Carbon Border Adjustment Mechanism (CBAM). The objectives of these meetings include: informing companies in the region with updates on the progress of the international climate agenda and the projections for COP27; disseminating information on the different ways of combating climate change (reduction approaches, compensation, and so on) in particular through the Qualit'Air Charter; presenting the carbon footprint tool and the existing support tools for business; and providing information on the eligible carbon offset actions and projects in the portfolio of voluntary carbon offset projects carried out by the Foundation.

In the same context is a project called 'Mobilizing civil society to support dialogue in order to adapt to climate change in Morocco', launched in 2018 under the auspices of the World Wildlife Fund office in North Africa. The project involves the active participation of 16 associations representing various regions of Morocco, and aims to support, train and strengthen their capacities. In addition, it aims to inform the authorities about the importance of integrating climate change adaptation into public policies for development, particularly in the areas of water, coast and forest.[29]

However, despite the importance of these initiatives, they fail to address the impact of climate litigation in strengthening the state's commitment to mitigating the effects of climate change. As a result, no association has filed a legal claim against the state or an economic actor regarding this issue.

One reason for this state of affairs, is that Moroccan law does not allow civil society associations to present legal actions to defend the general interest and the right to live in a healthy environment,[30] which largely limits the scope for any legal actions to be brought. Furthermore, disputes related to the climate

---

[29] It is clear that it is the role approved by Framework Law No. 99.12 for associations when referred to in the provision of the art. 22: 'Civil society associations working mainly in the fields of the environment and sustainable development contribute to achieving the goals stipulated in this Law-Framework. To this end, it undertakes to carry out, either on its own initiative or in partnership with the state, territorial collectivities, public institutions, state companies and private contractors, every informative, sensitizing or proposing process that is capable of: Supporting the population's keenness to respect the environment, natural resources, cultural heritage and the values of sustainable development, through awareness-raising and education processes; By ensuring the development and evaluation of tested methods and practices in the field of sustainable management of natural resources at the level of local communities; By contributing to the continuous improvement of the mechanisms in force in the field of population participation in environmental decision-making and access to environmental information.'

[30] Contrary to what was stipulated in art. 36 of Law No.10.03 related to environmental protection and sustainable development in Algeria.

are very expensive in terms of expert evidence-gathering and the costs of legal proceedings; an individual cannot bear the entirety of their expense.

Peculiarities of Morocco's legal system

Morocco's legal system is based on civil law. Therefore, justiciability is codified according to legal texts, and there are a set of conditions that must be met by the parties. According to article 1 of the Civil Procedure Code,[31] to bring a case to a court of law a plaintiff must have capacity and standing. Standing refers to the set of requirements that a plaintiff must meet to demonstrate that they are entitled to bring a claim before the court.

Legal definitions of those who have standing vary across different jurisdictions. In Morocco, it is mandatory to initiate the lawsuit, and it must be done by the right holder, his successor or his legal representative. Standing refers also to the advantage that the plaintiff would obtain if the judge recognizes the validity of his claim. The plaintiff has to prove that they were injured and that their injury was caused by the defendant's actions. In addition, their injury must be actual and specific.

We might imagine that a natural or legal person can have the interest and the capacity to seek justice to protect their right to a healthy environment, in accordance with article 31 of the Moroccan Constitution of 2011. This article states: 'The State, public institutions and local authorities are committed to mobilizing all available resources to facilitate equal access for citizens to the conditions necessary for enjoying the rights to access water and a healthy environment'. However, these are general terms, which cannot be used as a basis for asking the state to respect its climate change commitments. For instance, under article 31, a citizen had demanded that the state guarantee her the right to healthcare as provided by the Constitution. The Court of Cassation, the highest court in Morocco, held that if the administration is required to perform a public service, which is the healthcare service, it does so within the limits of its available means.[32]

Of course, it is desirable to have an explicit text that states clearly how to claim the right to live in a healthy environment. In the same context, it is also essential to ensure the effective implementation of existing legal texts, by issuing the necessary regulations. For example, the preventive role of EISs must be effectively enforced. Therefore, the implementation of legal texts must be ensured. The contents of these texts refer to a series

[31] Dahir Carrying Law No. 1-74-447 of 28 September 1974 approving the text of the Civil Procedure Code, as amended and supplemented.

[32] Decision No. 3/1550 dated 17 October 2019 issued in file No. 1/4/1583/2018.

of decrees and decisions that have not been taken yet, or are being delayed by the government, which adversely affects the enforcement of the laws.

In Morocco, the implementation of legal texts requires application texts (decrees, orders and decisions), and without these texts the law cannot be implemented. The application of the Environmental Assessment Law requires the issuance of 13 applicable texts. Some legal texts had never been enforced because they were awaiting the issuance of practical texts such as Law No. 08.01 on quarries of 2002, which had not entered into force and had been replaced in 2015 by an entirely new Law No. 27.13.

The absence of applicable texts not only impedes the application of the law, but also prevents the introduction of the National Strategy for Environmental Conservation and Sustainable Development, and thus hampers the fulfillment of the state's commitments in dealing with climate change. This may lead to its responsibility being raised in front of the national judiciary and the international community. This responsibility can be established under the concept of nonfeasance or delay in legislation. Here we refer to the executive's legal rules in the exercise of its regulatory powers as a subsidiary legislative authority.[33]

This type of case is frequent in comparative law, including a decision of the Belgian Court of Cassation dated 28 September 2006, which states that the courts have the power to monitor the appropriate and adequate enactment of laws by the legislature.[34] This respects the right to be tried within the reasonable time limit established under article 6.1 of the European Convention on Human Rights.[35]

The French judiciary has also held the state accountable for its failure to take the necessary measures for the implementation of the law. It has issued a ruling to repeal the implicit decision of the Department not to issue implementing decrees regarding child protection funds in accordance with a 2007 law. The court instructed the state to enact this decree under the threat of a fine and to compensate for damages caused by the absence of such funds.[36]

To the best of our knowledge, the Moroccan judiciary has not discussed any issue related to the slow pace of legislation in the environmental field or

---

[33] Chapter 72 of the Constitution defines the government's competence in the field of legislation.

[34] Decision cited by M Buhru, 'State Responsibility for the Actions of the Legislature' (2020) 4 *Journal of the Kingdom's Judicial Agency, Issue of Liability Cases*, p. 603.

[35] Decision of the Belgian Court of Cassation No. C.02. 0570, dated 28 September 2006, www.cass.be.

[36] Decision of the French Conseil d'Etat No. 325824; The French Conseil d'Etat issued a decision of 25 July 1936, in which it was held that the failure of the Ministry of Agriculture to intervene to apply the requirements of a particular law constituted a 'grave error which would raise the responsibility of the State'. For more details check, Mustafa Buhru (n 34), p. 624 and below.

climate change. The absence of legislation and delays in its implementation constitute a violation of constitutional obligations. The enactment of a legal text is not considered complete until its implementing regulations are issued. The partial regulation of a matter is tantamount to a lack of regulation, especially concerning the rights and freedoms enshrined in the Constitution, such as the right to live in a healthy environment and the right to sustainable development.

Conclusion

Climate litigation is directly linked to the concept of sustainable development and a country's compliance with its climate change obligations.[37] Despite Morocco's considerable legislative effort to adapt to climate change and reduce GHG emissions, the legislative system alone cannot succeed in this challenge. It requires a judiciary aware of the challenge and capable of implementing legal texts in all instances to accomplish the objective of safeguarding the environment and addressing climate change. To safeguard the rights of current and future generations to enjoy a particularly sound climate and environment, it is necessary to raise the public's sense of environmental responsibility, awareness of the negative impacts of climate change, and the consequences of environmentally harmful actions.

To approach the issue of climate change and the problems it causes to legislators, it has been necessary to make a thorough analysis of legal texts and the difficulties of taking legal action regarding climate. As a result, several observations can be made in this respect. Firstly, there is a range of legal texts that protect the environment and reduce the effects of climate change in Morocco. However, there are few legal texts directly concerned with climate issues. These texts mainly aim to reduce the effects of climate change. As we explain above, to be implemented laws need their application texts (decrees, orders and decisions) to be adopted. The absence of the applicable texts of many laws makes them ineffective and, therefore, incapable of being implemented

Secondly, there is a multiplicity of national and local environmental and climate institutions and bodies. The advisory and propositional nature undermines the authority of these bodies and institutions and highlights their lack of decision-making capabilities.

Thirdly, there should be a specific procedure in place to enforce state obligations in relation to climate change and provide compensation to the

[37] This year Morocco rose one spot to seventh – a top ten, high-performing country in this year's Climate Change Performance Index (CCPI). As in the previous two years Morocco rates high in three main CCPI categories: GHG emissions, energy use, and climate policy: https://ccpi.org/country/mar/.

victims of this phenomenon. However, in the Moroccan legal system, judges do not have extensive discretion when it comes to climate-related issues as, unlike common law jurisdictions, they cannot recognize new causes of action under suitable circumstances.

Finally, civil society's involvement in climate litigation is weak and ineffective. This is due to the weakness of the relevant laws and the vulnerability of the associations themselves in terms of the possibilities and resources available to them, as well as their technical knowledge of the environment and its requirements.

Government should work on strengthening the capacities of various actors and raising public awareness of environmental issues and related regulations. The potential actors that can be of help here are environmental monitoring and inspection officers, judges who are experts in the substantive and technical aspects of environmental issues, and environmental protection associations that care about environmental litigation, and are privileged by public benefit status.

It is also advisable to work on enhancing cooperation and coordination among various stakeholders, including observation and inspection agencies, executors and judges, law enforcement bodies and civil society. Last but not least, is crucial to recognize the existence of environmental damage independent of its impact on human beings within civil law. Prior to these efforts, the government has to ensure that the relevant laws are prepared prior to their promulgation, or at least by establishing a clear enactment programme.

13

Climate Litigation in South Africa and Nigeria: Legal Opportunities and Gender Perspectives

Pedi Obani

Introduction

Despite a lack of consensus over the meaning and types of climate litigation, the number of climate cases worldwide is on the rise. Across domestic courts in Africa, climate cases have been decided in South Africa, Nigeria and Kenya, with some cases pending before the domestic courts in South Africa and Uganda. These cases mainly involve a direct reference to climate change in the framing of parties' claims. It is, however, possible that a broad consideration of domestic cases involving the environmental impact of hydrocarbon exploration and production would expand the volume of climate change cases across the continent. For instance, although the plethora of oil spillage cases in Niger Delta communities in Nigeria have not been historically argued as climate change claims before the courts, the climate change implications of oil spill incidents are widely considered in the scholarly literature and public discourse.[1] An in-depth consideration of

[1] Cases involving the prosecution of suspects of illegal bunkering activities could also be relevant for this purpose. The rationale for this argument is in line with the submission of Morgenthau and Reisch that: 'Cases that focus on stopping the upstream drivers of climate change, such as oil, gas, and coal extraction and deforestation, can slow global warming *at least as effectively* as conventional climate cases that aim at securing policy commitments to reduce downstream emissions'. See T Morganthau and N Reisch, 'Litigating the Frontlines: Why African Community Rights Cases Are Climate Change Cases' (2020) 25(1) *UCLA Journal of International Law & Foreign Affairs* 85, 86; K Bouwer, 'Substantial Justice?: Transnational Torts as Climate Litigation' (2021) *15 Carbon & Climate Law Review* 188.

climate litigation in Africa is imperative, given the high exposure to climate change-related developmental risks of most economies on the continent.[2] Political economy issues associated with low carbon transitions could disincentivize carbon-dependent economies, such as Nigeria and South Africa.[3] Conversely, climate litigation could impose significant liabilities on governments whose (investments) plans for fossil fuel production are inconsistent with global greenhouse gas (GHG) emissions targets.

This chapter explores climate change cases from South Africa and Nigeria through a legal opportunity structures (LOS) lens. Understanding the effects of LOS is critical for sustaining climate litigation momentum across countries. Further, the academic literature on climate litigation hardly covers gender issues, even though women's vulnerability to adverse climate change impacts and limited access to resources for adaptation are widely acknowledged. The (lack of) receptivity of the existing LOS to women's unique experiences affects their ability to engage in climate litigation and prospects for accessing climate justice through the courts. The chapter, therefore, undertakes a gender-sensitive analysis of the relevant literature and decisions of courts from South Africa and Nigeria to conceptualize the LOS for climate litigation.

The chapter is in five sections including this introduction. The second section identifies the main features of LOS based on the literature: structural and contingent dimensions. The third section analyses the LOS for climate litigation in South Africa and Nigeria from a feminist perspective, to demonstrate the anomalies women face. Following the analysis is a reflection on the broader implications for LOS and the conclusion.

Conceptualizing legal opportunity structures

Hilson outlines a range of factors impacting a movement's choice of legal or alternative strategies for advancing any cause.[4] The factors could be intrinsic, external or a combination of both. Intrinsic factors influence the preferable

---

2 UNU-INRA, *Africa's Development in the Age of Stranded Assets* (UNU-INRA 2019).

3 I Gençsü, G Walls, A Picciariello and IJ Alasia, 'Nigeria's Energy Transition: Reforming Fossil Fuel Subsidies and other Financing Opportunities' (2022) ODI Working Paper www.odi.org/en/publications/nigerias-energy-transition-reforming-fossil-fuel-subsidies-and-other-financing-opportunities, accessed 2 January 2022; Jesse Burton, Tara Caetano, and Bryce McCall, *Coal Transition in South Africa – Understanding the Implications of a 2°C-compatible Coal Phase-out for South Africa* (IDDRI & Climate Strategies 2018) https://coaltransitions.org/reports/, accessed 2 January 2022; Kathryn Hochstetler, *Political Economies of Energy Transition: Wind and Solar Power in Brazil and South Africa* (Cambridge University Press 2020).

4 C Hilson, 'New Social Movements: The Role of Legal Opportunity' (2002) 9 *Journal of European Public Policy* 238.

advocacy strategy.[5] One intrinsic factor is the movement's access to resources such as finances, knowledge and legitimacy. A second intrinsic factor is the movement's identity; this could be either instrumental or counter/sub-cultural. An instrumental identity is likely to favour lobbying, litigation or other conventional strategies, while counter-cultural and sub-cultural identities are more likely to select direct action. Other intrinsic factors are ideology and values. Anarchists are less likely to utilize lobbying, litigation and similar conventional strategies than movements that respect formal legal institutions.

On the other hand, the accessibility of strategies or platforms (political opportunity) is an essential external factor that may influence the movement's choice.[6] However, access does not guarantee receptivity, and using (favourable) LOS does not guarantee a successful outcome. The progression from political to legal opportunities is not necessarily linear, and a movement may adopt protest or other alternative strategies following an unfavourable court decision.[7] Even 'unsuccessful' climate change cases could nonetheless advance narrative building and future success in claims for climate action.[8]

Further, within multi-level governance systems, opportunities (legal or political) could exist at various levels, and a lack of opportunities at one level (for instance, the national) may be compensated by reference to other governance levels. For example, following the Paris Agreement (international level), there has been an increase in the momentum of state action, and legal and political mobilization at the domestic level. This highlights the role of national institutions in implementing global climate change governance mechanisms.[9] LOS portrays how the individual's ability and decision to institute legal action is often a function of the constraints and incentives presented by formal institutions.[10] Within the context of social

5 Hilson (n 4).

6 Hilson (n 4); E Lehoucq, 'Legal Threats and the Emergence of Legal Mobilization: Conservative Mobilization in Colombia' (2021) 46 *Law & Social Inquiry* 299.

7 S Keller and B Bornemann, 'New Climate Activism between Politics and Law: Analyzing the Strategy of the KlimaSeniorinnen Schweiz' (2021) 9(2) *Politics Gov* 124 DOI: 10.17645/pag.v9i2.3819.

8 K Bouwer and J Setzer, 'Climate Litigation as Climate Activism: What Works?', British Academy 2020, https://www.thebritishacademy.ac.uk/publications/knowledge-frontiers-cop26-briefings-climate-litigation-climate-activism-what-works/.

9 J Setzer and LC Vanhala, 'Climate Change Litigation: A Review of Research on Courts and Litigants in Climate Governance', 2019, WIREs Climate Change, https://doi.org/10.1002/wcc.580; J de Moor *et al*, 'New Kids on the Block: Taking Stock of the Recent Cycle of Climate Activism (2021) 20(5) *Social Movement Studies* 619 DOI: 10.1080/14742837.2020.1836617.

10 L Conant *et al*., 'Mobilizing European Law' (2018) 25(9) *Journal of European Public Policy* 1376; F Kahraman, 'A New Era for Labor Activism? Strategic Mobilization of Human Rights Against Blacklisting' (2018) 43(4) *Law & Social Inquiry* 1279; CL Arrington, 'Hiding in Plain Sight: Pseudonymity and Participation in Legal Mobilization' (2019) 52(2) *Comparative Political Studies* 310.

movement legal mobilization, De Fazio states: 'LOS refers to the features of the legal system which facilitate/hinder social movements' chances to have their grievances redressed through the judiciary'.[11] LOS has two main elements: structural features (ranging from rule on standing, access to legal aid, to courts and justiciability of rights) and contingent features (mainly the receptiveness of the judiciary toward the claims of litigants).[12]

Other relevant structural features include the extent to which existing laws support a cause of action and affect the potential for a successful outcome and rules on legal costs, which could invariably dissuade less-resourced organizations or poorer individuals from instituting action.[13] Further, in terms of the receptivity of the judiciary, De Fazio asserts:

> [A] judicial culture averse to confer certain rights, together with judges and courts mostly impervious to claims promoting those rights, provides an uncongenial scenario for legal mobilization. Vice versa, courts' judicial activism in favour of certain issues may signal to social movements that a legal opportunity exists to undertake litigation, activists usually being aware of judges' ideological leaning and planning accordingly their legal tactics.[14]

Overall, LOS theory supports a better understanding of the factors within a legal system that influence the choice of litigation in a given context and the enabling factors and deterrents that may result in some individuals or groups being unable or less likely to employ legal strategies. The line between structural and contingent features is sometimes blurred as the latter may be affected by the separation of powers of government and the limits of judicial authority, which are structural or systemic factors. Further, there may be a difference in the attitude of different courts within a country. Even with a favourable legal opportunity, intrinsic factors such as a counter-cultural identity may prevent a movement's adoption of litigation as a strategy.[15]

It is also important to emphasize that the broader socio-economic, cultural and political context beyond the legal framework is equally critical for

---

[11] G De Fazio, 'Legal Opportunity Structure and Social Movement Strategy in Northern Ireland and Southern United States' (2012) 53(1) *International Journal of Comparative Sociology* 3 DOI: 10.1177/00207152124393114.

[12] Hilson (n 4); L Vanhala, 'Legal Opportunity Structures and the Paradox of Legal Mobilization by the Environmental Movement in the UK' (2012) 46(3) *Law & Society Review* 523, https://doi.org/10.1111/j.1540-5893.2012.00505.x.

[13] Lehoucq (n 6).

[14] De Fazio (n 11), 7.

[15] Hilson (n 4).

understanding the intricacies of LOS. This points to the relevance of the positionality of individuals and groups in relation to the legal system. The historically low representation of women, ethnic minorities, disabled persons and other groups in vulnerable situations, despite recent progress in some aspects, impacts LOS in at least two ways. First, the lack of representation erodes the legitimacy of the system and its robustness to appreciate and respond to the unique underrepresented interests. Second, it may hinder the ability, interest and confidence of excluded groups in engaging with the legal system without legal aid and other relevant support.

Analysis of legal opportunity structures for climate litigation in South Africa and Nigeria

South Africa

South Africa experiences extreme vulnerability and exposure to climate change impacts, ranging from water scarcity to low agricultural productivity, impacts on biodiversity and adverse health outcomes due to high temperatures and the spread of diseases.[16] Further, the heavy reliance on coal adversely affects the environment and human health. It directly threatens the environment and related human rights, mainly through the significant GHG emissions and potential climate change impacts.[17] South Africa ranks top in Africa for the number of climate change cases decided by the domestic courts, suggesting a positive LOS overall.

Structural dimension

Standing

The departure from the rigid common law stance on locus standi has significantly improved the prospects for public interest environmental litigation and the ability of various individuals and groups to enforce the government's commitments for climate action under different international and domestic frameworks. Under the common law, a private legal action could only be sustained where individual rights were threatened or violated. However, this became a stumbling block for instituting legal actions to protect the environment and other issues that affect not only an individual's or group's right but the general public interest. The position has been altered by the constitution and environmental law provisions.

---

16 Academy of Science of South Africa (ASSAf), *First Biennial Report to Cabinet on the State of Climate Change: Science and Technology in South Africa*, ASSAf, 2017, http://dx.doi.org/10.17159/assaf.2016/0015.

17 Burton, Caetano and McCall (n 3).

The Constitution of the Republic of South Africa 1996 (the SA Constitution) protects the right of everyone to an environment that is not harmful to their health or wellbeing, and mandates the state to enforce this right. By virtue of section 38 of the SA Constitution, anyone acting in their personal interest, or acting on behalf of someone 'who cannot act in their own name or a group, or acting in the public interest' or an association representing its members', has a right to institute legal action to protect a right in the Bill of Rights.[18] Further, section 32(1) of the National Environmental Management Act 1998 (NEMA) grants any person or group of persons the right to seek appropriate relief in respect of any breach or threatened breach of any provision of the NEMA or other statutory provisions on environmental protection or the use of natural resources. This can be done in the interest of a person or group of persons; on behalf of another person who cannot institute such proceedings for practical reasons or a group whose interests are affected; or in the interest of the public for the protection of the environment. These provisions have enabled increasing public interest climate litigation in the domestic courts (Table 13.1). While the SA Constitution does not go so far as to protect women's rights expressly, it prohibits discrimination on the grounds of sex or gender. So far, none of the climate cases in South Africa have been instituted on the grounds of women's rights.

Legal aid and representation in environmental governance

There is a significant focus on women's empowerment, capacity building and participation in the environmental sector, including the targeted recruitment of women in South Africa's environmental sector.[19] This empowerment narrative is buttressed with examples of women-led environmental conservation initiatives and social mobilization for climate action.[20] While

---

[18] Section 24.

[19] Submission by South Africa on Gender and Climate Change: Priority Area E on Monitoring and Reporting under the Gender Action Plan, 8 May 2019, unfccc.int, accessed 3 January 2022.

[20] I Dankelman, 'Introduction: Exploring Gender, Environment and Climate Change' in I Dankelman (ed), *Gender and Climate Change: An Introduction* (Routledge, 2010). In line with the empowerment narrative, natural disasters, presumably including climate change related crisis, can potentially trigger a change in women's gendered status in the society and transform women into key actors in climate action. See generally E Enarson, Crisis Response and Reconstruction and ILO, 'Gender and Natural Disasters' (2000) IPCRR Working Paper N1 Document1 (ilo.org), accessed 3 January 2023; Úrsula Oswald Spring, 'Contextualisation on Gender, Peace, Security and Environment. Earth at Risk in the 21st Century: Rethinking Peace, Environment, Gender, and Human, Water, Health, Food, Energy Security, and Migration' (2020) 18 PMCID: PMC7153461 3 doi: 10.1007/978-3-030-38569-9_1.

Table 13.1: Overview of climate cases in South Africa

Case and year	Issue
EarthLife Africa Johannesburg v Minister of Environmental Affair (2016)[a]	Failure to consider climate change in environmental impacts statements.
Philippi Horticultural Area Food & Farming Campaign v MEC for Local Government, Environmental Affairs and Development Planning: Western Cape (2019)[b]	Court remanded an administrative decision approving urban development 'in the context of climate change and water scarcity'.
Sustaining the Wild Coast NPC v Minister of Mineral Resources and Energy (2021)[c]	Decision granting exploration right was subject to review and climate change impacts was an essential consideration in awarding the exploration right.
Pending	
Trustees for the Time Being of GroundWork v Minister of Environmental Affairs, ACWA Power Khanyisa Thermal Power Station RF (Pty) Ltd (2017)[d]	Failure to consider climate change in environmental impacts statements
Trustees for the Time Being of the GroundWork Trust v Minister of Environmental Affairs, KiPower (Pty) Ltd (2017)[e]	Failure to consider climate change in environmental impacts statements
City of Cape Town v National Energy Regulator of South Africa and Minister of Energy (2017)[f]	Intergovernmental dispute over approval for the purchase of solar and wind power from an independent power producer.
SDCEA & Groundwork v Minister of Forestry, Fisheries, and the Environment (2021)[g]	Failure of the government to adequately consider climate impacts and the full cycle emissions in approving a natural gas power plant.
South Durban Community Environmental Alliance v Minister of Environment (2021)[h]	Failure to consider the climate impacts of offshore oil and gas exploration.
Africa Climate Alliance v Minister of Mineral Resources & Energy (2021)[i]	Constitutional challenge of the of the government's decision to procure new coal-fired power.

[a] Case No. 65662/16.

[b] Case No. 16779/17.

[c] (3491/2021) [2022] ZAECMKHC 55.

[d] Case No. 61561/17.

[e] Case No. 54087/17.

[f] Case No. 1765/17.

[g] The Sabin Center for Climate Change Law, http://climatecasechart.com/non-us-case/sdcea-groundwork-v-minister-of-forestry-fisheries-and-the-environment/, accessed 3 January 2023.

[h] Grantham Research Institute on Climate Change and the Environment, https://www.climate-laws.org/geographies/south-africa/litigation_cases/south-durban-community-environmental-alliance-v-minister-of-environment-and-others, accessed 3 January 2023.

[i] Case No. 56907/21.

it is vital to avoid essentializing women's experiences as victims or somehow more connected to nature, or imposing on them more responsibilities for climate action, examples of legal mobilization by women underscore the importance of empowerment and enabling structures. Empowerment requires addressing poverty, a significant cause and outcome of women's vulnerabilities to climate change, exclusion from access to and governance of various productive resources and environmental governance structures, and the resulting constraints on women's resilience to climate impacts.[21]

Sub-Saharan Africa accounts for 62.8 per cent of the world's extremely poor women and girls in South Africa.[22] Most employed people who live below the international poverty line are also women.[23] The prevalence of poverty among women and women-led household adversely affects their capacity to engage LOS and, therefore, they require support from legal aid or other forms of third sector funding. No recorded climate change case has been brought by women yet, despite the direct links to environmental impacts and, ultimately, women's productive and reproductive roles. Nonetheless, 'women-led and majority' organizations such as the Centre for Environmental Rights (CER) continue to play a significant role in climate litigation and other projects to support communities to advance environmental justice, democratize environmental and development planning and decisions, and challenge coal power plants projects.[24] Also, feminist initiatives such as the Initiative for Strategic Litigation in Africa (ISLA), which is based in South Africa but has a regional focus, use strategic litigation to advance access to justice and women's rights.[25] ISLA's priority themes for litigation are violence against women, sexual rights and women's socio-economic rights, which can all be impacted by climate change and could therefore form intersecting grounds for climate litigation.

Legal Aid South Africa, established under the Legal Aid South Africa Act 2013, provides state-funded legal aid and legal advice, legal representation, and education and information about legal rights and obligations to eligible persons.[26] Under this Act, there appears to be a lot of emphasis on access

---

21 S Haseem, 'Grass in the Cracks: Gender, Social Reproduction and Climate Justice in the Xolobeni Struggle' (Carleton University 2022 Spring Shannon Lecture Series 24 June 2022) (108) 'Grass in the Cracks: Gender, Social Reproduction and Climate Justice in the Xolobeni Struggle', YouTube, accessed 2 January 2023.

22 UN Women, South Africa, https://data.unwomen.org/country/south-africa, accessed 8 May 2023.

23 UN Women (n 22).

24 See more at Pollution & Climate Change – Centre for Environmental Rights (cer.org.za). CER has been involved in around 20 cases that directly involve challenges to decisions on coal-fired power plants projects, gas developments, or air pollution and emissions standards, most of which are not captured in the mainstream global climate change databases.

25 Cases – ISLA (the-isla.org).

26 Section 3 of the Legal Aid South Africa Act 2013.

to legal aid in criminal cases; however, Legal Aid South Africa supports a variety of claims, including land matters. For instance, South Africa's Fifth Periodic Report under Article 18 of the Convention on the Elimination of Discrimination against Women 1979[27] highlights the right to legal representation for indigent persons under detention at state expense. Women and children's rights and land issues have also been earmarked 'as deserving of special attention in the provision of' legal aid services. This guarantee does not directly promote women's LOS for climate litigation without detention or climate-induced threats to land rights. Nonetheless, legal aid is available for criminal and civil matters, including women's land rights cases which presumably could coincide with climate change adaptation or mitigation under certain circumstances.

Justiciability

South Africa is a state party to the United Nations Framework Convention on Climate Change (UNFCCC) and the Paris Agreement. South Africa has committed to climate change adaptation and mitigation goals in its Nationally Determined Contribution (NDC). Consequently, development plans and projects must be carefully assessed to ensure coherence with the country's NDC. Further, NEMA section 24(1), requires: '[I]n order to give effect to the general objectives of integrated environmental management laid down in this Chapter, the potential impact on the environment of listed activities must be considered, investigated, assessed and reported to the competent authority charged by this Act with granting the relevant environmental authorization'. The Environmental Impact Assessment Regulations made under the NEMA guide the procedures and criteria for obtaining environmental authorization from the competent authority before the commencement of the specified activities that could significantly affect the environment. Relevant to the application process for environmental authorization are the constitutionally guaranteed rights to information (section 32) and administrative justice (section 33). These rights have been operationalized through the Promotion of Access to Information Act 2000 (PAIA) and the Promotion of Administrative Justice Act 2000 (PAJA) respectively.[28]

27 Article 18 mandates states to report on the implementation measures which they have adopted for the Convention and their progress.

28 The PAIA provides access to certain information held by public bodies and by private bodies, while the PAJA was enacted to implement the right to administrative justice concerning any decision or failure to decide by an organ of state exercising a power under the Constitution, or any legislation.

Under the rules on legal standing already highlighted, various individuals and legal persons can institute private action to protect these rights. In the case of *EarthLife Africa Johannesburg v Minister of Environmental Affairs* (the *Thabametsi* case),[29] the applicant, a non-profit organization for environmental matters, instituted the action to challenge the Minister's approval of a new 1,200 MW coal-fired Thabametsi power project because of the project's climate impacts. The applicant had legal standing to institute a review of environmental decisions on its behalf as an interested and affected party, and in the interest of the public and environmental protection under section 24(4)(v)(a) and section 32(1) of NEMA.[30] Relying further on the legal provisions on administrative review,[31] the applicant challenged the decision of the Minister of Environmental Affairs, who upheld the environmental authorization granted by the Chief Director of the Department of Environmental Affairs (who was the third respondent) for the development of a coal-fired power station. The applicant subsequently approached the High Court to review the initial environmental authorization and the Minister's decision on the appeal. Given the circumstances, the High Court ruled it appropriate to remit the matter to the Minister for a reconstituted appeal process to consider whether the potential climate change impacts of the project should affect the granting of an environmental authorization.[32]

In the case of *Philippi Horticultural Area Food & Farming Campaign v MEC for Local Government, Environmental Affairs and Development Planning: Western Cape*,[33] the respondent Minister and the City of Cape Town took steps to approve urban development in the Philippi Horticultural Area (PHA). The applicants asked the court to review the environmental authorization and exemption granted for the development project, under section 6(2)(e)(ii) of the PAJA; this was because relevant considerations, including the impacts of the proposed development on the aquifer/groundwater and climate change, were not taken into account in granting the environmental authorization and the related exemption applications. The applicants also contended that the decisions taken were not rationally connected to the information available to the decision maker, as required under section 6(2)(f) of the PAJA. They successfully sought a declaration that the scoping and environmental impact assessment process was 'insufficient/fatally flawed/non-compliant'.

29 Case No. 65662/16 [2017] ZAGPPHC 58.

30 Para. 3.

31 The PAJA, s. 6, stipulates grounds for a judicial review of administrative action to include where the competent authority fails to comply with a mandatory and material procedure or condition, and the act was procedurally unfair, amounts to a failure to decide within the prescribed period or, if no period is specified, without an unreasonable delay.

32 Paras 117, 122.

33 Case No. 16779/17.

Contingent dimension

The courts' receptivity to climate cases in South Africa is supported by an enabling domestic legal and regulatory framework and good LOS. In reaching its decision in the *Thabametsi* case, the court, relying on South Africa's commitments under the Paris Agreement, held that climate change is a relevant consideration for the project's environmental review.[34] The court also found non-compliance with section 240(1) of NEMA because the Chief Director had relied on a statement that the climate change impact of the project was relatively low without a climate change impact assessment. The *Thabametsi* judgment significantly expanded the LOS in climate cases by recognizing: (1) the need for an environmental impact assessment, including the broader climate impact of each project with potentially significant climate impacts, as well as assessment of the impact of climate change on the project's viability; (2) the environmental regulator's duty to independently exercise its discretion on approval of a project with significant climate change impacts, and (3) the need to determine the measures that are required to reduce emissions and climate impacts of the project as part of the decision-making process. In subsequent cases, the courts have relied on this decision, as well as existing constitutional rights and environmental and administrative laws, to review environmental authorizations for projects where potential climate impacts have not been considered[35] and mandate air pollution regulation for coal infrastructure.[36]

Nigeria

Nigeria is a major exporter of oil and gas in Africa; the oil and gas sector accounts for around 10 per cent of the gross domestic product, and petroleum exports generate approximately 86 per cent of the country's total export revenue.[37] Nigeria's historical emissions from 1850 until 2010 are estimated at 2,564.02 million tonnes (Nigeria's NDC), less than 1 per cent of total global emissions as of 2010 (Nigeria's NDC). Climate change impacts in the form of extreme weather events and violent conflicts are already occurring across the country.[38] Despite litigation over the environmental and human

---

[34] Paras 90 and 91.

[35] For instance in the *PHA* case.

[36] For instance in the *Deadly Air* litigation, *The Trustees for the time being of Groundwork Trust v The Minister of Environmental Affairs* Case No. 39724/2019 DeadlyAir-High-court-judgment-18-March-2022.pdf (cer.org.za).

[37] NAN, 'Oil Accounts for 10% GDP, 86% Export Earnings – Sylva', *The Guardian*, 9 August 2021, https://guardian.ng/news/oil-accounts-for-10-gdp-86-export-earnings-sylva/, accessed 2 January 2023.

[38] Carbon Brief, 'The Carbon Brief Profile: Nigeria', 21 August 2020, https://www.carbonbrief.org/the-carbon-brief-profile-nigeria, accessed 2 January 2023.

rights impacts of pollution from the oil and gas industry, particularly in the Niger Delta region, there is only one climate case on record for Nigeria in the mainstream climate litigation databases. While this raises questions about definitions and categorization,[39] it also raises questions about the state of LOS for climate cases in the country.

Structural dimension

Standing

Historically, the restrictive common law rules on legal standing have also applied in Nigeria, restricting the prospects for public interest litigation for environmental protection. However, in the case of *Centre for Oil Pollution Watch v Nigerian National Petroleum Corpn*[40] the Nigerian Supreme Court upheld the right of everyone, including NGOs, to institute legal action for performance of statutory obligations or enforcement of legal provisions for environmental protection. The facts of the case are briefly that the appellant, a registered NGO in Nigeria, instituted an action for the reinstatement, restoration and remediation of the environment in the Acha autonomous community of the Isukwuato local government area of Abia state of Nigeria. The environmental degradation was allegedly caused by oil spillage resulting from the respondent's negligence. The Court of Appeal upheld the decision of the trial court striking out the suit for lack of locus standi. On further appeal, the Supreme Court overturned the decision. Eko, JSC, on the issue of locus standi in environmental protection litigation, stated:

> Once in his pleadings [the plaintiff shows] his genuine interest, as the present appellant has, it is disclosed that the defendant is transgressing the law or is about to transgress it by his objectionable conduct which injures or impairs human lives and/or endangers the environment the plaintiff, be he an individual or an NGO should be accorded the standing to enforce the law and thereby save lives and the environment.[41]

NGOs such as Friends of the Earth, Nigeria/Environmental Rights Action have already been instituting transnational climate cases for Nigerian host communities, in the home country of carbon majors.

The liberalization of the rule on standing will improve the prospects for private entities and NGOs to initiate climate litigation before domestic courts, also on behalf of women and girls. To date, the plethora of cases for

[39] See the editors discussion of this in the introductory chapter of this volume.

[40] [2019] 5 NWLR [Pt.1666] 518.

[41] [2019] 5 NWLR [Pt.1666] 601.

environmental protection and remediation of degradation from oil spillage and gas flaring, mainly from the Niger Delta region in Nigeria, have been instituted primarily by either men (in a personal or representative capacity) or NGOs. The major litigation related to oil exploration and production activities in the Niger Delta that women have instituted focus on allegations of complicity in human rights abuses by Royal Dutch Shell. The cases – *Wiwa v Royal Dutch Petroleum*,[42] *Wiwa v Anderson*,[43] *Wiwa v Shell Petroleum Development Co*,[44] and *Kiobel v Royal Dutch Petroleum Co.*,[45] – have each occurred in a foreign jurisdiction and have been prosecuted by the affected women with the support of international NGOs.

Legal aid

The Legal Aid Council, Nigeria was established in 1976. The Legal Aid Act 2011 enables the provision of free legal advice and representation and alternative dispute resolution for eligible persons. The legal aid applies to specific, restricted criminal cases, but also civil cases, including claims for breach of fundamental human rights, employee's compensation, and civil claims linked to eligible criminal matters under the Legal Aid Act. The restricted categories limit the prospects of applying legal aid to climate cases and environmental protection broadly in Nigeria. This significantly limits the LOS for poor women and other eligible members of society who cannot fund their climate litigation without financial and legal assistance.

Justiciability

Nigeria is a party to the UNFCCC and the Paris Agreement. Nigeria's Nationally Determined Contributions (NDC) are designed to deliver 20 per cent unconditional and 45 per cent conditional emissions reductions by 2030. The right to environment is not expressly recognized in the Constitution of Nigeria.[46] Although environmental protection provisions under the

42 226 F3d 88 – Court of Appeals, 2nd Cir. 2000.

43 *Center for Constitutional Rights, Wiwa v Royal Dutch Petroleum*, https://ccrjustice.org/home/what-we-do/our-cases/wiwa-et-al-v-royal-dutch-petroleum-et-al, accessed 2 January 2023.

44 Center for Constitutional Rights (n 43).

45 569 US 108, Supreme Court 2013.

46 E Emeseh, 'Mainstreaming Enforcement for the Victims of Environmental Pollution: Towards Effective Allocation of Legislative Competence under a Federal Constitution' (2012) 14 *Environmental Law Review* 185, interrogates the allocation of legislative competence in a federal state and the implications for enforcement of environmental laws.

fundamental objectives and directive principles of state policy are rendered non-justiciable by virtue of section 6(6)(c) of the Nigerian Constitution, the African Charter on Human and Peoples Rights guarantees the right to a general satisfactory environment. Further, the constitutional guarantee of freedom of information, subject to exceptions that are 'reasonably justifiable in a democratic society', operationalized through the Freedom of Information Act 2011, makes 'public records and information more freely available' to the public. This requirement would apply to public records and information on climate change and generally supports procedural environmental rights.

Also relevant is the Environmental Impact Assessment Act 1992 (EIA), which requires an environmental impact assessment to be conducted before implementation or authorization 'where the extent, nature or location of a proposed project or activity is such that is likely to significantly affect the environment'.[47] An environmental assessment is not required where: (1) the executive arm of government considers that the environmental effects of the project is likely to be minimal; (2) the project is to be implemented during a national emergency for which the government has taken temporary measures; or (3) the regulatory agency considers that the project is in the interest of public health or safety.[48] Though the EIA, section 7 requires the Agency to provide an opportunity to government agencies, the public, experts and interested groups to comment on the environmental impact assessment before giving a decision on an activity that is the subject of the environmental impact assessment, there are concerns regarding the effectiveness of public participation and the incoherence from multiple regulators, particularly in the oil and gas industry, that detract from the EIA process. This provision exposes the process to broad discretionary powers by the executive and the risk of abuse.[49]

In the popularly cited climate case from Nigeria, *Gbemre v Shell Petroleum Development Co. of Nigeria Ltd*,[50] the applicants sought declarations from the court that their rights to life and the dignity of the human person extended to the right to a 'clean poison-free, pollution-free and healthy environment'; continued flaring of gas by the first and second respondents violated the

[47] Environmental Impact Act 1992 (EIA), s. 2(2). The list of mandatory study activities under the EIA Act includes oil and gas fields development; construction of off-shore pipelines over 50 kilometres long; construction of facilities for oil and gas separation, processing, handling, and storage; construction of oil refineries; and construction of steam generated power stations burning fossil fuels and having a capacity of more than 10 megawatts. See EIA, Sch., para. 12.

[48] EIA, s. 14(1).

[49] OA Ogunba, 'EIA Systems in Nigeria: Evolution, Current Practice and Shortcomings' (2004) 24(6) *Environmental Impact Assessment Review* 643.

[50] FHC/B/CS/53/05.

applicants' rights to life and dignity. The applicants also relied on the EIA regulations. Additionally, they argued that the Associated Gas Re-injection Act provisions permitting continued gas flaring were unconstitutional. Section 3(1) of that Act expressly prohibits gas flaring, but section 3(2)(b) empowers the Minister to issue a certificate that allows oil and gas companies to flare gas having paid the prescribed fees. Subsequently, in 2018, the Flare Gas (Prevention of Waste and Pollution) Regulations were introduced to reduce the environmental and social impacts of gas flaring and ensure social and economic benefits from gas flare capture. The Regulations vest the Federal Government of Nigeria with the right to take all associated natural gas free of charge at the flare, stipulate the commercialization process for flare gas, while prohibiting the flaring of gas, except under a certificate issued under the Act.

In a similar vein, the Petroleum Industry Act 2021 also enables the relevant authority to permit gas flaring, but requires operating companies to submit natural gas flare elimination and monetization plans, among other provisions for environmental protection and restoration.[51] These statutory provisions would enable legal action to compel action by the government and oil and gas companies to mitigate and prevent the adverse impacts of the oil and gas sector on humans and the environment by eliminating gas flaring, managing the adverse impacts of their operations through an environmental management planning process,[52] and funding environmental remediation.[53] The legal relevance of the provisions enabling justiciability of climate and environmental 'wrongs' cannot be overemphasized, as Nigeria is included in the ten countries responsible for 75 per cent of total gas flaring globally,[54] and the environment and human health particularly in the Niger Delta region where most of the oil and gas exploration occurs has been severely degraded by the sector.[55]

Additionally, Nigeria's Climate Change Act 2021 (CCA) offers a framework for mainstreaming climate actions, including a carbon budgeting system, and imposes climate obligations on public entities and private entities having at least 50 employees. It establishes a National Council on Climate Change and specifies 2050–2070 as the timeline for realizing the

51 Petroleum Industry Act 2021 (PIA), s. 108.

52 PIA, s, 102.

53 PIA, s. 103.

54 'World Bank, 2022 Global Gas Flaring Tracker Report', World Bank 2022, https://www.worldbank.org/en/topic/extractiveindustries/publication/2022-global-gas-flaring-tracker-report, accessed 2 January 2023.

55 'The Bayelsa State Oil & Environmental Commission, An Environmental Genocide: Counting the Human and Environmental Cost of Oil in Bayelsa, Nigeria', bayelsacommission.org, accessed 28 May 2023.

country's net-zero GHG emissions target.[56] The CCA further provides for women's participation in climate governance, which also advances the goal of the National Action Plan on Gender and Climate Action for Nigeria to mainstream gender considerations in domestic initiatives, programmes and policies for climate action.[57] These gender-inclusive legislative and policy provisions enable a positive structural dimension of LOS for climate litigation for women in Nigeria.

Contingent dimension

Nigerian courts have displayed a mixed attitude in climate cases. In *Gbemre*, the Federal High Court in the city of Benin upheld the applicant's arguments to declare gas flaring unconstitutional. The court issued an injunction against the continuance of the practice in the applicants' community by the respondents. The Federal High Court in Port Harcourt reached a different outcome in the case of *Ikechukwu Okpara v Shell Petroleum Development Co. of Nigeria Ltd,*[58] where the plaintiffs sought similar relief as in *Gbemre*. The court adopted a narrow interpretation of constitutional and statutory rights guarantees, holding that: (1) the fundamental rights provisions did not apply to section 2(2) of the Environmental Impact Assessment Act and section 3(2)(a) and (b) of the Associated Gas Re-Injection Act; (2) the Fundamental Right (Enforcement Procedure) Rules did not apply to the provisions of the African Charter on Human and Peoples Rights (Ratification and Enforcement) Act; and (3) the term 'dignity of his person' under section 34(1) of the Constitution did not extend to community group rights.[59]

Under the CCA, courts have the power to issue a range of orders in cases involving climate change or environmental matters, including orders:

> (a) to prevent, stop or discontinue the performance of any act that is harmful to the environment; (b) compelling any public official to act in order to prevent or stop the performance of any act that is harmful

56 Climate Change Act 2021, s. 1(f). Remarkably, this is at variance with the government's stated climate policy objectives, such as: Nigeria's Long-Term Vision, in response to art. 4.19 of the Paris Agreement, indicative of the end of the century as the target for achieving net zero in various sectors of the economy, including energy and oil and gas.

57 Department of Climate Change – Federal Ministry of Environment, *National Action Plan on Gender and Climate Change for Nigeria* (Federal Ministry of Environment 2020).

58 Suit No. FHC/PH/CS/518/2005 (unreported).

59 A Morocco-Clarke, 'The Case of Gbemre v Shell As A Catalyst for Change in Environmental Pollution Litigation?' 12(2) *Nnamdi Azikiwe University Journal of International Law and Jurisprudence* 28.

to the environment; (c) compensation to the victim directly affected by the acts that are harmful to the environment.[60]

This further strengthens the potential for climate litigation to enhance climate action and remedy adverse environmental impacts, in addition to other statutory and common law remedies. The practical effect of this is yet to be seen, as there has been no litigation involving the Climate Change Act yet.

Broader implications for women and LOS for climate litigation

Given the variety of factors that often limit women's access to formal justice institutions, women's legal opportunity warrants special consideration.[61] Over the past decades, the gendered nature of climate change has been increasingly recognized, both within global institutions for climate change governance (as highlighted in the preamble to the Paris Agreement) and in national policies for mainstreaming gender in climate change governance and the environmental sectors broadly. In analysing the LOS available to women, it is necessary to adopt an intersectional approach to recognize the differential experiences of women based on their social identities, access to resources and other structural factors. This is even more so as, despite liberal rules on legal standing, justiciable legal rights and a receptive judiciary, there could be other structural limitations affecting vulnerable groups' ability and the decision to engage in legal mobilization, such as a lack of legal aid.

The literature suggests ways of understanding the impacts of climate change on women's productive and reproductive roles and wellbeing,[62] which have also informed the approaches to gender mainstreaming in legal and policy frameworks.[63] Without this understanding, the outcome is that

[60] Climate Change Act 2021, s. 34.

[61] CEDAW, 'Concluding Observations on the Combined Seventh and Eighth Periodic Reports of Nigeria', CEDAW/C/NGA/CO/7-8, 24 July 2017.

[62] See for instance C Sorensen *et al*, 'Climate Change and Women's Health: Impacts and Policy Directions' (2018) *PLoS Medicine* 15(7): e1002603, https://doi.org/10.1371/journal.pmed.1002603; World Health Organization (WHO), *Gender, Climate Change and Health* (WHO 2014).

[63] See generally UN Women, 'Explainer: How Gender Inequality and Climate Change Are Interconnected', 2 February 2022; Chidiebere J, 'Patriarchy and Women Vulnerability to Adverse Climate Change in Nigeria' (2019) 9(1) *SAGE Open*, https://doi.org/10.1177/2158244019825914; P Obani, 'Gender and Africa's Low-Carbon Transition', Green Finance Platform 2020, https://greenfinanceplatform.org/blog/gender-and-africa%E2%80%99s-low-carbon-transition, accessed 2 January 2023; J Pedro, C Devine and M Wallner, 'Gender, Climate and Finance: How Investing in Women can Help Combat Climate Change (UN Environment Programme – Finance Initiative', 4 November 2022' unepfi.org.

the existing LOS for climate litigation remains poorly suited to respond to the underlying differences in the climate change-related impacts, needs and priorities of women and girls and could exacerbate gender inequities. For instance, women's limited access to land and other productive resources in patriarchal governance structures common in indigenous communities and health impacts, displacement and security constraints from climate change compound their vulnerability.[64] Additionally, women are underrepresented in the ownership structures, workforce and governance of male-dominated sectors such as the oil and gas industry.[65] These may be linked to the intrinsic factors that affect political or legal mobilization. Consequently, some women may lack the skills and resources to utilize an otherwise favourable LOS for climate litigation.[66]

The mainstream climate litigation databases do not disaggregate the cases according to the gender of the parties. Therefore, it is not possible to get a full picture at this stage of existing LOS affect women's legal mobilization in response to climate change. Nonetheless, there have been a few examples of climate litigation instituted by women, predominantly from Europe and Asia, which are instructive for understanding the related LOS issues. One of the cases that has already been decided – at least in the domestic courts – on gender and climate change is *Verein KlimaSeniorinnen Schweiz. v Federal Department of the Environment, Transport, Energy and Communications (DETEC).* The *KlimaSeniorinnen* case has been heard by the European Court of Human Rights on human rights grounds, which is also becoming an essential legal strategy both within and outside the European Union (Table 13.2). Overall, the outcome of climate change cases focused on women's rights would be instructive for understanding the legal opportunity for human rights-based climate litigation by other vulnerable groups, as this area of law is far from settled (Table 13.2).[67]

The *KlimaSeniorinnen* case illustrates the difficulties presented by locus standi for a group of elderly women. The applicants relied on scientific evidence of their vulnerability to climate change impacts – increased mortality rate from heatwaves compared to similar-aged men – to challenge the failure of the Swiss government to reduce GHG emissions by 2020 to an extent that supports the realization of global temperature targets. They relied on the legal duties of the Swiss government under the Paris

---

64 See sources above in n 63.

65 S Arora-Jonsson, 'Virtue and Vulnerability: Discourses on Women, Gender and Climate Change' (2011) 21 *Global Environmental Change* 744; International Labour Organization, *Skills for a Greener Future. Key Findings* (International Labour Organization 2019); IRENA, *Renewable Energy: A Gender Perspective* (IRENA 2019).

66 Z Habtezion, *Overview of Linkages between Gender and Climate Change* (UNDP 2013).

67 No. A-2992/2017.

Table 13.2: Pending climate change cases for involving the rights of women and youths, respectively

Case name	*Mbabazi v Attorney General and National Environmental Management Authority*[a]
Jurisdiction and filing date	Uganda, 2012
Summary of claims	The applicants are seeking a declaratory and injunctive relief on behalf of four Ugandan minors based on the government's constitutional duty as a public trustee of the country's natural resources.
Comments on LOS	Mixed: Successful institution of the claim in court in 2012 is indicative of judicial receptivity, however hearing in the matter is still pending.
Case name	*Maria Khan v Pakistan*[b]
Jurisdiction and filing date	Pakistan, 2018
Summary of claims	A group of women have filed a constitutional petition against the government of Pakistan on their behalf and on behalf of future generations. Their claim incudes human rights violation due to the government's inaction on climate change.
Comments on LOS	Favourable: Government's climate obligations under international and domestic laws and policy frameworks (structural); previous pronouncements of domestic courts on the commitments for climate action and human rights protections (judicial receptivity).
Case name	*Cláudia Duarte Agostinho v 33 States*[c]
Jurisdiction and filing date	European Union, 2020
Summary of claims	The applicants, six Portuguese youths, relying on human rights grounds have filed a complaint in the European Court of Human Rights against the failure of Portugal and 32 other high-emitting countries in Europe to take more ambitious climate action.
Comments on LOS	Favourable: Human rights protections under the European Convention on Human Rights; accessibility of the European Court of Human Rights.

[a] Civil Suit No. 283 of 2012. See also Our Children's Trust, Youth.Gov: Uganda https://www.ourchildrenstrust.org/uganda, accessed 2 January 2022.

[b] No. 8960 of 2019.

[c] (39371/20).

Agreement; the provisions of the Swiss Federal Constitution on the right to life (article 10(1)), the principle of sustainable development (article 3), the precautionary principle (article 74(2)); and the European Convention on Human Rights provisions on the right to life (article 2) and the right to respect private and family life (article 8). In the first instance, DETEC alleged that the applicants lacked legal standing as their 'rights had not been affected as required by article 25*a* APA, and did not enter into the case'.[68] In dismissing the appeal, the Federal Supreme Court held that the appellants' rights did not appear sufficiently endangered by the alleged failings of the government. Remarkably, in addition to relying on LOS, the applicants have also relied on the substantive obligation to protect future generations by adopting an ambitious climate policy as part of the strategy for mobilizing support within the political system.[69]

Within the context of the two focus countries for this chapter, women remain underrepresented in climate litigation. In South Africa, climate litigation has been led mainly by environmental NGOs, and brought under enabling domestic administrative law, and constitutional and statutory provisions. Most cases have either challenged the process for authorization of coal-fired power stations and urban development or the failure of the administrative authority to conduct adequate climate change impact assessments before granting environmental permission (and subsequent amendments). The respondents are mostly government departments and private investors in energy projects at the centre of the litigation. In Nigeria, prominent climate litigation was challenging gas flaring on human rights grounds. The relatively positive outcome in the *Gbemre case* did not translate into a pro-environmental outcome in the *Ikechukwu Okpara* case. Further, gas flares are still prevalent in the Niger Delta region of Nigeria, policy reforms such as the Flare Gas (Prevention of Waste and Pollution) Regulations 2018 are increasingly focused on gas flares commercialization.

Despite the indications of some positive structural factors and judicial receptivity in South Africa and Nigeria, women are still underrepresented in climate litigation. While there are no formal barriers, the underrepresentation of vulnerable groups, particularly women and children, in climate litigation is evident, especially in Nigeria. The underrepresentation of women is unsurprising given that their access to and control of natural resources and property in traditional societies often depends mainly on their relationship with male authority figures, including their male relations or community head. Women, particularly those who are poor and live in rural areas where

68 Verein KlimaSeniorinnen Schweiz (n 67).

69 Keller and Bornemann (n 7).

oil and gas extraction often occurs, are therefore unlikely to directly control or have the capacity to exercise decision making for climate litigation independently. The limited access to legal aid compounds the challenge.

Overall, three trends emerge from the cases analysed in this chapter. The trends can give some insights into elements for successful climate litigation and women's limitations in adopting legal strategies for climate justice. First, the litigants who access the courts are often environmental NGOs or well-resourced individuals with the legal standing to maintain the action. Climate litigation, therefore, stands to benefit from improvements in access to justice and the removal of the legal barriers to litigation that populations in vulnerable situations experience. To this end, the relaxation of the common law rules on legal standing in environmental protection litigation – as has occurred in Nigeria – improves access to the courts for individuals and NGOs interested in litigating.

Second, climate change litigants increasingly rely upon domestic legislation (including administrative law and environmental protection legislation) and international climate change agreements to inform legal arguments. This trend underscores the importance of advocacy for climate change mitigation and adaptation legislation and the need to ensure that the domestic legal framework integrates ambitious climate action targets linked to the international climate change discourse. It is further essential to ensure that existing LOS are protected and any underlying barriers to participating in environmental impact assessment processes, pursuing judicial review and accessing any other judicial mechanisms for climate action are addressed in the interest of women and other vulnerable groups.

Third, a favourable decision by the courts can only fully impact on climate action through enforcement. Inaction or non-implementation of court decisions by the responsible actors undermines the impact of litigation on the mitigation of emissions. This was, for instance, reflected in the approval of high-emitting projects without sufficient climate change assessment in South Africa and the continuation of gas flaring in Nigeria. In light of this, the enforcement of court decisions should also be considered a crucial dimension of LOS because non-compliance with court decisions may lead to the erosion of public confidence in the judicial process.

Conclusion

Following the global climate litigation trend, Africa will likely experience increased legal mobilization for climate action. Strategies for climate litigation across Africa have consisted of challenging either proposed or approved high GHG emissions infrastructure or development based on the legal validity of their environmental impact assessments process; opposing high GHG-emitting activities on account of the impacts on fundamental rights;

and directly seeking to compel the government to take proactive steps for climate action based on the public trust doctrine and the protection of the interest of present and future generations. Given the central role of fossil fuels in the energy mix and the economic development of countries such as South Africa and Nigeria, litigants seeking GHG emission regulation and the closure of fossil fuel exploration and production activities are likely to meet significant resistance from some quarters. Nonetheless, there has been a rise in renewable energy and energy efficiency laws and policies, and innovative funding mechanisms such as green bonds, which could inform additional strategies for successful climate litigation.

Three lessons are evident from the South African and Nigerian cases. The success of climate litigation depends on positive LOS. The mainstreaming of women's rights in climate change policy in South Africa has not yet translated into a significant rise in women instituting climate litigation, though women-led organizations such as CER are driving climate litigation. Nigeria's situation also indicates judicial receptivity to environmental litigation, and the new legal and policy instruments on climate change and gender are promising for LOS. However, there are few recognized 'climate' cases in Nigeria, none have been brought by women. The advances in climate change laws and rules on legal standing need to be supported with access to legal aid for women who lack the resources to pursue climate litigation.

Even where there are structural enablers of LOS for climate litigation, the outcomes of the cases may not advance climate action for other reasons. The spectrum of climate litigation may encounter different LOS within the same jurisdiction, as indicated by the differences in the court decision in the *Gbemre* case and the *Ikechukwu* case from the Nigeria Federal High Court. As seen in South Africa, the impacts of judicial receptivity and administrative review on environmental impact assessment grounds may be limited where the respondents demonstrate recourse to climate impacts for their decision. The resulting threats to climate action underscore the importance of the legislature and executive demonstrating a solid commitment to reducing GHG emissions, particularly from the energy sector, which accounts for a significant portion of emissions in South Africa and Nigeria.

Finally, it is necessary to disaggregate the climate litigation discourse in ways that allow for understanding the context of vulnerable groups and the strategies most likely to address their vulnerabilities to climate change impacts and advance their climate justice interests. Particularly for vulnerable groups such as women, it is also essential to ensure access to resources and the mitigation of intervening inequalities that could impede legal mobilization for climate justice.

14

Future Citizens: Intergenerational Equity in Climate Activism

Bright Nkrumah

Introduction

Africa is a climate change hotspot, warming at double the global average rate.[1] The landscape of the region has been punctuated by deluges, drought and heatwaves.[2] Accordingly, the continent is inevitably witnessing the evolution of youth advocating for a sustainable environmental resource.[3] Yet, whereas a growing number of their peers in the Global North tirelessly use courtrooms to press for a reduction of greenhouse gas (GHG) emissions, Africa's young population rarely use courtrooms to pursue this end.[4] Ultimately, the limited legal (grassroots) mobilization has not pressured African states to commit to low carbon development paths or take far more decisive adaptation action.[5] More importantly, although the Global North is responsible for 92 per cent of GHG emissions, an introspection

1 B Nkrumah, 'Africa's Future: Demarginalizing Urban Agriculture in the Era of Climate Change' (2019) 7(1) *Future of Food: Journal on Food, Agriculture and Society* 8.

2 SB Bedeke, 'Climate Change Vulnerability and Adaptation of Crop Producers in Sub-Saharan Africa: a Review on Concepts, Approaches, and Methods' (2022) *Environment, Development, and Sustainability* 1.

3 B Nkrumah, 'Eco-Activism: Youth and Climate Justice in South Africa' (2021) 33(4) *Environmental Claims Journal* 328.

4 B Nkrumah, 'Courting Emissions: Climate Adjudication and South Africa's youth' (2021) 11(1) *Energy, Sustainability and Society* 1.

5 AO Acheampong, J Dzator, and DA Savage, 'Renewable Energy, CO_2 Emissions and Economic Growth in Sub-Saharan Africa: Does Institutional Quality Matter?' (2021) 43(5) *Journal of Policy Modeling* 1073.

of Africa's climate action is important for three reasons: (1) the notion of intergenerational equity has been extensively construed in American and European literature; (2) an increase in emissions is likely to hit Africans harder than their peers in the Global North; and (3) the growing population in Africa, in contrast to the Global North, implies that the former will need more arable lands, freshwater to sustain its animal husbandry, crops and human population.[6] Thus, a focus on the climate change implications for Africa is timely.

While a number of African countries are relying on big hydropower as their primary source of 'renewable' energy, a smaller sub-set of countries is heavily reliant, or seeking to increase their reliance, on coal. Besides South Africa, where about 90 per cent of its energy comes from coal, Tanzania, Mozambique and Botswana have resorted to coal production as major source of energy.[7] That being the case, it is imaginable that the continent's energy sector is going to exacerbate the socio-economic consequences of climate change over the next three decades. With the average global temperature projected to increase to about 2.5°C above industrial levels in 2050, it is likely that the resultant heatwaves and drought will impact people who are currently young, and their access to basic needs, such as food, housing and water.[8] As discussed elsewhere, the notion of youth implies individuals between the ages of 15 and 24.[9] Given that the age bracket implies young people, words such as young generation, youth and young adults will be used interchangeably.

---

6 J Wrigley, 'It's Time for the Global North to Take Responsibly for Climate Change' (2022) *Global Social Challenges*, https://sites.manchester.ac.uk/global-social-challenges/2022/07/16/its-time-for-the-global-north-to-take-responsibly-for-climate-change, accessed 18 January 2023; K Shrader-Frechette, *Environmental Justice: Creating Equality, Reclaiming Democracy* (Oxford University Press 2002); L Collins, 'Environmental Rights for the Future? Intergenerational Equity in the EU' (2007a) 16(3) *Review of European Community & International Environmental Law* 321–31.

7 DW 'Africa Digs for Coal to Meet Energy Demands Amid Climate Concerns', 2021, https://www.dw.com/en/africa-digs-for-coal-to-meet-energy-demands-amid-climate-concerns/a-57086116, accessed 18 January 2023.

8 M Collins, R Knutti, J Arblaster, JL Dufresne, T Fichefet, P Friedlingstein, X Gao, WJ Gutowski, T Johns, G Krinner, M Shongwe, C Tebaldi, AJ Weaver and M Wehner, 'Long-Term Climate Change: Projections, Commitments and Irreversibility' in TF Stocker, D Qin, GK Plattner, M Tignor, SK Allen, J Boschung, A Nauels, Y Xia, V Bex and PM Midgley (eds), *Climate Change 2013: The Physical Science Basis. Contribution of Working Group I to the Fifth Assessment Report of the Intergovernmental Panel on Climate Change* (Cambridge University Press 2013) 1033.

9 Nkrumah (n 3) 332.

On that account, bearing in mind that climatic effects have been projected to worsen over the next three decades, the urgency to transition to renewable energy becomes more pressing.[10] The use of coal for electricity in some countries has had a considerable impact on the value of the environment, and might worsen if immediate steps are not taken to transition from coal to other renewables. While the entire African population will ultimately be impacted by the negative ramifications of fluctuating climate, the plight of the young and future generations in poor communities deserves special consideration for two reasons. First, despite being the least emitters, they will be heavily impacted as they have poor housing to withstand the torrential cyclones or heatwaves that loom. Second, insufficient financial resources to cope with food and water price hikes might result considering the escalating droughts and floods across the region.

In this context, the chapter explores the conceptual arguments that could be invoked by the young and future generations in poor communities to press for climate action in (inter)national courtrooms, with a particular focus on the notion of intergenerational equity (IE). Since its emergence over half a century ago,[11] IE has evolved to become a rallying principle around which disempowered groups and grassroots environmental movements mobilize. Sadly, despite its legitimacy, and recognition that the future generation have a stake in the environment, the practical efficacy of IE to climate litigation remains on the fringes in Africa. Given that the term itself is seldomly invoked in environmental proceedings, the chapter seeks to understand the meaning of IE, and how it can be creatively invoked by African activists and public interest litigators who use litigation to get states to transition to renewable energy sources.

The rest of the chapter is divided into five parts. The next section provides an overview of the meaning of IE. The third section surveys the interlinkage between IE and the rights of young people to a clean environment, in contrast to the obligations of states, to fulfill this right. The section that follows interrogates how the developed principle of IE can be useful for contemporary climate activism. Then the chapter surveys some of the dominant challenges that might militate against attempts towards pressing for IE and climate action through legal channels. The final section serves as a conclusion and suggests ways by which young activists can effectively articulate IE.

---

10 B Nkrumah, 'Beyond Tokenism: The "Born Frees" and Climate Change in South Africa' (2021c) 2021(8831677) *International Journal of Ecology* 2; B Nkrumah 'Ecojustice: Reframing climate justice as racial justice' (2023) *Journal of Law, Society and Development* (forthcoming).

11 J Rawls, *A Theory of Justice* (Harvard University Press 1971) 284.

What is intergenerational equity?

IE has emerged as an important concept in climate change discourse and activism.[12] But what does this principle mean, and to what extent has it been articulated in African narratives? As its name implies, IE may be broadly construed as the use of available natural resources to meet the needs of the present generation without compromising the ability of the future generation to sustain themselves using similar resources.[13] In some articulations, the existing resources are jointly shared by both generations, and given that the future generations (yet unborn) are not yet here to claim their portion of existing natural resources (air, land and water), the current generation have an obligation to hold in trust the environment or natural resources on behalf of the former.[14] The earth is, then, a trust granted to the present generation, which ought to be passed on to the next generation in its original form or a better shape. For this reason, IE could be said to be attained if the quantity and quality of natural resources received by the present generation are passed on to subsequent generations.[15] Over time, the latter will take over and administer the affairs of the planet. The concept may be seen as the entitlement of the future generation to enjoy the same quantity and quality of resources that nature provided the former generation.[16]

IE is premised on the understanding that in every society the principle of equality ought to apply to all individuals regardless of age.[17] In other words, the adult, young and yet unborn generations ought to have a fair share in the use of collective resources. Such a common understanding of a minimum standard of distribution will ensure that everyone gets to enjoy their entitlement without unduly being deprived.[18] To that end, it behooves the current generation to use natural resources in moderation. IE imposes a

---

12 E Padilla 'Intergenerational Equity and Sustainability' (2002) 41(1) *Ecological Economics* 69–83; RN Stavins, AF Wagner, and G Wagner, 'Interpreting Sustainability in Economic Terms: Dynamic Efficiency Plus Intergenerational Equity' (2003) 79(3) *Economics Letters* 339–43; B Zuindeau, 'Territorial Equity and Sustainable Development' (2007) 16(2) *Environmental Values* 253–68.

13 GB Asheim, 'Intergenerational Equity' (2010) 2(1) *Annual Review of Economics* 197–222; AU (African Union), African Youth Charter, 2 July 2006.

14 JM Hartwick, 'Intergenerational Equity and the Investing of Rents from Exhaustible Resources' (1977) 67(5) *The American Economic Review* 972–4.

15 Stavins, Wagner and Wagner (n 12).

16 JK Summers and LM Smith, 'The Role of Social and Intergenerational Equity in Making Changes in Human Well-Being Sustainable' (2014) 43(6) *Ambio* 718–28.

17 S Dasgupta and T Mitra, 'Intergenerational Equity and Efficient Allocation of Exhaustible Resources' (1983) 24(1) *International Economic Review* 133–53.

18 A Williams, 'Intergenerational Equity: an Exploration of the "Fair Innings" Argument' (1997) 6(2) *Health Economics* 117–32.

moral obligation on the present generation to ensure their successors have adequate natural resources to meet their daily needs.[19]

Put differently, IE is the fair split of resources among members within a social setting. Weiss's work emphases that this principle underscores the pursuit of three aspirations: (1) preservation of choices – sustaining the diversity of the cultural and natural resources base; (2) preservation of quality – banqueting an environment that is clean to the next generation; and (3) preservation of access – fair access and sharing of the benefits accruing from the inherited planet.[20] In this light, IE would result in communal allocation of resources among people of different age categories.[21]

In Africa, the principle of IE echoes in the African adage that the elderly ought to take care of the earth, because they 'borrowed' it from their children. Simply put, an African man who loves his children would cherish the land and not deplete it, because he knows the children will depend on its resources, and not simply because he is duty bound. Such a man will adopt measures that contribute towards conservation (regardless of how small in scope) and set a good example for the children to follow in the usage of such resources (for the benefit of their own children).

As an illustration of such measures, Rawls admonishes that besides the conventional preservation of cultural norms and traditions, the elderly ought to put aside or persevere sufficient goods for the generation yet unborn.[22] For a century, the Rawlsian theory has been adopted by a series of activists and environmental scholars advocating for sustainable consumption. Their understanding is that natural resources belong to everyone on the planet, and ought to be shared equally or fairly. With the present generation preceding the future generation, and having ready access to the varied natural goods, the former has a moral and legal obligation to preserve the natural resources for the use of the subsequent generation. In the context of climate change, the principle implies that the current generation ought not to exceed emitting their share of hydrocarbons as a means of preserving the environment. Preservation may be classified into three camps: (1) preserving biodiversity or the various types of living organisms that nature offers; (2) preserving the quality of air, land, and water to nurture living beings; and (3) improving or retaining the quantity of natural resources for the sustenance of the community.

---

[19] WR Zame, 'Can Intergenerational Equity Be Operationalized?' (2007) 2(2) *Theoretical Economics* 187–202.

[20] EB Weiss, 'Intergenerational Equity in International Law' (1987) 81 *Proceedings of the ASIL Annual Meeting* 126–33.

[21] EB Weiss, 'Climate Change, Intergenerational Equity, and International Law' (2008) 9(3) *Vermont Journal of Environmental Law* 615–27.

[22] Rawls (n 11), 283.

The community in this regard has three layers: the old generation (25+ years), the young (-25 years) and the unborn.[23] In the spirit of the preceding discussions, one could collapse these species into two main brackets: (1) the *present generation*, representing the first two clusters, that is the younger and older adults; and (2) the future generation, embodying hypothetical others already conceived or yet to be conceived in their mothers' wombs.

Bearing in mind that these two camps have equal entitlement to the earth, it is in the interest of justice that natural resources are equally shared across all the generations.[24] However, because the young lack the maturity and capacity to fully exploit natural resources and the unborn are not yet in existence, their forebears ought to ensure that the portion of resources meant for them is preserved for their future.[25] A simple analogy is a distribution of an estate to three heirs: an adult, a teenager and an unborn baby. Even though the latter two recipients might not immediately be able to fully utilize their allocated shares, the elderly is obliged to refrain from appropriating the possessions of the others. It is this thought that gave rise to the concept of IE, as conserving the earth by the present generation is the only means of sustaining or guaranteeing the existence of future generations.[26] As the labels

23 Nkrumah (n 3), 332. Whereas the United Nations or its General Assembly did not clearly set out a rationale for the age classification, one may argue that in a social context, youth is a period of transition from a child's dependence to adult independence (UNGA 1981: para. 8 of the annex; UNGA 1985: para. 19 of the annex). In deconstructing as well as constructing generational identities in a manner that erases complexities and contradictions, the unborn may be distinguished as (1) babies yet to be conceived; and (2) babies in their mother's womb. Beyond this, one is eligible to claim young(hood) or younger generation from the moment one is born up to the age of 24. This demography may be seen as the young adults (rising generation), encompasses children, juvenile and youth. Since persons beyond the age of 25 fall outside the first two camps, the paper will leave the question of who is an older adult open to debate.

24 JK Summers, and LM Smith, 'The Role of Social and Intergenerational Equity in Making Changes in Human Well-Being Sustainable' (2014) 43(6) *Ambio* 718–28.

25 Dasgupta and Mitra (n 17).

26 The notion of inter-generational equity is often complemented by another term, *intra*-generational equity. Whereas the former implies fairness across different generations, the latter connotes fairness in the distribution of resources within a generation. Intra-generational equity is particularly pronounced in terms of relationships between the current generation: see S Rayner and EL Malone, 'Climate Change, Poverty, and Intragenerational Equity: the National Level' (2001) 1(2) *International Journal of Global Environmental* 175–202. Despite one's geographic location, the present generation (young and old) are all entitled to an equal share of the natural resources, whether in an affluent or less developed society. States, consequently, ought to ensure a fair allocation of these resources, as unfair use of the environment by a few affluent groups could threaten the existence of other community members. Intra-generational equity, akin to its sister concept, intergenerational equity, imposes a legal obligation on the state and affluent societies to refrain from excessive resource consumption as it compromises the

connote, while present generation refers to a human currently inhabiting the planet, future generations may be construed as individuals yet unborn. As a consequence, although young adults are part of the present generation, they have a role to play in holding the older generation accountable for their use or misuse of the environment, inter alia, their share of GHG emissions which have caused climate change, and the need for them to address this.

Intergenerational equity and human rights to a safe environment

This section engages with the question whether regimes for the protection of human rights and/or the environment affirm the inherent rights of Africa's young and future generations to clean air or environment? In this respect, the next sections will survey to what extent this principle could be considered as justiciable under international (and regional) human rights and environmental treaties.

Intergenerational equity and human rights regimes

The notion of human rights may be understood as the basic entitlement of every individual. While this entitlement imposes duties on states to refrain from actions that may impinge on the enjoyment of these entitlements, they also place positive obligations on states to take steps to protect the welfare of both present and subsequent generations.[27]

As a normative framework, human rights sets out legal provisions regulating the relationship between the state and young people and, as a practical framework, gives rise to the establishment of institutions to ensure compliance with these normative frameworks. It is now well established that the conceptual and practical frameworks of human rights could serve as the platform through which the suffering of vulnerable populations, particularly youth and the unborn, could be ameliorated by reducing global

quality of the environment and the biodiversity: see I Vojnovic, 'Intergenerational and Intragenerational Equity Requirements for Sustainability' (1995) 22(3) *Environmental Conservation* 223–8. It is this perspective of fairness that has been adduced to by youth movements as a launchpad to popularize or advocate for a climate *just*(ice). This view maintains that whereas the affluent and privileged members of society consume a large portion of natural resources, it is the least advantaged that bear the brunt of atmospheric depletion. AR Pearson, CG Tsai and S Clayton, 'Ethics, Morality, and the Psychology of Climate Justice' (2021) 42 *Current Opinion in Psychology* 36–42.

27 SF Kreimer, 'Allocational Sanctions: The Problem of Negative Rights in a Positive State' (1984) 132(6) *University of Pennsylvania Law Review* 1293–397.

warming.[28] The impact of climate change on rights could be grouped into two layers. The first layer comprises direct impacts, inter alia heatwaves, drought and flood that could threaten the civil rights (life) and socio/economic rights (food, health, water, education, housing) of individuals. The second layer references infringements on cultural and groups rights, as extreme weather patterns could impact herders, indigenous communities and cultural heritage.[29]

IE, as set out in article 19 of the African Youth Charter, encompasses two key layers in terms of the environment and resource use.[30] The first advocates for state measures to enhance the lives of the young generation as a means of carving a better future for their successors. To this end, the instrument recognizes the young generation as next in line to take over the stewardship of the earth and, figuratively, be accorded a seat at the decision-making table.[31] Such decision-making processes may encompass framing strategies towards attaining fairness in the use of natural resources or striking a balance between meeting the needs of the present generation without unduly limiting the prospects of the unborn to equally utilize similar resources to meet their consumptive demands.

Ironically, whereas a plethora of (inter)national and regional human rights instruments contain provisions broaching the issue of food and water insecurity, IE as creating any kind of a substantive right has not been clearly articulated in these documents.[32] This may be tied to two conditions: (1) at the time of drafting some of the international environmental and human rights instruments, intergenerational rights had not been conceptualized. Some of the key human rights instruments (including the International Covenant on Civil and Political Rights, and International Covenant on Economic, Social and Cultural Rights) predate much of the writing on the

28 GF Maggio, 'Inter/Intra-Generational Equity: Current Applications Under International Law for Promoting the Sustainable Development of Natural Resources' (1996) 4(2) *Buffalo Environmental Law Journal* 161–223; R Fambasayi and M Addaney, 'Cascading Impacts of Climate Change and the Rights of Children in Africa: A Reflection on the Principle of Intergenerational Equity' (2021) 21(1) *African Human Rights Law Journal* 29–51.

29 DM David-Chavez and MC Gavin, 'A Global Assessment of Indigenous Community Engagement in Climate Research' (2018) 13(12) *Environmental Research Letters* 1–17; JD Ford, N King, EK Galappaththi, T Pearce, G McDowell and SL Harper, 'The Resilience of Indigenous Peoples to Environmental Change' (2020) 2(6) *One Earth* 532–43. Also in relation to the protection of cultural rights of indigenous people see the chapter by Fiona Batt in this volume.

30 African Union, African Youth Charter, 2 July 2006, https://www.refworld.org/docid/493fe0b72.html, accessed 18 January 2023.

31 African Union, African Youth Charter (n 30), art. 2.

32 B Nkrumah, *Seeking the Right to Food: Food Activism in South Africa* (Cambridge University Press 2021) 77.

principle of IE; and (2) the problem of climate change, which brings to the fore serious questions about future generations and resource use, would not have occupied the thoughts of the framers of the instrument. Having said that, a reader could hammer out a counter-argument that while a range of regional and global human rights agreements have evolved post-1970s, there is no protection of IE as a substantive right.[33]

Intergenerational equity in environmental treaties

While not entrenched as a formal 'right' in environmental treaties, IE is recognized as a principle in a number of international environmental and climate change laws.[34] The 1972 Stockholm Declaration is the first international instrument to do so.[35] Under principles 1 and 2, the document implores states to take required measures to safeguard biodiversity for present and subsequent generations.[36]

Undoubtedly in recognition of the far-reaching implications of climate change and risks it causes to future generations, the 1994 United Nations Framework Convention on Climate Change (UNFCCC) made direct reference to the needs of the future generation.[37] Article 3(1) of the UNFCCC reflects state parties' agreement to safeguard the climate systems for present and future generations. The provision further confirms the agreement of high emission states to take initiatives in addressing the adverse effects triggered by climate change, to forestall the depletion of the environment. The UNFCCC may be considered groundbreaking in the arena of safeguarding future generations' interests as this reference shifts away from the more conventional practice of mentioning IE in the preamble. This does not, of course, create any kind of justiciable right.

That being said, the 2015 Paris Agreement regressed from this position by inserting a reference to IE in the preamble.[38] This section further makes references to the protection of children's right to a clean environment in framing strategies to mitigate climate change.[39] The consolation one could derive from this lamentable setback is its reaffirmation of state parties' need

33 O Spijkers, 'Intergenerational Equity and the Sustainable Development Goals' (2018) 10(11) *Sustainability* 9.

34 A Boyle and C Redgwell, *International Law and the Environment* (OUP 2021) 4th ed.

35 UN Doc. A/CONF. 48/14, at 2 and Corr. 1 (1972).

36 N 35, ch. 1, s. II, Principles.

37 UN General Assembly, United Nations Framework Convention on Climate Change: resolution/adopted by the General Assembly, 20 January 1994, A/RES/48/189.

38 FCCC/CP/2015/10/Add.1.

39 UNFCCC (n 37) Preamble, para. 11.

to promote sustainable development.[40] The very concept of sustainable development in itself entails the use of natural resources for development that address the needs of the current generation without undermining the prospects of the unborn to equally rely on such resource. Therefore, one could make the claim that IE is implicitly contemplated in the Paris Agreement.

At the regional level, the pursuit of environmental sustainability 'for all peoples' is reflected in the protection of the right to a healthy environment in article 24 of the 1981 African Charter on Human and People's Rights.[41] Whereas the provision departs from specific recognition of the unborn as an entity, one could advance an affirmative argument or creatively interpret 'all peoples' as encompassing the current and future peoples of the continent.[42] The principle of IE is also recognized in the 2003 Revised African Convention on the Conservation of Nature and Natural Resources.[43] As its name implies, the overarching ambition of the document is to enhance conservation of natural resources, ultimately for continual and future use. Article IV of the Convention imposes a duty on state parties to take immediate steps to, among others, forestall pollution in accordance with the best 'interest of present and future generations'. Even so, although the insertion of the right of future generations means the importance of IE is legally recognized, the failure of the instrument to provide clear guidelines on what practical measures ought to be adopted somewhat undercuts its fulfillment.

At the national level, although some constitutions expressly protect the right to a healthy environment, there is no recognition of intergenerational equity as any kind of substantive right across all the 54 African states.[44] This remains a pipedream. From the southern to northern parts of the region, only three documents may be identified as reflecting strong protection for the principle of IE. These are South Africa's 1996 Constitution, Kenya's 2010 Constitution, and Zimbabwe's 2013 Constitution.[45] The documents begin with a plethora of provisions that seek to safeguard and advance a list of

---

40 UNFCCC (n 37) arts 2, 4, 6 and 7.

41 Organization of African Unity (OAU), African Charter on Human and Peoples' Rights ('Banjul Charter'), 27 June 1981, CAB/LEG/67/3 rev. 5, 21 ILM 58 (1982).

42 LM Collins, 'Revisiting the Doctrine of Intergenerational Equity in Global Environmental Governance' (2007) 30 *Dalhousie Law Journal* 81.

43 Adopted by the Second Ordinary Session of the Assembly Maputo, Mozambique, 11 July 2003, entered into force on 23 July 2016.

44 There is no 'inherent' reason why representative proceedings on behalf of the unborn could not be brought – see Boyle and Redgwell (n 34), 123.

45 Constitution of the Republic of South Africa, 10 December 1996; Constitution of Kenya, 27 August 2010; Constitution of Zimbabwe Amendment (No. 20) Act, 2013, 22 May 2013.

civil and political, socio-economic and environmental rights. Subsequently, section 24 of South Africa's Constitution, article 42 of Kenya's Constitution, and article 73 of Zimbabwe's 2013 Constitution allude to IE by obliging the government to protect the environment for the benefit of current and future generations. The provisions oblige the respective states to avert ecological degradation, and foster conservation and sustainable development, for the good of the present and future generations. The wording of the provisions specify that in its pursuit of socio-economic development, states ought to be cognizant of the negative impact of a polluted environment on the survival of the current population and the unborn.[46] The references to future generations in these provisions opens up debate as to whether IE is entrenched in justiciable rights in these jurisdictions. Put differently, if any of these states pursue climate-related projects that threatens or substantially undercuts the prospects of future generations to draw from these resources, can that be construed as violating the rights of the unborn to a healthy environment? How can one advance claims based on IE in local courts where there is no enforceable entitlement?

Perhaps the answer to the above questions lies in drawing from local, regional and (inter)national jurisprudence that emphasizes the significance of the principle of IE in the way existing rights are interpreted. This we can see clearly in climate change jurisprudence. The next section offers an overview on some of the key judicial decisions that demonstrate how IE is recognized and protected in climate litigation in contemporary Africa.

Intergenerational equity in jurisprudence

While the recognition of IE in the instruments discussed above is commendable, its recognition at the national level has been scanty. This observation was made by Weeramantry J (*New Zealand v France*) in an International Court of Justice ruling. In his dissenting opinion, he observed that IE ought to be of great concern to local courts, as they are the guardians of the generations not yet present to assert their rights. The assertion by the judge supports the emergence of IE as an international norm that could be invoked by activists and public interest litigators to press for the entitlements of contemporary and future generations. In this regard, local courts could draw inspiration from the jurisprudence of international courts, and apply

[46] Section 24(b) of South Africa's Constitution stipulates that everyone has the right to 'to have the environment protected, for the benefit of present and future generations'. Article 42 of Kenya's Constitution reiterates that every person has the right 'to have the environment protected for the benefit of present and future generations'. Ultimately, art. 73 of Zimbabwe's 2013 Constitution echoes that 'every person has the right 'to have the environment protected for the benefit of present and future generations'.

the principle when making their decisions. Nonetheless, although the judge's opinion was not captured in the majority decision of the International Court of Justice, it arguably continues to serve as an important source of international customary law, particularly on matters relating to IE.[47]

In that regard, it is important to consider to what extent the principles of IE are reflected in African climate jurisprudence. But before that a caveat ought to be inserted. Aside from a single case, virtually all the lawsuits under this discussion were filed by individuals or non-governmental organizations (NGOs) against the state, for its (in)direct engagement in harmful environmental practices. The next two sections of the chapter will explore instances where explicit and implicit references to IE were made to support plaintiffs' arguments that enhanced action on climate change should be taken.

Explicit reference to intergenerational equity

The notion of IE does not have broad recognition in regional and (inter)national jurisprudence. Therefore, its status as a legal principle is uncertain.[48] At the time of writing, only one case invoked this concept in its jurisprudence. The Philippines Supreme Court has been the arena where the justiciability of IE was put to the test. In the early 1990s, a group of young people approached the Supreme Court requesting an order to terminate and halt the continued issuance of licences for timber felling.[49] The defendant's continual granting of timber licences agreements to corporations was leading to deforestation of nearly four million hectares of rain forest. Section 16 of article II of the country's 1987 Constitution prescribes that the government ought to advance and safeguard the right of citizens to a balanced and healthy environment 'in accord with the rhythm and harmony of nature'. As a response to growing concern and local rumblings over rapid deforestation, the Philippine Ecological Network filed a suit against the Secretary of the Department of Environment and Natural Resources (DENR).[50] Representing several minors, the petition filed in March 1990 mooted that the defendant's conduct breached the constitutional obligation to hold in trust natural resources for sustaining the plaintiff minors and their descendants.[51] The plaintiff sought to enjoin the department to halt the acceptance, approval or renewal of timber licences as a means of sustaining

47 See Boyle and Redgwell (n 34), 122–3.

48 Although see Boyle and Redgwell (n 34), 122.

49 *Minors Oposa v Factoran* 101083, 224 SCRA 792 (1993).

50 *Minors Oposa* (n 49), Preamble.

51 *Minors Oposa* (n 49), paras 16.

the ecology for 'their generation as well as generations yet unborn'.[52] Commencing with procedural issues, the Supreme Court held that 'based on the concept of intergenerational responsibility' it 'find[s] no difficulty in ruling that [the minor petitioners] can, for themselves, for others of their generation and for the succeeding generations, file a class suit'.[53] It underscored that 'the minors' assertion of their right to a sound environment constitutes, at the same time, the performance of their obligation to ensure the protection of that right for the generations to come'.[54] The Supreme Court found that IE had become a recognized principle of customary international law and the government ought to be cognizant of the impact of deforestation on the sustainability of the ecosystem and the survival of future generations. Finding in favour of the youth, it held that the future generation is entitled to a clean ecology, and the present generation ought to sustain the harmony and rhythm of a healthy environment. The decision of the court continues to be internationally recognized particularly in the areas of climate justice and sustainable development.

Implicit reference to intergenerational equity

While such explicit reference and reliance on the principle of IE is rare in pronouncements of the African judiciary, some African courts have indirectly contemplated the relevance of IE to environmental conservation. The following section surveys some of these cases, observing that the principle of IE is implicit in many African climate change decisions, even if the courts do not undertake an exposition of the nature of the principle.

In *SERAC v Nigeria*, the applicant approached the African Commission on Human and People's Rights with an application alleging a violation of their rights under articles 2, 4, 5, 6, 7, 14, 15, 16, 17, 18, 22 and 24 of the African Charter on Human and Peoples' Rights (ACHPR).[55] The rights contemplated in the communication were the rights to life, human dignity, security of the person, housing, property, to have one's cause heard, health, family, education, work, development and a healthy environment. The applicant alleged that infringements occurred against the backdrop of the Nigerian National Petroleum Company's (NNPC) oil leaks and disposing of hazardous wastes into the environment.[56] The practice resulted in health problems due to the contamination of air, soil and water in Ogoniland,

[52] *Minors Oposa* (n 49), para. 6.
[53] *Minors Oposa* (n 49), para. 22.
[54] *Minors Oposa* (n 49).
[55] AHRLR 60 (ACHPR 2001), para. 43.
[56] ACHPR 2001, para. 1.

violating the aforementioned rights. The communication was submitted against the government on two grounds, as: (1) the proprietor of the oil company; and (2) facilitating the harmful operations through the use of military forces to attack, burn and destroy food crops in local villages. The communication alleged that this development infringed on the local populations' rights to health and a satisfactory environment. In affirming the claim of the applicants, the Commission held that the state's inaction breached residents' basic entitlements to life and a clean environment as entrenched in articles 4 and 24 of the ACHPR respectively. Although IE, and more broadly climate change, was not the central argument of the plaintiff, three important observations can be made: (1) there is an inextricable link between the environment and other human entitlements, including livelihood, health, education and housing; (2) the failure to safeguard the environment could have other adverse ramifications, not just for the present generation, but the unborn; and (3) oil leaks and hazardous waste disposal could have a cascading or knock-on climate change impact.[57] As a result it makes sense to bring this case into the discussion at hand, considering that rising temperatures, deluges and drought could equally impact the current and future generations' right to food, water and health condition.

Four years after the conclusion of the *SERAC* case, Nigeria's High Court handed down a similar oil-pollution decision against the NNPC and its parent, Shell. The applicants sought to interdict the two entities from flaring gas in the Niger Delta.[58] Filed by Gbemre, for himself and the Iwherekan Community in Delta State, the petition alleged that during the oil explorations, the defendant oil companies have conducted extreme and continuous gas flaring that poisoned the environment and depleted a large section of the air in the Iwherekan community. They added that the pollution would not only exacerbate climate change but threaten the life and dignity of the community. In its decision, the High Court held that the continuous flaring of gas by the oil companies is a gross infringement on the applicant's community's right to dignity, environment and life as set out in the Constitution.[59] While there was no discussion of the principle of IE, it was evident that the continuous gas flaring would impact not only the current residents of the community, but their future generations. The High Court emphasized the importance of the principle of sustainable development, and the right to a healthy and sustainable environment as protected in the

[57] K Bouwer 'The Influence of Human Rights on Climate Litigation in Africa' (2022) 13(1) *Journal of Human Rights and the Environment* 157–77.

[58] *Gbemre v Shell Petroleum Dev. Corp. & the Nigerian National Petroleum Corpn* (2005) 6 AHRLR 152 (Nigeria).

[59] *Gbemre* (n 58), para. 5(4).

African Charter.[60] As discussed above, the principle of IE is implicit in the concept of sustainable development and, as such, the way the environmental right is formulated in the African context requires that a court give effect to this. Ultimately, the court proscribed the respondents from further flaring of gas in the affected community with immediate effect.[61]

More recently, Nigeria's Supreme Court handed down a significant decision which broadened the basis on which locus standi could exist in applications concerning environmental issues. In the *Centre for Oil Pollution Watch v NNPC*, the appellant alleged that the respondent had neglected its pipelines in Abia State, leading to oil spillage and contamination of its water sources, the Ineh/Aku Rivers.[62] The company has failed to take steps to reinstate or clean the water body. Before this case, a plaintiff had locus standi if: (1) the issue at hand falls within the direct provisions of the Constitution; and (2) the plaintiff has or will suffer an actual injury stemming from the matter in question. A person failing to satisfy these thresholds was perceived as a busybody interloper. Yet, the *COPW v NNPC* was a turning point. Drawing from international jurisprudence, the Supreme Court decided that any person with a genuine commitment to safeguard issues relating to public interest ought to be permitted to approach it. Thus, since the petition seeks to safeguard the environment for the benefit of the citizens, the appellant has the right to institute the action. Beyond the procedural issues before it, the Supreme Court bemoaned the interrelation of the respondent's activities to global warming amid burgeoning ozone layer depletion and climate change.[63] It found that the environmental protection afforded by the section 24 of the Africa Charter was enforceable in the Nigerian courts.[64] The Supreme Court also made oblique reference to the principle of IE, noting that the earth's resources must be protected for the sustenance of 'present and future generations'.[65] It concluded that environment conservation obliges the state to adopt and operationalize strategies that are feasible for containing climate change and ultimately fostering the interests of present and future generations.[66]

60 See the discussion in the chapter by Elsabé Boshoff in this volume.

61 *Gbemre* (n 58), para. 6.

62 *COPW v NNPC, Centre for Oil Pollution Watch v NNPC* [2019] 5 NWLR (Pt. 1666) 518. The implications of this case for climate justice in Nigeria are considered in this volume, in the chapter by Eghosa Ekhator and Edward Okumagba.

63 U Etemire, 'The Future of Climate Change Litigation in Nigeria: COPW v NNPC in the Spotlight' (2021) 15(2) *Carbon & Climate Law Review* 160.

64 COPW (n 62), 597–8. See discussion in Etemire (n 63).

65 COPW (n 62).

66 COPW (n 62).

In 2012, the NGO Greenwatch approached the Ugandan High Court on behalf of four minor claimants, with a suit against the state.[67] The complaint was based on the fact that the Ugandan government's failure to take action both toward mitigation and adaptation of climate change, was a failure to comply with its constitutional obligation to promote a clean and healthy environment.[68] The inaction was construed as endangering the right to life and health of present and future generations. The youngsters further argued that as a trustee of the people's natural resources, the 1995 Constitution imposes a duty on the state to avert the depletion of these resources for present and future members of society. The complainants alleged that the government has reneged on this duty, leading to intermittent weather patterns. Ultimately, the youngsters requested the High Court for injunctive relief, including for the development of an action plan to immediately cut GHG emissions and various declarations. While this case has not as yet been substantively heard, it remains live. It also makes strong representations of IE. Throughout, the plaintiffs argue that the Ugandan government has not sustainably used resources, which, as mentioned above, is an implicit reference to IE. However, there are more explicit references in the declarations sought. The plaintiffs specifically ask for relief for 'children of Uganda', and expressly ask for recognition that all shared resources, including the atmosphere, are held in trust for 'the people of Uganda present and future generations'. Conclusively, one can discern that this case holds much promise for Africa's climate litigation landscape, particularly as the principle of IE was invoked by the plaintiffs.[69]

In *Earthlife Africa Johannesburg* an NGO approached the Pretoria High Court with a petition against the Minister of Environmental Affairs relating to the ecological effect of constructing a 1,200MW coal-fired power station near Lephalale in the Limpopo province.[70] The complainant alleged that the decision of the Department of Environmental Affairs (DEA) to grant authorization for the erection of a 1,200MW Thabametsi coal-fired power plant was unlawful.[71] The plaintiff relied on section 24 of the Constitution and international climate change instruments.[72] The High Court interpreted the relevant statutory provisions taking section 24 of the Constitution into

[67] *Mbabazi v The Attorney General and National Environmental Management* Civil Suit No. 283 of 2012.

[68] *Mbabazi* (n 67), para. 15(6).

[69] In the chapter by Elsabé Boshoff in this volume, she discusses potential future directions for the *Mbabazi* case.

[70] *Earthlife Africa Johannesburg v Minister of Environmental Affairs*, Case No. 65662/16, para. 1.

[71] This case is discussed in more depth in various of the chapters in this collection, including by Nicole Loser and Sanita van Wyk.

[72] *Earthlife* (n 70), para. 12.

account. It opined that the recognition of IE in section 24 of the Constitution (as discussed above) entails that development projects, despite any financial gains ought to be balanced by the notion of sustainable consumption and 'intergenerational justice' for the 'benefit of the present and future generations'.[73] The state, for that reason, ought to consider the long-term impact of additional emissions before granting licences for the construction of such a plant. The High Court concluded that the DEA's preliminary assessment of the project's impact on climate change 'was wholly insufficient', and that it ought to 'consider a climate change impact assessment report' to possibly determine and avert the potential impact of such a fossil fuel project on the neighbouring communities.[74]

Challenges to intergenerational equity in litigation

The recognition of the rights of future generations serves as a focal point for environmentalists, and especially youth claimants, to press their demands for IE in courtrooms. In climate cases in the African court, these arguments are often successful. But these victories should not distract from the challenges that might undercut the prospects cases against the state. A few of these key challenges that might threaten possible climate litigation in Africa countries follow.

First, there are unsettled debates around the conceptualization of IE.[75] While the principle is recognized in international customary law, its lack of use means it remains largely incoherent. Domestic lawyers and judges, without adequate legal precedence to provide guidance, may not want to use or make reference to the principle. Even in cases where judges and parties to the lawsuit are privy to the term, it remains burdensome to speak of the preservation of resources for future inhabitants due to some unresolved – and unresolvable – questions: (1) how many generations are yet to come; (2) when will each arrive; (3) what will be the demography of these generations; (4) what will be the gender composition; and (5) what quantity of resources is sufficient and ought to be preserved. The annual population growth in Africa arguably indicates that the future demography will be more than double the present population. In any event, since the framing of (sub) national climate action plans are within the ambit of the state, the political will of the executive and legislative branches of governments is crucial in

---

73 *Earthlife Africa* (n 70), para. 82.

74 *Earthlife Africa* (n 70), para. 94, 126.3.1.

75 Williams (n 18); Asheim (n 13); TM Andersen and MH Gestsson, 'Longevity, Growth, and Intergenerational Equity: the Deterministic Case' (2016) 20(4) *Macroeconomic Dynamics* 985–1021.

shifting countries' energy production, and public and private behaviour, towards more sustainable practices. In the meantime, it falls to local courts to adopt an activist approach or creatively interpret national constitutions and relevant laws to give effect to IE.[76] As outlined above, they frequently do this with reference to human rights protections that allow reference to sustainable use of resources, in which the principle of IE is implicit.

Second, there are access to justice concerns. A high percentage of Africa's population has insufficient access to resources for legal fees (including due to the high cost of living and growing unemployment), publicly funded lawyers or access to private lawyers willing and able to conduct complex climate change cases. The challenge is exacerbated by two separate but somewhat related factors. On the one hand, pressures on publicly funded legal resources mean these usually only support criminal defence cases, rather than 'optional' environmental complaints. On the other hand, there are few public interest lawyers and think tanks that are keen to take on environmental lawsuits. With insufficient resources and several other pressing civil and political, and socio-economic issues, climate issues rarely make it to the priority list.[77] This setback may be fueled by insufficient funding, as some donors may be unwilling to fund legal actions against the state for fear of retribution or being labeled as an anti-government agency. Even where a private attorney decides to take on the case pro bono, limited funding may impact the capacity of collecting evidence, hiring expert witnesses, and accessing required information to submit a viable legal action.[78]

The third concern is prolonged litigation. It is a common phenomenon that environmental suits, akin to others, could be lengthy. Due to the accompanying frustration, some litigants are prone to abandon the cause in pursuit of other personal aspirations. Abandonment of cases may be tied to several overlapping factors: (1) litigants seeking job prospects rather than following lengthy proceedings and cross-examinations; (2) the case concerns not just themselves, but others as well; and (3) the daily cost of attending hearings. Ultimately, where the lead litigant is compromised or unwilling

76 *New Zealand v France*. 1995. *Request for an Examination of the Situation in Accordance with Paragraph 63 of the Court's Judgment of 20 December* 1974 in the Nuclear Tests (*New Zealand v France*) Case, Order of 22 September 1995 (Dissenting Opinion of Judge Weeramantry) [1995] ICJ Rep. 317 at 317–62, http://www.icj-cij.org/docket/files/97/7567.pdf, accessed 18 January 2023.

77 C Konkes, 'Green Lawfare: Environmental Public Interest Litigation and Mediatized Environmental Conflict' (2018) 12(2) *Environmental Communication* 192.

78 J Setzer and L Benjamin, 'Climate Litigation in the Global South: Constraints and Innovations' (2020) 9(1) *Transnational Environmental Law* 78; B Nkrumah, 'Think Tanks and Democratisation in South Africa' (2022) 14(1) *Cosmopolitan Civil Societies: An Interdisciplinary Journal* 25.

to see the case through, the case is likely to be struck off the register, even if the lawyer is willing to proceed. Consequently, with a history of dealing with such 'bad clients', some lawyers may not be keen on taking on pro bono cases as they may see it as a waste of time and financial resources. In this regard, it is essential that after being approached with a climate complaint, the public interest litigator ought to mobilize the affected community into one social entity or constituency for the litigation. Where the case is filed on behalf of a community or social movement, even if some members lose momentum along the way, it is likely that there will be other members that could still act as the spokesperson for the legal action.

In sum, while a case can be made that formal rights protections to some extent reflect the principle of IE, the litigation process has some weaknesses that might undercut activists' attempts to make extensive use of it. This is particularly the case for young claimants, who are disproportionately poor, and may face several hurdles in their attempt to explore legal remedies. These setbacks may span from internal factors, inter alia, lawyers' and judges' understanding of complex theories such as IE, but also the contextual factors discussed in this section, including insufficient financial support and the prolonged ligation process. Although they are separate, these challenges overlap and could undermine young claimants' potential to contribute to the development of jurisprudence protecting the rights of the future generations of Africa.

Conclusion

The success of climate litigation in some African countries is likely to inspire similar legal activism in other parts of the continent. But, until such a time that IE becomes justiciable in its own right, existing rights protections will continue to be used as the basis for making arguments about IE. This is seen clearly in the cases discussed, and it would be hoped that similar claims could be filed at the regional level where the local courts are opposed to or oblivious to the need to ensure the state takes sufficient action on climate change to protect the interests of future generations. In these cases, it will be useful for potential litigants to frame their claim within the ambit of existing human rights protections, including the rights to life, health and a healthy environment as protected in (some) national constitutions and the African Charter. As outlined above, the implicit protection for IE through these rights is the best avenue for activists to protect the rights of future generations through the courts.

Index

References to tables appear in **bold** type. References to footnotes show both the page number and the note number (131n30).

D

T